THE ALERT, GREY TWINKLING EYES OF C.J. DeGARIS

Also by David Nichols

Dig: Australian Popular Music 1960–1985
Trendyville (with Renate Howe and Graeme Davison)
Pop Life (with Marc Andrews and Claire Isaac)
The Bogan Delusion
The Go-Betweens

Edited:

Urban Australia and Post-Punk: Exploring Dogs in Space (with Sophie Perillo)
Cultural Sustainability in Rural Communities: Rethinking Australian Country Towns (with Catherine Driscoll and Kate Darian-Smith)
Community: Building Modern Australia (with Hannah Lewi)
Deeper Leads: new approaches to goldfields history (with Keir Reeves)

THE ALERT, GREY TWINKLING EYES OF C. J. DeGARIS

David Nichols

UWA PUBLISHING

First published in 2022 by
UWA Publishing
Crawley, Western Australia 6009
www.uwap.uwa.edu.au

UWAP is an imprint of UWA Publishing
a division of The University of Western Australia

This book is copyright. Apart from any fair dealing for the purpose of private study, research, criticism or review, as permitted under the *Copyright Act 1968*, no part may be reproduced by any process without written permission. Enquiries should be made to the publisher.

Copyright © David Nichols 2022

The moral right of the author has been asserted.

ISBN: 978-1-76080-165-6

 A catalogue record for this book is available from the National Library of Australia

Cover designed by Carolyn Hawkins
Typeset in 12 point Bembo
Printed by Lightning Source

To Nancy

Contents

List of Illustrations		ix
How do you spell 'DeGaris'?		xi
Foreword		xiii
1	'The pleasantest and surest death'	1
2	'As many sides as the Kohinoor'	11
3	'Smile with your eyes', 1898–1910	25
4	Establishing an empire, 1913–20	39
5	'The Aussie Glide'	77
6	The C. J. DeGaris Publishing House, 1920	101
7	My town Kendenup, where everybody smiles	121
8	A great smash, 1921–23	143
9	The alert, grey twinkling eyes of C. J. DeGaris	177
10	'The Long Vision'	201
11	Eight lost days	219
12	Infamy	237
13	'Fell down on a big job'	257
14	'The essence of kindness'	265
Notes		281
Bibliography		319
Acknowledgements		345
Index		349

List of Illustrations

The note left in C. J.'s Packard on the shore at Mentone.	2
The sheet music to 'Moonooloo', 1924.	3
DeGaris family tree.	14
DeGaris family, probably circa 1900. Left–right: Bessie, C. J., Elizabeth, Lilian (at rear), George (at front), Alfred, Mary.	22
This image of the Corbould family from mid-1916 is one of the few extant photographs of Rene DeGaris. The back row is of Bean, Robert, Harold – who was a close associate of C. J.'s – Clarence and Charles, and at the front, Rene, Clara and Mollie. Vera DeGaris is on the right.	35
Pyap Hall, built by C. J. in 1913, in 2007.	46
Sunraysed film announcement.	60
Grant Hervey, in Sydney *Truth*.	64
The sheet music to 'Proposing', 1921, with *F. F. F.* branding.	85
The most spectacular of C. J.'s aeroplane crashes.	87
C. J. saluting those who served, in his introduction to Harold Hansell's *The Everlasting Ballads*.	105
Joseph Furphy's *Rigby's Romance*, the most enduring of the C. J. DeGaris Publishing House novels.	113
The Kendenup *Index*.	125
Leaving Perth for Sydney, from *The Victories of Failure*.	130
'Old Aussie admiring his new beauty spot'.	132
'Take a tip from this', *Mildura and Merbein Sun*, 22 October 1921.	146
C. J. caricature by K. Wallace Crabbe in the *Sunraysia Daily*.	156

LIST OF ILLUSTRATIONS

The DeGaris–Austin wedding, 27 June 1923. Ernie Bye and Jean Wenborn are the children; the adults are, left–right, Ewan Tate, Wilga Austin, C. J., Violet, Roy MacGregor, Marjorie Austin.	189
Violet DeGaris, an unsourced clipping.	194
C. J. at his desk.	202
Corio's 'big day', Melbourne *Sun*, 22 September 1924.	209
C. J., Violet, Veema and Prince.	242
The Victories of Failure, with C. J.'s inscription.	245
C. J.'s grave, Brighton Cemetery.	266

How do you spell 'DeGaris'?

Newspapers and other texts have had considerable trouble with the name DeGaris. Over more than a century it has been presented in the Australian media as DeGaris, Degaris, deGaris, de Garis and so on. I have chosen to use 'DeGaris', the mode chosen by some (by no means all) of the family in Australia, and C. J. himself – sometimes! To make reading easier, I have also formalised all quotes to reflect this rendering.

I have also chosen to refer to my subject as 'C. J.' for 'Clement John', throughout. This is the name he, and the public and media, tended to use although those closest to him (and occasionally, the press) called him 'Jack'. I have eschewed the convention of referring to him by last name because there are too many DeGarises in this book to make that simple, though of course he would be referred to this way in the 'serious' press and this will be evident in some quotes. I have similarly formalised the presentation of film and book titles in quoted passages. This does not always necessarily reflect the manner in which these titles were presented in original texts. Once again, this has been done for ease of reading.

Readers may be interested to note that almost all people who knew C. J. and the DeGaris family in the 1920s pronounced the name with the 'a' as in 'Harris', rather than as in 'cigar'. I have not encountered any attempt to silence the final 's' as one might in French.

Foreword

For a few exciting years in the early 1920s, C. J. DeGaris was a household word in Australia. Like a comet, he streaked across the national horizon, sparking adulation, enmity and controversy. Charming, enterprising and charismatic, he seemed to be a man perfectly in tune with the aspirations of the age. Australia had emerged from the Great War disillusioned with the old world but uncertain of its direction in the new. C. J. was a man with answers, almost too many it sometimes seemed. A restless innovator, he was in love with everything modern and mechanical – cars, aeroplanes, radio, movies, musicals – but deeply attached, too, to some old ideals – health, community and the virtues of country life. He seemed, in that moment of transition, to have intuited how new and old could be combined to make a new Australia. But, then as suddenly as he had appeared, he was gone, leaving a shocked public wondering whether they had lost a flawed genius or a brilliant scoundrel.

As David Nichols shows in this wonderful book, the life of C. J. DeGaris is not just a rollicking good yarn but a fascinating window into the tangled dreams and nightmares, fads and follies of an anxious age. DeGaris often seemed to be the hero in a drama of his own making, a highwire performer hungry for the plaudits of the crowd, a daredevil tempting the disaster that was only a misstep away. It's a tale replete with excitement and suspense, along with touches of tragedy, scandal and absurdity. It has all the ingredients – attempted murder, adultery, staged disappearances and fake identity – of a modern melodrama. In telling it, David registers all these notes together with a grudging respect for a man whose ambition, however ill-governed, was always mixed with an apparently sincere desire to do good.

Born the son of a preacher named Elisha, he seemed almost predestined to the mantel of a prophet. While he would stray from Methodist morality, he retained something of Methodism's evangelical mission to redeem a broken world. From Mildura, where he absorbed his father's utopian faith in the regenerative power of irrigation, C. J. gradually broadened his mission, establishing his own irrigation business at Pyap in South Australia's Riverland, before launching his most ambitious scheme – 'the dream of his life' – a combined agricultural and manufacturing settlement at Kendenup in Western Australia. With its own school, hospital, church, playgrounds and owner-occupied cottages, Kendenup was to be at once beautiful, harmonious and prosperous, 'a slumless town and a slumpless settlement'.

Over the years, many Australians had hoped to reverse the harmful drift of population to the coastal cities. Most had failed. DeGaris believed that with the application of modern technology and business methods, he could regenerate rural Australia. Kendenup's patented dehydrator would enable its irrigated fruit to be transported to markets all over the world. Its knitlock brick-making machine, designed by the American architect Walter Burley Griffin, would house its residents more cheaply. DeGaris's exploits as a long distance car driver and aviator were not only self-indulgent publicity stunts but – he for one believed – demonstrations of the power of modern transport to tame the tyranny of distance. It was a vision shared by many of his contemporaries, including some now revered as saints and patriots, like John Flynn of the Inland.

Reformer and huckster, the community organiser and entrepreneur, DeGaris may look more like a character from the American West than from the Australian Bush. Detroit and Hollywood, Madison Avenue and Broadway were his spiritual homes. When his business empire faltered, it was to New York rather than London or Melbourne that he looked for a rescuer. And when it finally crashed, he fled assuming the implausible disguise of a travelling American businessman. Yet, we should remind ourselves, such characters are not entirely unknown in our history. From the land boomers of Marvellous Melbourne to the White Shoe Brigade of Queensland's Gold Coast, boosters and hucksters have always played a prominent part in Australian urban and rural development.

FOREWORD

The history of urban planning is often written dialectically, as a contest between planners, inspired by expert knowledge and a commitment to public good, and developers, motivated by low cunning and self-interest. Sometimes the planners triumph; although more often they fail, while living to fight another day. This Manichean perspective has been serviceable to an underdog profession, reinforcing its self-worth and offering hope of future vindication, but it hardly reflects the real urban world in which planners and developers, ideals and self-interest are so inextricably intertwined that it is sometimes hard to draw any lessons at all.

Perhaps that's why David Nichols, who knows the history of Australian planning and real estate development like few others, approaches the mercurial life and sudden death of C. J. DeGaris with a light touch, acknowledging his personal and business failings as well as the complicated mixture of motives – power, recognition, altruism and, yes, money – that drove him. He has provided the evidence for every reader of this absorbing book to draw their own conclusions about the brilliant, fascinating, ill-fated character behind 'the alert, grey, twinkling eyes of C. J. DeGaris'.

Graeme Davison, OA
Emeritus Professor of History
Monash University

1

'The pleasantest and surest death'

He had banked on the shore being entirely empty, and there was no-one on Beach Road at 5 am on Monday 4 January 1925 when a brand-new double-seated blue Packard turned right onto Mundy Street, in the Melbourne beach side suburb of Mentone.[1] An observer might well have recognised Clement John 'C. J.' DeGaris, a famous and flamboyant figure whose photograph or caricature had frequently appeared in newspapers over the previous five years. He was 39 years old, 1.52 m tall, with an athletic build, square shoulders, brown hair turning grey and thinning at the temples,[2] and was regarded by many, including himself, as handsome.

He was also, typically, well-dressed. After parking in a clearing in the tea-tree, he stood by the car and removed his light grey hat, his dark grey check suit, his tie, collar, waistcoat, shirt, and trousers.[3] All were folded neatly and placed on the front seat of the Packard. He pinned a note to the suit's lapel. It read: 'Whoever finds this car and clothing please communicate at once with Mrs C. J. DeGaris of Wahgunyah, Rosebud and tell her to look in the small drawer in the chest of drawers in her bedroom'.[4] There was a similar note in the waistcoat. Other pockets contained the Packard's registration certificate, C. J.'s driver's licence, two newspaper cuttings – one headed 'What is efficiency?'[5] and another, a picture of C. J. himself, from the *Buffalo Times*[6] – and two stock certificates from Kendenup, the West Australian fruit growing settlement he had founded less than five years previously, one of them bearing the name of Alice Austin.[7] There were also, on scraps of paper, some verses he had written:

> On fancy's wing my thoughts will often wander,
> To one dear spot where Romance came to dwell,
> There is no spot on earth of which I am fonder,
> For all is happy as a marriage bell.
>
> Not all the wealth of fabulous Golconda
> Could weave o'er me a greater magic spell,
> And when upon the memories I ponder
> Of that dear place that I remember well.[8]

The note left in C. J.'s Packard on the shore at Mentone. Sydney *Evening News*, 6 January 1925, p. 1.

They were lyrics to the song 'Moonooloo'. They veered between the sentimental – above – and a chorus that embodied the kind of silliness that might have fit in his musical, *F. F. F.*:

> That happy Moonooloo
> Where we would Boonalloo
> And run down to Noonaloo
> In happy Tunaloo.

He had high hopes for sheet music sales for the song.[9]

The sheet music to 'Moonooloo', 1924. National Library of Australia.

The car also contained a piece of thin rope, freshly cut[10], a motor tube, and a booklet of views of his Corio Garden Suburb.[11]

C. J. had become convinced over the previous six weeks that he had 'slipped a cog in his thinking machine'[12] since the fade in financial fortunes of the Melbourne Sub-Divisions Company, known as the MSD. Concerned over his obligation to shareholders – many of them old friends – and distressed about his wife Violet's illness following the birth of their first child, Veema, he had compounded his problems by making rash financial decisions, borrowing from MSD accounts to repay personal debts.[13] A month earlier, the MSD had announced a restructure, entailing the removal of C. J. himself from the day-to-day operations of the company.

Only a few weeks before, he had been travelling with his 18-year-old chauffeur Albert de Pledge on an elevated section of the Nepean Highway overlooking the sea; C. J. had mused out loud 'what a spectacular death it would be' to simply drive off the road. De Pledge, probably glad *he* was driving, had nervously agreed.[14] Additionally, C. J. had considered taking prussic acid (hydrogen cyanide), and had bought some at a chemist in Glenferrie a few days prior on the pretext that he wished to poison a dog.[15] In conversation with one of the MSD's employees, James Keogh, C. J. had mentioned 'drowning was the easiest way to take one's life'.[16] 'I am assured it is a pleasant death', he had written to a friend. The previous month, a boy had been drowned in the spot C. J. had chosen, and the body had washed to shore in less than an hour.[17]

C. J. and Violet had been at the seaside resort of Rosebud for a week and a half with Veema, friends, relations and, for part of the time, C. J.'s three daughters from his first marriage: Winnie, Dulcie and Vera. Violet's illness was abating. As he had suggested in the notes on his clothing, C. J. had placed two letters in her drawer in their holiday home in Mitchell Street from which he commanded the 'Heart of Rosebud' Estate. She came across them while looking for a handkerchief after he had left the house at 3 am, and before police contacted her.[18] One letter, to explain the other, had been written the previous evening, along with hundreds more posted to friends and colleagues. It read:

> Sweetheart Vyzie.
> Enclosed letter has been written for some days, preparing for my departure from this world. I have decided on drowning as the pleasantest and surest death. I am eager for it now to be all over. I am not drowning myself at Rosebud, because I do not want the place to be associated with a tragedy in your memory. It has so many happy recollections, and we have had such a wonderful ten days now that I want the end to be relieved of some of its distressful results. Hence, fully dressed, early on Monday morning, but with my bath togs underneath, I will motor along the bay to some spot where I will soon be out of my depth – and end it all. It is the first time I have been glad that I cannot swim, for the end will be only a matter of moments, and everyone who has been nearly drowned tells me that it is a beautiful panorama of past events, from which they dislike being awakened. Therefore, my angel, do not worry over me, and, if you can, remember only the few attractive phases of my character, and overlook, with your usual generosity and love the many shortcomings.
> Dearest love, the hardest part will be to say good-bye without betraying myself.
> Your loving Jack.

The second letter – apparently written some days earlier – said:

> My way of spending Christmas has been to try to appear as happy as possible, while all the time I am preparing to "shuffle off" on Sunday or Monday morning. But for you, my sweetheart, this would have been done weeks ago. You and little Veema have been the only restraining forces that made me want to live. You have been all that love and a devout wife

could be – an inspiration, a gift of God, a gift, unfortunately, of which I have proved unworthy. It is the last bitter fight against Fate – apparently a well-deserved fate, though my intentions have always been of the best. I have come to realise that while alive I am a source of worry and anxiety and trouble to those I love the most and who trust me the most, and, unfortunately, that characteristic increases with every year of my age. Dead, I can at least leave some memories, some redeeming features which with things as they are and as they promise to be, would disappear if I lived. I would rather you be the widow of a dead man than the wife of a lunatic – and this I am afraid I would become if I had to stand the constant pressure of the squealers of the past six weeks – and the knowledge that I, for another five or seven years at least, would not be normal to you under the fearful pressure of trying to satisfy every creditor and every investor, each one of whom seems to desire and expect special treatment, which it is truly impossible for me to give.

I think my life policy assigned to you is worth about £3,500 and is secured from your creditors, and this is all I have to leave you besides the miserable few personal belongings you have. This insurance money, invested in Government bonds, should bring you in about £3 a week. Use it as income and not as capital. Do not make the same mistake as I did and would do again if I were alive. It is because I see that my continuation of life would bring you grief and long unhappiness that I am determined to finish it and leave you free to some day find a better man.

We have been so very very happy. Your illness started my fears for you, and their effect undoubtedly gave the impression of financial worry. At the time I was for three weeks consolidating. This would have meant security and profit to them and to us. But then came preparations for the journey that has no return ticket.

I felt in advance your sorrow, those many reproaches. But both would be dear if I lived, as my sub-normality for the past two months has made me do things that normally I would not do to you, not, thank God, in matters of domestic morality.

It has never been hard to be true to you, but because I have gambled in futures and had no right to.

Sweetheart, though the whole of me is weak, teach Veema that her daddy had some good in him, which good was never more manifest than when you, my angel, were near.

From this love, millions of kisses, from your loving husband, Jack – Daddy – "C. J."[19]

There were numerous other business and creative partners to whom he had written, explaining his decision to die. To another friend, C. J. wrote, 'I cannot face the hard work, worry, anxiety and suspicion of a prolonged reconstruction, and so I'm jamming out tonight – in the bay'.[20]

To the company's directors, he wrote a rambling message, reading in part:

> If anyone ever tells you that the man who commits suicide is a coward, you can emphatically deny it...I naturally often wish now that I had been killed in some of our plane smashes, at which dangers we used to laugh. These were the days of my prosperity, and death then in 1920 would have left my name untarnished, my integrity undoubted, and my commercial status assured, and yet I can truly say that in the period 1920 to 1924 I have worked more for Australia and less for myself than at any other period in my history, and have lost all, and gained nothing by so doing.[21]

To Joseph Woolf, who had recently become heavily involved in the MSD reconstruction, C. J. offered:

> Your unworthy protégé is ridding you of a big responsibility to-night by cutting the painter and making his exit from this life beneath the waves...I know you are optimistic and

enthusiastic about reconstruction, but the tenor of the replies to your letters, and the fiasco of the Rosebud sales make success impossible, and in any case I'd be in the way. Therefore, to all concerned I'm passing out.[22]

Reginald Stoneham, who C. J. had commissioned to write the music for the 'Sun-Raysed Waltz', 'Moonooloo' and all the songs in *F. F. F.*, also received a note. C. J. didn't break the habit of giving Stoneham a jovial honorific:

> Dear Sir Reg...The strain has been too long and too strong, and I have cracked up under it.
> I hope for dear Vi's sake that Moonooloo turns out a winner, for she will need to get every penny she can.
> Think as pleasantly as you can of me, who came nearer to being a big success than people think, and who consequently, became the greatest failure.
> Regards and regrets – C. J. DeGaris.[23]

He had not forgotten the staff at the MSD. To them he wrote:

> A short goodbye message to the office staff, to whom I have not had ability to write separately. Sorry we had no final hand grip...Remember me with as fragrant a memory as you can.[24]

He wrote a note to de Pledge, who had come from Kendenup to Melbourne to find work and had been put in charge of the MSD's car fleet. It asked him to help C. J.'s wife and her sisters back to Melbourne, and included a five pound note.[25] He apparently did not write to J. S. Schwartz, the New York investor who had touched him so deeply, but let him down so severely. In 1922 Schwartz had written to C. J.'s close associate J. J. Simons: 'Keep his mind from brooding, for he has seemingly great burdens to bear...'.[26]

A dog was barking on shore.[27] We cannot know if the 'beautiful panorama of past events', which C. J. had written about to Violet, took hold. If they had, the times he would look back on most fondly were surely his boyhood in the infant settlement of Mildura, when he was responsible for his beloved father's businesses; the camaraderie of his scant few years at Wesley College; his social life as the popular eldest son of a leading local family in Mildura; the happy early days of his first marriage and the births of his children; his times spent speeding on the barely built roads between Melbourne, Mildura and Pyap and flying across Australia between the east and west coasts, breaking records between state capitals. He might have lingered on the time when assorted gentlemen of the press, who he so impressed while touring the Sunraysia districts, coined names for him like 'The Sultan of Sunraysia', 'The Monarch of the Murray', 'The Ball of Energy', or 'The Restless Genius'.[28]

Notwithstanding his present situation his mind would also, still, be obsessing on the operations of the MSD and its cornerstone Corio estate, which he knew would be a success once Ford established its colossal automobile factory on its east side. Perhaps, though, his reflections centred on the most satisfying and hopeful time of his forty years on Earth: when he was the 'Chief' of Kendenup, where 700 settlers esteemed and depended on him.

Mentone returned to a silent dawn, broken only by the occasional vehicle passing on Beach Road. One of them was driven by a Mr Montague, an MSD staff member, with de Pledge in the passenger seat; they were following the coast, looking for the Packard, but didn't spot its hiding place.[29] Instead it was found by a Mr Swann, of Merino Road, Rosebud, passing by in his own car; he roused the owners of a nearby house in Beach Road, and one Sergeant Tenant was called to the scene. Violet DeGaris was contacted, the newspapers were alerted and a furore began.

Three days after C. J.'s disappearance, a school of large sharks was observed near the beach.[30] Some observers suggested they may have been attracted by a body; others were adamant that no evidence of C. J. would be found, because a sea lion would quickly eat his remains. Certainly, systematic searching of the bay at Mentone, south of Beaumaris Pier, over the next few days failed to discover a corpse. Yet C. J. DeGaris had definitely gone. He had left behind a wife, four daughters, three sisters, two brothers, his revered father Elisha, scores of friends and enemies, the nascent Kendenup settlement, and hundreds of creditors.

2

'As many sides as the Kohinoor'

C. J. described his father, Elisha, as having 'as many sides as the Kohinoor', but he might have been talking about himself. At a time when Elisha was at his business peak, C. J. declared pseudonymously and whimsically, 'He is the ablest and most gifted man we have ever met. That statement is definite, concise and true'.[1]

This good-humoured assessment of Elisha is even richer coupled with the knowledge that his eldest son was modelling himself strongly on his father. Elisha's ability to function in different spheres of thought and society were, C. J. claimed, just like 'the various facets of that famous pebble'. He went on:

> The man is so versatile, it does not give us a fair chance to reckon him up…An excellent preacher, a powerful platform speaker and an able journalist; surely this was a large enough field to content him! But not so…the colony of Victoria owes him a debt it can never repay.[2]

Certainly, the everyday lives and ambitions of Elisha Clement and Clement John were intertwined. This was true not only of the way that their main joint businesses – the growing and selling of fruit, and the selling of land for others to grow fruit – was transacted over thirty years, but also of their expectations of the value of such business. Tycoons and entrepreneurs are usually concerned primarily with their own wealth and prospects. The DeGarises were exceptions. They saw themselves as facilitators for greater prosperity, comfort and happiness for the wider community.

Outside their business concern, the DeGaris men's approaches contrasted – Elisha was a minister of religion and also had ambitions to run for office. In this he was, ultimately, disillusioned: 'One man with the best of intentions in Parliament is almost helpless, and to carry out his own ideas he has to convert an entire party, and nobody but a prophet with the power to work miracles could do that'.[3] It's not surprising C. J. chose not to follow him there.

Elisha was born in 1848, the son of another Elisha, in Guernsey, UK. He was 3 years old when his family travelled on the ship *Pestonjee Bomangee*[4] to Australia to settle in Adelaide. Many of these family members, including Elisha's brother Lucas, and their father made their mark, still visible today in the South Australian town of Naracoorte.

Elisha was educated at St Peter's College, Adelaide. When C. J. wrote about Elisha in 1925, he described it as an education funded 'by means of his own modest savings and some assistance' from Elisha senior, with additional income 'from cleaning the boots of the college masters'.[5] Elisha relocated from Naracoorte to Melbourne in 1872, when he was 23, and for three years studied architecture at the prolific firm of Crouch and Wilson. C. J. later depicted his father's architectural forays as successful – he won 'first and second cash prizes' in architectural competitions and drew a good salary.[6] But the work was spiritually unsatisfying, so Elisha studied for and entered the Methodist ministry. He was to serve as a minister for 14 years.[7] While Elisha's route to his eventual central role in both the promotion of irrigation and the foundation of the city of Mildura was circuitous, one can see him picking the various elements of his holistic approach to social engineering for the greater good as he went. The leap from architecture to Methodist preaching, with its emphasis on religious work and stated ambition to consistently stand 'in the forefront of the fight for the purification of public and social life' is no great stretch when triangulated with his eventual great achievements in helping to create the city of Mildura.[8]

Elisha married Elizabeth Buncle, whose family had arrived in Australia from Scotland thirty years earlier, in early 1881.[9] Their non-identical twin daughters Mary Clementina (Clemmie) and Bessie arrived in the same year as their parents' wedding – decently at the far end of that year. Mary would remember not only their dedication to equality but also a domestic life founded on respect for the individual, rather than gender roles.[10]

The couple's first son, Clement John, was born on 27 December 1884 in the working-class suburb of Hotham, now known as North Melbourne. C. J. begins his fictionalised autobiography with a telling portrait of his 4½-year-old self preaching to bystanders there 'with all the unction and pride of a well-satisfied and highly sincere Minister of the Gospel'.[11] To listeners' 'delight and amazement, and his own extreme gratification, he would reel off word for word the eloquent prayers to which his gifted father had given utterance the previous day' and which, in style, 'depended wholly on his imitation of his father's address to his God'.[12] The story ends, as C. J. tells it, with discovery by a furious father, and punishment drumming the entire incident into the boy's head.

Religion was a key element in DeGaris life, never far from the family's daily existence. C. J. later recalled:

> Grace at each meal, Morning and Evening Family Prayers, Band of Hope classes, regular Sunday school attendances and Church twice each Sunday. At early ages the family had

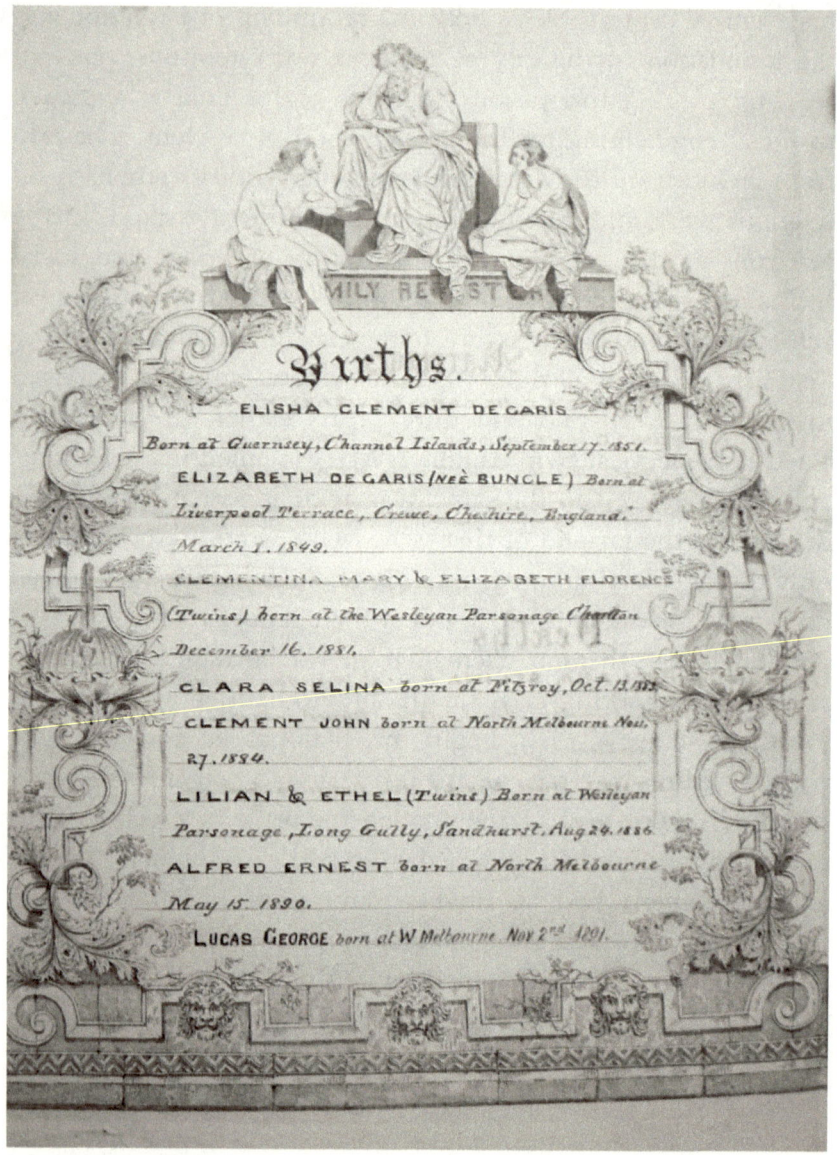

DeGaris family tree, in Lucas George DeGaris papers, National Library of Australia.

absorbed the Old and New Testaments, and could, and did, quote from them freely. They knew almost every Wesleyan hymn and tune by heart.[13]

Yet there was also a touch of the pagan. Another story from this era tells of the young C. J. – a 'baby' but able to speak – having a 'serious infantile complaint' to the degree that his father built him a coffin. He was saved by the healing hands of his mother, who Mary DeGaris wrote of as a font of knowledge on infant health.[14]

Elisha's ministries included the affluent and fashionable beachside suburb of St Kilda; Sandhurst, now Bendigo; and two towns to its north, Durham Ox and the more substantial regional centre and railway village of Kerang.[15] He was particularly popular with Kerang's congregation,[16] and here the next phase of his career came upon him. The region was stricken by drought and, noting that 'the only thing that could save the district was the conservation and utilisation of the streams',[17] Elisha became convinced of the 'national necessity of irrigation'.[18] He had become acquainted with the Scottish-born irrigation advocate Hugh McColl, eager to develop capacity in Australia for huge engineering works distributing river water across the country in large canals. Later, C. J. would write of Elisha:

> He saw that he could not only minister to the sacred requirements of the individual, but could also minister to the national requirements of a huge, but comparatively empty, continent, which, by the scientific addition of water to the soil, would become a land without a rival the world over.[19]

Elisha wrote that he met McColl:

> and studied the plans which he brought which were huge affairs, several ft long and my impression with regard to him up to that point was that he was a fanatic and there was really

no practical basis for the theories which he was expounding...
However...I became enthusiastic about the things which he
advocated.[20]

Turning to journalism and publishing, Elisha founded the *Australian Irrigationist* – 'a useful journal',[21] C. J. later described it – as well as irrigation leagues to agitate for government funding for infrastructure. He 'corresponded with all the Irrigation countries of the world and received some valuable information', building up a 'small library of books' on the topic.[22] Elisha relayed a story about Bishop Moorehouse – asked to pray to end drought, Moorehouse had simply responded, 'Dig bigger dams'.[23] Elisha agreed: God sent the 'blessing of water', and Australians should develop the skills to retain and control it.

For the *Irrigationist,* Elisha created an alter ego known as 'Simon Seedy', a name he would still be publishing under sixty years later. In 1883 he became president of the Central Irrigation League of Victoria, insisting that 'the conservation and distribution of the water in the colony should be in the hands of the state, and so managed that its beneficial influences might be as fairly and widely diffused as possible'.[24]

A notebook of musings of 1924–26 preserved in Elisha's collected papers, seem to give a flavour of the man. He's certainly patrician, and religious with a mystical bent, but he is also imaginative, aware and not without good humour. A list of figures recording agent sales of sultanas and peaches in the first half of 1924 is augmented by notes for a work entitled 'Inner Secret' ('My faith is firm inner assurance of V beneficence of that Infinite Reality')[25], possibly intended for anonymous publication (one page is headed 'by Mr X'). The same pages contain the text of an inspirational speech given at Yarra Street State School in the Melbourne suburb of Alphington on 2 May 1926, wherein Elisha told Yarra Street students that 'Thinking is hard work. It takes time and effort. It's a great thing when a boy or a girl begins to think'.[26] Incongruously – it's probably not part of his speech to the Yarra Street children – this is followed in the notes by 'Dried Fruit Statistics'. Elisha's collected papers also feature numerous ideas for sermons sketched out on gutted envelopes; the co-existence of tallies and sales projections on the same page as a thorough exploration of autosuggestion is entirely typical. He saw his society, its means of economic support, its religious and intellectual underpinnings, and its intellectual and physical sustenance, as one package.

In 1887, Elisha augmented his passion for irrigation with a related creation, the Associated Australian Yeomanry (AAY), with branches in several rural centres.[27] It strove to improve the farmer's lot through a combination of primary producer unionism and professional association. One AAY prospectus suggests that it was not 'proposed as another so-called "co-operative company" to do business with farmers, but as an ASSOCIATION OF FARMERS TO DO THEIR OWN BUSINESS'.[28] An impressive and fast-growing organisation, its various branches merged in the early twentieth century into related but more specialised co-operatives and bodies.

Elisha used whatever means he could to promote the lot of the man on the land, particularly the cause of irrigation: 'Irrigation lectures, irrigation pictures – even irrigation excursion trains were among his devices'[29], wrote C. J. admiringly. Elisha's activities included the chairing of the Tragowel Plains Irrigation Trust, the first to be established under Victoria's Irrigation Act.[30] Elisha was of the opinion that 'half-heartedness' had 'never succeeded anywhere and certainly it will not succeed in such a battle as is involved in a struggle against aridity'. He continued:

> Unless a farmer throws himself into the work with enthusiasm + hope he had better remain out of it altogether + make way for a better man but a way is shown of overcome [sic] the essential difficulties of the situation of winning a considerable personal reward + of conferring a national advantage in mean dimensions.[31]

He was one of a number of distinguished and dedicated men who had pressed government – specifically a young member of colonial parliament, Alfred Deakin – to investigate international irrigation activities. Deakin adopted irrigation as a special passion, publishing books on the intricacies of the subject as a key component of national growth. In California in early 1885, Deakin encountered two Canadian brothers. The Chaffeys – William and George – had made a large-scale success of closely adjoined settlements, Ontario and Etiwanda, dedicated primarily to citrus produce. Both towns blended social engineering – alcohol, for instance, was banned – with the scientific marvel of the irrigation works as well as novelty in the form of the donkey tram, pulled by the animal up a low incline for some miles, then returned by gravity, the donkey riding aboard. Deakin encouraged the Chaffeys to investigate conditions he saw as similar to California's in northern Victoria, where a large river flowed through dry landscapes. At Deakin's recommendation, the Chaffeys sent an emissary, Stephen Cureton, to survey the Murray between Echuca and the South Australian border, and became of the opinion that a riverside sheep station, known as Mildura, was the best place for fruit growing.[32] Their decision was swayed, they would later claim, by the misinformation that nearby Wentworth was to be the site of the federal capital.[33]

The Victorian government vacillated on granting Mildura to the Chaffeys, and South Australia took the opportunity to invite them to set up at Renmark, 250 km northeast of Adelaide and 140 km west of the Mildura site. Victoria then offered them 250,000 acres (101,171 hectares) of the 'Mildura run' in May 1887.[34] The Chaffeys took on both projects. Their publicity vehicle was the 'Red Book', *Australian Irrigation Colonies on the River Murray*, published in 1889.

The Chaffeys did not need to advertise to attract Elisha to Mildura; he knew them, admired their work, and spent time at their experimental irrigation farm 6 km from Werribee.[35] However, he did not relocate immediately, and Mildura had been under Chaffey control for four years when the DeGarises moved there in 1891. Elisha undertook 'the work of a philanthropist and a patriot rather than that of a business man'.[36] While philanthropy may have been his prime motivator, he was to become a business success. Elisha began his association with Mildura simultaneously with his 'retirement' from the Methodist ministry[37], though he continued to preach in a lay capacity for the rest of his long life.

Elisha took key administrative positions at the local hospital and the Mechanics Institute Hall and Library. But while he was engaged in the politics of local development and worked successfully as an administrator in the 'city father' mould in Mildura, his political forays at state level were far less successful. In an Australia where party politics was embryonic, Elisha was traditionally an independent. He did not join the Liberal Party but saw himself as a liberal in the classic mould, believing that 'Liberalism from its very nature must endure, and in the end gain a great triumph'. Liberalism's principles were, in Elisha's mind, 'The supremacy of conscience...Freedom in conviction and action...Preservation of personal individuality'.[38] That said, in 1910 he would stand for the seat of Yarra as a candidate for the short-lived Fusion party. 'Fusion candidates are strong for the Federation; but theirs is not the Commonwealth Federation but the Employer's Federation', wrote one critic, opining that Elisha therefore 'ranges himself alongside these champions of land and industrial monopoly'.[39]

Mildura, a new town created from scratch, publicised by the Chaffeys as a 'colony' and seemingly combining science and technology with ancient agricultural crafts, was a perfect venture in which Elisha could throw his (and his family's) lot. Yet the transition from an advocate for irrigation to an actual irrigationist – that is, to a large-scale farmer (or even a yeoman) of irrigated lands – was long. The first plantings in Mildura were in 1888; between 25 per cent and 50 per cent of the new settlers planted vines, the remainder deciduous trees and citrus trees.[40]

Though Elisha was a grower, operating a large landholding, he was to make his fortune in packing, preservation and distribution, as well as in real estate. Of those pursuits preservation was the most important, and the science of drying fruit was of great value for an industry dependent so strongly on the transport of its produce to major markets.

The town grew rapidly in the first few years. The Grand Coffee Palace was erected in 1890, a Chaffey Agricultural College was in the preparation stages and £1,000 had been subscribed for a public institute to include a free library and a horticultural museum.[41] It was in the irrigation works themselves, however, that most of the important work was being done, as one early visitor discovered in 1889. The *Daily Telegraph's* journalist arrived in Mildura and was personally escorted across 45 miles (72 km) of the operational section of the estate. He saw a pump that could throw up to 80,000 gallons (364 kilolitres) of water in a minute, and another with a capacity of 120,000 gallons (546 kilolitres). Chaffey told him all village land had been sold, and close to 10,000 acres (4,047 hectares) surrounding it had been bought for cultivation. 1,200 people were living there, 'all of a very superior class'.[42]

Relying primarily on the river for contact with the outside world and using new and expensive technology for which solvency depended on fast returns was a gamble, which nearly did not pay off. The Chaffeys were soon in grave financial trouble and the very existence of Mildura was threatened. C. J. later reminisced that the early 1890s Depression in Victoria left Elisha 'on the brink of disaster, with no assets whatever, and an income that was almost negligible'[43]; indeed, the whole Mildura settlement seemed for a time in 1893–94 to be over before it had started. Even George Chaffey left the settlement to return to California. At the age of eight, C. J. saw an opportunity and filled it. He later recalled:

> By December, 1894, the successful business...had dwindled down to a mere matter of a few auction sales (all sellers and no

buyers) and an ever-decreasing insurance department, while its main support was an increasingly difficult rent round.

In C. J.'s recollection, this state of affairs puts him in a position of power. He had, he claimed, learnt arithmetic and writing from his tallying of business transactions[44], and:

> knowing full well by the bread-and-treacle diet at home that things were disastrously low, and proud of his newly-acquired exemption from school, volunteered to enter his father's office, and to help keep the flag flying until "Pa's ship came in"…

> It therefore became quite a common sight to see father and son (hand in hand) going to work early in the morning, dividing the indoor and the outdoor work during the day, and returning to the office at night to answer any correspondence, and put the few entries through the books.[45]

The fortunes of the company did, indeed, repair as the last decade of the nineteenth century wore on. Yet C. J. was also a child of the 1890s Depression, and this period of hardship haunted him psychologically. It certainly seems that he was also physically affected by the family's financial problems, and it is likely that despite his parents' best intentions he was a malnourished child. He was so short as a boy that there was every expectation he would be a dwarf.[46] Writing about himself later (in the third person), C. J. reflected that:

> In physique he was a "weed", being rather sickly in appearance, of stunted growth, but still possessed of the pink cheeks and the smiling blue-grey eyes, and the engaging frankness that won him friends wherever he went.[47]

The eyes were not only smiling, he wrote, but 'frank', though his face was 'wistful'.[48] C. J. believed it was beneficial for him to cultivate charming and personable ways that would make it easier for him to do business with local renters and others related to his family's business interests.[49]

This, and other examples of his 'university of life' education – most notably his abilities in mental arithmetic – meant that he had 'shown sufficient knowledge by examination' by the age of ten to complete his compulsory education long before the common school leaving age of 14.[50] He saw nonetheless a deficiency in his schooling that he would strive to redress later in his teens, in much the same way as his own father did – that is, by paying from his own money to attend school.

What we see from the DeGaris family's late-nineteenth-century experience, then, is a group of people – some still infants as the century draws to a close, some, like C. J., also old beyond their years – ensconced in their father's compelling vision of public service and individual responsibility. As already mentioned,

DeGaris family, probably circa 1900. Left–right: Bessie, C. J., Elizabeth, Lilian (at rear), George (at front), Elisha, Alfred, Mary. COURTESY RUTH LEE.

the family was extremely religious, but as was common in many Methodist families this was never to dull their intellectual curiosity, and in fact probably heightened it. All read widely and were often in conversation on diverse topics.

Elizabeth and Elisha were highly progressive, and their children's fortunes were to range between respectable, distinguished and notorious. They emerged at the start of the new century, prosperous within Mildura and famous across Victoria. Elisha's abilities to move within a range of spheres – religious, governmental and business – was, if not unique, certainly remarkable. One can imagine C. J.'s observation of, and reverence for, his father, alongside his numerous quirks – his short stature, his drive to entertain and engage, and his head for figures – spurring him to equal, if not better, Elisha's achievements. The coming Australian nation of the twentieth century would surely be the stage where C. J. would shine.

3

'Smile with your eyes', 1898–1910

School

Elisha and Elizabeth DeGaris' ambitions to send all their children to university to achieve an education appropriate to the brand-new century were dashed, in part, by the Depression. Only one child, Mary, was able to achieve the type of outcome her parents had wished for all. She had attended Methodist Ladies College in the Melbourne suburb of Kew for two years in 1898–99, achieving the rank of dux. Most of her education was funded through scholarships. C. J. was later to claim that this 'trait of independence' was a 'marked characteristic of every member' of his family.[1] He would prove to be no exception.

Ten-year-old C. J. was a blend of canniness and ignorance. He was 'accountant, the confidential correspondent, the copier and indexer of letters and general right hand' to his father in business dealings, yet in his early teens, his 'general knowledge… was lamentably deficient'.[2] Many years later he was to claim that as a youth he 'could not have told anything about other nations unless they happened to produce dried fruit in competition with

Mildura...As for history – other than the history of Mildura, which he knew backwards', he claims to have been 'totally ignorant'.[3] It was hardly surprising that he would be well-versed in the history of Mildura: the town was the same age as C. J. himself, and he had lived there for most of his sentient life. But the point of his self-assessment was, of course, that he was very able in some areas, and self-centred and provincial in others, but that his intelligence was not low for being uneducated.

Elisha pulled strings amongst his Methodist contacts to get C. J. into Melbourne's Wesley College, Australia's oldest registered school, at a reduced rate. C. J. was torn between his family, its business and his own interests, but realised that it would be a good investment. Like Mary, C. J. paid much of his own school expenses – almost £44 per year – from his savings, earned from his time working with his father.

A phrenologist friend, reading the bumps on C. J.'s head and, presumably, noting that the boy was short, warned Elisha and Elizabeth that their son would become a 'stunted dwarf' if he did not take up sport.[4] He did so with gusto. Cricket, football, tennis, boxing and running all became part of his daily regime. Taking stock of himself, C. J. found that he had:

> Four years of business training behind him; no knowledge of other boys; no training to obedience (except to his father, who treated him as an equal); no friends to consult; no stamina to withstand physical hurt; and no learning...[5]

As it transpired, his Wesley experience was to take only two and a half years out of three, in 1899–1901, but that time appears to have had an enormous impact. His memoir suggests a particularly emotionally immature boy, used to being recognised for his special skills in Mildura where he was both widely known and respected. It is hard to imagine that he was not teased for his short stature.

Elisha gave C. J. tips on ingratiating himself with others: 'A smile from the lips only may be forced. The eyes reflect the heart.

Smile with your eyes'.[6] At Wesley he was told by a friend, 'When in doubt, smile, and when you've got a smile like yours, keep smiling'.[7] Another boy discussed C. J. within his hearing: 'I like his smile – he's hot stuff'.[8]

C. J.'s account of his time at Wesley is banal. He would later suggest that his experiences 'and the wonderful band of vigorous and talented young Australians who were [my] contemporaries at Wesley College'[9] warranted a full-length novel. The few episodes he puts forward as notable Wesley experiences – such as a fight with a student with the unlikely name of Sourland, who he knocks out with a lucky punch,[10] and some extended accounts of football games – do not suggest anything compelling.[11] Wesley probably had a sentimental place in C. J.'s affections as representing a time when he was able to retreat from responsibility for anyone other than himself: a second childhood, *in* childhood. With a winning smile and ability to negotiate numerous difficult social environments, C. J. learnt about status and society at school.

Postcards home – the surviving ones are addressed to 'Papa' alone – are brief and, in contrast to the ripping yarns of the adult C. J.'s memoir, often sad. 'I have not yet got over that feeling of homesickness and would still like to be a day-boy', he writes in April 1899.[12] Mary was also in Melbourne, and was clearly in frequent contact with her brother: 'Clemmie and I were rather surprised at not getting a letter on Friday,' he writes in August of the same year, 'But I was pleased to get the long welcome letter today'.[13] He did well; it would not have been easy to learn enough history to receive an exam grade of 98 in his first year of formal schooling in five years, and indeed this result implies that the adult C. J. was overstating his boyish ignorance. In another letter he records an award in his Latin exam of 92 out of 100; 'Whitlam and Morgan were top with 100'.[14] 'Whitlam' was Fred Whitlam, destined to be father to a prime minister.

C. J. appears to have benefited from the Wesley experience, though it does not seem that many friends from this time lasted into adulthood. A year and a half into his studies, in July 1900,

C. J. took a six-month break, returning to Mildura to assist his father in business. During this time, he writes, he 'was able to apply the public school boy's psychology to every transaction'.[15] He had also become a proud Empire patriot, precociously writing a letter of support to Lord Roberts fighting in the South African War in July 1900.[16]

At Elisha's insistence, C. J. continued boxing.[17] Though he does not seem to have consulted any doctors, C. J. was naturally concerned about his short stature. At age 14, he was 4 ft 9 in (1.45 m) and weighed less than 6 stone (38 kg). When he left school at the end of 1901 he had gained 2 inches, to become 4 ft 11 in (1.5 m). A *Mildura Cultivator* report from that year, of a cricket match between Wesley and Geelong, is illustrative:

> DeGaris, a very small "man" at square-leg, was very noticeable, and frequently stopped strokes which must have been "boundaries." A procession to the wickets was kept up, and a smart return from little DeGaris at square-leg resulted in the last man being run out, and the innings closed for 53, amidst intense excitement. Wesley won by 4 runs. The "little DeGaris" referred to is "Jack DeGaris" of this town.[18]

Returning to Mildura, C. J. continued to play cricket regularly, and was a feature of the local 'Methodists vs Presbyterians' games in 1902.[19] Additionally, he played tennis and occasionally football, for instance at the 'Coronation Day Charity Match' on 26 June 1902.[20]

The year 1902 was one of change and development. Bicycles were not new (they had first been discussed in the Melbourne *Age*, for instance, in 1869) but were still gaining ubiquity.[21] C. J. used his to rapidly traverse areas around Mildura. Apparently it was his own idea to make his seat higher so he had to reach further to the pedals, in the hope it would make his legs grow longer. This, or better nutrition as the family's fortunes recovered, or simply late development, made the difference: he grew 7 inches (18 cm) in

1902, to reach nearly 5 ft 6 in or 1.67 m: not a tall man, but 'little DeGaris' no more.

In April 1902, fruit growers' associations in Mildura and Renmark formed the Australian Dried Fruits Association (ADFA), a cooperative venture to aid growers. The ADFA was not a commercial enterprise in and of itself; it was a trade body formed to further the collective interests of its members.[22] In the same month as the ADFA was formed, Elisha fulfilled a long-held ambition of returning to Britain. He travelled with his brother Lucas, who still lived in Naracoorte. The two men hoped to witness the August coronation of Edward VII, as well as to undertake work relevant to their respective businesses.[23] Elisha also intended to visit Guernsey, where he had been born fifty-one years earlier.

Naturally, C. J. was left holding the fort. Though he was still too young, at 17, to undertake certain transactions – such as signing cheques – his mother and family friends were to operate under his instruction. Elisha expected that C. J. would merely keep the family firm afloat; however, C. J. told him that 'Mother and I will make things hum'.[24] Persistently ambitious to a self-punishing degree, and dedicated to impressing his father, C. J. made a rule not to sleep on any single working day unless that day's earnings exceeded the same day of the previous year's.[25] This ridiculously gruelling scheme, fortunately for C. J.'s health, was made possible by imaginatively expanding underdeveloped aspects of the DeGaris company. Life insurance, for instance, had been a component of the business since Elisha set it up in 1891.[26] C. J. thought life insurance was invaluable, and in fact believed every man should present his bride with a policy on his own life on their wedding day.[27] The no-nonsense farmers of the Mildura district 'either laughed outright, or were positively rude' when the subject of life insurance came up; but he discovered ways to ingratiate himself into their lives, largely through false camaraderie, feigning interest in their hobbies.[28] A core principle of salesmanship was thus initiated for C. J. Customers liked to be courted, and then, perhaps, persuaded. It was one of the seductive processes his smiling eyes seemed made for.

Another was literal seduction. It is hard to imagine that a bright country boy brought up in a pioneering settlement, engaging as an equal with adults and with enlightened parents concerned that he receive a holistic education, a sister at medical school and two and a half years' experience as a boarder at a boys' school, would be entirely ignorant of procreation. Yet C. J. insists in his memoir that he had no interest in, or understanding of, sex until he was 20 (in 1904). It never arose for discussion with either parent, he claims, adding that his 'age of maturity in this direction was unusually delayed, probably because of the intense concentration in business directions'. This, he says, was how he 'avoided the pitfalls that so beset most youths between the age of 14 and 20'.[29] He is presumably referring to the 'great masturbation panic' in its final throes in the early decades of the twentieth century.[30] It saw male masturbation as a sap on strength, vitality and physical development. C. J. claims that his lack of sexual knowledge and experience gave him great energy, and a respect for women.

It was on his return to Mildura that, perhaps in spite of himself, he became interested in girls. He still did not need to shave, however, and his interest in the women he dated was, he later claimed, 'purely that of calf-love...entirely sexless'.[31] His mother, he felt, was alarmed by his naiveté but unwilling to educate him in case this made him eager to experiment.[32]

While Mary apparently chose not to enlighten him, her achievements, bravery and persistence must have had a significant role in his emotional development and his outlook. She was headstrong and intellectual, and a 'serious' person – interested in broad social change, particularly as it related to the rights of women – and was proactive where C. J. was often reactive.[33] The DeGaris siblings were competitive when it came to the outside world, and C. J. relished competition more than any of them. Once Mary chose to study for the medical profession (she began at the University of Melbourne in 1900) C. J. could discount her as a rival in any of the spheres he cherished. Indeed, medicine had just become open to women; it would be a lot longer before women could work in 'business' or take on many of the other occupations in which C. J. specialised. The only field in which C. J. and his doctor sister both engaged was writing.

Elisha returned on 8 August 1902,[34] and was persuaded by Mildura's polite society to formulate a lecture, 'An Australian Across the Seas', illustrated with a series of collected-to-order slides from 'a Melbourne lanternist'.[35] The lecture included what were described in the press at the time as 'racy anecdotes'; they were unlikely to be risqué, but were perhaps thrilling.[36]

Family historian Ken DeGaris' account of the DeGarises in Australia claims it was the 'systematic brilliance of the father combined with the quiet achiever-like patience of the mother Elizabeth' which meant their children were, 'one way or another… destined to leave their mark on the world'.[37] The results of the Mildura Musical and Elocutionary competition, held in the Shire Hall on 7 September 1903, show their precocity: all DeGaris siblings with the exception of the eldest two, twins Mary and Bessie, were performing.[38] Such entertainments were part and parcel of life in rural towns, and included not only the singing and recitations the title suggested, but also exhibits of painting, drawing, needlework and cooking, down to the deceptively simple, such as Best Ironed White Shirt; no DeGaris child stooped to this. It was a community's inclusive nurturing of young people, a way of taking pride in achievement, and showing that Mildura – still a new town in a very new nation – could produce spirited, hearty, talented Australians. The DeGarises were not ones for musical items (C. J. claimed his singing voice was 'like a foghorn in distress'),[39] but in 1903 George, the youngest child, came second place in 'reading at sight' and 'recitation under 13', also tying with his brother Alfred in 'recitation boys under 17'. Alfred additionally won the 'temperance recitation'. A 'Miss DeGaris' (perhaps Lilian, who would become a nurse) won in the Ambulance Bandaging category. C. J. won the gentleman's 'recitation' category, and with two others, the best 'Original tale'.[40]

Eight months later, in July 1904, the competition was repeated to raise £25 for charity. This time, the DeGarises were even more involved, now in the organisation as well as the entertainment, which stretched over a week of evenings and afternoons. Elisha presided over one program, and C. J. was treasurer for the events. This time, George won in the recitation-under-14 category with a piece entitled 'Boys' Rights'; Alfred won in the boys-under-18 category with 'The Road to the Trenches' (George came second). Both boys won in the 'Temperance Recitation' section, Alfred with 'The Burst Bubble' and George with 'The Drunkard's Dream'. George also came first in 'Reading at First Sight'. Yet C. J. was not outdone by his younger brothers. He came second in the adult section of the temperance recitation with 'Sims' Little Girl' – he was to take this piece to another recital, the state championships in Ballarat, the following year.[41] This brief piece, by Ohio-born Mary Hartwell Catherwood, in the voice of a man who accidentally kills his beloved daughter through drunkenness, was calculated to deliver maximum impact in the telling. It also, as a first-person monologue, allowed the speaker to show ability in American accents.[42] C. J.'s recitation of 'Othello's Address to the Senate' came first in the gentleman's category, and he also won the 'Prepared reading' section with 'Universal Adoration', as well as tying for the best humorous recitation. He also came second in the 'Coon song' category, the only musical category in which any DeGaris ranked.[43]

Clearly C. J.'s willingness and ability to entertain, beguile and entrance was picking up pace. His winning smile was twinned with a winning ability to coerce and manage all around him: be they sceptical farmers and other reluctant customers; prospective romantic partners; a crowd of people wishing to be captivated; or his own parents and family. He was a showman.

He was also a rising star within the business-community leaders of Mildura, while his father was continuing to act in commercial and leadership roles in the town. Elisha had long agitated on behalf of the Mildura Railway League, pressing for the building of a line between Bendigo and Mildura.[44] He was pleased to see this become an 'accomplished and profitable fact' in 1903.[45] ('Well done! Good gentlemen and true...' exulted a poem in the *Mildura Cultivator*, welcoming the railway and namechecking Elisha).[46] Although still a 24-hour trip from Melbourne, the improvement over other forms of travel (river boat and/or road) was immeasurable, and the symbolism of state investment mattered.

A good example of the progressivism of the region – exemplified by families like the DeGarises – was Mildura Shire Council's request to the industrialist–philanthropist Andrew Carnegie to fund, as he had done around the world, a free lending library for their town. Council went too far in the first instance, proposing Carnegie pay for a two-storey building with a museum on the upper floor; he insisted it be a more modest single-storey structure.[47] Recently returned from a second international voyage,[48] Elisha DeGaris was shire president in 1906 when Carnegie donated £2,000 for the library, on condition that council contribute £100 a year to its upkeep and stock.[49] Free libraries were a rarity, and the cities and suburbs receiving such a gift – from a prominent and popular Scottish-born American ('splashing his millions about', one Orange journalist observed snidely)[50] – were doubly advantaged, both in their reputation and the cultural value of the thing itself. The *Mildura Cultivator* hoped that the books it held would be 'of a class which will make it valuable in the various departments of literature, science and art', and saw the library's contents – initially based on local donations – as indicative of the community's qualities.[51] Pride in the library, and in the town itself, were inextricable: no doubt many hearts were stirred when Lieutenant-Governor of Victoria John Madden, laying a foundation stone, praised 'the energy and persistence of the Mildura settlers':

Sir John Madden said he was amazed at the reclamation of a wilderness accomplished at Mildura. Coming through the desert that morning to Mildura seemed to him like passing through a weary life to Paradise. Certainly, leaving the desert, and finding oneself amidst citrus groves and vineyards, was like coming to Paradise.[52]

Marriage

In August 1907, C. J. wrote to his sister Mary:

> The wedding may seem to you, no doubt, to be an early + a hurried one. Even if it be speedy, you can be assured it is not hasty. Plenty of thought was devoted to the subject before we decided on what is looked on by some as an early marriage. I have very decided opinions of my own in reference to that phase of the question + as you know, my opinions, once logically founded, take some shifting before they will waver or alter.
>
> As to our happiness I have no fears. There is a perfect understanding between us. We have a thorough knowledge of each others' foibles + therefore are not liable to "a great awakening" as are those who walk blindly into matrimony, trusting to Providence to extricate them from any troubles, which unexpected + hitherto undiscovered disagreeable traits in each other, may bring about.
>
> We will be happy. This statement I make now + confidently expect to be able to affirm + confirm it on our Golden Wedding day.[53]

C. J.'s autobiographical novel *The Victories of Failure* is sorely tempting. On the one hand, it seems to hold answers to most of the questions one might have about his inner life; on the other, it has to be said that not only is it a justification (and on rare occasions, a *j'accuse*), it also proclaims from the very beginning that it is 'a business romance of fiction, blended with, and based on, fact'.⁵⁴ That said, if we did not have this book, we would have little more than the letter quoted above and news reports that on Thursday 26 September, at 8pm, C. J. married Rene Corbould at the Ninth Street Methodist Church, Rev F. Flentje presiding.⁵⁵ C. J.'s sister Lily, Rene's sister Marianne and another woman, Elsie Glasson, were bridesmaids. One of Rene's brothers, Harold, and C. J.'s brother Alfred, were best man and groomsman respectively. The reception was held at the Shire Hall. The listing of wedding gifts took up columns in the *Mildura Cultivator*.

The Corboulds preceded the DeGarises in Mildura; Robert Rutter Corbould, a milliner and haberdasher like his father in Ballarat, came to the town in 1890 with his wife Clara. Robert and Elisha would have been known to each other for well over

This image of the Corbould family from mid-1916 is one of the few extant photographs of Rene DeGaris. The back row is of Bean, Robert, Harold – who was a close associate of C. J.'s – Clarence and Charles, and at the front, Rene, Clara and Mollie. Vera DeGaris is on the far right. COURTESY HAL CORBOULD.

a decade, having served on diverse boards and committees as civic leaders in Mildura since that time. The Corboulds lived on Deakin Ave between 11th and 12th streets, and had six children. Rene, born in 1888, was the second. Rene was her full name, and it rhymed with 'Bean' which was, incidentally, both her mother's maiden name and the given name of one of her brothers.[56]

C. J.'s memoir is less reticent about his romantic and domestic life than most middle-class men would have been in the first decade of the twentieth century; he relays some stories from this period that give a sense of the lead-up to his marriage to Rene. He claims to have had a drawn-out sexual relationship in 1904–05 with a woman he calls Gertrude James. The two do not love each other enough to marry but were what a century later would be called 'friends with benefits'. Gertrude, we are told, finds C. J. 'nicer, cleaner and better than her first lover'.[57] Their affair allows Gertrude to taste 'just enough of the spice of life to enable her to settle down happily' with a long-term admirer.[58] That said, the arrangement (as C. J. tells it) was on- and off-again for some time as they met in diverse country towns for secret assignations.[59] His performance at the popular South Street talent competition – along with 'Sims' little girl', he gave a recitation on the topic of the Mt Etna volcano[60] – in October 1905 was, he says, coloured by the affair's revival. There is no further evidence that the woman he calls Gertrude James existed.

In January of 1906, C. J. had been best man to Robert Alexander, who married Elizabeth (Bessie) DeGaris at the Ninth Street church.[61] Seeing a sibling marry may have inspired him, though he does not say so. Nonetheless in taking stock, he writes, he found himself 'realising…that his temperament demanded early mating' so 'he began to look around, in all seriousness, for a girl with whom he could keep company, and whom he could ultimately (and soon) marry'.[62]

He had, he claims, known Rene (called 'Grace Mordant' in his book) since they were children. He describes her as 'most charming and attractive at times' though at others prone to illness, and 'a business girl, being her mother's right hand in managing a big drapery business'. She knew, he says, that he was 'an unconscionable flirt', but she, too, 'had a habit of "stringing on the boys"'. Neatly, when they 'each decided to try their arts on the other...both fell victims to the other's powers of conquest'.[63]

When Elisha returned from his second international trip, he presented his eldest son with the opportunity to travel to the USA. C. J. waited a day to respond, and while he and Elisha cycled to his cricket match, 'going over a sand hill with wobbling wheels', he told his father of his wish to marry.[64] Elisha's response is recorded thus:

> "I won't withhold my consent; but I advise against your engagement until you go to America, and come back."
> "It's this way, father...I don't know whether it's my French blood or unusual temperament, or what it is; but I want to get married early, and I want to marry Grace."
> "Why?"
> "Because I want to keep straight, and I have too many temptations, and I'd have more if I travelled. I want to keep straight, and I find it mighty hard."

Relieved by the 'plain speaking' with his father, C. J. – in his recollection – went on to make 70 not out and took five wickets for eight runs.

C. J. records a happy courtship, only 'marred by Grace's frequent indispositions...arising from weakness of blood'. In his opinion, this would be remedied by 'home life' and her 'retirement from business, plenty of outdoor environment and marriage bliss'.[65] Once married they lived 'about one and a half miles from the township', commuting to town 'in a hooded buggy, drawn by a spirited grey horse named "Theodore" – shortened to "Do"'. C. J. claims that for the first seven months of their marriage they 'lived without a maid', sharing home duties (even including C. J. himself 'chain-cleaning and sand-soaping the saucepans and frying pans' on Sundays).⁶⁶ Whether this was a deliberately bohemian choice is unclear; C. J. did write to Mary insisting the marital home was 'not going to be an Aladdin's Palace'.⁶⁷

Their daughter Dulcie Estelle was born on the 20 July 1908. Three weeks after her birth, C. J. wrote to Mary, who was travelling in Britain, that:

> She can see, hear and feel so that everything seems to be A1... Rene looks tip top and feels in splendid health. She is a real brick...If anyone doubted the wisdom of our early marriage, they have only to see us now, + they must admit their error.⁶⁸

4

Establishing an empire, 1913–20

Pillars of the community

If you lived in Mildura in the early 'nineteen-teens' and had any interest in popular entertainment, technology, fruit growing, fruit marketing, real estate, or in more genteel local sport, you knew about C. J. DeGaris. If he did not dominate all of these fields, he was a frequent presence in each. His fingers were in an outlandishly large number of pies, and he kept locating more pies and spare fingers.

The DeGarises were members of a select elite of businesspeople in Mildura in the second decade of the twentieth century. It was a town still young enough – it turned 25 in 1912 – that many residents would have remembered its creation. Indeed, its co-founder William Chaffey was still active and Alfred Deakin, who had facilitated the Chaffeys' move to Australia, had just completed his third term as prime minister. It already had a host of middle-class families: the names Bowring, Cameron, Cater, Corbould, Couttie, Davey, Desailly, Hawkes, Hollick, Pelloe, Sutton and Watmuff – and, of course, DeGaris – were prominent in the town's businesses. Their owners were associated with arts and other social events.

Tennis provides an example of middle-class social clubs where business decisions were made and networks forged or reinforced in between games. C. J. and his brother Alfred, who was moving up in the ranks in the family companies, were keen players and members of the Austral Tennis Club. Retiring as president of the Austral in April[1], C. J. was elected president of the Mildura Lawn Tennis Association in May 1913, at a meeting held at his home.[2] Mildura won the Provincial Tennis Championship in that year, thanks in part to C. J.'s skill as a player.[3] The association's vice-presidents were, similarly, a roll call of prominent Mildurans: for example, W. Rupert Cater[4] was a lawyer who would represent another association member, Richard Midgley, in a debt collection case that very month.[5] P. T. Hollick was a grower active in the Irrigation Trust.[6] Dr. Cameron was the director at the town's Agricultural High School[7] and also proud defender of his ethnic heritage: he was Chieftain of the Mildura Caledonian Society.[8] C. J.'s brother-in-law Harold Corbould, the Tennis Association's auditor, was president of the Mildura District Hospital committee, and Bowring, Pelloe and Hawkes were committee members.[9]

A strong presence in local activities, fundraising, political and 'progress' bodies was a combination of the DeGarises' Methodism and their business nous. This required not only a prominent public life but also a need to be good role models for others. Mildura was as much the DeGarises' creation as anyone else's; they recognised their responsibility to make it work as a society. C. J.'s public persona was amplified up to eleven by a wish to contribute to both his family and his local community, as well as by his own superhuman energy.

Mildura life in the first few years of the nineteen-teens was good. C. J. wrote an epistle of sweet domesticity to Mary in 1912. He began with the news that 'Mildura is having a very prosperous time at present, and everybody seems in the very best humour possible'.[10] He told his sister:

Rene and Mary have been enjoying roller skating – I say "enjoying" advisedly, as they have not had as many falls yet as some others whose names we won't mention...Rene, as in most things, is the personification of caution, and very seldom ventures out amongst the crowd, but prefers to take her exercise in the mornings and afternoons when the spectators are fewer, and the rink not nearly as much occupied as at night.

The 'Mary' referred to was almost certainly Rene's sister Marianne, later to be known as Molly or Mollie, possibly to avoid confusion with Mary DeGaris.[11] Rollerskates were not new – they'd been available for local purchase since at least 1899[12] – but rollerskating 'caught on' as a social event in 1909.[13] People played rollerskating tricks and games day and night at the Shire Hall and also at S. J. Pugsley's Olympia Hall.[14] Rene may have been the 'personification of caution', but it was a sign of her modern nature that she would embrace such activities at all. Meanwhile C. J. was promising Dulcie, who was days away from turning four, rollerskates, ponies, bicycles and jinkers 'when she is a "big girl"'. He also wrote that Dulcie's sister Winnie (Winifred Rene, born 21 January 1911), who was not yet one, 'enjoys life in every possible way'.[15]

In case there was, as C. J. feared, any tut-tutting locally about his and Rene's 'speedy' marriage[16], he made it his duty to be a pillar of the local community. He was as much a leader when merely participating as he was when he occupied the role of chair or president. His activities as reported in the local press were prodigious, and it is hard to imagine any Milduran mentioned or discussed more often, unless it was 'the boss', William Chaffey.[17] But Chaffey was an eminence, unlikely to be rolling up his sleeves to be part of the throng. Whenever there was a fundraiser for the hospital, the rowing club, the tennis club or other important institutions, C. J. was an eager participant. He was prominent in the Rechabites, the renowned 'friendly society' well-known for requiring its members to commit to complete abstinence from alcohol; later in the decade he would continue anti-drinking activities as a committee member for the Mildura branch of the Early Closing Movement.[18] He was involved in publicity for one of the town's cinemas in Pugsley's Olympia (as well as owning his own 'home cinematograph'). He was also, it is clear, keen to be seen as decisive and determined: C. J. embraced the fast pace of the twentieth century, and newspapers often carried mention of his 'well-known Russell car' frequently driven at breakneck speed through the Mallee, to Renmark, Pyap or the new settlement of Loxton.[19]

When he participated in amateur concerts, his specialty was monologues. These were in good supply: short dramatic pieces were circulated through the Anglosphere, written and published specifically to be recited in public. In the course of the 1910 Mildura Musical and Elocutionary Competitions in 'the hall', C. J. played Sir Geoffrey Bloomfield opposite Doris Bowring as Lady Gwendoline in a 'duologue' entitled 'Drifted Apart'; the *Mildura Cultivator* lauded their stoic persistence despite 'a violent storm which occurred during the course of the performance'. They won third prize the next night.[20] On the occasion of the visit of (Catholic) Archbishop Carr in mid-1912, C. J. recited Arthur Conan Doyle's eighty-line humorous verse piece 'The Groom's Story'.[21] Written in an approximation of Cockney, this is an account of a man who hitches his horse to pull a broken-down automobile. The automobile recovers and starts up, destroying the horse's tail and much more. This piece allowed the speaker the opportunity to display dramatic and comic talent. C. J. considered it 'remarkably funny'.[22]

A concert in aid of the Mildura Rowing club at the Shire Hall, including 'a New Romantic Play' *Fennel* by Jerome K. Jerome, provided similar opportunity. Here, C. J. appeared as the hunchback Filippo, and 'sustained the character admirably and put plenty of fervour into his addresses. He has never appeared locally to better advantage. The audience pitied him for his deformity and admired him for his self-effacement'.[23] The pieces C. J. and his friends chose to perform were slight, amusing, reassuring and rarely provocative; they always confirmed, never challenged, prejudices about the outside world and reinforced Mildura's place as an Australian component of the British Empire. The only reason not to enjoy 'minstrelsy' or 'coon songs', for instance, would be that they were coarse, and almost no-one objected to everyday racism. With exceptions of (for instance) Indian-born or influenced writers such as Tagore or Kipling, theatre and concert programs were generally made up of British, American and occasionally Australian content. Mildura performers rarely wrote their own material, although they sometimes added 'topical' verses to well-known songs or dropped locally relevant asides into their repertoire. C. J. became adept at this.[24] The point was not to make an artistic or individual statement, but to hammer the cultures of the English-speaking peoples home in a new and often inhospitable land. This was doubly important in Mildura, where everyone was new(ish).

In *Fennel,* Filippo was enamoured of Giannina, played by Susie Sutton. Susie and C. J. often appeared together. She was C. J.'s age, the wife of a local dentist and, with a 'charming personality and a bright, happy disposition'[25] well-regarded as a keen amateur singer and actor.[26] She and C. J. were also partners in mixed doubles tennis.[27] In a small town like Mildura, it can only be imagined that eyebrows would have been occasionally raised over C. J.'s frequent stage and court collaborations with Mrs Sutton. The truth of this relationship can never be known, and its substance is less important than the light it sheds on C. J.'s public persona and the blithe way he flew close to scandal. 'Mrs C. J. DeGaris' made occasional appearances in the *Cultivator's* social pages, providing a tea for ladies, or writing a charity cheque. In most instances, however, she is in C. J.'s shadow.

When C. J. accompanied Rene and Marianne on their skating expedition, he may also have been scoping new business opportunities. In January 1913, the Olympia committed itself to showing films two nights a week. The event has all the hallmarks of a C. J. enterprise: the opening night was a 'big splash' and included *Black Cat* (a film which had 'Caused Crowded Houses in the City'), with the support of a 'Mildura industrial picture, showing work in the vineyards and orchards and in the packing sheds'. Australians had already been long engaged in the excitement of seeing themselves, and places they knew, on screen. C. J. devised a voting competition to win 'a trip to England and back' that required frequent attendance at shows and nomination campaigns.[28] The Thomson brothers, owners of the Wonderland cinema in Langtree Avenue[29], were unhappy with the extravagance of the new enterprise. They were quick to accuse the Pugsleys and C. J. of underhand behaviour – specifically, handing out flyers for their 'show' to Wonderland customers on the premises.[30] This was one of C. J.'s early public experiences of competition and controversy. He claimed in later writing to have not been overly fazed by the situation. After all, the Olympia was not his business but the Pugsleys', and his competition was a great success.

Nevertheless, he might have been glad to stretch his wings beyond Mildura and test the waters in other parts of the region away from petty rivalries and accusations. In December 1912, C. J. and his co-driver Tommy Joy drove his father and another companion from Melbourne to Pyap, via Mildura: 490 miles (790 km) in just under 24 hours. Newspapers like the *Cultivator* were happy to report extraordinary feats such as this, testament to C. J.'s capacities for endurance, skill and risk-taking, as well as the quality of the Russell car.[31] The trip was an excuse to give the Russell a workout and Elisha had been commissioned to value Pyap by its Melbourne owners. Long, fast drives were exhilarating, and C. J. was wont to break into snatches of popular song while driving. Gifford Hall, an émigré British journalist who wrote for the Mildura press under the name 'Steele Blayde', would note that travel in a car with C. J. meant the silence of the open plain was 'broken by the drumming whirr of rubber tyres and broken snatches of vaudeville choruses'.[32]

Pyap was not, it had to be said, a remarkable place: barely even a dot on the map. It was one of a number of settlements established on the Murray by the South Australian government in the 1890s. Minimal horticulture had taken place there and it was essentially moribund. 'Properly managed and controlled', C. J. wrote, 'it had a wonderful future; but, continuing on its then course, it would depreciate to the ordinary value of unused river frontage lands'.[33] He saw potential in both the region, and in himself as its conductor.

The following February, against the wishes of his father, and after considerable debate with his bank, C. J. bought the 12,000 acres (4856 hectares) of Pyap. Unsurprisingly, he had big ideas: he would maximise the production to 'full capacity' with increased infrastructure such as pumping and channelling. It was a four-hour drive from Mildura, and C. J. intended to maintain all his Mildura interests as well as putting regular visits in to his new property. C. J. wrote that he had long hoped to 'take a wilderness and turn it into a garden, and Pyap seems to me to be the best place I've seen for that purpose'.[34]

As in most things, C. J. moved fast at Pyap. Within a few months, he had initiated Sunday School and church services in a settlement with no community buildings (and then, he commissioned the building of a hall for the area).[35] He would go on to commission a brickworks and new pumping infrastructure.[36] In June, he installed Milduran Gerald Beverley as estate manager.[37] His ducks in a line, C. J. was able to achieve more towards the end of 1913: the pumping station was completed by the end of October. His and Rene's third daughter, Vera Elizabeth, was born on 30 November.

The Great War

In 1913, a halting attempt had been made to create a local branch of the Legion of Frontiersmen, a British organisation with elements of the 'citizen army'.[38] C. J., Beverley, Hall and Alfred E. Lloyd

Pyap Hall, built by C. J. in 1913, photo taken in 2007. AUTHOR PHOTO.

were all fellow travellers with this group; Hall had been active in the London branch. Yet Milduran men – usually keen joiners – were not in the mood for playing soldier. Possibly they could see the Frontiersmen's militaristic play would soon be replaced by real fighting in Europe, where there was constant expectation of military action.

His Australian–British patriotism was as strong as any, but C. J. did not relish war. He *did* blithely muse to the *Mildura Cultivator* 18 months before its onset that a 'war in Europe should "boost" Australian sales' of dried fruit 'a little'.[39] From a business point of view, he suggested, the prospect of a war causing limits on imports of products like Greek sultanas would be a positive development.

In what was to be the last gasp of frayed credibility, the Frontiersmen called a 'Patriotic Meeting' regarding the war on 10 August. C. J. led from behind. He seconded the first motion approving the 'offer of assistance to the Imperial government during the war'. He then added, to applause, that 'Mildura had proved in the past to be loyal, and would always be found so'.[40] He went on:

> Anyone who failed to support [the motion] could hardly be called an Australian or a Britisher...It was patriotism to the mother land that brought them there. This was the most critical period in the world's history and people everywhere in the Empire were giving men, money or ships. Mildura was no exception.[41]

It was suggested that twenty tons of fruit might be donated 'for use on the field', an idea C. J. turned into a motion and that was carried.[42] There were, of course, some minor issues to iron out: no-one was so gauche as to mention that Shire President George Wittmann had a German name. A Mr Iredale acknowledged:

> There were Germans in their midst whom they admired as much as any English (Loud Applause). He was glad they echoed that sentiment. But Germany's deliberate policy was aggressive, and she was seeking expansion by conquest. The war was against the will of half the German people. He did not think the war would be long...The outcome of the war would be greater solidification of the British Empire.[43]

Talk was moulded to engage outrage over the unfairness of 'the attack of the huge German Empire on the little state of Belgium'.[44]

Once again, C. J. was wearing numerous hats. He wrote to the *Cultivator* proposing that he and Rene would be donating a pound each every month for the relief of Belgium, and urged others to do the same.[45] Business continued to be important, such as when he protested new railway timetabling from Mildura to Melbourne which meant fruit – a delicate cargo – was delayed or rerouted on its way to market.[46] Difficulties such as a drought, now 'a certainty', a lack of fruit pickers (and the fact that those available were asking for more money) and predictions of a smaller than usual crop, were his concern.[47] Nevertheless he found time to play in the annual tennis tournament in Melbourne in November.[48]

C. J. could not help wanting to become involved in dialogue about the war and its consequences. Inspired, perhaps, by the nationalist quandaries posed by the German and British origins of his own community, he penned the first half of a play, *Ambition Run Mad*. C. J. sent it to J. C. Williamson, Australia's best-known theatrical company. Word came back that if the conclusion was as good as the initial scenes, there was definite interest. He completed it and drove to see them; however, it was rejected, because he was unknown as a playwright, and Australian, and it was felt the play would read better than it would act.[49]

The play was published, presumably paid for by C. J. himself as a vanity project; the *Mildura Telegraph and Lower Murray Advocate* for 9 April 1915 reports receiving a copy 'turned out very neatly by our South Australian contemporary, the *Murray Pioneer*'.[50] The book claims on its title page that 'a copyright performance of the play' had taken place.[51] It is not clear where or when this might have happened, and *Ambition Run Mad* did not appear in any other form. It seems likely that, even a few months into the war, few Australians were in the mood for a philosophical drama about its futility in which rapid-fire dialogue paused only for speeches correctly identified by Williamson as lengthy. More problematically, the play features arguably sympathetic German characters, such as the comically uptight Lieutenant Froitzer and his subordinate, Captain Hertsman, whose family are all ensconced German–Australians.

The play begins in May 1914, at the brink of war, with conversations between military men and the effete upper classes. Its action largely takes place in, or on the way to, Australia. Philosophising takes forms such as this, delivered by Lord Debonaire to Lieutenant Froitzer:

> I have a premonition that when, if ever the time comes it will be found that German–Australians are Australians in every sense of the word…no grateful child can hate even an adopted parent, if that parent is kind, just and generous.[52]

Although there is little doubt that these words – as per C. J.'s speech in the Shire Hall in August 1914 – are strongly against the 'German Empire', such appeasement towards the German 'race' would have been increasingly difficult to swallow in the heightened pitch of war fever. Many Australians of German extraction were changing or disguising their names. It is surprising that C. J. was still trying to find his play an audience in April 1915; he dropped the project thereafter.

As an aside, it is notable that two of the minor characters in the play are named for Mr and Mrs C. J. DeGaris: 'Jack Thompson', a 'young Australian millionaire', and 'Rene Thompson' – his sister. This is doubly unusual because the Thomsons (without the 'p') were operators of the open-air Wonderland cinema, and T. W. Thomson had at times been a public rival of both C. J. and his father. Elisha had replaced Thomson as councillor in the Mildura Riding in August 1902.[53] If the naming was not for Thomson, it may have been for Mary DeGaris' fiancé, Colin Thompson – or it may have been random.

Much is made of the notion of the Anzacs' struggle, bravery and persistence in Europe as forging the spirit of the young nation of Australia. C. J. said in 1916: 'Two years ago Australia was just a country: now it [is] a nation because of what the Anzacs had done at Gallipoli, and on the west front'.[54] Less attention is paid to the importance of the two conscription referendums held during the course of the war, in October 1916 and December the following year. C. J. was pro-conscription, but did not seek to enlist.[55] He would later suggest that loose cartilage in his left knee made service impossible.[56] This did not affect his frequent sporting activities. Many took the attitude that single men should be the first to sign up, then married men without children, then married men with dependent families – C. J. was, then, in the 'safest' category. At one meeting, it was reported, he stated that he 'felt certain that if the war continued for another year the married men would be called up, and why should they not?'[57]

Mary's fiancé, Colin Thompson, and Rene's brother, Bean, served in Europe. C. J. was to state that he 'felt proud to be able to introduce his brother-in-law as an Anzac'.[58] He could not have known, when speaking these words, that Thompson had died at Pozières a few days earlier.[59]

With his firm engagement in the war effort, how then did C. J. avoid the question of his own (lack of) service? If he was a natural leader, wasn't it his destiny to fight for the country he loved? If he was asked these questions directly, his answers are not recorded. At another meeting, seeking support for a 'war loan' by Mildura residents investing in Australia's cause, he cast himself firmly as 'employer' – implying that his role was to keep the wheels turning for a vital industry – although he tried to also pitch his position as 'citizen' at the same time.

> Everyone felt their blood run high when they heard of the Anzacs' victory, and were glad the casualties were slight...These men were our friends and relatives, who were playing such a gallant part in the "big push", which we hoped would end in peace being signed in Berlin...Let Mildura set an example to Victoria in this war loan, and show the people of Australia that we were as wholehearted in this as in sending our men to the front. (Applause)[60]

Late in 1915 Elisha and Elizabeth DeGaris relocated yet again, this time to Guernsey where, C. J. wrote, they would be 'nearer the big events' and would 'watch most carefully the interests of growers under the ever-changing conditions...'.[61] They made Mildura's 'boys' their particular interest. On Friday 20 October 1916, at the Shire Hall supper room, C. J. was one of five men to deliver papers, each purporting to explore the 'Effects of the War'.[62]

Having attempted to insert himself into the discussion about nationalism and ethnic conflict in the war with *Ambition Run Mad*, and providing frequent commentary from a Mildura grower's point of view, C. J. now turned his mind to the returned soldier. He penned a pamphlet engaging with the soldier settlement schemes of federal government. *Repatriation: A Gigantic Problem, a Practical Scheme* was probably (it is not dated) published in mid-1917.

C. J. opined that while all political parties encouraged decentralisation and immigration after the war, they were less likely to concern themselves with repatriation of soldiers and the practicalities of harnessing and redistributing the population in practical fashion. The nation owed returned soldiers, whose number he estimated at 170,000, their dependents making the number up to 700,000.[63] He believed 'the repatriation problem is the most serious one Australia has ever faced' and that it was 'therefore necessary to see BIG':

> This is demonstrated by illustration. A progressive business man, dissatisfied with his balance-sheet, does not reduce his staff, but widens its scope, and probably increases its number even if it means a temporary rise of overdraft. That is, he puts forward extra efforts, and even incurs more expense to produce better results.[64]

He used the example of the USA, as many other Australians had done before him, and implored his nation to follow its example, using the common trope that 'We stand now where America stood 100 years ago'.[65] Irrigation, he believed, would allow the population to expand inland, and utilise areas lacking only two important components – water and hard-working people – to become productive. 'Centres with a population of 20,000 are all too rare in this country', he wrote, yet added that any such settlement would offer 'unlimited opportunity for every class of business, trade or profession'.[66] He added:

> They should have every modern convenience with railways and special freights, motor transport, electric light, good roads (especially good roads), telephones, sewerage, all attractive features of city life that can be transferred to the country should attach to these settlements, making each a "city in the country".[67]

In works such as his repatriation pamphlet C. J. was all care and no responsibility; he did not have to outline a payment scheme for his plans. His argument, ultimately, was that to *not* fund it would ultimately be more expensive; additionally, it was Australia's moral duty to provide appropriate care and livelihoods for returned soldiers.

Alice Lapthorne, the daughter of the *Mildura Cultivator's* editor–publisher, was 17 at the end of the war. She writes of a 'monster picnic' ten days after the signing of the Armistice, and a two-thousand-strong parade of schoolchildren headed by the town's brass band, marching to the recreation ground 'singing patriotic songs and waving flags'.[68]

Naturally the lives of everyone touched in any way by the Great War were altered. But other facets of the realities of human existence also got in the way. It was just as the war was drawing to a close that one important woman entered C. J.'s life, a relationship with another was irrevocably changed, and a third departed. The Mildura–Ouyen Concert Party, on 5 September 1917, included C. J. as a star attraction with 15 minutes of 'Humorous Stories', 'Lasca' ('Character Recital' – presumably, Frank Desprez's 1882 cowboy poem), 'Topical Verses' – a 'Humorous item' entitled 'In 1999' – and a 'Sneezing Song'. The Ouyen *Mail* rejoiced:

> As to Mr DeGaris – well he is a host in himself. As a raconteur we have heard few better on the professional stage, and should Fortune withdraw her smiles, the stage would gain an artist. He has escaped the nasality of the professional, and that is saying a lot. The much backed "Lasca" in his hands is a gem

(mostly it is an infliction). In humorous story he served up many of the ancients, but somehow the clothing wore a modern appearance, and the local topical song caused roars of laughter as one or another of our residents went to the toasting. Finally his versatility showed out in the monologue sketch with Miss Davey, "A Pair of Lunatics". In this the histrionic talent shone out...[69]

Also on the bill was 21-year-old Violet Austin, with *her* humorous recitation, 'They Didn't', a 'Musical Monologue', and another song, 'The Game of Life'.[70] Whether this was the moment C. J. encountered Violet is uncertain. No doubt the five Austin sisters were well-known about town; Violet would be chosen the 'Prettiest Girl in Mildura' in 1919.[71] She would soon be working for C. J. as his secretary.

What was certain – or at least, what C. J. later made sure to be certain in the minds of anyone with a stake in his private life – was that his marriage to Rene had effectively ended some years before, on 26 September 1916.[72] He is definite about this in his memoir, stating that she committed an act he does not describe on a date seared into his memory. This rendered their marriage henceforth a sham, kept in play for the sake of their children and, perhaps, the need for social probity. He claimed it was not the 'act, but the circumstances and the individual connected with it' which were offensive, but this does not enlighten.[73] If Rene had been in Mildura that 'fateful' day in late 1916 she may have attended a farewell to Mrs Harold Levien at Mrs Percy Hollick's home in the afternoon[74], or a 'farewell social' to the Presbyterian clergyman Rev. J. A. Burns and his wife at the Shire Hall in the evening.[75] However, whatever Rene's wrong, C. J. did not feel entitled to do anything similar, or so he claims.[76]

The woman to exit C. J.'s life was his mother, Elizabeth, who died 'at home' in Guernsey in July 1918, from a heart attack following a long bout of pneumonia. Elisha's letters to family and well-wishers are poignant. To William Chaffey, he mourned 'a humble Christian, a devoted mother, a loving wife, a sympathetic confidante, an enjoyable comrade, and a wonderfully patient companion'.[77]

C. J. wrote to his sister Bessie:

I cannot picture Mother as dead. I see her happy + smiling + she seems very close. For that reason I am glad the end came while she was far away. We can still picture her as living. We know she is happy. She always prayed she would not live to be over 70 + that her end would be painless and peaceful. God bless her sweet memory.[78]

To his children, Elisha confessed: 'Mother did not say goodbye'.[79]

Publicity machine

Frankly speaking, we had expected to see a pushful American, because of his really "big stunts", and we said so.

"No," replied Mr. DeGaris, "I'm an Australian – was born in Victoria, in fact, and am thoroughly proud of my nationality, though there is a sprinkling of French blood in the roots of the family tree."

"But your business training has been American, surely?" we suggested.

"No again, I certainly admire the Americans, but I don't grant that they have a monopoly of all the brains and business enterprise on this old earth. In fact Australians who go to the United States all do well in that land of hustle, showing that we have really capital material to make a great nation if only we can cultivate an unfailing faith in our own great country. Personally, I am passionately fond of Australia, and all things Australian."[80]

Perth *Australian* 1920

When his interest in publicity turned from mere local 'ideas' – promoting the Olympia, for instance – C. J. was often discussed in terms of his 'American' approach. But while he believed American cultural producers were 'mighty clever', he was opposed to any attempt to 'Americanise Australia' culturally.[81] He was a patriot in the 'colonial nationalist' mould. 'The fibre of the Australian is as good as that of the Yankee', the Angaston *Leader* editorialised in March 1919, 'and if only our sunny land would develop that big stick together and progressive concentration element, what a prosperous people we would be'.[82]

What C. J. had, he believed, was an innate ability to publicise. 'The publicity sense', he said, 'is as much a gift as the artistic sense. It is the ability to tell the public something you want them to know, and tell them in such a way that they will accept it, and not throw it aside'.[83]

The years immediately following his alienation from Rene and the death of Elizabeth were C. J.'s most frenetic – and this from a base of already furious activity. Observing his father as a politician, leader and businessman, C. J. had carved out a public persona for himself as a man who did not back down from a fight, kept to his word and, most importantly for him, used reason and logic to win the day.

Sarnia Topics, edited and, apparently, written almost entirely by C. J., was an upbeat, persuasive organ for the growers of Mildura. It also sold the modern nature of Mildura and associated ideals he held dear. In February 1919 he trumpeted *Sarnia Topics*' increase in circulation (from 200 copies in the war years to 2,000 at the end of the decade).[84] Initially intended as a 'medium of news from Sarnia Packing Pty Ltd, and E. DeGaris & Co. Pty. Ltd. to their clients' and, later, customers of the 'Sarnia Motor Garage', it gradually took on the role of announcing 'Dried Fruits matters to all ADFA growers, merchants, agents, packing houses, to newspapers with whom the ADFA advertisements have been placed' and beyond.[85] Just as C. J. (and Elisha) seemed unable to distinguish their various interests, personal, public and pecuniary, from each other, so too their Sarnia business was unable to extract itself from C. J.'s own work for ADFA. It is perhaps unsurprising that there was some rivalry and jealousy expressed, in some quarters, against the DeGaris concern which might justifiably be seen to be claiming credit for the successes of the irrigation areas' growers.

C. J. had long been associated with the ADFA, formed from smaller organisations in 1902 to pursue, primarily, Renmark and Mildura growers' needs in production, distribution and marketing.[86] The ADFA would negotiate with international and local markets and seek to regulate prices on behalf of its members. In the years just before the war, ADFA members had been debating the value of employing spruikers to visit homes to discuss the value of dried fruit. This would not be a salesperson but a one-on-one influencer; the householder would subsequently, ideally, incorporate dried fruit into their regular shopping. C. J. was in favour of this style of publicity, and in late 1913 he wrote to Mary that he had 'Had a good time @ Adelaide Fruit Conference + got House-to-House canvassing scheme thro' @ last'.[87]

The ADFA's reluctance to advertise was strange. There was no shortage of advertising in the Australia of the nineteen-teens; its newspapers, cinemas and city streets were awash with publicity slogans, images and ideas. Newspaper columns would break off from actual news into single-sentence assertions about the value of particular tonics or news of a local shoe sale. There was, in short, no shame to advertising – but many members of the ADFA seem to have been extremely bothered by the notion that dried fruit might be tainted with such commercialism.

While this reticence might in itself seem strange, one important aspect of the objections of many was that promotion cost money up front, and its specific advantages were not easily gauged. However, in early 1918 desperate measures seemed called for. Dried fruit was, C. J. writes, 'placed on the "Prohibited list" for exportation'. He continues:

No shipping space! Big stocks on hand! Increased areas under production! Record crop in sight, and within five months of harvesting! No chance of export! Only an Australian market to rely upon![88]

For some time, C. J. had been agitating for the ADFA to consider promotion of its wares. It was, he writes, his 'hobby horse', though it vied with the establishment of commercial flight in his affections. At the conference, in October 1918, he argued for 'The Magic Wand of Publicity'. He was opposed, he said, to lowering prices as the main motivator for sales. Instead, he urged his fellow members to support a plan to interest the general public in Lexias ('our most unpopular and yet our most tasty product') in preparation for the availability of the new season's crop.[89] 'Our fruit', he said 'has been running round for years like an illegitimate child'. It needed a name, and his first priority was to 'get the public interested by giving them an incentive to choose the name'.[90]

C. J. may have been lobbying behind the scenes to become selected as publicity manager. He was the obvious choice – one only had to look, for instance, at his Olympia successes. His stipulations were that he only be compensated on a 'payment-by-result' plan, have completely free rein, and a budget – based on a levy on sales – to work with. He wrote that he would 'strive to gain the results' he was confident could be achieved 'and which should establish the Dried Fruits Industry on a firm foundation for all time'.[91]

The 'catchy name' was his first concern, as he looked to Californian innovations like the 'Sunkist Orange' (1907) and 'Sun-Maid Raisin' (1912). Both of these trade names incorporated subtle puns for copyright purposes. The ADFA's 'Wanted! A Name' campaign invited Australians to send in either a 3/- postal order, receiving in return a 'package of fruit', or grocers' dockets proving they had bought a pound each of sultanas, currants and lexias. These were to be accompanied by their proposal for a brand name for the ADFA's product.[92] Two weeks into the competition, the Great War came to an end.

This first rally of C. J.'s publicity enterprise was an instant success, both in the resulting name, 'Sun-Raysed' (the region was henceforth known as 'Sunraysia') and in the ways that the result was promoted. 'It is so strikingly appropriate that its selection presented no difficulty', was the verdict.[93] Thirty-three contestants came up with the name (others imagined variations, such as 'Sunraysd' and 'Sun-Razed') and shared in the £50 prize. In his forthright, somewhat meta approach to advertising, C. J. explained his reasons for choosing 'Sun-Raysed' as a term in initial advertising in mid-December 1918: 'It lends itself particularly well to advertising and to future publicity work', he wrote. 'It is NOVEL enough yet ATTRACTIVE enough to become a household name'.[94]

The period immediately following the Great War was tumultuous, not least because of the Spanish Flu, which killed up to 170,000 Australians. The virus' spread was a mystery – and so, then, was prevention. There were two waves over 1918–20, the second more deadly. Measures included quarantining at state borders. Places like cinemas, where people might assemble en masse, were closed. Masks were made compulsory at church services. At the end of 1918 the DeGarises held garden parties and other entertainments at their home in 12th Street – perhaps to counter the lack of public entertainment venues.[95] At the same time, they changed its name from 'Roseneath' to 'Windulva' (a portmanteau, of course, of 'Winnie', 'Dulcie' and 'Vera').

Publicity director DeGaris moved fast. Within weeks of the 'Sun-Raysed' announcement, the name was a household word. 'Advertisements of Sun-Raysed Fruits meet the eye everywhere', wrote a columnist for the *Mildura Cultivator* in February 1919:

> Tuesday's *Age* has a good-sized advertisement urging the Melbourne public to follow the doctor's advice and keep their bodies fit and their constitutional organs naturally lubricated

by eating every day Sun-Raysed Dried Fruits...The good Australian will eat them and fit himself to withstand the onslaughts of disease. Readers are asked to say over and over again "I fear no more the dreaded 'flu, for Sun-raysed fruits will pull me through." So they will, if given a chance.[96]

C. J. made sure that the 'Sun-Raysed' name was consistently in the public eye. Advertisements appeared in theatre programs; on slides at cinemas and the theatre; magazine advertising; 'Leaflets to 200,000 troops on incoming ships'; balloons and kite displays above cities; advertising on public transport and railway stations; posters on hoardings; flyers; and catchy sloganeering; 'it is astonishing how many thousands of people know the phrase and use it', the *Murray Pioneer* observed. 'As an experiment in a railway carriage just mention "Get the Habit" and four out of five will finish the slogan for you.'[97]

Newspapers featured two kinds of Sun-Raysed advertising. It might promote the product itself, or engage readers through competitions. These could be word games, or more complex endeavours such as guessing the amount of lexias in a particular pound. This necessitated purchase of the relevant amount of fruit and counting it for a 'ballpark' figure – then hoping to be lucky to guess a number close enough. C. J. had promoted the Olympia cinema with an elaborate voting competition some years before; he embarked on a Sun-Raysed promotion for Australians to vote for 'the most popular birthday'. His competitions were innovative, and tended to give the participant the sense that both chance and skill were involved. Those who did not win were still part of something remarkable: the expansion of an industry producing a nutritious and delicious product, aiding the economy and the nation. C. J. believed 'the public knew that the fruit was grown and prepared under hygienic conditions, on the eight-hours day principle in one of the highest paid industries in the world'.[98] The campaign, and the product, became the subject of nationwide conversation and fascination.

His 'Big Stunt' of guesstimating the number of lexias in a pound was partially successful; he anticipated 250,000 entries but received only 75,000. Australians, he said, were ambivalent or suspicious about the prizes, and he felt that 'the effort of counting was too much for many people – making it plain that any similar "stunt" must be so simple as to require no time and little energy'. Nevertheless, he believed the Big Stunt had 'achieved its purpose': raising awareness of the lexia. He told the *Murray Pioneer:* 'I'll guarantee 20 babies are called Lexia in the next 12 months. It's a pretty name, too, when you "get the habit"'.[99] No new parents seem to have taken up this suggestion.

Two major publicity enterprises were hampered by the flu outbreak. C. J. commissioned the *Sun-Raysed Film* and a major media junket in February 1919. The filmmaker Charles Herschell visited Mildura and Merbein to film the 'Sun-Raysed' operations there, but ADFA straddled three states; Herschell was 'smuggled' 25 km north-west across the Murray to Curlwaa for an hour, breaking quarantine rules. Later he visited South Australia to make the film 'as representative as possible'.[100]

Sunraysed film announcement, in Lucas George DeGaris papers, National Library of Australia.

An excellent Normey

In July 1919, a *Smith's Weekly* journalist grilled C. J. about his latest ploy: '"Why?" I asked him, "why did you call the sweets 'The Good Little Normey'?"' C. J., once again, could not resist revealing the workings behind the dial. 'That's the very reason, because everyone would ask – why. Get the public curious, and you have created the demand'.[101]

C. J. had noted that in the USA, novel ideas such as 'Raisin Bread', 'Raisin Cakes' and a 'Victory Loaf' had almost doubled dried fruit consumption. He set about devising a similarly ubiquitous food item. The result was a confectionery, increasing dried fruit's popularity during the postwar sugar shortage. In an interview with the *Daily Commercial News,* C. J. said Australians ate 4 lbs of fruit a year, but regarded dried fruit as a Christmas luxury. 'If they can be persuaded to eat 8 lbs a head', he mused, 'Australia will not be producing enough to supply the Commonwealth demands'. He went on to detail 'our new sweets, "The Good Little Normey" – which we sell at 1s per 8 oz carton', and the '"Molly Sandwich" for picnics and school luncheons... It is made of fruits. The girls who make it receive £2 2s. per week – and yet it is the cheapest and most wholesome sweet on the market'.[102]

The Good Little Normey could be bought prepackaged or made at home by mincing, in equal quantities, currants, sultanas and seeded lexias. When formed into balls and coated with desiccated coconut, 'children clamour for them'.[103] C. J. never claimed credit for the 'Normey' recipe, only the name. The ADFA engaged the popular Sydney cartoonist and animator Harry Julius to produce a short film to display at cinemas. Julius had made his name with a series of topical short films about the war, combining live action, cartoons and sped-up film.[104] Julius's cartoons were more like twenty-first century PowerPoint presentations than animations, but they were stylish and often funny. There were also lantern slides, featuring the recipes for the Normey and the Molly Sandwich.[105]

C. J. was initially tentative with Normey production. The sweet was made at the ADFA premises in Deakin Ave, and motor seeders and mincers were brought in to make the product in 8 oz (226 g) packets; the idea was, however, only to produce a model, 'just sufficient to show people how easily they can be made in the home'.[106] Yet soon ADFA outlets were stocking not only Normeys in ½ lb cartons but also other packaged goods direct to the consumer: Sun-Raysed currants, sultanas and lexias; Sun-Raysed show boxes of assorted dried fruits; the *Sun-Raysed Children's Book*; a recipe book; a kettle holder; writing pads and envelopes.[107] By September 1919 the Perth *Sunday Times* was observing that Normeys were 'a splendid substitute for ordinary sweets':

> Indeed, the Good Little Normey has been such an excellent little Normey that the A.D.F.A. now brings it forward in a new and gay packet. This, with its decoration of grapes, is sure to please the kiddies.[108]

The Normey phenomenon ran the risk of overtaking the whole of C. J.'s campaign, unless the cult of C. J. DeGaris got there first. As if to hammer home C. J.'s conquering of Mildura, in early 1920 the Urban Trust Water Tower, a local landmark adjoining the railway station, was adorned with the advertising message: 'Get the Habit – Sun-Raysed Fruit and Good Little Normey'.[109]

Although the Molly sandwich was never quite as successful as the Normey – but then, it was not sold as a packaged product – the fact that there were 'male' and 'female' products to promote allowed satirists to imagine romantic conversations between the two:

> "Normey, dear" purred Molly, as she nestled more snugly against the second button of his new chocolate coloured waistcoat, "you don't know how much I love you." Normey coughed deprecatingly as he replied as modestly as he knew

how. "They all do old heart. I'm simply the rage just at present; the girls all absolutely adore me..."[110]

C. J. had copyrighted the 'Good Little Normey' name on ADFA's behalf.[111] Within a year, new varieties were being produced: 'Crystallised Normey' and 'Chocolate Normey'. Perth's *Australian* declared them 'tray-bong'.[112] From hesitant beginnings, suddenly at the peak of Normey fame there were *seventy* new varieties of the confection proposed.[113]

Any ADFA member who would have preferred the association stay in the background would have had a horrible 1919. C. J. ensured that ADFA was in the public eye at all times. In October of that year, he opened a pop-up shop, the Sun-Raysed Café, in Collins Street, Melbourne.[114] It was always intended to be a temporary awareness-raising exercise, featuring a staff of 'Sun-Raysed girls' and a window display of a 'Sun-Raysed store' itself made from fruit 'with tiny kewpies popping up from the chimney, and walking the biscuit tiled verandah'.[115] The cafe, managed by Violet Austin, was an instant success[116]; 25,000 people visited the shop and 10,000 frequented the premises.[117] C. J. later claimed that the cafe caused controversy amongst the Mildura growers who believed that he had been spending ADFA funds enjoying himself amongst a 'harem' of 'Sun-Raysed girls'. He responded that 'whenever the time comes that I am too old to appreciate a pretty girl, I want to die', adding that where some men might be secretive and sly, his trustworthiness came from his honesty – 'I'm perfectly open in my love for the ladies'.[118]

Neither C. J. nor the ADFA wished to enter the cafe business in perpetuity, but aspired to educate the public away from the notion that dried fruit was a Christmas luxury.[119] It was also a retail outlet for the Normeys that C. J. had ordered for that year's agricultural shows, which had been cancelled due to the pandemic.[120] The cafe showed the value of imaginative publicity in tangible form.

Enter Grant Hervey

Grant Hervey's interruption of C. J.'s world was cataclysmic and definitive. Had Hervey not gone to Mildura in 1919, it is highly unlikely C. J. would have been leaving his clothes in a Packard at Mentone six years later. At the same time, they were two sides of the same coin – and both men, though they only met once, appear to have recognised this. They were both playwrights, performers and orators, and both had visions for the future of their region and their country. They both admired the USA, respected the British Empire, and loved Australia. Examining Hervey shines a light on C. J.'s public persona and the new Australian man.

George Cochrane was born in 1880 in Casterton, Victoria, 460 km south of where Mildura was to be founded a few years

Grant Hervey, in Sydney *Truth*, 16 June 1929, p. 24.

later. As a youth, he worked as a wheelwright, but 'had always strong tendencies towards journalism'.[121] He claimed he had 'the taint of insanity in my blood':

> For from, say six to nine months of the year, I can go about my business and pleasure the same as any rational man; then there comes a time when I have to go away from the city, out into the bush, and hide myself from my fellow-men. I must do this to keep my brain upon its balance...Perhaps such men are more to be pitied than blamed, I-do-not-know. Sometimes...men are gifted with special ability in certain lines, and they have to pay for it in another way.[122]

At the turn of the twentieth century, Cochrane adopted the exotic name Grant Madison Hervey. The first and middle names were, surely, references to the eighteenth and fourth US presidents (the famous New York eugenicist and conservationist Madison Grant was active but not yet internationally known). 'Hervey' is not easy to pin to a source or reference; he appears to have pronounced it 'Harvey'.

In July 1902 announcements were made regarding 22-year-old Hervey's marriage to 31-year-old Maggie Sullivan[123], a poet and 'clever journalist' once of the *Catholic Press*[124] but who he worked alongside at the Sydney *Truth*. She often wrote under the pen-name Altiora Peto: a Latin phrase meaning 'I seek higher things'. 'They met', one gossip columnist claimed, 'they loved at first sight, and – they hurriedly married'.[125] It is not clear if a marriage actually took place.

'Oh, we leave the girl a-crying and we "well it" with the chum', Hervey's poem 'Steerage to the West' exulted.[126] Hervey was in Western Australia by the time those words were published in the Perth *Sunday Times*; the paper was most pleased with its new contributor.[127] He remained there for three years, producing (for instance) an extensive overview of West Australian media for the Wagga *Worker* in early 1904 which saw him wittily dismiss the Kalgoorlie *Argus* ('edited by the office-cat in spare mouse-moments'), the *Western Mail* ('the impious say "Wail"') and the Perth *Spectator* (its 'leading articles lead nowhere, like blind alleys...'). For Hervey, the *Spectator*'s greatest asset was cartoonist Fred Booty: 'perhaps the best decorative artist'.[128] Hervey returned to Melbourne in early 1905, 'sharing a Bohemian attic' with Booty in Queen Street, Melbourne.[129]

'Whenever I have got into trouble before', Hervey was to say, 'a woman has been responsible, or, rather, a woman has been at the bottom of it'.[130] The events of 9 November 1905 were a case in point.

Walter Baker, a 42-year-old actor whose real name was Alfred Sadler[131], often played lover or hero roles in the popular and successful Bland Holt company. Baker and his wife Carlotta lived what she called 'a divided life'.[132] A Catholic, Carlotta refused to grant her husband the divorce he sought.[133] In early November 1905 Walter was appearing in Sutton Vane's play *The Betting Book* at the 'New' Theatre Royal in Bourke Street, Melbourne.[134] One Thursday night in November, Baker left the theatre and caught a tram towards Spring Street. Near the corner of Exhibition Street, he saw Carlotta walking arm in arm and 'chatting pleasantly' with Grant Hervey, a man whose picture (Carlotta would later attest) was displayed on the wall of the Bakers' Sydney drawing room[135] and whose verse Baker believed to be 'particularly clever' but who he had never met.[136] Baker alighted from his tram at the corner of Spring and Bourke and intercepted the pair. He asked Hervey 'What are you doing with my wife?' then punched the younger man on the jaw in what he described as 'a sort of upper cut'.[137] Hervey staggered and, as he steadied himself, brought a Webley .450 revolver out from his hip pocket and pointed it squarely at Baker's chest. Baker – theatrically – 'dodged' Hervey's gun for ten seconds.[138] 'Oh Walter!' Carlotta cried.[139] Baker grabbed his wife (both she and Hervey testified that he deliberately put her between himself and Hervey's pistol) and, as Baker decried Hervey as a 'murdering bastard',[140] husband and wife fled for the corner of Spring Street. Hervey fired but missed.[141] Detective Howard, a passer-by, disarmed him: 'Oh, it's alright', Hervey said, 'I'm not going to fire again'. ('Better not', Howard replied.) At the watchhouse Hervey claimed that he had been arrested for 'trying to rid the Earth of a skunk'.[142]

At his trial the following month for shooting at Baker 'with intent to murder'[143], Hervey explained he found it necessary to carry a pistol because of 'threatening letters' received in the course of his journalistic work. He claimed that the slow drawing-out of the Webley and his firing at a pillar were calculated to frighten Baker, and were not an attempt to kill him. After a two-and-a-half-hour deliberation the jury returned a verdict of not guilty.[144]

Hervey organised the Decentralisation League for Western Victoria in April 1910, taking the office of 'general organiser'.[145] His primary goal at this time was to effect a railway 'extension' from Branxholme (his mother's birthplace), north of Portland, to Dimboola – something in the region of 300 km. He told an enthused crowd at Natimuk, close to the Dimboola end of the proposed route, that 'the urgent need of the Wimmera was direct communication with the sea'.[146] Landed interests were resentful of the need to take their produce through the metropolis, and railways usually seemed calculated to make capital cities beneficiaries of primary industry through taxes, handling and storage costs. None of these, detractors felt, were deserved. In early 1911 the Casterton *News* announced that Hervey had been 'appointed general organiser' in the Glenelg (south-west Victoria) district 'for the People's Party'.[147] Although its members were standing for election, the People's Party seems to have been a paper tiger: it was avowedly not connected to any established political entity, yet received backing from the Victorian Employer's Federation.[148] Hervey was 'organiser' of a campaign by non-Labor forces to defeat a referendum to dissolve the states, and instead institute an array of provinces with federal and local as the only two tiers of government. Hervey was adamant that the people of Australia vote 'no'. There was talk that Hervey may become the Liberal member for the area, and in 1913 he attempted to enter politics as the candidate for Wannon, where he had spent his childhood.[149]

Hervey was easily offended and unable to let animosities rest. He hated, for instance, the Casterton *News*.[150] In April 1912, while standing as the Liberal candidate for Wannon, Hervey sued the editor of the *News*, William Little, for 'malicious libel', seeking £1,800 damages.[151] The report provoking Hervey appears to have been the apparently innocuous observation that, during an inspection meeting at Casterton, Railway Commissioner Fitzpatrick became impatient with Hervey's extensive list of improvements.[152] The libel case came to nothing, but Hervey fumed.

The year 1912 had begun with Hervey writing to the Hamilton *Spectator* to announce his retreat from politics due to the 'instantaneous success of my drama, *A Sportsman and a Man*, which the Harry Craig Company is presenting'.[153] He also had 'journalistic work for the *National Review*, the *New Age* and other leading periodicals in London and New York to keep up'.[154] The script of *A Sportsman and a Man* does not appear to have survived; it was a self-consciously Australian piece of theatre celebrating the legacy of the poet Adam Lindsay Gordon who, bankrupt, had shot himself in St Kilda tea-tree in 1870. Gordon had lived and worked in Mount Gambier – Hervey claimed to have spent six months 'collecting valuable material' for the play there.[155] It was filled with Hervey's obsessions: character, reputation, the press, and ethnic vilification, in this case a 'Jewish scoundrel', Goody Levy. An unscrupulous newspaper editor, named Smooge, disparages Gordon's work; Levy, in cahoots with Smooge, attempts to bribe and then to 'compromise Gordon by enticing him to a house of ill fame' in Mount Gambier. The five-act play was 'illustrated in action with popular songs and verses specially written by Mr. Grant Hervey, and rendered in character by members of the company'.[156] It was a moderate success – touring for at least six months in small halls and other humble venues.

Hervey's 'taint of insanity' was not going to let him settle into respectability. On 9 November 1914, in George Street, Sydney, he encountered a journalist friend, Charles Jeffries[157], and asked him to help compose a pamphlet on the political career of *Truth*'s publisher and his employer, John Norton. They used Jeffries' typewriter in his home; when Jeffries left to use the lavatory, Hervey composed a telegram, signing it 'Michael Denis Livingstone',[158] and paid a theatrical agent he barely knew, Michael Josephs, two shillings to send it to the Casterton *News*.[159] The telegram read:

> Morning papers report insolvency of Mount Gambier prodigy Grant Hervey, Liabilities £327/14/9, assets nil.

Once this information was published in the *News*, Hervey sued its proprietor, Edward Gazzard, for £2,000 damages. Hervey was arrested.[160] He had persuaded Jeffries to throw the incriminating evidence – the typewriter's distinctive shuttle – from the Milson's Point ferry ('If it is discovered and I go down, you go down with me').[161]

Hervey could either give up, or gamble on an escalation. He asked Norton for £100 so that he could 'nobble' witnesses.[162] Norton declined. Knowing Norton was hoping to divorce his wife, Ada, Hervey told Norton that he had already 'misconducted himself on two occasions with Mrs. Norton'[163] a few days previously.[164] For £200, Norton would be given information whereby 'his spies'[165] could discover his wife 'in an act of misconduct with Grant Hervey'.[166] It is unclear why Hervey's proposal wasn't worthwhile for Norton, who arranged to have Hervey repeat it within earshot of hidden police witnesses; Hervey was again arrested. 'I can hardly believe that you should say such a thing about me,' Ada told Hervey. 'You knew that I was very fond of you.'[167] It apparently suited Norton better to divorce Ada on the grounds of his own adultery (principle amongst those named, his niece).[168] The divorce took place the following year, and he died soon afterwards.

The telegram trial was fought twice six months apart, the guilty verdict having been overturned the first time. Initially Hervey defended himself, poorly; he blamed Jeffries, Josephs and at least one other man for arranging the telegram and damned them as being 'as black as Hell'.[169] On being given an extensive jail term, he claimed that in 'this Norton case':

> I was striving to help a woman. I admit now, after thinking the affair over in my saner moments, that the thing was impossible. My motive was right, but my methods were wrong, and I have paid the penalty.[170]

He spent almost four years in three prisons, subject to indignities insufferable to a man with his views on race, such as being shackled to Chinese and Indigenous prisoners. Inspired by a Californian religious tract he became fervently Christian.[171]

On his release he married Anne Crowe, a widow from his hometown. He had also formulated a new scheme blending longstanding obsessions (such as the economic and infrastructural development of western Victoria, from Mildura to Portland) with his own search for recognition. The new Mildura Memorial State would, Hervey believed, be his vindication.

If Hervey had any public profile in 1919, it was as the author of the poetry volume *Australians Yet* and as a prison reform campaigner.[172] He would have meant very little to most Mildurans, even those who noted the similarity in name between the poet-journalist and the newly arrived American journalist 'G. Madison Harvey'. C. J. described his impressions of 'Harvey':

> He was tall, well built, good looking, and of excellent address. He was well educated, and had the gift of facile expression. He possessed a strong, clean-shaven face, and a determined jaw. His mouth, ears and forehead were rather a contradiction to the rest of his physical make-up, as they indicated weakness of character.[173]

Harvey claimed connection to the Butterick publishing house – the company responsible for magazines such as *Everybody's*

Magazine and *The Delineator* — and as proof brandished a picture postcard of the company's extensive New York headquarters. He appeared in Council Chamber to announce a bold new proposal; councillors, the shire president, and C. J. were in attendance.

Harvey's rhetoric was impressive. He appealed to patriotism and the memory of the war. He also appealed to the hip pockets of Mildurans, and the general sense of optimism in a nation now, in its own estimation, matured through the 'blooding' of war and ready to face the 1920s with vision and purpose.

He praised the visionary Chaffeys, noting the high land values of the once almost worthless Mildura land, and citing the example of Ohio, a state he claimed had been built by soldier–settlers of the American Civil War. A Mildura Soldiers Memorial State, he claimed, would section off a portion of the west of Victoria. Produce would not go through Melbourne but would travel to the world via Portland. Although his proposal had no connection to the ADFA, Harvey announced that, whatever C. J. received for his role as publicist, he demanded twice as much, 'because I have the knowledge, plus ability, plus energy to arouse the attention of thoughtful men'.[174] A public meeting was held in the Mildura rotunda on a Saturday evening, the 2nd of August, to deliver his pitch to the people.

Harvey's rotunda address was stirring. He implored the people of Mildura to do their bit in saving the Empire from poverty and disaster by seizing their destiny and developing the area to the hilt, through further irrigation measures (across a million acres) and new railway infrastructure. He suggested that the first and most important plank in the project was to send a deputised mission to Prime Minister Hughes to negotiate the creation of the state in question. He also, in the manner of a travelling preacher, led what C. J. called a 'magnificently delivered'[175] prayer for God to give all present adequate courage and intelligence to follow Harvey.

In outlining his scheme, Harvey described the ADFA as a 'damned farce' and demanded the right to ask 'a big series of questions' about the ADFA's operations. C. J. then mounted the platform and declared that he 'should like to be allowed to answer' but that first he had 'a couple of questions himself'. In fact, there were three:

> Who was it who asked the questions? And whom did he represent? Would he give some account of his movements for the last seven years?[176]

'Then', *Smith's Weekly* recounted, 'the orator saw his hopes of power and pelf vanish like the baseless fabric of a dream'.[177] 'Harvey' immediately confessed to being 'Hervey' and further admitted that he had been in prison for half of the period mentioned, blaming Norton for a 'swindle' for which he 'swung the man a double cross which broke him up but which incidentally led to his own imprisonment'. He claimed that he had conceived of Greater Mildura in prison (not mentioning that he had put forward a modest version of the same idea in 1912) and said that pretending to be American was a calculation that Australians would pay more attention to 'a man from abroad' than a local.[178]

Grant Hervey left Mildura by the next train but continued to write cajoling and threatening letters to Mildura newspapers from various central Melbourne addresses, usually under his 'American' name of Harvey, proclaiming himself 'Mildura's single-purposed Chief and King'. He claimed, for instance, to have met with Hughes in Bendigo and 'dictated a policy to him, since he has none, himself'. 'Now,' he wrote, 'since I have captured the imagination of Mildura, the city is mine'.[179]

C. J. was the hero of the hour; his sleuthing and connections had allowed him to identify and bring down an enemy in an instant. He said his suspicions had been aroused by flaws in the man's American accent; 'as an amateur actor and raconteur', C. J. knew accents well.[180] His friend Gifford Hall, a man of the world with experience of Americans, claimed to have identified 'Harvey' as a fraud almost immediately; Hall also claimed that a 'girl' from Casterton had recognised George Cochrane on his arrival.[181] C. J. later described his encounter with Hervey as 'the clashing of two supreme Egoists'.[182]

Ending a remarkable decade

C. J.'s *The Victories of Failure* periodically sees its narrator, 'K. J.', take stock of his own successes at key moments. His nineteen-teens had certainly seen him rise from big fish in the small pond of Mildura to a nationally famous success. Not only was he a demonstrated 'business mind' of great capacity; he was also cloaked in the kind of glamour normally reserved for film or theatre stars; he drove fast cars, was dreaming about aviation, and was never resting, on his laurels or anything else. He was a driven and unique individual.

He had already dreamed up the Big Stunt for 1920, 'Three Magic Letters'. With typical candour – and a slight pinch of arrogance – he announced that with the 1919 stunt, he and his staff had learned that 'Australians, as a whole, are too lazy to count 6,000 berries in the hope of winning over £1,000':

> Therefore in planning the "stunt" for next year we have devised something so simple and yet so appealing in its attractiveness, that it can be completed in 20 seconds by anyone over the age of six. The 1920 stunt will not be released until Saturday, April 19…it will be introduced to public notice somewhat earlier by "The Three Magic Letters". These three magic letters will be transformed…into three magic words, with cash in every syllable.[183]

C. J. assumed that, as long as he explained the thought processes behind all his 'stunts', the public would continue to trust him. He was fighting the good fight: not only on behalf of his fellow ADFA members, but also for Australia's economic and physical health, and repatriation – that is, the settling of returned soldiers on the land. It was not, he may have figured, his fault if press coverage sometimes crept close to comparing him to Christ ('What a day of revelation the 29th will be' the Angaston *Leader* had declared of the first 'Big Stunt').[184]

In October 1919, C. J. was unanimously re-elected ADFA publicity director for 1920.[185] Soon after, however, two growers by name of Schmidt and Paulson were publicly critical of the campaign and new financing arrangements which saw C. J. receive a lump sum payment.[186] He called a meeting to address their concerns. Here, he mused on his recent trip to Western Australia and his visit to Mundaring Weir:

> It was designed by a prince of engineers, named O'Connor. I was given his history. He had devoted years of his life – all his energy, enthusiasm and ability, to the design and construction of this wonderful weir. He was a victim of tremendous criticism, and was accused of faulty construction and bad administration. Complete disaster was prophesied for his weir. One Perth paper slated him to a full page. He was found dead one Sunday morning with his head lying across this printed condemnation of himself. A sensitive, earnest man, he committed suicide because of unkind and unwarranted criticism. After his death, it was found that the Mundaring Weir did all that he had prophesied for it, and a monument is erected at the entrance to the weir, so that all visitors may honour his memory.

He hastened to add that he wasn't comparing himself to C. Y. O'Connor precisely, but O'Connor's weir and the ADFA campaign 'both arouse criticism...That is where the comparison ends'.

'With me', he added, 'there is no sensitive soul, and no chance of suicide'. He would prefer, he said, to 'come right out in the open and face whatever critics there are...I'd give way to a better man'.[187]

Those present at the meeting – including Schmidt and Paulson – were satisfied by C. J.'s accounts, showing that his

£52,000 expenditure had returned up to £1.5 million in land value increase and crop sales 'as a direct tangible result'. C. J. received applause at various points of his address 'and at its conclusion the acclamation was long continued'.[188]

Even at the very beginning of the 1920s, however, C. J. was more than just changing the game in Mildura: he was going to gamble on his own career, reputation and life. He would go on to concentrate on a very different set of concerns in the new decade, and soon the acclamation from his old friends and enemies at ADFA would be a distant echo.

5

'The Aussie Glide'

"I say, Molly, girl", said Normey, "did you notice that the Almight – no, confound it! I mean C. J. DeGaris – I'm always mixing them up – said before the Cost of Living Commission the other day that there were only ten currants in an average baker's bun?"

"Wonderful, isn't he?" returned Molly. "In spite of the fact that he's running the biggest publicity campaign ever attempted in Australia, managing a huge packing-house, an estate agency, an irrigable estate capable of supporting a couple of thousand people, discovering Australia's Dickens, writing musical comedies, and acting as first assistant in the running of the university, he yet finds time to pick the currants out of bath buns. How many buns would he have to pick to pieces to obtain a true average, Normey lad?"[1]

The broad humour of 'Dip-Tin' in the 'Sun-Raysed Column' – scattered across a few South Australian newspapers – never missed a chance to poke fun at C. J. That said, C. J. was also happy to poke fun at himself. He published a series of what he termed 'quaint cusses' entered in his 'Sun-Raysed' nursery rhyme competition parodying the campaign: Little Jack Horner, for instance, suffers stomach pains from 'those dratted Sun-Raysed raisins'.[2] However, under almost any measure — his disastrous married life and the distasteful encounter with Hervey notwithstanding — C. J. entered the 1920s from the strongest base possible. He was a shooting star.

His success as a publicist for the ADFA having sprung, in no small part, from the exploration of a personal 'hobby horse', he decided to give himself a 'Christmas present' to make inroads with another enthusiasm. From his personal funds, he allocated £1,000 towards finding, and rewarding, a new breed of Australian novelist. £550 was to be prize money for first, second and third place; the remainder was to go towards advertising.[3]

In C. J.'s mind, the literature promoted would be of a world standard, presenting Australia as modern and progressive, rather than as exotic, primitive or marginal. Rather than works showing Australia as 'noted for bush, bushrangers, convicts, bushfires, droughts and aboriginals' it should be shown as 'a more modern civilisation' on par with any other.[4]

He claimed that the 'original idea' of the literary competition 'was because of a patriotic ideal; but I shall naturally try and turn it to good account, so that my losses may eventually change to profits'.[5] On a trip to Perth in the first week of 1920, he took time out from spruiking the ADFA's message, and talking up the West's own capacity to grow currants, to discuss this competition. He began by alluding to having written a novel himself, of which no other evidence exists — perhaps it was a version of *Ambition Run Mad* — 'and I know what a job it is to have a book published in Australia' without an English market. As authors, he claimed Australians had 'been terribly handicapped, and the result is that Australian literature has been neglected'. Yet, Australian sportsmen were the best in the world; Australian culture only needed some encouragement to flourish.

I am hopeful that this will be the commencement of a new era, and that soon we will be able to release Australian books monthly. This offers great possibilities for the cinematograph. The novels could be filmed – there is no country in the world better placed for that than Australia – and gradually we would build up the thing that is so seriously lacking today – a true Australian literature. Prospects are already very promising in connection with the competition I have promoted, and authors in larger numbers than I hoped for have announced their intention of competing.[6]

The *Murray Pioneer* reported at this time that C. J. – who it already believed to be 'the most gifted all-round man in Australia' – had received 'a proposal' from America 'to stage his powerful play *Ambition Run Mad*'.[7] No more seems to have come of this, and it may simply have been a rumour planted by C. J., or an acolyte, to excite attention.

While his literary competition percolated, C. J. took time – though not much time – to realise another dream, with a putative first. He would later claim that the idea for *F. F. F.* came during the ADFA press tour of the Sun-Raysed Districts, from a discussion with an unnamed Adelaide journalist picking his brains about the literary competition. C. J. noted (as so many have since) that Australians were cultural sponges, happily consuming songs, stories and art of, for instance, the USA. Australian concerts, he said, often involved audiences paying money to hear 'pretty Aussie girls and husky Aussie men' singing songs that 'Americanise Australia'.[8] Challenged by those present to produce Australian material on par with American work, C. J. spent the night writing lyrics for songs – 'The Aussie Glide' and 'The Magic Call – Coo-Ee'. The following day the pressmen 'chuckled over his made-to-order verses' and laughed louder when he told them he would incorporate both into a stage musical to be produced before the year was out.[9]

C. J. was once again seized by passion and had the wherewithal to make it happen. Reginald Stoneham, composer, had served in the South African War and worked as a fireman in Adelaide; he was 31 before his first composition was published. Five years older than C. J., Stoneham had been recruited to compose the 'Sun-Raysed Waltz' for the ADFA campaign; he was, of course, the natural musician for C. J. to turn to as a co-writer.[10] The two produced up to twenty songs for the new project.

Complexity was not required here, and C. J. did not spend an extraordinarily long time figuring out a plot. He invented a protagonist with a dash of DeGaris savoir faire; Fitzwilliam Ferguson, sent to Australia and an established 'Aussie' (and, in typical DeGaris self-referential fashion, a playwright). Ferguson meets a theatrical producer called Hugh D. Collins (impresario Hugh D. McIntosh was a challenger to Williamson – the company that had rejected *Ambition Run Mad*). Ferguson falls in love with his typist, Flo Hastings, and the two travel to Britain, an opportunity for C. J. to present, as he did in his previous dramatic work, scenes predicated on various possibilities for flirtation on an ocean liner. In London, Ferguson is told that his wealthy uncle will bestow him with riches if he becomes a 'dude' – that is, a member of the aristocracy; he tries, but fails, to take on the class pretentions of this type and ultimately confesses that he has become Australian through and through. This is what the wealthy uncle had hoped for all along, and the fortune is all Ferguson's.

Perhaps aware that his storyline was basic, C. J. returned to safer ground to add the frisson of what he knew best, and was indeed famous for. Not only, he hoped, would audiences love the songs and performers, there was also a bonus competition within the show itself: the audience member who could crack the code of *F. F. F.*, the show's final song would win a cash prize.

C. J.'s 1919–20 period was redolent with good and bad choices, happenstance and chance interactions or situations that impacted him extraordinarily. Theatre historian Frank van Straten posits that C. J. created 'Hugh D. Collins' to capture the imagination, or perhaps stroke the ego, of Hugh D. McIntosh; but van Straten points out that McIntosh saw C. J. coming a mile off. Financially troubled, McIntosh needed £10,000 to stay afloat; he banked on C. J.'s love of the theatre and his faith in *F. F. F.* He made C. J. Chairman of the Melbourne Board, sold him £12,000 of shares in the Tivoli theatre, and took on the production of *F. F. F.* to open in August of that year. C. J. was blithe about investing in his own production because he was strongly of the opinion that sales of his and Stoneham's songs would cover any losses; he also could not imagine the show itself would not be a success.

By Monday 24 May, *F. F. F.* was in solid enough form that C. J. and other 'Mildura artists' – including Violet Austin – were able to visit Pyap for its annual sports day and a concert for which the 'majority of the items' were songs from *F. F. F.*[11]

It was to be a Tivoli production using its 'Famous Players'. The romantic leads were British-born: Hugh Steyne was Fitzwilliam Ferguson; Minnie Love, Flo Hastings; Flo's aunt Maggie was played by Marie La Varre; and Ferguson's uncle, the unsubtly named Joseph Morgold, was played by Charles H. Workman. Flo's mother was played by Maggie Moore, beloved and, according to van Straten, 'definitely the show's biggest drawcard'.

F. F. F. was to premiere in Adelaide in August. Before this happened, C. J. realised yet another dream. During the Sunraysia press junket he had brought out a 'pet hobby map', showing Mildura as the 'Aviation Capital of Australia', with anticipated flying distances between the ADFA's home base and Australia's cities.[12] At the same time as he impressed the assembled men with his knowledge and ambition for air travel in Australia, he made an ally and friend in J. J. Simons, of the Perth *Call*.

C. J.'s aeroplane was called the *Sun-Raysed* and it bore ADFA advertising, although it was difficult now to tell whether C. J. was publicist for ADFA or the other way around. Certainly, his principal mission, as he described it, was to conduct business between cities, using not only air travel to lend glamour to his role and the company he represented, but also to reduce distance. Notably, C. J. received – and accepted – the kudos for his aviation feats, but he did not fly himself. He employed good pilots, principally Frank Briggs. However, the bravery it required to travel by air, whether long or short distance, was extraordinary at this time. in the 1920s' pilots, and their passengers, were not expected to make old bones.

His first trip was from Melbourne to Adelaide, undertaken in four stages, piloted by Lieutenant Arthur Long of Aviation Ltd, who had sold him the aircraft. C. J. was adamant that he was not interested in a novelty or pleasure trip; he wanted his first flight to demonstrate potential. At 9 am on 22 June, C. J. and Long left Melbourne for Mildura. The weather en route was daunting. C. J. was withering, however, when his pilot suggested he might not want to undertake the flight: 'We're supposed to be pioneering civil aviation…If a bit of weather is going to scare us, or knock the machine about, what good is flying ever going to be for the nation. We'll go if we drop'.[13] They stopped at Wedderburn briefly[14], thence to Mildura, where well-wishers scribbled messages in pencil on the plane; C. J. 'received a "mascot" from one of his children'.[15] C. J. and Long then travelled to Pyap, thence Adelaide. They may have been as close as 10 miles from their destination, though they did not have adequate maps to be certain, when they encountered storms and low-lying cloud. They were forced to take an emergency detour south-east to the Murray Bridge–Port Elliot region. They arrived in Adelaide that evening.[16]

C. J. had postcards printed of a photograph of his aeroplane and sent them to newspapers great and small around the continent. The postcard told recipients, who told their readers, that the plane was 'a Boulton and Paul, 100 h.p., two-seater and can do 104 miles per hour'. It was not a toy. C. J. was going to use it 'solely for private business flights between the State capitals and Sun-Raysed settlements'.[17] The *Mildura Cultivator's* 'Steel Blayde', Gifford Hall, did for his readers what C. J. would not: he went on a pleasure trip with Long in the 'bird-machine'. Long agreeably performed various aeronautical tricks, such as looping-the-loop.[18]

The following week, on Tuesday 29 June, a 'banquet-social' was held at Hudson's Cafeteria in Mildura. It was an 'Aero dinner' for a hundred of C. J.'s various staff members – people who worked at the family business, Sarnia; the ADFA; the Olympia Theatre; and Pyap – to celebrate their celestial employer's most recent triumph, a crowning achievement until the next one. DeGaris employee Alfred E. Lloyd noted in his speech how 'high in the clouds…he is held in the esteem and affection of all staff members present at this Aero Dinner…' His hopes for their 'pioneering and enterprising chief, C. J. DeGaris Esq.' were limitless:

> C. J., may this, your first trip skywards, be a forerunner of years of flights equally successful. May you never encounter a cloud so dark as to obscure your vision of further pioneering triumphs or dim your recollection of this pleasant gathering, inaugurated by your most staunch supporters, your combined staffs.

In response to Lloyd, C. J. said he went up in the sky thinking how big Australia was, and came down thinking how little he was. He paid tribute to his pilot Long – who had been invited to the Aero dinner, but had sent his apologies – and told those assembled that he had engaged Frank Briggs as Long's replacement.[19] Calcutta born and South Australia raised, Briggs had been an aviator in the Great War; afterwards he flew dignitaries between London and Paris to the Peace Conference; he had also worked as Billy Hughes' pilot.[20] C. J. had engaged his services in Adelaide the previous week.

On 6 July 1920 – a week after the Aero dinner – C. J. made another ambitious foray. He and Briggs travelled from Mildura to Sydney in five hours, stopping at Hay, Junee and Harden along the way for petrol. Trains would have taken fifty-four hours; an automobile would have taken thirty hours.[21] It was a heady time in Australian aviation: on Friday 9 July two aeroplanes left Mascot. One, for the Perdriau rubber company, was heading to Brisbane, and the other contained C. J. and Briggs, returning to Melbourne. Both broke records.[22]

F. F. F. opened on Saturday 28 August 1920 at Adelaide's Prince of Wales Theatre, resplendent with wattle blossom, before a 'large and appreciative audience'. The *Advertiser's* critic believed that Hugh Steyne's and Minnie Love's parts had been written especially for them. This may or may not have been true, but certainly confirms they were effective in the roles. The writer continued:

> The dressing, mounting, lighting and stage pageants were of the best, and it was evident that the comedy had been well rehearsed, for everything went with a rhythmic swing. There was an efficient orchestra, and the choruses gave the required strength and volume to the lyrics. Whatever the mystic initials of the title may represent, the comedy may accurately be described as Fresh, Fanciful and Frolicsome.[23]

The *Mildura Cultivator* – a paper not inclined, it is true, to criticise C. J. or his activities – praised both the show's plot and the way it brought Australia 'into its own as the Land of Romance. Hawaii, Ceylon, Japan and countless other spots have served in the past. Here is our own Australia'.[24] Much praise was bestowed on the artistic presentations in the show, such as for the scene for the song 'Murray Moon' presenting the glittering river in a panoramic vista. Reports suggest this captivated audiences so much that they begged that the scenery not be changed quickly after the song, so that they might take it all in.

DeGaris and Stoneham appeared before the audience hand in hand and, commenting briefly, C. J. praised all involved but would take little credit himself; he claimed he only 'wrote some of the words'. Of course, there would have been no show without C. J. rising to a challenge – largely of his own devising – and providing an impressive sum of money. *F. F. F.*, C. J. proudly stated, achieved its ambition of 'smashing precedent' by running for a fortnight in Adelaide, and broke the local record for a first-night house. 'We did it', he proclaimed.[25]

The sheet music to 'Proposing', 1921, with *F. F. F.* branding. National Library of Australia.

The meaning of the title *F. F. F.* was fluid. C. J. later wrote that he and Briggs had *F. F. F.* advertising painted on their aircraft and amused themselves during flights with interpretations.[26] The Adelaide *Herald* told its readers that C. J. had revealed at the end of the successful two-week Adelaide run that the answer was 'Fitzwilliam Ferguson, Fop' and that no-one had guessed it. This is unsurprising, since it ran directly counter to the actual message of the play – whatever Fitzwilliam was, a 'fine fellow', perhaps, it was definitively shown that he was *not* a fop. Each week the show ran, the competition needed a different answer.[27] While it's not clear how C. J. established the rules – in this regard it was like his literary competition – no-one could accuse him of changing things around to save paying up. In Adelaide, part-winners were announced and awarded portions of the prize money, and the remaining cash was given to a charity for blind soldiers.[28]

As well as basking in the glow of theatre's glamour, C. J. also came close to the golden light of royalty. The Prince of Wales (destined, the following decade, to be one of the Empire's shortest-reigning monarchs, Edward VIII) visited Australia to pay tribute to the nation's role in the Great War. Rumour had it that the Prince was being forced by his minders to stick to the coast during his visit. C. J. lobbied to have him visit at least one or two of the seventeen Sun-Raysed settlements. A presentation box of dried fruits and Curlwaa oranges intended for the Prince went on display at the Royal Melbourne Show.[29]

Just as Grant Hervey could not get Billy Hughes to Mildura, C. J. could not persuade the Prince towards Sunraysia. However a chance to impress him was laid at C. J.'s feet when tour organisers asked if he would fly the royal mail from Port Augusta in South Australia to Sydney.[30] Edward was presumably hoping for letters from his lover, the elegant, married Freda Dudley Ward. The Prince would wait on the HMAS *Franklin* at the Heads for C. J. and Briggs, and was keen to meet them.[31] They flew from Melbourne on Sunday 15 August in a De Havilland borrowed from the defence department. They suffered two forced landings,

The most spectacular of C. J.'s aeroplane crashes, from *The Victories of Failure*.

the second on Onkaparinga racecourse. Another flight having gone awry, C. J. departed by car to Renmark, to meet his own Sopwith flown from Mildura. On reaching Renmark, however, C. J. was told that the plane had misjudged and landed at Berri.[32] Arriving there by car, he and Briggs took off only to be thrown into the air by wind and forced to crash-land in a tree. C. J. later recounted that he took the opportunity, as the two men plummeted, to turn to Briggs and make an *F. F. F.* joke: 'falling frightfully fast'. He escaped easily, but Briggs was trapped in the craft and the fuel tank had become damaged; C. J. climbed the tree, stopped the leaking petrol and freed his pilot. Unable to fly – the plane was a write-off – they took a car to Mildura to find that Colonel Williams and Sergeant Chester, who were to travel with them, had left for Sydney an hour before. It was a comedy of almosts. The mail was delivered, though not by C. J., and the meeting with the Prince was not to be. C. J., who did not smoke, received a presentation cigarette case as a thank-you gift.[33]

The Golden West

> There is none of the aloofness which usually surrounds the stereotyped Great Man about DeGaris. He is just a young, young-looking man, typically Australian, strong-faced and bright-eyed, and his personality just radiates confidence – confidence in himself, in his work, in the country.[34]

By the time the Western Australian newspaper *The Call* published the above words, in September 1920, a casual observer of the popular media might have been moved to wonder who this C. J. DeGaris actually was – or wanted to be. The war was over, though still very much in the public mind. Australians were open to new ideas from optimistic and charismatic people about the way the nation should explore its newfound freedom and channel its new prosperity. C. J. had blasted himself into the public eye in 1919 at the head of a campaign to make people aware of, buy and consume dried fruit – on its own, reconstituted, or as part of bizarrely titled new sweets. He wanted Australians to think about dried fruit, cook with it, encourage their children to read stories about it, dance to the idea of it (the 'Sun-Raysed Waltz'), and exercise their minds on competitions for it. But before that message was fully absorbed, the dried fruit promoter announced a literary competition. Next, he was a pioneer of air travel, inviting all to imagine accelerated and unified national businesses, linked by aerial routes. Then he was suddenly the author of a musical comedy touring the country. He tried to bring them altogether under a patriotic umbrella, telling *The Call:* 'Take it from me the day of the home-made article is at hand, whether it be a pot of jam or a musical plan'.[35]

For C. J., 1920 was already frenetic. Why not add an entirely new element to blow him completely off course? While *F. F. F.* was still enjoying the full bloom of publicity, C. J. started talking about a place called 'Kendenup'.

C. J. was undoubtedly looking for something to take him far away from Mildura, Victoria and the vocal minority of always-critical, overfamiliar, ungrateful ADFA members. In February 1920, he made his first trip to Perth – the initial visit, by rail, on behalf of the ADFA. His impressions, recorded in the press, seemed almost tactically calculated to persuade himself, anyone around him, and any West Australian who was easily flattered, that the future for C. J. DeGaris lay in the West. He felt the West was too dependent on the eastern states for food, primary products and shipping. Yet, he said, the state had the best vineyard in Australia (Barrett-Leonard's, in the Upper Swan Valley), and more generally it was 'almost infinite in size just as its potentialities are almost limitless'.[36]

A land agent by the name of John Claffey offered a journalist in the Adelaide 'Sunraysia' office, Harold Taylor, £250 for an introduction to C. J.[37] Taylor having done so, Claffey told C. J. about an extraordinary opportunity that had just come on the market.[38] The Kendenup estate had been in the Hassell family for generations, and the Hassells had built a large, two-storey home in 1866, along with sundry other buildings on site. The family had established the Standard Gold Mining Company Ltd of Kendenup in 1874; it went into voluntary liquidation two years later, having produced nothing more than an unproductive shaft.[39] Sensibly, the Hassells stayed with their core business thereafter, and the area was a successful sheep station for close to ninety years. Some choice wool bales had, in fact, received an international award at the Paris Exhibition of 1890.[40] On John Hassell's death the estate, perfect for soldier settlement in the eyes of locals[41], sold to Daniel Edmunds, a mica miner with a long Western Australian career but now living in Adelaide.[42] Edmunds was seeking to quickly onsell.[43] Situated as it was on the railway line between Perth and Albany – two important centres – Kendenup was very accessible. It had ample water supply and good soil. But it also required capital for clearing and infrastructure. However great the potential, it would be a challenge to make Kendenup work.

Elisha travelled to Kendenup, in the company of Mildura shire engineer Ben Johnson. The two men arrived via train in Perth on the 16 August, less than a week after Edmunds had bought the property. Perth's *Australian* assumed that the DeGarises wanted Kendenup for closer settlement on Mildura and Pyap lines, and that 'where sheep once nibbled, splendid Australian families will be reared'.[44]

The Australia C. J. envisaged was one in which, by science or exploration, and through the machinations of private enterprise or government policy, areas of the continent would be populated in small 'closer settlement' villages, organised on democratic, communal lines. This conception linked to campaigns to increase the country's population for reasons of security (most commonly, typified as the nation's ability to resist overpowering populations from China and Japan). There was no shortage of racist fearmongering suggesting that 'the bosom of Australia' was being 'left naked to attacks from more populous countries, where people of different colour and different ideals to our own are looking for a new area'.⁴⁵ A diagram published in the Melbourne *Evening Sun* in 1924 was typical of the thinking of the time. It featured an outline of the coast of Australia filled with population figures of various European countries inside a jigsaw puzzle of hypothetical territories. Such depictions of the Australian continent fired the imagination of what the region might become with the perfection of certain technologies, ground and air transport and irrigation in particular.⁴⁶

C. J.'s Kendenup was also part and parcel of the assumption across the nation that returned soldiers, who had risked their lives and who in many cases were psychologically or physically damaged by the experience, were deserving of a chance for prosperity and property ownership. State governments were sponsoring soldier or 'closer' settlements in underdeveloped areas. This allied with the 'vigour' promoted by J. J. Simons in Kendenup advertising: 'DeGaris force! DeGaris Punch! And DeGaris enterprise!'⁴⁷

The egalitarian nature of closer settlement appealed to C. J.; for him 'community prosperity' was a feature of all 'Seventeen Sun-Raysed Settlements of Australia', described as 'the living examples of prosperous inland development. There are no rich men, but there are no paupers. There is a remarkably even distribution of prosperity'.⁴⁸ It also aspired to be as multicultural as was politically possible at the time: 'Cosmopolitanism is going to be a characteristic of Kendenup', and British, Belgian, Swedish, Anglo-Indian and Mexican settlers were anticipated to leaven the Anglo-Australians.⁴⁹ Under the thinking on 'racial hygiene' at the time, such a blend was as progressive as Australia could be and still stay 'pure'. The balance was between populating the nation with 'loyal' non-Anglo Europeans for the sake of defence, and retaining 'British' traditions.

Like many Australians – particularly those who identified with rural areas – C. J. subscribed to the enthusiasm for New States prevalent in the years after the Great War. Regional Australians and key politicians, such as the Country Party's leader Earle Page, espoused regional development based on the idea that smaller 'capital' cities in new states would be closer to the activities of rural producers. If smaller trading hubs (Albany, for instance) were able to deal directly, politically and economically, with their hinterlands, producers would be better served and there would be less opportunity for urban bureaucrats and middlemen of the larger cities to control and profit from things they either did not understand or in which their involvement was not required. New political designations were proposed around the nation divided, as everyone knew, on arbitrary colonial, now state, lines by cartographers with no knowledge of the country. New states – the first, it was popularly assumed, would be New England in northern New South Wales, though there was also a strong Riverina movement – were therefore calculated to create prosperity for regional areas by freeing them from the controlling and self-interested grasp of the capital cities. One version of this movement advocated the 'subdividing' of the six states of Australia into thirteen with three 'federal territories', becoming the 'United States of Australia'.[50] A central plank of Hervey's preposterous 1919 bid to lead the people of Mildura was predicated in large part on the creation of a Soldiers Memorial State in the west of Victoria; C. J. thwarted Hervey's campaign, but he was open to the notion of redrawing of state boundaries. At the same time as the Country Party pushed for new states, Labor party policy aspired to eliminate states altogether, to be replaced by an enhanced local government tier: provinces across the nation attending to the nuts and bolts of infrastructure, while the federal government looked after its core purposes such as defence and trade. This would probably have suited C. J.'s purposes just as well, if not more so.

A 'second Mildura'

The extremely tall (2.1 m) John Joseph 'J. J.' Simons was a man after C. J.'s heart. They were roughly the same age (Simons two years older) and had been stunningly successful in a broad range of innovative, socially progressive campaigns. Simons had come to Western Australia from Clare in South Australia[51] in 1896, aged 13, with his family.[52] Ten years later he founded the Young Australia League (YAL), an organisation for boys and girls, dedicated to travel and physical activity. Its headquarters were at Perth, but it would gain currency around the nation. Since 1909, Simons had been known as 'The Boss' or 'Boss Simons'.[53] He was a broad-brush patriot ('loving wattle, waratahs, West Australian daisies and eucalyptus')[54] who saw value in propaganda in song, story and poetry: he enjoyed the work of Grant Hervey, for instance, who he put in a category with Banjo Paterson, Henry Kendall, Henry Lawson, Barcroft Boake and 'others with…undoubted histrionic ability'.[55] In the early 1920s, he was active as publisher of *The Call*; a popular Labor politician and, of course, leader of the YAL. Simons had become a C. J. ally earlier in 1920, on the press tour of Sunraysia, representing *The Call*.

C. J. was in Perth in late September to promote *F. F. F.*'s run there. He was only able to attend the first half of the opening night, however, as he had to take the train back to Melbourne, the Prince of Wales fiasco having left him temporarily without an aeroplane.[56] He was also planning a trip to Kendenup to investigate its potential. He told *The Call* about his ambitions:

> Yes, I'm looking forward to seeing Kendenup all right, and, to use an Americanism, I have a hunch that I'll like it…a model settlement, smiling landscapes and all things poetical and practical are in our vision, and if Kendenup justifies our expectations the scheme will be put into operation right away.[57]

The Call's Office Shakespeare and Office Cat collaborated on a poem about C. J.:

> Oh Monarch of the Murray, you have tarried overlong
> You are welcome, doubly welcome with your Sun-Raysed and your song.

You say you hear us calling but it's nothing in the way
That the West will call its encores to your Myst'ry Music Play!

C. J.'s worldview, as he outlines it in his *The Victories of Failure,* is melodramatic, with himself as the central swashbuckler. He could have learnt something from Grant Hervey's self-administered cure to keep his 'brain upon its balance' – periodic retreat to solitude – although Hervey's worst behaviour was hardly the best advertisement for the practice. Instead, C. J. built on frenetic activity by whipping up more. Any objective observer would have seen it was a mistake to leap into Kendenup.

Once again, *The Victories of Failure* is an unreliable memoir. It is almost certainly based on C. J.'s copious and self-reflective diaries, but at the same time, C. J. wrote it with a desire not only to protect his own reputation but that of those around him.[58] In the midst of relating tales of F. F. F. and Kendenup, he indulges in a long anecdote in which he defends Violet's honour from attack by his bank manager, who has treated her disrespectfully then demands C. J. fire her. C. J. threatens to punch the man, who backs down in a cowardly manner.[59] Soon afterwards, C. J. makes some overtures towards reconciliation with Rene, in the context of discussing Kendenup ('the whole of the environment should lend itself to a new start in domestic happiness for both of us'), and encourages her to pursue a greater friendship with Violet, which she does.[60]

This discussion of personal issues is a small, titillating offering to distract from what was probably quite prevalent gossip in Mildura about his, Violet's and Rene's lives in the late 1910s to early 1920s. It seems apparent to the present-day reader that if C. J. and Violet were not in a sexual relationship – he would surely have had no particular moral objection to this, assuming his assertions about Rene's behaviour were true – he was in love with her, particularly as he protests far too much.

C. J.'s love life may also have had a direct impact on his decision to concentrate his energies on Kendenup. It was, as he claims in *Victories,* a chance to start over again, to remove himself from the gaze of eyes in a small pond where he was one of the few big fish to look at. With Rene in Kendenup (he suggests to her that she might 'look after the social and domestic side of the community')[61] and Violet part of his business, C. J. could remove the women from Mildura and better control his relationship with each. Moving to Kendenup was also an opportunity to cast a new 'colony' wherein he was leader, rather than the second generation in a city where older men – including his own father, keeping an eye on things from Melbourne – were still tangibly ensconced.

Kendenup was to include not one but two parks named for the Chaffeys, and C. J. was overt about Kendenup's status, in his mind, as a second Mildura: 'having put a storey onto Mildura, he wished to erect a complete edifice of his own'.[62] The naming of these parks as the 'Chaffey Lawns' would 'establish a sentimental link between the older and the new settlement'.[63] The common connection was the need for dehydration equipment to preserve the product for export. While both settlements were distant from their markets, Kendenup, to its economic advantage, was different from Mildura and Pyap in that it was in need of neither major irrigation works nor railway link. Kendenup was 40 miles (64 km) from Albany, 'the second finest harbour in Australia'. It was seven days nearer European markets than Victoria, and Java – another enormous population with a wealthy European-derived population – was six days away. The average Kendenup rainfall was 26 inches (66 cm) – much more than twice that of Mildura – and there was no drought in its recorded history. It was a comfortable climate for people, too; C. J. claimed residents needed blankets every night, and the regular cool evenings of the 'Albany Doctor' meant 'eight hours in the Land of Nod was a refreshing experience'.[64] It had a railway station and two sidings.[65] An advertisement for Kendenup shortly after its launch suggested that, on average, its land could produce 10 tons (9 tonnes) of onions to the acre; 15 tons (13.6 tonnes) of potatoes; 40 bushels of maize; 1½ tons (1.36 tonnes) of oats; and 160 cases of apples.[66]

Nearby Mount Barker was already known for its apples. C. J. saw economic value in the land price apparently predicated on the failure of previous owners to appreciate its economic worth once converted to an agricultural, rather than a pastoral, region – amplified and stabilised by the existence of new dehydration technology.[67]

Gerald Beverley thought C. J. was foolish to contemplate this new project. This was not so much because he did not think it would succeed but for what he would put in jeopardy in the east to invest in Kendenup. This, at least, is what he told C. J. on the train in late September on the way to inspect the property.[68] Once in Mount Barker, the men met with Frank Coote, who had been on site since mid-August and produced a range of high-quality, fine-grain maps and plans for the region.[69] Coote had an office in the old Hassell homestead and had networked in the area and at state level, gaining guarantees of government assistance in clearing the site, and from local roads boards in building the required subdivisional thoroughfares and bridges.[70]

C. J. writes of a conversation, at the Hassell homestead after four days of forensic examination of Kendenup, between himself, the Beverleys, Rene, Violet and Coote, about the advisability and the practicalities of a new farming settlement. The women are cautiously supportive; the men are talked around when Coote, professing himself to be 'in love with this place', offers to manage the estate while C. J. extracts himself from his Mildura businesses and the ADFA.

C. J. announced he was to purchase and develop Kendenup, with a view to moving to Western Australia within a few years.[71] Although it was typical of C. J. and the press to ascribe activities to him as though he were a lone agent, he raised money for the purchase from a syndicate and sold debentures to small investors. Additionally, he had some wealthy or famous friends to add cash or cachet to the project: Alfred Nicholas, a recent millionaire due to the success of his pain medication, Aspro, bought 954 acres in the area, and although C. J.'s partner in *F. F. F.* Hugh

D. McIntosh was probably not particularly solvent, he committed to 1,000 acres.[72] The directors of the Kendenup company came from diverse parts of the Anglo-Australian world: Nicholas was a recent business marvel; Harold Corbould was, of course, C. J.'s old friend and brother-in-law; and Alfred E. Lloyd was a veteran of the South African War, a Mildura viticulturalist and manager of a range of high-profile businesses.[73]

After seasons in Adelaide and Perth, *F. F. F.* played Melbourne in the second week of October. By this time it was clear that the show, while not a disaster, was not a colossal hit either. Deprived of the chance to play anywhere else on the east coast by scheduling problems, it would lose money, and the money lost would be C. J.'s. Nevertheless audiences, it was reported, continued to respond with 'marked approval and enthusiasm'. *Table Talk* noted kindly that it had not had time on the road being shaped and formed like the international product commonly seen in Australia, and that 'By the time *F. F. F.* has undergone this ordeal it should be brilliant, and quite out-rival the imported article'.[74] 'All through the performance the applause and laughter had been genuine', wrote the critic from the *Age,* who nevertheless found the lyrics (and therefore the songs) mediocre but, like *Table Talk,* felt that *F. F. F.* represented a solid first go.[75] How Rene might have felt during the 'Garden of Girls' number, with Hugh Steyne as a comedy version of her husband, amidst a 'chorus of beauty girls dressed as flowers' is hard to imagine. Perhaps, noting that C. J. had only a few weeks earlier been arguing for his desire to 'build a garden' and remembering that his secretary, also sitting in the author's box at the King's Theatre, was called Violet, she might have felt uneasy.[76] The first Melbourne show was, nonetheless, a triumph: 'Everybody felt like kissing everybody else that night', C. J. later recalled.[77]

C. J. had been promised a Sydney season, too, but *F. F. F.* was 'bumped' from both Sydney and Brisbane schedules. In the final analysis, he reasoned, he had lost something in the region of £2,000, although he made back almost a third of that on sheet music sales (there were also some gramophone recordings made, in Britain, of 'The Murray Moon' and 'Proposing').[78] Atypically for C. J., when looking back later at the show he had invested so much in, he blamed not himself but poor casting decisions.[79] The truth is, every new piece of art or commerce, and this was both, needs some luck, and *F. F. F.* didn't have enough. By happenstance (perhaps the Australian musical was even seen as a threat), other attractive shows featuring popular local and international stars were put up against it. There may also have been a suspicion, amongst prospective audiences, that at least *one* of those 'F's was for 'fruit' – and that the whole show was an extended product placement. In any event, after its Melbourne run concluded, *F. F. F.* ended altogether.

Having emerged from his Mildura cocoon, everything C. J. did in 1920 was too fast. An example of this is that in March, C. J. was so certain of his Mildura future that he had made yet another arrangement to modernise and energise a town which, until very recently, he had thought of as 'his'. Like *F. F. F.*, it emerged from a conversation with the journalists who had been covering the Sunraysia district as guests of the ADFA in May 1920. They had commented on the absence of a daily Mildura newspaper, and C. J., always alert to ideas, decided to act. He assembled a group of backers for a newspaper that would bring three local journals – the *Cultivator*, the *Telegraph and Darling and Lower Murray Advocate*, and the very recently established *Merbein Irrigationist* – into one paper.[80] The first issue of the *Sunraysia Daily* was produced on 2 October and utilised 'the most complete plant for a Daily paper outside the cities'.[81] Its managing editor was Harry J. Stephens, a member of the May press junket, and already a newspaper veteran of more than thirty years' experience. He had edited the Melbourne *War Cry*, the Launceston *Federalist* and the Sydney *Farmer and Settler*, and sometimes wrote under the pseudonym 'Uncle Wiseman'.[82] Stephens was eminent in rural politics (he was one of the formative figures in the creation of the Country Party)[83], as well as an advocate for decentralisation and regional development.[84] He was to be joined by W. F. Partridge, formerly of *The Diggers' Gazette*; A. Gilchrist, once of the *Carnavon Times*; Ken Wallace-Crabbe, formerly cartoonist and journalist for the Melbourne *Bayonet*; Frank Henty, of the Melbourne office of the Sydney *Bulletin*; and Miss L. Bladwell, of *The Farmer and Settler*.[85] This was a more than respectable line-up, and testament once again to C. J.'s charisma and Mildura's reputation that he could attract such people from diverse quarters to resettle in a remote river town. 'The new journal will stand for water conservation', gushed the Launceston *Examiner*, 'irrigation, production, population, decentralisation, repatriation and aviation'.[86] To these broad topics add Australian cinema, literature and theatre, and you would have in sum the obsessions of C. J. DeGaris.

C. J.'s memoir suggests that Mildura, and indeed the whole state of Victoria, was clinging jealously to the man. His Mildura bank manager having, he claims, cast aspersions on him higher up the chain, he finds his Melbourne manager hostile to his Kendenup plans 'We have no branch in Western Australia', he is told, 'and we object to you going there...we feel it our duty to put obstructions in your way, unless you can decide to sell Kendenup at once, and concentrate on Mildura'. To be precise:

> We did not like your theatrical venture. We greatly dislike your interest in aviation, and we certainly do not intend to encourage you to leave Mildura, and emigrate to another State.[87]

Though he did not mention it, the bank manager surely 'greatly disliked' the literary competition too. It distracted from the real world of primary produce, markets, advertising and land sales. Yet it was here that we see the best, most tangible illustration(s) of who C. J. DeGaris really wanted to be.

6

The C. J. DeGaris Publishing House, 1920

> Being ardently and enthusiastically interested in all things AUSTRALIAN, and being confident that this Great Young Country contains the mental genius, and all the material and scope for the production of A LITERARY MASTERPIECE equal to – if not superior to – Any of THE GREATEST NOVELS OF THE OLDER WORLD, I am glad to be able to offer a monetary incentive towards the production of A REALLY GREAT AUSTRALIAN NOVEL.[1]

Australian newspaper readers were confronted by this announcement in a series of grandiose advertisements in December 1919. Many must surely have assumed – it would be logical – that this was going to be another sensational tie-in to fruit-themed guessing games or word puzzles. For all that most Australian newspaper readers knew, the winning 'novel' would be a paragraph in length or feature Good Little Normey as its protagonist.

But C. J. was a modernist of a stamp rarely seen in Australia at that time. His tastes in literature were unapologetically populist – unsurprising in a man who so overtly craved mass acceptance himself – and his yen to further Australian literature was often ensconced in the rhetoric of proving that Australians had intrinsic talent to match that of British or American authors. This was a controversial opinion at the time when, as *F. F. F.* showed, Australian cultural producers were largely considered immature, imitative and inferior.

C. J., his sister Mary and their brother George – like their father Elisha – were extremely familiar with the world of writing and were also used to seeing their names, and words, in print. George published his first book, *Labour or Gold?*, at this time. Generally speaking, the material the DeGarises wrote aimed to inspire social betterment.[2]

The C. J. DeGaris Publishing House – an ostentatious name for a small enterprise without any office or employees – produced ten diverse publications, none of them by a DeGaris but all of them catering to C. J.'s agenda. Harold Hansell's *The Arising of Jimmie Munro* and *The Everlastin' Ballads*, J. Kauffman's *Sunraysia Wonder Book*, Frank A. Russell's *The Ashes of Achievement* and *Facing the Inevitable* by 'G. H. S.' were all published in 1920. The following year saw publication of J. M. Walsh's *The Lost Valley*, Joseph Furphy's *Rigby's Romance*, Ada A. Holman's *Sport of the Gods*, Ethel Jackson Morris' *The White Butterfly and Other Fairy Tales* and Emily Pelloe's *Wildflowers of Western Australia*.

C. J. did not envisage an immediate profit from publishing. Fifty years after the launch of the publishing house Michael Dugan, the only writer to date to have investigated C. J. the publisher, suggested that he represented 'a mass publisher in a country with no mass audience for books'[3], by which he must surely have meant no mass audience for *locally produced* books; the nation was already famous, as it remains today, for its voracious reading appetite.[4] C. J.'s forays into this field are based on a 'boosterist' desire to foster Australian cultural production. This, in C. J.'s view, was as important an arm of national development as economic expansion and another concern of the time, the 'need' for population increase.

Typically, C. J. could not wait for the competition's results to begin on this new enthusiasm. His first two publications were by Ballarat writer Harold Hansell, author of a series of well-received humorous verse volumes including *Dewdrop Danby* and *The Plum-Street Brethren*. Hansell had not published a full-length book for ten years. Neither of his publications via C. J. appears to have been entered in the competition, but then, neither of them was a novel – and the first is a very short short story. *The Arising of Jimmie Munro* had been published twice in 1916 by two different publishers. C. J. claimed he aspired to print a million copies of the twelve-page book 'for free distribution', suggesting that he could not accept 'such a sordid thing as money' for it.[5] He did, however, devote three of its sixteen pages to ADFA advertising, presumably offsetting the cost of production from sources outside C. J.'s own funds but also muddying the waters between C. J. DeGaris the publicist for ADFA, and C. J. DeGaris the literary Australianist.

The front of the booklet features C. J.'s testimonial. He begins by claiming that he had found an earlier edition of *Jimmie Munro* 'on a penny bookstall – but then, we find diamonds in the dust – I am circulating it by the thousands across Australia – and beyond. Read it and see WHY, then pass it on'.[6] The work in question is an extended riff on the notion of Australian patriotism. *Jimmie Munro* begins and ends with a patriotic rural schoolteacher who has decorated his small classroom with signs declaring 'Arise, Australians!' and 'Australians! Love your country'.[7] His career is ruined when a school inspector objects to his sloganeering.[8]

On the death of his wastrel father, Jimmie, aged 12, leaves this same school and finds work in a grocery.[9] Through hard work and dedication, he becomes a travelling salesman and prospers:

> His views grew wide, his mind grew broader and freer. He saw the vast continent with a fringe of human beings on the outer

edge of it, unchecked rivers pouring their priceless waters into the sea, millions and millions of untilled acres of fertile land spread out in the golden sunshine waiting for the hand of man to till them that they might start pouring forth their golden store...This was Australia, this was his country.[10]

Hansell takes time from the story of Jimmie to editorialise:

> We are telling the croakers who say that Australia is the land of the Never Never that they are right, and they'll never, never see anything as good as it again; never, never have the golden chance that lies at the feet of them and theirs to-day.[11]

Hansell and Jimmie also praise the advantages of advertising: 'If you are the best storekeeper in the town, let them know it...'[12], thus preparing the reader for the advertising that comes at the end of the book for ADFA fruit products such as the familiar 'Good Little Normey' ('Crystallised and Chocolated...is a FOOD'[13]), as well as a 'Sunraysed-NORMEY Stunt for CHILDREN!!!' – an essay competition for under-12s ('What I am doing for Australia – MY Country').[14] In essence, the publication is boosterism of a type that many commercial enterprises, governments and ideologues have found valuable as propaganda – just as the ADFA, through C. J., also found patriotic *spending* valuable.

Hansell's other publication through C. J. was entirely new. *The Everlastin' Ballads* is a collection of wartime poems in the guise of diggers' songs. It is not a folk archive. Hansell had, it appears, penned the ballads for performers seeking work that might stir, inspire or cheer diggers; he wrote on whatever came to hand – usually scrap paper, but in one case, a sheet of tin. There is equal parts comedy and reverence in the presentation of the collection; almost a third of the ninety-eight-page volume is introductory, featuring testimonials and explanatories from celebrities including the author and publisher, as well as 'entertainers' and senior military officers.

C. J. presents the *Ballads'* emergence as an outcome of his literary competition, claiming that having launched the competition he was urged by 'all classes of the community' – apparently unaware of what constitutes a novel – 'asking me to publish certain War Ballads in book form'. On reading the 'complete set' of Hansell's ballads, C. J. says:

> I could hardly believe my senses. Was it possible that to me, just starting as a publisher, with doors not yet opened for business, such an unlooked for piece of good fortune had happened as the discovery of this literary prize? I was amazed at my good luck.[15]

He continues in similar vein for seven more pages. The inference is that both this work and *Jimmie Munro* came to C. J. by separate means, and the fact that his first two publications were produced by the same writer is complete coincidence.

Those introducing Hansell's ballads are shown in war artist G. C. Benson's caricatures saluting the reader; C. J. is standing astride his roll-top desk. This is an effective, and suitably comedic touch; as the reader – perhaps a 'digger' too – proceeds through the book, he or she is saluted at every page, as if on parade.

Publication was rushed, as C. J. hoped to go to print in time to give a copy to the Prince of Wales and his aide-de-camp,

C. J. saluting those who served, in his introduction to Harold Hansell's *The Everlastin' Ballads*.

Admiral Halsey.[16] *The Everlastin' Ballads* were a critical success in most quarters: 'Every one of them is delightful, pathos is so interwoven with the humour, that they evoke tears and laughter almost simultaneously,' declared the *Burra Record*.[17] The Adelaide *Critic* believed the book 'should be in every household'[18] and the *Coffs Harbour Advocate,* published the same day – 3 November 1920 – agreed: 'If you ever see a thin, brown book with *The Everlastin' Ballads* on the cover, get it. Never mind how – just get it'.[19] The Sydney *Sun* was more circumspect, irritated by C. J.'s hyperbolic introduction ('It is Mr. Harold Hansell's misfortune that the publisher of his little verses boosts them as he would boost, say, raisins').[20] Yet Hansell found his reputation resoundingly revived. The 'gifted elocutionist'[21] Winifred Moverley incorporated Hansell's 'ballads' into her repertoire and when she presented her 'All-Australian Recital' at Melbourne's Athenaeum in mid-April 1921 she included Hansell's 'Upon the Road to Glory' in her selection of 'serious' material intended to demonstrate the value of Australian literature 'for the purposes of dramatic and humorous narration'.[22] *The Everlastin' Ballads* retained currency for more than a decade, and selections were used as radio entertainment but also in Anzac commemorations.[23] As much as the *Sun* might have scoffed, it's almost certain that C. J.'s extensive support of the book – it appears almost every regional newspaper in Australia received a review copy – played a large part in its fame.

It was the novel competition itself, however, that was to provide the most important of the publishing house content. The rules were straightforward: manuscripts were not to be submitted anonymously. 'Established reputations' would not 'affect the adjudication'. C. J. also opined that the competition 'may, and probably will, develop into the establishment of an Australian Publishing House, particularly designed to encourage all forms of genuine Australian literature'.[24] He asked that would-be competitors advise him of their intentions post haste, so that he could form an idea of the number of manuscripts he could expect.

The competition unleashed 428 'prize-aiming Austrazealand novels', as the *Bookfellow* was to announce early in 1921.[25] Only five titles, including the three winners, are known, although Presbyterian Ladies' College schoolgirl Jean Campbell began a literary career by writing her first novel for the competition, and later published *Brass and Cymbals* in 1933.[26] Grant Hervey claimed to have discussed submitting a novel, 'the story of the founding of Mildura', but refused to participate in the competition, as C. J. implied to him that he would not pay Hervey upfront, but that he would possibly receive 'special consideration' in the contest – the inference being that C. J. was willing to rig the competition. 'I replied, briefly, to the effect that Mr. C. J. DeGaris could go to blazes.'[27] The winning book was a work by a Melbourne journalist with Mildura connections, Frank A. Russell: *The Ashes of Achievement*.[28] Runners-up were J. M. Walsh's *The Lost Valley* (second prize) and Ada A. Holman's *Sport of the Gods* (third). *Bookfellow* magazine neglected to publish the name of the first prize winner or his book, preferring instead to discuss its own contributor, 'Wolla Meranda' (Gertrude Poyitt) whose book *In Mulga Town*, it claimed, was 'picked' by the company, though not awarded a prize.[29]

Some elements of the winning manuscripts appear to have been composed specifically by entrants to appeal to C. J. himself; some of the winners were also personally known to the DeGaris family. Russell's brother, Howard, was a Mildura clergyman.[30] C. J. and Frank Russell may also have been at school together, although Russell claimed in a letter to the *Mildura Cultivator* that they were recent acquaintances.[31]

'Donalbain', writing in the Sydney *Bulletin,* claimed that the novel was too long – exceeding the stated acceptable length of 100,000 words 'by a very wide margin'. 'Donalbain' went on to explain that, as Russell had accepted future royalties rather than the cash prize, C. J. was able to invest that money in publishing a longer book. 'Donalbain' summed *The Ashes of Achievement* up as a 'conventional story, which holds the attention fairly well' but which was 'overweighted with discursive crudities that have little bearing on the tale...the idealism is that of the Methody classroom'.[32] The West Australian *Call*, however, was more damning. The paper's editor Victor Courtney wrote:

> It is the sort of book that lovers of the real Australian [sic] and those who can appreciate the real Australian character will want to forget.
>
> It is neither a good book nor a clever book. It is a literary dud, and I as an Australian decline to believe that it represents the best Australian literary talent can produce.
>
> There must have been some dreadful mistake somewhere?[33]

The Ashes of Achievement begins by introducing a strong contrast between the English class system and Australian egalitarianism, in the pompous and priggish John Pascoe Lee and his actor/dramatist son Philip, whose life the novel purports to tell. Much of the novel explores the relationship between Phillip, his childhood friend Peter Wister, and one Margaret Gillies, who they both love but who Phillip marries.[34] The English–Australian divide aside, another element that must have appealed to C. J. is Lee's immersion in Australian and international theatre. There is a heated discussion between Lee and the theatre owner M. J. Field over a play of Lee's devising. At one point Field cries 'Australians can't write plays, there you have it in a – nutshell'.[35] Lee does, however, become an internationally acclaimed playwright. The book ends in New York, 'a city of Lies and Intrigue'[36] with Phillip, engaged in a farcical contretemps, allowing himself to be shot by a jealous husband to prevent the bullet from killing Margaret.[37]

Compared with the *The Everlastin' Ballads'* mass mail-out of review copies, there seem to have been far fewer reviews solicited for *The Ashes of Achievement*. The *W. A. Record* took exception to (and devoted fifty-four lines of a sixty-two-line review to critiquing) a 'gibe' against Catholicism.[38] But such critical response as there was generally found the work both engaging and significant: the *Sydney Morning Herald's* reviewer, for instance, declared it had 'merits out of the common'.[39] The Launceston *Daily Telegraph's* assessment might have been the most glowing:

> The book is alive and it speaks, extolling the ramifications of our existence with dramatic force, lightly touched pathos, trifling satire, and exquisite humour, and with it Australian literature finds a place at last.[40]

That the title of *The Ashes of Achievement* appealed to C. J. is clear from the name of his own autobiographical fiction five years later, inverting the concept to similar effect. Lee's tenacious pursuit of his own goals in the face of the 'doomsayers', and at the same time his sexual adventuring and vanity, are similarly explored in *The Victories of Failure*.[41] These reasons – along with the patriotic and 'modern' air of the novel – no doubt made *The Ashes of Achievement* irresistible to C. J. It was republished in London, as part of Fisher Unwin's 'First Novel Library', in 1922. As a Tivoli shareholder, C. J. arranged for Russell's play *The Skirts of Opportunity*, 'A Play of Laughter and Pathos of American Social Life', to be performed at Mildura's Shire Hall in October 1920 using Tivoli scenery.[42] 'A successful performance in Mildura will mean a professional production in the cities of Australia', claimed the *Murray Pioneer*, but nothing more was heard of the play, regardless of the Sydney *Mail's* eager reportage that it met with 'exceptional favour'.[43]

Few reviews were forthcoming for the second C. J. DeGaris Publishing House novel, second prize winner *The Lost Valley*. The *Queenslander* preferred it to *The Ashes of Achievement*'s 'tedious...sloppy sentimentality', finding Walsh's work to contain 'plenty of excitement'.[44] Its protagonist is one Jimmy Carstairs, an 'explorer by inclination, gentleman by instinct' who saves the life of a wealthy eccentric named Bryce on a remote beach.[45] Like C. J., Bryce is a fast driver, tempting Providence 'just for the sheer fun of the thing'.[46] The novel is in three parts; a central section dealing with a gold robbery explains much of the intrigue involving Carstairs, Bryce and a former lover of Carstairs', Moira – coincidentally, Bryce's niece.[47] The lost valley in question, a remote location hiding the bushrangers' treasure, is a device common to thousands of yarns.

An article in the Melbourne *Advocate* announcing Walsh's win informs the reader that his father, T. P. Walsh, is a 'Gaelic scholar' and served 'on the council of the Australian Catholic Federation'. Father and son were both in the 'stock and station line'.[48] A Geelong author, Walsh was the only member of the DeGaris 'stable' to go on to maintain a significant career in fiction, publishing over forty (and possibly up to a hundred) books under a variety of names, of which *The Lost Valley* was apparently only the second to appear between hard covers. It is unusual amongst the DeGaris-published novels as it is, essentially, a pure adventure romance, its characters 'doers' rather than 'thinkers'.

Sport of the Gods was another novel with much to appeal to C. J. Its author, Victorian-born Ada Holman, was both the daughter of a journalist and a journalist herself.[49] H. V. Evatt, in his life of Holman's husband, NSW Premier William Holman, describes her as belonging to 'a brilliant Melbourne family'.[50] William, a formative figure in the Australian Labor Party, abandoned it after a debate over conscription and like his associate Billy Hughes became a founder member of the United Australia Party, a forerunner to the Liberal Party. Both are considered turncoats in Labor history.

Ada Holman was 'always interested in the status of women'[51] and indeed had been an ally to Marion Mahony Griffin in her 1915 'battle' with the 'women's section' of the Town Planning Association of NSW.[52] Either through her friendship with Marion and her husband Walter or for other reasons, it seems likely that Ada Holman was known to C. J. Like *The Ashes of Achievement*, there are elements of the novel reflecting C. J.'s own interests. Whether these were included to appeal to the publisher or appear coincidentally as part of a host of contemporary concerns, is impossible to know. Holman's heroine, Cecil Eucalyptus 'Euky' Mapeson, is a woman with literary interests and limited funds. She relocates from her remote hometown of Goolibah, a fictional locale which was the subject of short pieces in the *Australasian* twenty years earlier that were almost certainly also Holman's work.[53] She becomes, firstly, secretary to and then secondly, romantically involved with her local member, Ivo Kimber. He is apparently, rigorously moral and too principled, certainly too complex, to be a successful politician. Kimber, like *The Lost Valley's* Bryce and of course C. J., is a recklessly fast driver; like C. J., he (and most other characters in the book) is a strong advocate of rural interests and the primary producer.[54] Kimber claims early in the work that:

> The backs of the people are bent under their load of debt, and the real mainstay of the State, the people of the bush, men and women like my long-suffering constituents of Goolibah, are crushed to earth by debts incurred for expenditure of which they have received not one penny of benefit.[55]

Indeed, fitting comfortably with the conventional bush ethos of the early twentieth century, Sydney, the town where Kimber plays politics, is to Euky 'remarkably ugly and dirty'[56] and there is suggestion elsewhere in the novel that Australia is in need of 'drastic decentralisation'.[57] Regional citizens 'were taxed that the City might pipe and dance'.[58] This was a line often pushed by the *Sunraysia Daily*, and not completely outside the DeGaris family's interests.

While Kimber's ideas are presented as sound, sadly the man himself is a fraud. Euky discovers Kimber has a wife back in Goolibah and ends her relationship with him.[59] He renounces politics and travels the world.[60] Euky marries a man she loves less than Kimber but who, it seems, is empathic and may prove a stable match.

It is possible that C. J. saw in Kimber a brilliant-yet-flawed figure with whom he could strongly identify. Other elements of the book — questions of class and 'respectability', the aforementioned championing of bush and regional interests above the city, and political intrigue — would also have struck a chord (and a man's romance with his secretary was a concept he understood). Additionally, like *The Ashes of Achievement,* the book fits with C. J.'s modernist idealism. An element of this modernism may also be reflected in what some critics tartly typified as an amorality; for a reviewer in the *Barrier Miner,* for instance, the book exhibited 'certain scenes which, however true to bagnio life they may or not be are quite outside the limit of conversation in the family circle'.[61] It would certainly seem that C. J. himself was unaffected by such 'immorality', which to present-day eyes is so innocent as to be unnoticeable.

Few would disagree that Joseph Furphy's *Rigby's Romance* is an entirely different beast to the populist fiction generally favoured by C. J. Furphy's *Such is Life* is an acknowledged classic. *Rigby's Romance* is a previously unpublished portion of that book, a lesser work but of inestimable value to Australian literature and in many ways as subversive as its parent novel. It was, it appears, submitted in C. J.'s competition by Furphy's literary executor Kate Baker, who — after it failed to receive a placing — then prevailed upon C. J. to publish it regardless. To his credit he did so, in an abridged form that omitted most of the content Furphy had dedicated to the discussion of state socialism.

Rigby's Romance not only features parodies of the conventions of romantic novels — for instance the classic bushranger story — but is, in fact, in structure and tone itself a parody of such works.[62] The reader is drawn in by the promise, early in the novel, of a classic story of love and, perhaps, betrayal. There is also a beautiful woman, in the form of Kate Vanderdecken, who holds a torch for the banished or exiled American, Rigby; many episodic 'romances' told around a campfire later, it transpires that Rigby is only slightly acquainted with the woman in question.

Joseph Furphy's *Rigby's Romance*, published under the pseudonym 'Tom Collins', and the most enduring of the C. J. DeGaris Publishing House novels.

Though he decides, after much prevarication and 'forgetting', that he will seek a further alliance with her, he never gets around to doing so. 'The thin trickle of plot is lost in the wilderness of conversation', wrote one reviewer, and the meandering, apparent formlessness of the work is an aspect of Furphy which anticipates elements of twenty-first century culture and humour.[63] In terms of the type of popular, commercial novel C. J. might have wished to promote, it was far from ideal. A novel more different from *The Lost Valley* could not be imagined. Yet both fit with C. J.'s public identity. He could make a place to enjoy both absurdist long-windedness and rip-roaring adventure.

The last fiction work from the C. J. DeGaris Publishing House was for children. C. J. had already produced, via the Melbourne publisher F. W. Niven and his own ADFA connections, the *Sun-Raysed Children's Fairy Story Book*.[64] It is unsurprising that he would aspire to publish further in this vein.

Ethel Jackson Morris was a Melbourne artist who exhibited with the Fine Art Society. She had produced another book, *All Among the Fairies,* in the previous decade; C. J. published her *The White Butterfly,* a 107-page large-format volume of stories, in 1921. Jackson's black and white illustrations have an arts-and-crafts feel (particularly the woodcut-style dropped capitals beginning each story); a number of her watercolours are also included as plates, and the book itself is as lush a production as an Australian children's author could have expected at this time. It would appear that Morris had been working on the book for some time; some of the plates are dated as far back as 1918. It was published at what must have been a particularly difficult period in her life. Her father, a merchant, had been thrown from a buggy and died in January 1920, and while driving the following year – this book substantially completed – she hit and killed a 6-year-old child.[65]

The book is filled with thinly veiled adult concerns, the most extreme example being a kidnap scene with overtones of rape fantasy involving a nymph perched daintily atop a large mushroom:

her skirt of rainbow-coloured gossamer outspread, and her little bare toes just touching the ground.

It was not long before Dwarf Trouble appeared, and when he saw the little wood-nymph, he became so excited that he... rushed forward...and seized the poor little thing, bound her hands behind her back, fastened a heavy chain about her waist, and laughing gleefully, led her away.[66]

Other stories mimic the temptation in the Garden of Eden (one 'Prince Fortunio' is attracted by a 'large orange tree'[67] and the Prince's reward for resisting is the opportunity to rescue a 12-year-old girl who has been turned into a golden duck as a punishment for indolence). Possibly the most disturbing of the stories is the tale of a lonely Chinese girl called 'Blue Eye' in the story of same name[68] who throws herself into the sea at the behest of a beautiful bystander and lives underwater to rule 'over our little water babies'.[69]

Australia is mentioned only once, as the location where stories such as these are definitely *not* taking place.[70] In this respect – and in the context, for instance, of *Jimmie Munro* – it is surprising. C. J. (who, admittedly, barely had a childhood) grew up in the outback; he was keen to encourage families to settle outside the cities. He would surely have seen the value in inviting young children to explore picture-books based on Australian themes. The title, too, is an unusual one from a publisher with an agricultural background – the white butterfly *(Pieris rapae)* was a costly and problematic pest.

Another novel was, apparently, in the planning stages but did not appear. This was a reprint of the revised *Mordecai MacCobber* by Abraham Samuel Gordon. Gordon had originally published his novel – 'the story of a Scotch Jew in Australia' – in 1921 and had since expanded it. In 1926, he told the *Riverina Recorder* that 'for some time' it 'was to have been issued and "boosted" by the C. J. DeGaris Publishing House, but the fates willed otherwise'.[71]

The 'Scotch Jew' concept was a common trope of the 1920s – the notion being that this combined the two most miserly races in the world – although in the case of Gordon's protagonist the only Scottish thing about this Russian Jewish émigré is his name.

The diversity of the publishing house works is extraordinary. It is difficult to know how to describe George Henry Shoebridge's *Facing the Inevitable* within any kind of genre aside from 'maudlin'. Published with the author's name anonymised to 'G. H. S.', it is a booklet of twenty-eight pages, seven devoted to an introduction by W. Farmer Whyte, editor of the Brisbane *Daily Mail*. Whyte explains that the author was a stockbroker who had died of cancer at the age of 44.[72] C. J. adds in a note that to his mind 'the booklet is worthy of universal acceptance and study' and both C. J. and Whyte note that the author's survivors were to benefit from royalties.[73] In fact, the work is a short musing on its author's impending death, and curiously, given that it is merely his own reaction to circumstances, Shoebridge gives away little of his own feelings on the matter, beyond being resigned to it as 'inevitable' – the title says it all. One reviewer in 1922 found it 'very poignant', another a 'touching human document'.[74] Perhaps the most interesting element to a contemporary reader is G. H. S.'s revelation that he saw Australian literature on the rise:

> Encouraged by the recent boom in Australian authors, I had even planned to write a novel, the plot of which I had developed with some completeness and which I had hoped to finish within the year. I simply could not persevere with it now...[75]

The main appeal of this text for C. J. – aside from, perhaps, an obligation of some sort to the Brisbane *Daily Mail* for serialising his three prize-winning novels – was the way it related to his own obsessions. *Facing the Inevitable* is, no doubt, evidence of this aspect of C. J.'s character allied to conventional notions of honour amongst civilised gentlemen, particularly when it came to providing for wives, children and other dependents.

Two books from the publishing house are non-fiction and very different in scope. Kauffman's photographic essay explores 'seventeen pearls' of the Sunraysia region, including Pyap.[76] The book's uncredited introduction was probably written by C. J.; it mentions the efforts of his father to promote irrigation in the 1890s.[77] Here C. J. (if he is indeed the writer) casts the real world of enterprise and business venture as suitable material for entertainment:

> The first ten years of their [the Chaffeys'] vicarious existence contain all the material of comedy, tragedy and melodrama – of mis-conception, mis-construction, mis-representation of motive and belittling of achievement – to construct one of the most human and yet startling novels, plays and picture films the world has seen.
>
> Some day the dramatist will arise to do the subject full justice.[78]

He also indulges in extensive discussion of a pet topic – not unlike Hansell's in *Jimmie Munro* – of the possibilities of wealth production in Australia and the limitations placed upon them by pessimistic 'doomsayers'. 'One hundred years from now', he writes, 'Australia will look back on the year 1920 with tolerant amusement, tempered with amazement' over what was *not* done.[79]

John Kauffman's photographs are lovingly presented, showing the Sunraysia region as a lush, idyllic netherworld, far more pre-industrial than the reality. There are some explanations of the fruit-drying process, as well as some explorations of, for instance, the value of Sunraysia operations to closer settlement and soldier-settlement schemes. In essence the book is an expensive piece of propaganda.

The bowdlerised *Rigby's Romance* notwithstanding, only one C. J. DeGaris Publishing House product has gone on to be recognised as a bona fide classic, reprinted in subsequent decades. This is *Wildflowers of Western Australia,* arguably not only a remarkable work in its own right but also the foundation of a genre and a national pastime. Emily Pelloe had lived in Mildura – her husband Theodore was a bank manager – and knew the DeGaris family there.[80] Emily and C. J. had even performed in a concert, *Queen of Sport*; they performed a skit called 'Thrown Together'. Theodore sang 'comic items' at the same event.[81] Both C. J. and Emily were endurance travellers – though his preferred means was motorised, whereas hers was horseback.

That she came to have a book published by C. J. was a confluence of circumstances: her book appeared under his imprint very soon after he had purchased the Kendenup estate. Visiting Kendenup, she had been taken to see wildflowers by the estate manager Fred Coote; she had also written and illustrated articles for the Perth *Sunday Times* under the heading 'Mountaineering in W. A.', describing a journey from C. J.'s Capecup estate through the Stirling Ranges.[82]

As with many other paternalistic entrepreneurs, C. J. assumed that his enthusiasms should be everyone's. His 'discovery' of Western Australia and its natural beauty (and bounty) was therefore the perfect subject for a book, even better a book under someone else's name. He must surely have been aware that promotion and increased awareness of WA's flora would serve multiple purposes, some of them to his direct advantage. It would aid in conquering perception of the west as arid; it would assist in building wider interest in the south-west of the state; and it would increase public knowledge to the good. C. J. was also of the opinion that those in WA undervalued their own state.[83] It is notable, however, that nowhere in Pelloe's book is there mention of Kendenup. A map showing southern WA does not feature it even as a reference point, and the book is divided into seasons and months, rather than into regions.[84] While its text uses the author's own experience, as well as Aboriginal legend ('The Legend of the Origin of the River now called the Margaret') and the work of Browning[85] in its discussion of landscape and flora, it is primarily an illustrated survey of its subject, apparently the first of its kind for the region and the nation. It was to go through over twenty editions.

C. J.'s name appears once, on the title page. This is important: while there must surely have been some self-promotional impulse in the entrepreneur's decision to publish, it was subtle in this instance. In this, the elegant production of the *Wildflowers of Western Australia* is a graceful contrast to (for instance) *Jimmie Munro* or even *The Sunraysia Wonder Book*.

It appears that C. J. spent £3,000 in publishing: for the same money he could have bought the equivalent of six shops in Hay Street West, in Perth, or a 'fashionable villa' in suburban Melbourne.[86] He did not see it as money squandered, however. In one of his suicide notes from early 1925 he claimed some credit for the progress of Australian literature which, he believed, 'has developed to the extent that the prize-winners of my contest have since become serial writers, and have successfully published in England and America'.[87]

The publishing house activities would be a side interest to C. J. in the early 1920s, as he became increasingly consumed by his involvement in Kendenup. Indeed, it is testament to the man that he was able to continue the project he started to such a professional and enterprising degree, given the worries and challenges that were to face him in Western Australia.

7

My town Kendenup, where everybody smiles

> There is a little germ called "Kendenupitis" that one breathes in with the air, and the visitor soon becomes infected.[1]

Less than a year after C. J. signed the contracts, Kendenup was well under way. The first store, D. E. Duff's, was built and functioning in June 1921. A brick building with a tiled roof, it was described as looking 'well against the green of the gum trees'.[2] Ridge Brothers' hardware store and plumbing business[3] opened soon afterwards and E. J. Smith built a shop to operate a newsagency and 'fancy goods store' incorporating dwelling-rooms. It was announced that a chemist would soon move to town from Boggabri in northern New South Wales.[4] Eight bungalow residences were to be erected on the street facing the station, and a large number of buildings were to be transported from Kalgoorlie or Boulder and re-erected.[5] But it was the potential for growth and productivity that really mattered; an anonymous 'American lady' wrote on visiting Kendenup:

> To the eye of faith...and that means to every Kendenupite, young people in white flannels are already playing on the velvet turf of the tennis courts, while across the way, the Administration Building rears its handsome façade above the trees of Central Park...somehow I began to see visions of the future likewise, and the present bush faded away like a shadow.[6]

Her florid and future-focused outlook shows the persuasive power of both C. J. and the people who followed him. If anything testifies to C. J.'s abilities to infect even the most conservative with his boundless enthusiasm, it is the excitement and delight that attended this scheme.

Daniel Edmunds bought the Kendenup Estate on 11 August 1920 for £37,000, with £500 paid by way of deposit. Less than two months later, on 29 September 1920 – the day before the closing date of his novel competition – Clement John DeGaris agreed to purchase Edmunds' interest in the land for £10,000. This was a £9,500 profit for Edmunds; after paying him, C. J. would then pay £36,500 for the land. Most of the money came from the Kendenup Development Company, although £4,880 was C. J.'s own.[7]

He met with government officials in December 1920 at the Palace Hotel in St Georges Terrace, Perth. Here he explained his hopes for Kendenup, listing 'practical ideals' such as maximising the potential of the land and the railways that served it; as well as attracting settlers of 'ability, energy and determination'. He would provide a happy atmosphere and the right facilities to assist in the preservation and packing of produce; establish a market; make a good product; 'encourage the community spirit of mutual helpfulness'; provide further expertise; and 'have a slumless town and a slumless settlement'.[8]

Western Australia's railway department responded earliest to the Kendenup challenge, remodelling the siding at the site. While this indicated a progressive railway authority, it also made good business sense – the Kendenup *Index* reported that Kendenup had raised rail revenue to the tune of £3345 in fares and £1,600 in freight in only five months.⁹

In early January 1921, C. J., Rene and their daughters moved to St Kilda; but C. J.'s mind was as far away from the old suburbs of Melbourne as one could be, while still in Australia.¹⁰ An advertisement in the Melbourne *Age* from that month declared:

> Last month C. J. DeGaris started his 'Kendenup' Community Scheme. Since then rapid strides have been made. Settlers are on the land and, as previously advertised, great progress has been made. Although £80,000 was the estimated land sales for the first year, in the first few weeks £57,463 worth of land… has been sold. Debentures are going off so freely that the closing date of the list is now announced as January 31, 1921.¹¹

Frank Coote was credited with designing the Kendenup township and lots, although the actual surveying work was done by E. H. B. Macartney, who also came to own two blocks of farmland.¹² The ambition was to create 1,042 farm areas and factory sites, and around 964 township blocks, although it would be possible to buy contiguous blocks, and consolidate them. The projected population was 10,000 and the optimism was rife. That said, Coote's jovial references to Mount Barker, 18 km away, as Kendenup's future suburb¹³ or 70 km distant Albany as 'the port of Kendenup'¹⁴ would have been recognisable to most Australians of the 1920s as no more than jovial boosterism. Australians had only recently emerged from a war in which simple sloganeering had guided and even enlightened their days; C. J.'s ADFA campaigns had capitalised on their readiness to see the simplest truths as perfect. Thus, the journalist and, now, Kendenup publicist J. J. Simons' announcement that 'Kendenup is slump-proof' was recognisable as 'good' propaganda. He went on to explain that slumps were impossible when one's enterprise has a 'basis representing the most permanent thing in human history – Agriculture'.¹⁵

C. J. had been the editor, and largely the writer, of *Sarnia Topics* in Mildura. This twelve-page journal, produced monthly, had been – like Elisha's notebooks – a curious blend of commercial information on the company's growing and packing activities, along with more inspirational material, notably pages of brief notes from Elisha's correspondence with Australian soldiers serving in Europe. C. J. established the Kendenup *Index*, edited by Simons, to operate in much the same way in peace time.[16] Not only did it tell the Kendenup community about its own activities, and reinforce to Kendenupites that they were a part of something bold, it also advertised Kendenup to the rest of the world. Distributed through the eastern states and elsewhere in Australia, the *Index* showed an idealised version of Kendenup and its remarkable progress. It made this credible – just as *Sarnia Topics* had – by occasionally reporting on negative criticism of DeGaris projects. It was also always quick to report in full on other papers' journalistic forays into Kendenup. Certainly the settlement had numerous visitors in its brief heyday, including politicians, reporters and bureaucrats as well as occasional anonymous reports from, for instance, the 'American lady':

> Strictly speaking, [Kendenup] consists of six or eight brick buildings with tiled roofs, and a large number of signboards which announce the sites of future buildings. One drives along an "Avenue", or "Street" and sees such signs as "Tennis Courts", "Central Park", "Municipal Buildings", all on posts in the bush, for Kendenup will not be a straggly country town that "just grew" like Topsy, but a municipality along the most modern lines of town planning.[17]

The 'American lady' (who may in any case have been a fabrication) was clearly not Marion Mahony Griffin. The anonymous 'lady' had no idea what constituted 'modern lines of town planning'; the town's design was as old-fashioned and pragmatic as any nineteenth-century colonial outpost. The site

The Kendenup *Index*, a loose copy in J. J. Simons papers, State Library of Western Australia.

sloped gently towards the north-west. A grid of six north–south 'avenues' and nine east–west streets was laid out 3 km from the Albany Highway, with the easternmost thoroughfare alongside the railway line. Hassell Ave, as it was to be known, would only have buildings on one side but they would be the shops and fine houses of a prosperous settlement, and include C. J., Rene, Winnie, Vera and Dulcie DeGaris' own home. C. J. was expected to settle permanently at Kendenup in September 1921, a year after the original contract to buy was signed. Here, Simons wrote in the Kendenup *Index*, 'he will be in close personal touch with the dream of his life – the growth of a new community, the centre of which will be an ideal town'.[18]

The avenues 'behind' Hassell, going west, would be numbered in an 'American' style like Mildura's, allowing for easy orientation. The other streets would be named for founders – DeGaris, of course, and Beverley, Coote, Simons and Austin – and inspirations, such as Mildura. The northernmost street, Pennifold, was named for C. J.'s Melbourne manager Frank Pennifold, who had begun working for E. DeGaris and Co. in 1920[19] and later became secretary of the Kendenup Development Company. It seems unlikely he ever visited Kendenup.[20] The grid, and its street naming, was egalitarian; perhaps C. J. should have insisted on honouring the state premier, James Mitchell, with a tree-lined avenue, in anticipation of favour. Even had he been inclined to do so – and Simons' Labor allegiances would have bristled – the volatility of state politics at this time meant that it was difficult to be certain how long a premier would stay in power. A street was named for John Monash, a politically neutral war hero. Elsewhere, C. J. railed off the grave of an Aboriginal man – regarded locally as the last of his tribe and recorded as King Qualbert – to protect it for posterity[21] and acknowledge an ancient human history for the region.

At the centre of the town site a 2 acre (0.8 hectare) area was to be dedicated to administrative buildings, and a much larger area – a central reserve – would include municipal offices, a theatre and churches, alongside parks, bowling greens, tennis courts and croquet lawns. To its east would be a new hostel designed to mimic an old English village inn. A hospital, police station and schools were also given sites. Factories were to be located in the south-east. Lawns would face the railway station, and four 5 acre (2 hectare) playgrounds would be found throughout the town. Native trees would be retained in park and playground spaces.

Homes on farm sites might be wood (often, Simons noted they were not mere wood, but jarrah), but the town itself was to be built of brick. This was an important ruling, and one sending messages about the permanence and value of the place. There would be no fly-by-nighters coming. New arrivals would need adequate resources to make a decent start. Kendenup would be respectable and durable. The shop sites, facing the station, were to be of a regular standard size, with 33 ft (10 m) frontages. There was to be a (DeGaris owned and operated) brickworks on the town site and new tile technology, too.

With the brick ruling in mind, C. J. entered into a contractual arrangement with some important new friends, Walter Burley and Marion Mahoney Griffin, to supply Kendenup with a Knitlock machine. This device allowed the manufacture of up to 400 large slab tiles a day on site using local materials: it was both practical and symbolic.[22] The Griffins had created a process by which tiles could be interlinked to create strong walls. The machine was small, portable and hand-operated, and while its success was dependent on the quality of the materials used, the output was generally judged a success. The first Knitlock construction was the roof of a branch outlet of the store owned by Alfred E. Lloyd, built opposite the dehydrator.[23] Simons, who commissioned Griffin to design a headquarters for the Young Australia League in Perth[24], wrote:

> It is expected the machine will be operating by the end of the month, and that the company will be in a position to accept orders for tiles for delivery during July. The tiles are of cement colour and blend splendidly with brick buildings. While it is

expected that the predominant roof colour will be terra cotta throughout the town, the grey Griffin tiles present a pleasing contrast.[25]

The use of this machine was practical – it was small, transportable, but productive. It was also symbolic – new technology for a new phase in Australia's history. It is possible, but perhaps unlikely, that C. J. saw the possibility of a greater Griffin presence in Kendenup. It was announced that Walter would be visiting.[26] In 1921, publicity also suggested that a 'leading Melbourne architect is preparing plans for 250 houses' in the town.[27] It is not apparent who this architect was. The Griffins – who led the field in Australia in small house design – were surely the only architects known personally by C. J. who had experience in such design, through their work at and around Canberra on (unrealised) designs for mass housing. Only a month prior to this announcement, the Albany *Advertiser* claimed that C. J. had promised Walter Griffin was to visit Western Australia: 'The primary object of Mr. Griffen's [sic] visit is to consult with Mr. Frank J. Coote, the administrator of the Kendenup country, regarding the architectural matters in connection with the development scheme'.[28] This is just one of a hundred intriguing but unresolved details of the Kendenup story; how well C. J. knew the Griffins, and how they came to know each other (it might have been through Ada Holman, who had long been a friend of Marion's; it may also have been through J. J. Simons)[29] is a mystery. Certainly C. J. and the Griffins were in the same room together – Labor politician King O'Malley's Melbourne office – on 21 November 1921, but the connection had been made long before.[30]

The Kendenup system

The postwar world was to be faster, more logical, and led by science. On 2 December 1920, C. J., Briggs and mechanic Sergeant Howard flew from Melbourne to Perth in 18½ hours, landing at the Belmont Racecourse to be greeted by Minister for Mines, Jack Scadden. Emily Pelloe's horse, Snowdrift, escaped from its tethers while the Pelloes were waiting to greet their friend; it was half an hour, and just before the plane was sighted, before Snowdrift was caught.[31] In January 1921 C. J. broke a new record by participating in a 'triple interstate journey' in one day. He, Briggs and a mechanic, Sergeant Bond, flew from Brisbane to Sydney and thence Melbourne, carrying letters and newspapers as proof of the way business could be transacted by aeroplane over an unprecedentedly short time.[32] In April 1921 C. J. announced that 'with great reluctance' he was giving up flying for three years at the request of Kendenup investors: 'my only reason for the step I am taking is to satisfy those who feel their money is in my hands and is safe as long as I keep out of a flying machine'. He felt, however, 'the wrench of abandoning the upstairs highway'.[33]

There was an extraordinary amount of press created for, by and about Kendenup. Much of it was preserved in scrapbooks by J. J. Simons as Kendenup's publicist. A large amount of it was print advertising, bought and paid for by the Kendenup Development Company to entice settler-buyers to the place. The film *Western Australia: Land of Opportunity* was also a popular attraction.[34] His experience of the successful Sunraysia film still fresh, C. J. commissioned an advertising film to show Kendenup to the world. Envisioned by J. J. Simons, it came from the Perth studio of Fred Murphy. In a novel piece of self-referential cinema, the film begins with a letter from C. J. asking Murphy to visit the township, and Murphy's camera crew assembling in Perth. They travel in comfort by train to Kendenup, where land is being cleared and families are arriving. The Albany highway is carrying new automobiles, and brick buildings are under construction. The film injects an element of comedy in a stereotypical 'upper class' tourist, boasting a monocle, jodhpurs and a riding crop, stumbling through the landscape. C. J. appears – initially from the cockpit of an aeroplane – and then, finally, shaking hands with Kendenup men. It ends with the comedy fop tripping and falling down the steps of the Hassell homestead to boisterous laughter from all assembled. The messages, though multiple, were clear: this was a place for men and women of substance and grit, but also a hearty, healthy and inclusive place for anyone willing to be part of a community, as long as they were able to abandon any decadent ways. While the fop is almost certainly *not* Hugh Steyne in his Fitzwilliam Ferguson 'dude' guise – F. F. F. had left town long before C. J. formally purchased Kendenup – Simons must have been inspired by the contrast between the effete fool of broad comedy and the 'real' Australian man to suggest someone play the part.

C. J., clearly, generated a large amount of publicity purely by being C. J., flying around Australia and operating his literary competition and publishing house. He had become a celebrity in a short space of time, and while he personally often talked about detractors – politicians in particular – who unfairly denigrated both himself and his enterprise, it could be said that the best publicity these antagonists received was C. J.'s discussion of them: there was little criticism in the mainstream press. Exceptions

Leaving Perth for Sydney, from *The Victories of Failure*.

include an individual, styling his or herself 'A practical farmer', who wrote to the *West Australian:*

> Why can't the truth be told about Kendenup? It is not suitable for closer settlement, and because a rich man with a flying machine bought it, that doesn't make it suitable. It's the long, dreary, wet, cold winter that dooms it, only two months of spring and three months of summer…Kendenup and Mt Barker are cursed with a very intricate and unnatural drainage. The clay is 3in. from the surface at one point and 3ft down 12 yards away. When Mr. DeGaris bought Kendenup…he did the worst possible thing for Western Australia…[35]

The Kendenup *Index*, as lively and positive a journal as it was, often depicted Kendenup as under siege from detractors. Simons wrote, for instance:

> To those anxious mortals with both hands deeply protecting their money pockets who wish us success but who forecast failure I would urge a larger sense of Australianism, so that the Kendenups of the future will receive more general and helpful assistance than "wishes handicapped by fears".[36]

C. J.'s greatest profit from Kendenup was never intended to be financial. He had grown up with Mildura, successfully rescued Pyap, and was now hoping to go his own way and start from scratch. He was committed to populating Australia with a network of farming communities via closer settlement, for returned soldiers, migrants, and of course urban Australians seeking a new life.

A secondary benefit would be through the Kendenup Development Company, based in Melbourne. It had authorised capital of £200,000, and C. J. was its managing director. Its primary purpose was to sell Kendenup land, of course, though it also operated a brickworks, the Hassell homestead known as the

Old Aussie Admiring His New Beauty Spot

'Old Aussie admiring his new beauty spot', *Sunraysia Daily*, 9 September 1921, in J. J. Simons' scrapbook.

'hostel', and some other low-key, moneymaking ventures, all in Kendenup, and although these were only slightly profitable, they were not loss-making.

The Kendenup Development Company had a symbiotic relationship at Kendenup with the Packing Company. C. J. was once again managing director and also the majority shareholder – in 1922, he held 1,501 out of the 1,507 shares issued. In general, the Packing Company was responsible for purchasing, dehydrating and distributing produce from Kendenup to the rest of Australia and international markets. Beans, peas, potatoes and tomatoes – marketable root crops – were the stock in trade of Kendenup; while fruit would be as easily grown in the region, perhaps there was a wish to be distinct from the famously successful apple district of nearby Mt Barker, both for the purposes of brand recognition and not hurting one's neighbour's business. The goods were paid for in cash by the company, and were dehydrated and stored in its warehouse before being transported by rail to Albany, then shipped to and distributed from Melbourne. Here the firm of DeGaris (Kendenup) was registered, and it was where the company had its distribution contracts. Kendenup had thousands of supporters. They were well-wishers, heralds of its potential, investors, and consumers of its produce.

Settlers, current and future

The masthead of the Kendenup *Index* featured an illustration of the overflowing 'horn of plenty'. Simons made it his business to catalogue the comings and goings of as many new arrivals as possible, introducing them to the wider world and each other through the pages of the Kendenup *Index*.

It is through the *Index* that we meet 26-year-old Fred Allen, originally from Perth, who had moved to Kendenup with his family (he was father to four children) to manage the hostel.[37] Allen was soon assistant secretary of the Settlers' Association[38] and a member of the Kendenup Kostume Koncert Komedy Kompany.[39] W. H. Barnett and his son were from Sunshine, west of Melbourne[40]; the Barrows were from Cardiff[41]; H. J. Bessant and his wife were migrants from London's Covent Garden who'd arrived in Australia via the *Zealandie* and were ensconced at Kendenup within six months.[42] Cecil Button, the assistant manager for the Kendenup Development Company, had been an orchard supervisor in Kyabram and East Burwood, Melbourne; he'd taken on the Omrah and Wicklow estates some years earlier and Omrah had become prominent in the Mt Barker apple industry. Button was often the new settlers' first contact with Kendenup, as he would help them choose their lots.[43] E. Caldwell and his wife had come from Footscray[44]; R. G. Cameron and his son Harcourt were from Mildura[45]; T. H. Cooper and his wife had come from Shepparton and his daughter was the first child born at the town[46] (she was given the first name 'Kendenup').[47] T. De Pledge had come from Victoria with his wife, daughter and 'three hefty sons'.[48] F. H. Hull and family came from Milthorpe, New South Wales, and purchased not only a farm block but a lot in town where he built a brick bakehouse, with an oven partly underground and a flour room above.[49] R. W. Peggs was an ex-soldier from Broomehill[50]; Ern Phillips brought his horses and cart from Subiaco[51]; the Robinson family had come from England[52]; Fred and Gertrude Rowe had come from the goldfields[53]; and the Sandilands family from Boulder, including their five children, occupied a five-roomed house at the settlement.[54] Bill White, his wife and their four children had moved from Victoria Park in Perth; he had previously been a building contractor.[55] The Rev. Humphrey Wightwick was possibly the most unusual Kendenup settler. He had been the headmaster of Princetown College, Calcutta, and had published a book entitled *God, My Neighbour and Myself* in 1902.[56]

In August 1921 C. J., Rene and Winnie travelled to Ceylon via the *Osterley* for a holiday. A holiday was necessary for C. J., according to his doctor who believed him to be on the verge of a nervous breakdown. C. J. was, of course, unable to do anything that was not work-related, and part of the Ceylon trip was about locating potential new settlers for Kendenup. As he passed through Perth to visit Kendenup en route to his trip, *The Call* discussed his 'great dream of attracting Anglo-Indians to the West'. By 'Anglo-Indian' no-one seems to have meant anything other than ethnically 'English': 'The average Anglo-Indian comes from England', explained the newspaper, 'and his sojourn in the tropics has made him constitutionally unfit for the colder climes of Europe'.[57]

The degree of ignorance amongst non-Australians about the nation he loved shocked C. J. Amongst other things, most of the men he met in Ceylon believed Australia to be 'three-quarters black'. 'It is not their fault, it is ours', he said, advocating for a 'little magazine containing up-to-date news about Australia' to be available to ocean vessels.[58] The notions of the Anglo-Indian settlers and of broader awareness of Australia were interconnected:

Kendenup specifically, and Australia generally, needed migration, and potential migrants needed to be informed.

Another point of information was how cut off a regional town in Western Australia might be from the rest of civilisation. Those who did accept the Kendenup challenge were undertaking what was surely one of the biggest risks they could have imagined, not only relocating to but investing in an entirely new place. Few of them were unused to hard work, but many were surely newcomers to agriculture. They were undoubtedly a motley community. Yet in the initial burst of Kendenup's development, a 'colonist' protested enthusiastically that:

> We are alive, we are progressive, and we are happy and intensely satisfied with the enjoyment we can make for ourselves. We live a useful, healthy existence here, in the very heart of Nature's rarest treasures, yet we are not isolated, not cut off from civilisation.[59]

Building a modern community

The economic centre of the town was the dehydrator, where all food grown on the blocks was to be processed for distribution. It is perhaps logical that the dehydrator building was also established in the first months of Kendenup as its social centre; its concrete surface also made it a very satisfactory dance floor. The old Hassell family homestead, though not in the main town itself, was also a social centre, as was the newly erected boarding house.

C. J. was future-proofing Kendenup by use of modern technology. Drying produce would allow it to be stored indefinitely, rather than letting a particular fruit or vegetable rot while consumers either had so much of it they could command a very low price or ignore it altogether. Mount Barker growers brought their apples to a 'trial run' of Kendenup's Morton Efficiency Dehydrator. Simons wrote:

> The dehydrator represents to the Kendenup vegetable-grower and orchardist a standing monument, reminding him that so long as he plants the right varieties he is secure against a glut, and that he has a market within a very short distance of his producing area. In other words, the dehydrator makes gluts impossible. After all, the great spectre of the producer, more especially the fruit-grower, is the glutted market...the dehydrator is the slayer of gluts.[60]

It was suggested that dehydrated fruit and vegetables were in a state of suspension once all moisture was removed; that texture, flavour and colour would all remain preserved. Immersion in water would see the tomato, potato or pea (for instance) rehydrate through its fibres and return to, for all intents and purposes, the fresh product it had been. At a time before home refrigeration, when food kept in a domestic larder was threatened by pests and ageing, anything that could be suspended as edible until cooked and eaten was an advance.

The Kendenup Dehydrator was to the specifications of a Mr J. Morton who, it was stated, 'came to Australia in December and immediately placed his invention before Mr. DeGaris, who commissioned him to construct the first modern dehydrator to operate in Australia, thus putting Kendenup right ahead of any other producing settlement in the Commonwealth'. Morton agreed to construct the building before the end of the apple season:

> There were many who reckoned he had attempted the impossible, yet from the day the first brick was laid down up to the hour when the works were under steam and apples were being actually treated, only 57 days had elapsed...nearly 100,000 bricks were used in the construction.[61]

Constructed with a tubular frame, its interior had no posts or girders. The building was 30 m by 15 m, and its floor 22 m by

7.6 m, making it additionally ideal as a hall for public events 'larger than many country halls in Western Australia'.[62]

'What impressed me the most', one visitor said at the very beginnings of Kendenup, 'was the rapidity with which the community spirit has grown'. Citing the Progress Association, the sports club, and Kendenup's first football match, she or he described a night at the dehydrator when over 200 people 'were enjoying the social pleasures of a dance evening…A perfectly toned piano has been installed, and electric light makes the scene one of brightness and colour'.[63]

There was, it is clear, no shortage of entertainment, and indeed the company made community its business. Most of the citizens appeared to have relocated from cities and towns and had modern expectations of social leisure. As was so often the case in early twentieth century western societies, individuals were entertainers as well as audiences: they would take turns contributing pieces to an evening of amusements involving singing, playing a musical instrument, or recitation. Pieces might be original compositions, learned works or a combination of the two; for instance, a parody based on a familiar favourite.

The Kendenup Development Company provided a library and a billiard room for settlers. C. J. gave Violet the job of creating the Kendenup Kostume Koncert Komedy Kompany.[64] The KKKKK performed at numerous social events in Kendenup itself and in the wider district – as far as Albany. It was primarily populated by the young women of the district, either the daughters of the more leisured settlers or members of the administration, such as Violet and her sister, Marjorie. The performance officially welcoming C. J., Rene and their daughters to Kendenup, while including the KKKKK, was presumably typical of the time: the DeGarises themselves featured prominently as performers in amongst the other settlers. Here, C. J. caused what was described as 'genuine merriment' with a parodic piece he had prepared. It was entitled 'In Nineteen-Hundred and Ninety-Nine' and was probably an adaptation of a popular poem from the period, perhaps the same piece which C. J. delivered at the Mildura–Ouyen concert in 1917 where he shared the bill with Violet. This time, it contained observations on various Kendenupites – some of whom he was meeting for the first time but who he had researched. At another concert Grace Geddes sang C. J.'s song from the *F. F. F.* musical, 'The Murray Moon', while the DeGaris daughters sang 'I'd love to live in Loveland'. Rene performed a ukulele solo. Another song by C. J. and Stoneham, 'Garden of Girls', saw him at the centre of young women from the area, each playing a different flower. Violet, notably, did not play her floral namesake or any other fixture in this set piece, dampening any notion that she was part of C. J.'s 'garden'. C. J. told stories of 'Men I Knew'. Other pieces were performed by Violet, Frank Coote and his son Ronald, a noted pianist.[65] Simons' Young Australia League (YAL) also connected to Kendenup, and its general secretary E. R. Marle visited accompanied by an instrumental quartet derived from the YAL band, playing for a dance social in the dehydrator.[66]

In mid-1921 a ground was cleared to make a football field, and new Kendenupites came to watch the region's first football match. 'Here was witnessed the crowd, the play, the barrackers', Simons wrote, 'all features of an athletic gathering usually found online in old settled localities'. Dancing followed that evening; the next day, the Rev S. B. Fellows visited to preach and to provide 'a fine word story of missionary experience in the Solomon Islands, where he was stationed for a considerable period'.[67]

The first year at Kendenup
There is no record of C. J. ever expressing regret at his decision to take on the Kendenup project; he only rarely suggested that he made particular mistakes there, aside from broad self-flagellation over his own vanity. Mistakes came from others' shortsightedness, self-interestedness, faithlessness or malice.

The director's first report to shareholders, for 1921, reports 'most successful results'. C. J. goes on:

Upon the launching of the Company, the main criticisms resolved themselves into-
1. "They will never sell the land."
2. "They cannot get £10 per acre."
3. "They will never attract the settlers."
4. "If they do attract settlers, they will never satisfy them."
5. "The soil will not produce. It is only good for sheep."

Whereas the position to-day is-

1. The quantity of land sold was twice the quantity your directors estimated for the period.
2. The average price realized exceeded £14 per acre.
3. At the end of the first year there were 166 settlers on Kendenup – a population of 581 as against seven a year before.
4. One hundred per cent. of the settlers issued a public statement to Parliament and Press that they were absolutely satisfied with –
    (a) The land values;
    (b) The quality of the soil;
    (c) Its productivity;
    (d) The bona fides of the Company and C. J. DeGaris.
5. Some settlers were clearing £20 to £50 per acre net in eight months from taking possession, proving the soil did and will produce.
6. The railway revenue increased from £49 for 12 months to over £10,000 for 12 months.

Surely these results prove sufficient to answer to those chronic pessimists whose doleful dirge would (if paid heed to) kill any and every Australian enterprise.

Your directors claim that what Governments are talking of, your Company is doing, thereby showing the practical solution

of the immigration problem. The opposition from the very inception of the Company did, however, entail your Company in extra expenses which the first year has had to bear, but which should not recur in succeeding years.

C. J. announced a profit of £4,886 15s 9d, to be carried forward. He asked investors to consider the long term: 120 homes had been erected by settlers, and Kendenup was 'one of the busiest and happiest centres in the Commonwealth'. He continued:

> Your Company is not in business simply to make a profit, but aims not only at attracting the settlers but also at ensuring their success. For this reason, it provides (free of charge to the settlers) fruit and vegetable experts, and an administrative staff who advise the settler when, what and where to plant or sow; who supervise harvesting, and who are at all times at the settlers' call.
>
> This involves heavier administration expense in the first two years, when such costs fall on a comparatively small area, but ensures greater productivity and eliminates failure amongst the settlers. In later years this wise course also rebounds to the advantage of the Company through the proved excellence of the soil quality and improved prices obtainable for the land.
>
> Greater capital would naturally mean greater and speedier development.
>
> That is why the sudden stoppage in the sale of debentures last October, after an insane and unwarranted attack on your Company's credit, proved to be such a handicap. For this reason it is confidently hoped that the remaining £20,000 of first mortgage debentures (carrying 8 per cent. per annum interest, and a profit limited to £50 for each £100 debenture) will be promptly taken up by the investing public, who can now be

satisfied that Kendenup is no longer an experiment, but is an accomplished and flourishing fact.

C. J. DeGaris, Chairman.[68]

C. J. knew Mildura's history back to front, and he knew that the Mildura story was one of battle and fortitude in crisis; the creation of *that* town as an 'accomplished and flourishing fact' took decades of toil and anguish – there may also have been considerable luck in there, too. He could justifiably feel that a critical mass of settlers to Kendenup was the most important element of its future success.

The 'insane and unwarranted attack' was, however, the elephant in the room. C. J.'s bête noir, Grant Hervey, had returned to meddle further in his affairs with a scheme with no firm logical purpose or aim aside from the upsetting of the DeGaris applecart, and it was to prove the biggest challenge of C. J.'s career to date.

8

A great smash, 1921–23

The trip to Ceylon restored C. J. constitutionally but weakened his grip on supporters. He writes that his absence 'left the way clear for all the antagonistic forces' marshalling against him 'to act in concert, and to show this self-anointed superman that he was very, very vulnerable, after all'.[1]

But Ceylon aside, C. J. was planning to exit Victoria altogether. Until the end of the nineteen-teens, he had been as much 'for' the ADFA and Mildura as he had been 'for', and all about, C. J. – the three were inseparable. When he began to concentrate on activities outside his particular patch of Sunraysia – a place he had named – a leadership hole was left. The Ceylon trip only focused the problem, particularly as rumours grew that he may not return.

A small weekly paper, the Mildura and Merbein *Sun,* had been established by George Veall in Deakin Avenue in early 1921. Little can be gleaned about Veall, other than that he fought in both the South African and Great Wars; he may have come originally from Violet Town.[2] It is clear that he had a problem with C. J. DeGaris, or was at any rate open to being persuaded towards hostility. The *Sun* was an unexciting publication, surely struggling until the middle of 1921 when it suddenly suspended publication to install new printing equipment — there had been large-scale investment in the paper, with gusto, and there were now funds enough to employ a new editor. Western Australia's *The Call* was of the opinion that the investors were 'financiers who have opposed the Kendenup scheme'.[3] Grant Hervey was installed not only in charge of the paper's content, but also as its advertising manager. Hervey had his sights on the man who had embarrassed him, and chose initially to use C. J.'s modern and popular newspaper, *Sunraysia Daily,* as the point of attack. C. J. writes that his absence from Australia was 'like a gift from the gods' to Hervey.[4]

Having been so comprehensively exposed and, effectively, run out of Mildura in 1919, a less driven and delusional man than Hervey might have figured he had used up his opportunities in that region. Hervey had no affiliation with Mildura or even, it seems, any familiarity with it. But Hervey seemed unable to cast off his old obsession with both Sunraysia and C. J., and in any case he plainly relished walking into a whirlwind. He returned in August 1921, two years from his original unmasking and embarrassment, this time to live in Sarnia Avenue, a street named for the DeGarises' company and homeland. He was accompanied by a woman named Florence Lockwood, who he claimed as his wife, although he was still married to Annie Crowe. Lockwood was pregnant.

Hervey kept the *Sun* afloat by inviting potential advertisers into his office to show them two articles — one damning, one full of praise — and advising them to advertise to ensure the positive story would run. Given Hervey's unique flourish, the *Sun* had become entertaining reading, particularly if you were cynical when it came to C. J. DeGaris and his family. Hervey announced, for instance that 'if the necessity should arise', the *Sun* had 'got one special article ready for C. J....which would paralyse Mildura'.

The afterthought, that 'we like and respect Mr. DeGaris all the same, in certain directions'[5] was an unconvincing attempt to confuse reader and subject alike in Hervey's cat-and-mouse game. It is difficult to understand why Mildurans would be favourable towards something 'paralysing' their town, although Violet tells C. J. in *The Victories of Failure* that Hervey is 'as welcome as the flowers in May to some of your antagonists. They just lie low, and smile, and let him say what he likes, and the public is eating it up'.[6]

Hervey could not have been more of a stage villain if he had tried: pompous, whining and Machiavellian. He would claim to be defending himself from provocation; C. J. had 'for years past endeavoured to hound him down and make it impossible for him to live'. Whatever C. J. had done – typically, Hervey gave no detail – it was 'the most beastly thing one man could do to another', whereas Hervey 'had done nothing against DeGaris in any form'.[7] Hervey would also suggest that C. J. had 'made £250,000 by stealing some of my ideas'.[8] The conflict between the men over the novel competition did not account for most of these assertions.

Initially, Hervey's public vitriol was reserved in the main part for Harry Stephens, the *Sunraysia Daily's* editor: Hervey may have often worked as an editor but he clearly did not respect the office. One extraordinary example of the anti-Stephens propaganda was an appropriation of a drawing featuring the characters from the American comic strip *Mutt and Jeff*. This extremely famous and popular pair might have been better known to readers in Mildura as stars of a series of animated cartoons. In the *Sun's* version, a diminutive C. J. was 'little Jeff' at the racetrack, riding a horse labelled *Sunraysia Daily*, its tail tied to a rope wrapped around a post labelled 'public opinion' and held by Stephens in the form of 'Mutt'.[9] The purloined drawing appeared each issue, with a different caption (or 'slogan'), all of them obtusely provocative. In one 'open letter' to C. J., Hervey wrote:

'Take a tip from this', Mildura and Merbein *Sun*, 22 October 1921, p. 7.

Mildura has been your seedbed. Be grateful to it. Fire Mildura's worst public enemy – or else Mildura may fire the boss, along with that bending Stephensonian parasite at your door.[10]

Privately, Hervey was writing letters to C. J. threatening 'fearful revelation unless he went on his knees as to the Lord Jesus Christ'. C. J. ignored him.[11]

Hervey and C. J. were similar in the importance both gave to rousing stories of good and evil. There weren't many vital social issues that couldn't be conveyed in a parable. Hervey began serialisation of a 'novel', *A Don Quixote of the Saltbush,* in the pages of the *Sun*. This was his first attempt to mythologise the foundation of Mildura; the second would come in his novel *An Eden of the Good*. In *A Don Quixote of the Saltbush*, Hervey related the internal monologue of an American fugitive, Stephen Puritan (clearly modelled on the Chaffeys' associate, who first 'discovered' Mildura, Stephen Cureton) wandering through the dry red landscape of pre-development Mildura. He is accompanied by an Aboriginal man, Pinggali, a stereotype of the noble savage ill-equipped for modern Australia. They encounter a white woman, Hazel Neild, living in a hut with two Indigenous servants. There is some suggestion, vaguely expressed, that Neild's mother has been killed by squatters many years before. Puritan, enraged upon hearing of this brutal act, vows retribution will be rained upon them. This would come in the (ludicrous) form of modernisation through irrigation and agriculture. Had it been completed, *A Don Quixote of the Saltbush* might well have been a compelling, though naturally bizarre, work. Hervey was presumably composing this scattershot serial week by week.

Considering how unstable Hervey's world was, he seemed to have no problem bringing others on board for bizarre projects, though cajoling and threats were a strong feature of his armoury. In September 1921 he inveigled Veall, along with clergymen James Legge and Howard Russell, into a campaign to persuade Lord Northcliffe to tour the Sunraysia district. It was later suggested in court that Hervey had blackmailed the Rev. Russell into participating in this campaign.[12] Howard was brother to Frank Russell, who had won C. J.'s literary competition the same month.

Northcliffe – Alfred Harmsworth – began as a comics and light magazine publisher becoming spectacularly successful in newspapers, dominating the British market with papers both high and lowbrow. Coincidentally, like C. J., he was known to his staff as 'Chief'.[13] During the Great War Northcliffe had distinguished himself as a propagandist. He was visiting Australia to confer on postwar diplomacy and migration (as well as hoping to 'solve the riddle of the Pacific and White Australia').[14] Hervey's team aimed to enlist him into a campaign to invite Britons to 'become pioneer settlers of Greater Mildura, Australia's coming inland State'.[15] An advertisement written in Hervey's style appeared above Veall's name in the Melbourne *Argus*. Amongst other things, it announced that the 'red rock of Empire called Mildura…herewith repudiates the foolish and unmeaning term "Sunraysia"', applied to the Murray Valley, as having 'an Asiatic and pro-alien sound', and that a public meeting of returned soldiers 'and others' requests him to visit Mildura, Renmark and other irrigation settlements. 'Come to our camp-fire at Mildura, Comrade', the ad bellowed. 'Let us talk things over.'[16] A further advertisement featured what purported to be a letter from Northcliffe – regretting his inability to accept the invitation and suggesting his interest was in migration to all of Australia, rather than merely the 'Murray Valley'. Hervey and Veall chose to interpret Northcliffe's willingness even to communicate with them as positive alignment with their bumptious racketeering. His engagement with them may have mattered even less than the fact that they had attached his name to their project. The section of the advertisement featuring Northcliffe's polite evasion led to a rambling story about one Harold Crisp, who made an extraordinary profit from tomato-growing land in Merbein; 'and the editor of the "Sun" now lives, by the way, in Mr. Crisp's Sarnia avenue house'. This banal information segues into an invitation to all Victorians to subscribe to the *Sun* for its investment advice; 'The Special Feature of this week's edition' was an exposé on 'Clause 20 in the Kendenup Country Home Buyer's Agreement'.[17]

Hervey was adamant that the *Sun* would take over the *Sunraysia Daily* and become installed in its premises 'on or about' 15 October. At this time, he wrote, 'the financial undertaker will knock at Editor Stephens' door. Very reverently, but in hopes of a glorious resurrection, poor old *Funraysia* will be laid to rest. It will reappear, presently, under entirely different editorial managements, as the *Morning Sun*'.[18] Three days after the magical date – that is, on 18 October – having failed to cross the *Sunraysia Daily's* doorstep to take possession, Hervey and Veall launched an attack guaranteed to hurt. Hervey sent a telegram to one William Owen, asking him to meet Hervey at Spencer Street Station and bring a bucket of paste, and brushes. Owen and Hervey spent the night on a trip to Warragul, possibly to pick up posters from a printer, then headed back to Melbourne. They then travelled from Balaclava to Brighton Beach (where they stopped for a while at William Dance's tea rooms) and North Brighton, and finally to thirty-three 'business houses in the city', for the purpose of pasting up notices under the Mildura and Merbein *Sun* banner stating:

Extraordinary
The Mildura and Merbein Sun
Thursday, October 20, 1921.
The Great Smash.
C. J. DeGaris Bankrupt.
Enormous Losses.

"The Sun" learns on the highest financial authority that the bankruptcy of Mr. C. J. DeGaris will be announced this morning. Although the figures are not yet available, it is expected that the net deficiency will be at least a quarter of a million pounds. Further information is expected today.

C. J. relates that Hervey drove past the Kendenup company's Melbourne offices 'smoking a huge cigar' in a car bearing posters proclaiming 'Kendenup has smashed'.[19] News accounts suggest that the car displaying statements about the 'smash' did travel the city that day. If Hervey was aboard, smoking a cigar or otherwise, C. J.'s announcements of a £1,000 reward for information leading to the conviction of the person responsible was ingenuous.[20] Hervey claimed the reward money, which was not paid. 'Statements concerning myself circulated in the city', C. J. told the Melbourne *Argus*, 'are absolutely false…Steps are being taken to prevent a repetition of this offence. I have been overwhelmed with expressions of confidence and good will'.[21] C. J. was selling off Pyap to fund his Kendenup activities: Hervey and Veall's acolytes also took *Sun* posters to the sale of lots at that estate, effectively shutting it down as C. J. refused to sell under such conditions.[22] C. J. reportedly lost a considerable amount on the Pyap sale.

What did Hervey expect would happen to him on his return to Sarnia Avenue? He courted disaster. As soon as he was seen at Mildura railway station, car loads of angry local men descended on him, chasing him to his home. He locked the doors and windows and threatened to shoot anyone who entered. Florence Lockwood was allowed to leave; she called on a neighbour and used the telephone to summon the police, who urged the crowd to disperse. They did, but scouts remained and alerted the mob when Hervey left the house in a car heading for Ouyen. On crossing a culvert, his exit was blocked by a drayload of wood. Here a large number of men emerged from beneath the bridge, having driven there earlier and parked their cars out of sight in nearby pepper trees. Hervey was commanded to 'Come out of that car'. The police were powerless against the crowd, who seized Hervey, tied him by the hands and feet, and conveyed him to the airstrip in a parade of motor vehicles. Here, they ordered him to remove his coat, vest and shirt while a tin of tar was opened. Hervey, wearing only trousers, socks and boots, asked

'Do you want the pants pulled off?' He was told, 'No, you can slip them over your knees'. He was then told to take his boots off, and replied that the ground was 'rather rough to sit on'. He then asked, 'Now, is there anything else that you want to do?'

'Yes', a member of the crowd replied, 'we are going to give you the time of your life'. A tar brush was then 'slapped over his shoulders' and tar applied over his body and legs. He was then covered in kapok – mattress feathers – so that, in the words of one observer, he resembled a 'huge gorilla', his arms outstretched beseeching God to forgive those who had assaulted him. In the midst of this furore, a random aeroplane landed. Some of Hervey's assailants drove to the fire station, rang the bell, and announced to the thousand assembled people that Hervey had been tarred and feathered. Mildura offered 'continuous cheers'.[23]

Hervey was nothing if not resourceful. He attempted to turn his experience into advertising endorsements, beginning with a rip-roaring adventure in which he was 'attacked by about one hundred "men"'. He claimed to have 'knocked-out about half a dozen of them' but was then overpowered and 'lifted bodily – I weigh about 19 stone – into a motor-car; taken some miles away, and tarred and feathered'. For days, he claims, he 'could scarcely walk from Sarnia Avenue to my office' due to nervous exhaustion. He found his succour, he says, in the well-known iron supplement Clement's Tonic.[24] 'Clement' was, of course, C. J.'s first name, but Hervey avoided any temptation to mention his bête noire. He similarly used his notoriety to provide a testimonial for a brand of soap: 'Inside half-an-hour the last vestige of the stuff was off me'.[25]

Two court cases followed: one a prosecution of Hervey for postering, and the other against twelve of the men who tarred and feathered him. The first, at Brighton Police Court, saw Hervey expostulate furiously in the witness box. He was fined only a pound.[26] The second took place the following month. Fourteen men were accused, reduced early in the trial to twelve.[27] Justice McArthur was under no illusion regarding Hervey's willingness to use blackmail and described his behaviour in the witness box as exhibiting 'repulsive hypocrisy'. He also claimed Hervey had published the most 'foul and filthy' articles he had ever read, apparently a reference to an article in the *Sun* that other newspapers were too polite to identify.[28] Resorting to an obfuscatory tactic that had worked for him in the past, Hervey referred to relevant information given to him by a 'lady' whose name he refused to reveal to the court. He would say only that she was a soldier's widow who might come to harm from the 'DeGaris gang' should she be identified.[29] Press reports made much of the 'lady' and her anonymity ('Was the lady Liza Harris?' asked the *Cairns Post* in a peculiar non sequitur; whatever this meant is lost in the mists of time) yet even the relevance of her supposed information remained undiscussed.[30] The twelve accused were each fined £25. All men were adamant that they did not attack Hervey under orders from C. J. but rather from natural outrage at his actions, including the bigamy and blackmail.[31] The majority, if not the entirety, of their fines were paid by Mildura's business community and private citizens.

Hervey relocated to Sydney. He had long been a contributor to the smart, intellectual London journal *New Age*. In 1922, it published his two-part article damning the colonial ('Georgian') backwardness of Sydney and New South Wales, in comparison to Victoria. In the pages of *New Age*, he rubbed shoulders with writers as renowned as Ezra Pound, Hilaire Belloc and Michael J. Arlen; Clifford Douglas was working out his temporarily fashionable 'social credit' schemes within its pages. Hervey, as the author of 'From Sydney to the Golden Mile' was pretending, once again, to be an American; he also claimed to still be editor of the Mildura and Merbein *Sun*.[32] The *Sun* had not endured beyond Hervey's tarring and feathering at Mildura airfield. Presumably its backers had no use for it, or Hervey, the damage having been comprehensively achieved.

Starting downwards

Hervey loved to destroy, and had hit C. J. in his most vulnerable place: it was quickly obvious that the C. J. myth was propped up by the belief and goodwill of those around him. Like a run on a bank, lack of customer faith saw the C. J. edifice crumble.

Once again, *The Victories of Failure* is probably our best source of information on the days following the Hervey libel. C. J. entitles one chapter on this time in his life 'Starting Downwards'. Even before the Hervey intervention, those who had supported C. J. in Mildura and Melbourne were hotly resentful of his desire to leave for the West, and were unwilling to help him depart. C. J. had not examined the optics – in most Australians' minds, including the ADFA's, he was essentially a dried-fruit publicist – and while he had packed a lot into two years, two years is a short time to engage a large group of people when you are delivering a somewhat complicated message, especially when it includes asking for their money. The initial Hervey attack was damaging, and the tarring and feathering looked more like frontier retribution than civilised justice. Nevertheless, looking back some years later in his memoir, C. J. seems unable to recognise that even when he sees the 'friends' and 'foes' recalibrated in his world of golf course and gentleman's club agreements, the 'friends' are still only *barely* friends. He is a newcomer in Melbourne, and no doubt there had been resentment against him among the establishment since his arrival. 'One of our Board was playing golf yesterday afternoon with a very prominent Western Australian', a bank manager says, 'who told him that Kendenup was valueless, being nothing but wind-swept clay'.[33] On the basis of that casual misinformation, a promised loan to Kendenup of £40,000 evaporates.

After the Hervey attack on 15 October, Kendenup debentures, which C. J. said had been selling to the tune of £1,500 a week, stopped immediately.[34] He explains that, after spending a day on the telephone or in conversation with Kendenup investors assuring them of the sustainability and resilience of the project, he lost his voice. This was just when it was most required, for a meeting with the ADFA at which he intended to justify his actions during the second year of the dried-fruit campaign, which had been less successful than the first. Soon afterwards he severed all connection with the ADFA.

He details a series of frustrating and unhappy conversations in the weeks after the Hervey 'smash'. A syndicate of well-wishers, for instance, suggest raising a cushioning line of credit which will get him through tough times; suddenly, his supporters get cold feet when it is rumoured that he is a spiritualist. Alfred Deakin, who had died in 1919, was unabashedly aligned with spiritualism and it had not spoiled his political career – but times had changed. C. J. denies allegiance to this movement fervently, but his informant responds that spiritualists always *do* deny their belief.

Perhaps in light of his father's experience with local government and bureaucracy, C. J. was uncomfortable with the needling and pedantic ways of public servants, not to mention what he (and many Australians) saw as the populist hypocrisy of politicians. Yet Kendenup needed constant cash to keep it solvent. Mildura was in a nosedive in the 1890s, until colonial government money was injected into the project in recognition that there was a critical mass of settlers and enough infrastructure to make it harder for Victoria to withdraw than to fully invest. C. J. claims in *The Victories of Failure* that the premier of Western Australia offhandedly mentioned to him that Kendenup had brought £30,000 to the state without government having to raise a finger. Of course, there were roads and railway lines in the district already, but the point is essentially well made. There seemed to have been, therefore, good sense in asking the Western Australian government to prop up the settlement until it could get firmly on its feet; indeed, in C. J.'s mind there was almost a gentleman's agreement that this was the logical way forward.

But C. J. quickly regretted an approach to the Western Australian government for a loan of £30,000 to shore up Kendenup in its first year. The parliamentary discussions on the request – C. J. was present, taking notes – put forward good arguments for positive or negative responses. Mr Mann, who put forward the motion that an inquiry be made into the settlement and who argued in favour of assistance, did so in part from the logical argument that, as public confidence was necessary for the venture to succeed, government backing was the perfect solution. He also noted that were Kendenup to fail, this would reflect poorly on Western Australia itself.

Others were far less sympathetic. Mr Walker felt that the 'advertising campaign carried out by the company under the seas and up in the heavens...were the methods of showmen, not those of solid businessmen...Was it the duty of the State, when the bubble of a company promoter who came to the state with flowing prospectuses burst, to come to his assistance?' Other parliamentarians presented variations on these themes: the positions, essentially, being whether to prop up Kendenup was to reward recklessness with public funds, or whether it was to respond to human need. Should the settlers be punished for trusting C. J.? Was the state government responsible for rescuing people like C. J. who, up till this point, had tried to work outside state government programs?[35]

A royal commission into the settlement began in January 1922 under William Grogan, Assistant General Manager of the Industries Assistance Board in Western Australia, and associated with the Agricultural Bank.[36] The Grogan Royal Commission became an awkward nuisance to C. J., who was painfully aware of the potential for negative publicity to hurt, and during most of 1922 – as he became confident of other funding sources – it was a distraction, requiring him to testify or to supply financial records. These were not, it is clear, in the most robust shape.

The Grogan Royal Commission was not kind to C. J., but it was probably honest about him. It found that Kendenup was precarious; that 'financial control has been improvident; its methods spectacular and expensive'. Of course, Kendenup's supporters suggested this was entirely appropriate – spectacle and expense were what an extraordinary project like this needed. 'Its

C. J. caricatured by K. Wallace Crabbe in the *Sunraysia Daily*. J. J. Simons' scrapbook, State Library of Western Australia.

ideals of settlement are admirable and its dealing with its clients just and considerate', Grogan also found. But this was not a story of good and evil, or pluck and luck; it was a business proposition, and people had to live. The consumption of Kendenup's products had not, Grogan felt, 'attained dimensions to prove the existence of a market for a large scale production'.[37] It was probably Simons, writing in the *The Call,* who theorised that Grogan was under the thumb of a hostile Agricultural Department preventing him from reporting 'in favour of the scheme', adding that he 'would moreover by inference condemn the apathy or worse of the Government which employs him, and it is a hard thing to expect an employee to condemn his employers even by inference...It wasn't fair to him'.[38]

The commission had, in any case, exposed the settlement in a snapshot, yet if the settlement was, indeed, as ramshackle as it appeared, it was also beloved. The settlers were almost all happy with their situation and spoke with admiration about their treatment.

While the Grogan Royal Commission was ongoing, C. J. also attempted to appeal to the goodwill of a pool of businessmen and middle-class people he might have considered his colleagues. He composed a form letter, beginning with the unpromising line, 'A serious crisis has arisen in my affairs'. He had battled, he said, for six months from an attack on his credit. He was close to overcoming it, but liquidation loomed. He needed the 'comparatively small sum (considering the big interests involved)' of £40,000; he hoped that 400 'friends' would each lend him £100 thus assuring 'absolute success...not only for me personally, but for big Australian enterprises'.

He went on:

> I am not claiming to have made no mistakes, but do claim it would be a pity to allow Big Australian enterprises to go under for the sake of what 400 people could do.
> If you make one of the 400 – the greatest risk you run is that you may lose £100. Against this you have the following facts.
> 1. I am young (37), Insured for £30,0000, inspired with ambition + determination to pay 20% in £1, plus interest.
> 2. In a 20 years business career, handling big concerns, no one has ever lost a penny thru' association with me.
> 3. At Kendenup, In the face of all malicious statements from people who have never seen the place, the SETTLERS (100% of them) voluntarily issued a public statement to the Press of Australia that they were absolutely satisfied with: -
> (a) The Value of the Land
> (b) The quality of the soil
> (c) The productivity
> (d) My own integrity[39]

He later wrote this letter elicited 'only two replies – both refusals'.[40] This was, at best, poetic license: the response came back as £4,950 – not enough, of course, but not insubstantial.[41]

As the commission revealed, the settlement's apparent prosperity was highly dependent on continuing land sales and investment. These were (despite the visions of a 10,000 strong 'colony') unlikely to continue at their initial strength. In March 1920 the surplus of assets was £74,000, whereas by June 1922 it had declined to £12,000.[42] The Hervey provocation was the biggest factor here, but the fact that sales enthusiasm was so fragile was naturally a matter for concern. As the *Sunday Times* pointed out, the state government 'had never shown any sympathy' for C. J. 'or extended him any moral support in his venture,' particularly because he appeared to be in competition with the government's own group settlements.[43] Yet as the *West Australian* editorialised:

> There is no reason to question the bonafides of the promoter. His scheme had in it the elements of a great and beneficent enterprise, but his impulsive optimism led him to underestimate the obstacles in the way of success, and to make insufficient provision for surmounting them. Had public confidence in the scheme not been undermined at a critical period the settlement might, in a year or two, have won through to a position of established security, and been acclaimed as a triumph of boldness of conception and vigor of execution. But the methods of the promoters savoured too much of those of the gambler, who pins his faith to fortunate chance.[44]

The royal commission revealed many positive sides to the administration and operation of the project that arguably put similar state government projects to shame: for instance, that C. J. made it policy to personally visit and talk with all settlers on the estate. Roads, the responsibility of local government, had instead been constructed by an impatient company. DeGaris (Kendenup) also provided advisors for growers unfamiliar with all aspects of their chosen work. Features like this were a sign of a progressive and practical outlook.

The fascinations of a young admirer

There was such a thing as being too progressive, however. C. J. was indulging in what many people saw as an inappropriately close relationship with his private secretary, Violet. As it happened, the DeGaris marriage did fall victim of a scandal in mid-1922, but not directly because of C. J. or Violet.

In January 1922, having installed Rene and their children – and Violet, too, in her role as official DeGaris (Kendenup) employee – at Kendenup, C. J. was required to travel back east for business. C. J. contends that his marriage to Rene was chimeric by the time of Kendenup. Yet C. J.'s lack of attention to his wife could not help but leave her feeling unappreciated and lonely. He seems to have been unaware, or unconcerned, about this.

Ron Coote returned to Kendenup. His father, Frank, was at the estate without his family for some time in the second half of 1921, but Ron had also lived there for a brief period that year, before the DeGarises arrived to stay. Twenty years old, Ron had been commended for his piano playing at the Kendenup Koncerts and his 'sympathetic expression [of] the "Right sound at the right time"'.[45]

While C. J. was away, he and Rene corresponded every second day, and she would give him news of settlers and their progress. He claims to have had little inkling of what was in store when, returning to Kendenup, he found well-wishers warning him of a shock to come.

Rene had briefly become entangled with Ron Coote some months before. C. J. quizzed Rene on the rumours that Ron had kissed her and, more damningly, had 'left her room in his pyjamas at 2 o'clock in the morning'. Ron himself confirmed that he had been to Rene's room, although only 'to return something she had left in his car, in which they had been riding'. Confronted with this admission, Rene continued to deny all for three days until finally she 'admitted that Coote had kissed her a score of times, and that they had had immoral relations together three times during April'. C. J. then brought Ron and Rene together with Ron's parents (at 20, he was still a minor) and Rene admitted that they had slept together. After a few days staying elsewhere in Kendenup, C. J. travelled to Perth and instituted divorce proceedings. He told Rene 'he did not wish to be hard, and would make ample provision for her and the children'.[46] Rene was to be allowed '£15 per week and custody of the children so long as she behaved herself'. He claimed that he believed her 'misconduct...was an isolated instance'.[47]

In his own account of these events in *The Victories of Failure*, C. J. spends less time on the seedy detail. Perhaps considering the feelings of his children who might one day read his book, he says merely that Rene had 'succumbed to the fascinations of a young admirer'.[48] He suggests that it is the public nature of it, rather than the fact itself, that upset him: he apparently found it tacky. In his memoir he claims to have insisted on a divorce, to be had either from the truth of Rene's infidelity or C. J.'s fantasy list of his own improprieties. In this account, Rene opts to be truthful, but keeps the made-up list for her own unstated purposes.

No doubt Frank Coote was mortified by his son's involvement in the break-up of his employer's marriage, and he and his wife left Kendenup for a three-month holiday in New Zealand in June 1922. C. J. writes that Coote was close to nervous breakdown before the trip, a similar situation to his own before his Ceylon venture.[49] The Cootes' send-off was held at the boarding house, where each settler 'expressed his individual sorrow that Mr Coote should be leaving, even though for a short period'.[50] C. J. felt the need to assure the settlers that 'his personal relations with Mr Coote are of the best nature'.[51] Nor did Rene leave under a cloud, but in a public farewell much later in the year, on 9 December 1922, with musical-items, competitions and a 'very dainty afternoon tea'. She gave a speech to the settlers wishing them all 'prosperity and longevity'. It was clear she would not return.[52] She and the children went east again, to Ballarat, where her parents were now living; the settlers later sent her a 'signed autograph book as a present'.[53] C. J. and his daughters would be able to easily visit each other, and while their relocation to Ballarat was, plainly, not entirely satisfactory for a fond father it was more liberal than many comparable arrangements.

Although Rene had confessed to an affair with Coote, and she and C. J. were granted a divorce in late 1922 on these grounds, there is surely more to these events than meets the eye – or at least many at the time believed so. A significant number of Kendenup settlers, better placed than anyone now living to have an opinion, were described as feeling 'very bitter towards Mr. DeGaris in consequence of what they heard concerning his treatment of his first wife'.[54] In the misogynist world of 1920s Australia a man would have to be treating his wife extremely poorly for wider society to care. *The Victories of Failure* account of Rene is surely propaganda for the wider world, to protect C. J.'s and Violet's reputations.

Neither Violet nor Rene spoke publicly on the issue of the divorce, but C. J. does present a conversation – stilted, like most conversations in *The Victories of Failure* – between himself and Violet in which he tells her he is going to divorce Rene, and suggests that many 'who've criticised our supposed relationship' will expect them to marry. 'But I don't want to marry you', she replies; 'I think we'd be unhappy married...I admire you, but I'm not blind to your faults, and, in my present mood, there are several men I'd marry in preference to you, though there is no-one I admire so much'.[55] For reasons unstated, C. J. then asks for, and receives, a photograph of Violet which he takes on his next adventure: a trip to the USA.

The Americans

The Western Australian government was not going to assist Kendenup, only hinder it; C. J. continued to search for backers.

He found a guarantee from the City Mutual Assurance Co for 'the amount required'. C. J. told the Perth *Daily News* that in February his guarantors at City Mutual had met with a specific 'Western Australian...who told them that Kendenup was a useless piece of country, and I was either a misguided man, a fool or a knave'. This nearly spoilt his chances, he said, as did 'self-appointed destructionists' who contacted City Mutual directors to warn them 'that the company was assisting a wild-cat proposition'. 'I have some prominent people financially interested, and with the exercise of a little patience and a little less interference from "the croakers", Kendenup will be OK., and the "I Told You So's" retired to the dust heap'.[56] Ultimately, City Mutual bowed out.

Of course, C. J. did not give up. In the second week of May 1922, he was in Perth with some new friends: Dr Stanley P. Woodard and Mr J. Baxter. Of Baxter, little is known; in *The Victories of Failure* he is no more than Woodard's friend, though papers at the time suggested he was a 'capitalist' who was willing and able to match Woodard's investments. Woodard was 'an American manufacturer and banker,' representing 'immense financial interests in the United States'; he was probably originally from Eudora, Kansas[57], maintaining a sentimental interest in his hometown[58], but had worked his way up to become President of the Gillette Safety Tire Company[59] and vice-president of the Gotham National Bank.[60] The Gotham Bank of New York was a reputable and credible institution, soon to become known as the State Manufacturers Trust Company. It became a component, through mergers, of what is now JP Morgan Chase. Within a short time of these gentlemen's visit, there were suggestions that Kendenup's saviours would be the men from Gotham.

Woodard was, he told the *News,* in Australasia largely because of a rubber business in New Zealand, but he was in Melbourne looking for investment opportunities. He read one of C. J.'s 'serious crisis' appeals for funds, which he considered the 'most audacious, original, and unconventional effort' he had seen.[61] Additionally, the idea of Kendenup 'appealed to him'. This may have been less because of the project itself and more because – like so many others – he believed Australia needed to address its imbalance of population between the overcrowded cities and the underpopulated regions. Other nations with 'hardly enough room to breathe', he felt, would not tolerate this situation indefinitely.

On Thursday 11 May, Woodard crammed Kendenup into the very end of his Australian trip. He told the Perth *Daily News* he was 'convinced' about the 'tremendous possibilities of the proposition' and was likely to suggest an arrangement that day 'regarding the financial side of the venture'.[62]

'I went there sceptical, quite sceptical', he told a reporter who had interviewed him at Perth's Savoy.[63] Travelling across Kendenup by car – he made his own way, so as not to be guided by C. J. – he was impressed by the potential of the place to grow crops; 'even the poorest' soil in Kendenup was, he felt, 'certainly good'.[64] 'The country round about there is really California over again. Why, in California that land would be worth £300 an acre!'[65] He had conversed, the *News* reported, with 'nearly all the settlers' – he obviously hadn't, as this would have entailed hundreds of conversations in a few short hours – and 'had not found one who was discontented. They were all optimistic, and had done splendid work. The scheme had been well laid out, and already excellent crops were being produced'.[66]

If Woodard had been an actor paid by C. J. to infuse broader confidence into Kendenup he could not have done a better job. He told the *News* reporter that from 'what he had seen of him and his work he regarded Mr. DeGaris as a man of very great vision…Men who did things like that should be encouraged'. He added:

> People who had advanced ideas were, unfortunately, generally regarded as extremists and radicals, but there was no denying

the fact that Mr. DeGaris had established a splendid work, which could benefit not only the people of Kendenup and Western Australia, but of Australia as a whole. The vacant lands had to be occupied. There was no scheme similar to Kendenup in America. The assured market for produce was a good idea, and must play an important part in the development of the place.[67]

Before Woodard, his wife and Baxter boarded the *Naldera* at Fremantle they met with C. J. and Simons and agreed to contribute £250,000 to Kendenup. 'Dr. Woodard has committed himself in writing to find the necessary finance immediately he arrives in New York', C. J. told a reporter for the *West Australian* who had buttonholed him at a Perth railway station. 'Mr. Baxter, his companion, thinks so much of the place that he is willing to go half with him, or with his bank, in anything that is done.' The reporter suggested this undertaking 'must have lifted a load of worry from your mind': '"Believe me, it has", smiled Mr. DeGaris as he stepped on the train'.[68]

Even when the settlement was publicly in trouble, people still flocked to buy Kendenup land. 'The whole proposition in the matter of quality of soil and productivity has exceeded our expectations', Frank Coote told the Grogan Royal Commission. 'Everywhere it is turning out better than we expected. It is marvellous how potatoes, tomatoes, and peas particularly grow here...The majority [of settlers] are desirous of bringing their friends here and making known the advantages of settling here'. They would ask, he said, for samples of dehydrated products to send to friends to persuade them.[69]

C. J. resolved to travel to the US to seal the Gotham deal (the Perth *Truth* put it more damningly, reporting that he was pursuing the 'elusive phantom of Yankee cash').[70] During his short Ceylonese trip the previous year, there had been rumours he did not intend to return to Australia; in light of this, and no doubt also in the interests of general openness, he convened a meeting of Kendenupites to consult on the advisability of the four-and-a-half-month trip, to be funded by still-loyal creditors. At the meeting, the Kendenup *Index* reported, C. J. was frank yet still buoyant. Many times, he said, he had been 'tempted to give up the fight, but the thought of the way the settlers had stuck to him and to the Kendenup scheme had spurred him on'.[71] He arranged with Alfred Nicholas to provide funding to 'carry Kendenup on' for five months on the strength of Woodard's promises.[72]

On 22 June, C. J. left Sydney on the SS *Niagara*. In his absence, Kendenup continued to attract a constant flow of visitors keen to see the development of this new miracle town, sprung up in less than two years and grown in population from seven to 700. A distinguished Melbourne stationer and printer, Ernest Peacock,[73] wrote to the *West Australian* in defence of C. J. and his settlement:

> Purely for general interest, I visited Kendenup and spent four days among the settlers, and say, without hesitation, that it is the most interesting study in closer settlement in Australia, and the most sound co-operative enterprise in the Commonwealth. It follows very closely the principles of the world example of successful co-operation in Denmark [the nation – not the nearby township] where the producer is helped by scientific experts in the first stages of production right up to marketing. The achievements at Kendenup so far demonstrate beyond question the soundness of the scheme.[74]

Peacock's opinion was that Kendenup was bounteous and inexhaustible:

> Kendenup cannot be "over-boomed". Neither can Western Australia be over-boomed. "Without vision the people perish". With vision, genius, energy and enthusiasm, and natural advantages, Western Australia can speedily lead the whole of the Commonwealth in prosperity.[75]

One of the most unusual visitors was a fairground attraction, a 12-year-old savant by the name of Argus, who came to Kendenup in July 1922. Argus' presence in Kendenup was just one more amazing moment in the early history of an amazing place. He was guest of honour at an event on Wednesday 5 July that gives us a flavour of Kendenup in full flight. It was 'the monthly social dance of the sports club in the boarding house', involving a euchre party – the card game was still enjoying great popularity around Australia – and dancing. 'The floor for dancing was excellent, and the snap of the atmosphere added just the necessary zest to this exercise', it was reported in the Albany *Dispatch*.[76] Many expected Argus, the guest of honour, to be 'some uncanny gnome, with a wizard-looking knowing face'. But he was a 'strongly built handsome little chap...essentially a youngster, and one to whom we all took to immediately'. The *Dispatch* reporter continued:

> The concert in which Argus was featuring was to be held in the drier. Without hesitation or delay Argus, as well as the others of his party, clambered on to a two-horse lorry which was leaving the Hostel at 7.15, seated himself among all the others, and was immediately thoroughly at home. At the dehydrator a large crowd of nearly 250 were eagerly awaiting his arrival, anxious...to get only one glimpse of his face.[77]

Before Argus' turn, the Kendenup Kostume Koncert Komedy Kompany were scheduled to perform. Their repertoire featured new material, such as 'I want to go to Bye-Bye'.

> [T]he fair maids with baskets filled with wild flowers and shrubs, dancing alluringly around Mr. Tate dressed effectively as a "three o'clock in the morning" gentleman, made an extremely beautiful stage effect. Mrs. W. L. Nelson's sweet voice received special appreciation, and Mrs. Cook's splendid soprano called forth vociferous encores.

Argus' show elicited 'gasps of astonishment and exclamations of amazement and admiration' from those present. Argus would be blindfolded on stage, and his father would go through the crowd holding up articles of jewellery and clothing to be described in minute detail by the young boy. Next, he communed with spirits and answered questions on wills, legacies, meteorology, matrimony and finance, all of which convinced those present. There was certainly no C. J. DeGaris waiting in the wings to debunk the young man's performance (but then, perhaps C. J. was a spiritualist...).[78] When quizzed on the future prospects of Kendenup, he envisaged a flow of American capital into the town.[79]

C. J. was, by this time, already on his way to the USA on the *Niagara*. He published an anonymous newsletter, *The Niagara Daily Spotlight*, producing three copies of each issue a day, and placing them surreptitiously around the ship. He had passed through Auckland in late June continuing to boost Kendenup, and 'incidentally mentioned that he was considering a proposition for establishing a similar settlement in the far north of New Zealand, although the matter had not been definitely settled'.[80] This idea was never publicly discussed again.

His next stop was in Canada, disembarking at Vancouver, then travelling south to Atascadero, Bakersfield and Fresno and thence to the larger cities of Los Angeles and San Francisco.[81]

The Californian irrigation town of Atascadero was of particular interest; J. J. Simons had visited it, and was surely behind C. J.'s decision to inspect the region.[82] 'The "lay-out" of Atascadero, its fine buildings, and noble conceptions, appealed...enormously,' he wrote, and mused that, with merely half that settlement's capital 'he could make a vastly more productive settlement'.[83]

He later claimed to have written a book, *Ten Weeks in Wonderful America*, although it was not published.[84] One item from this time that did appear, curiously, was a long piece about the cultural differences between the US and Australia, submitted on spec to the *New York Times* – 'I walked in to the *Times* office on the day I arrived in New York, and said I had written some impressions while travelling overland'[85] – published in its 22 August 1922 edition as 'The New Australia'.[86] Here he drew connections many would observe even today: 'the same healthy optimism; the same confidence in one's own country; the same opportunity for and encouragement of initiative', for instance. He discussed the domination of Australian cinemas by American films during the war, and the resulting subconscious creep of 'Americanism'. Australians mainly drove American cars, too, and were culturally aware and receptive to the USA. He was surprised nonetheless at American ignorance of the investment potential in Australia, when 'another California' could be 'created overseas'. He was, ultimately, 'boosting' Kendenup:

> The southern and south-western portions of Western Australia have all the potentialities of California, and they are practically untouched. I speak that which I know. I have just arrived from California and I reiterate that we have in Western Australia its equal in soil, water, coast line, harbours, productive possibilities and climate. We have not got your wonderful roads.[87]

He was perturbed, and made much of, the complete ignorance of so many Americans about Australia and found the ideas of Australia he encountered to be 'crude and weird'.[88] It was clearly important to him financially that people in the US didn't find Australia exceptionally exotic – the first impediment to investment was fear of the unknown – but he was as offended as an Australian and British Empire patriot as he had been on his Ceylon trip. 'I have been here three weeks, and find the prevailing impression here is that Australia is a little island, the population of which mainly consists of black people, except for a few white people, who are soldiers, or tennis players'.[89]

Interviewed by the *Pennsylvania Register*, C. J. was able to wax euphoric on his favourite topic. 'When railway revenue jumps from two hundred and fifty dollars to fifty thousand dollars in twelve months, it is enough to make people take an interest', he told his interviewer.

> That is what happened in the settlement of Kendenup. For eighty-two years it was a sheep ranch, a tract of land comprising about fifty-thousand acres, with a total population of seven people. That was sixteen months ago and the change today is almost unbelievable. It is now a model community of two hundred houses built of brick and concrete with tiled roofs, and the population has increased to seven hundred and seventy inhabitants...We, who are interested in and responsible for this settlement, have spared no pains to give the best that can be obtained. We have had the soil analysed by experts, have ascertained what fruits and vegetables are best suited for that particular kind of soil, and we have established a dehydrator for extracting moisture from the fruit which makes it imperishable...Australia is a great country, and we want as many real Americans as we can get to come and settle there permanently.[90]

The financiers C. J. met with in New York are some of the very few figures whose names were not changed in *The Victories of Failure*. Woodard was his original point of contact, and introduced him to his broker J. S. Schwarz, vice-president of R. J. McClelland and Co, and acting president while McClelland was on holiday in Europe. *The Victories of Failure* is a wealth of detail on the ideas bandied about by Woodard, Schwarz and McClelland, three men who featured prominently in C. J.'s world but about whom little else is discoverable.

Ross McClelland had the most public life of the New York contacts. He had been the chief engineer of the Electric Bond and Share Company from 1909 to 1919, and formed R. J. McClelland and Co. in 1919.[91] He was chairman of the technical section of the National Electric Light Association during the Great War[92]; and he was *probably* a Baptist, or at least was happy to give an address on 'The Road to Financial Independence' to the Baptist Men's Club of the Lenox Road Baptist Church, Brooklyn in March 1922.[93] C. J. had little to do with him personally, but his influence is apparent on the actions of others in Schwartz's circle.

Schwartz, however, is a mystery, and the fact that Schwartz is a very common name is not helpful to tracking his career. A man called J. S. Schwarz was charged with embezzlement of funds at the Pittsburgh Park Bank in 1919 and subsequently suffered a 'mental break-down'.[94] It seems highly unlikely that, three years later, such an individual would be associated with a reputable Broadway institution such as McClelland's, much less as vice-president. The Pittsburgh 'J. S. Schwarz' is also referred to in the press at the time as 'J. S. Swartz' and 'J. B. Swarz'.[95] No other 'J. S. Schwartz' has a profile in the USA financial sector (or, indeed, anywhere!) in the years leading up to 1922. Schwartz, in particular, is singled out in *The Victories of Failure* as a man with whom C. J. felt a strong empathy. C. J.'s description of a night spent in conversation with Schwarz during which they 'interchanged confidences of a most intimate nature'[96] is intriguing. Schwartz's affection and support for C. J. is apparent.

C. J. was perturbed when, just as negotiations were concluding in New York, the details of the Grogan Royal Commission were publicised. He went to Schwartz ready to be told that the deal was now, necessarily, off. Schwartz told him that he already knew about the Grogan findings.

'And what will you do?'

'Do!' replied Schwartz, 'Why, see this thing through. When a man is down because people disagree with him he wants help. We are prepared to help him. When a man has a vision of the future of a locality he wants to be assisted to realise it'.[97]

There was one further element to the Americans' interest in Kendenup. After viewing the site, Woodard told C. J. that he believed there were 'big lagoons of oil' under Kendenup.[98] Schwartz was also 'confident that the oil was there'.[99] C. J. had, apparently, already come to the same opinion.

There had been rumours of oil in the wider region for almost fifty years. A surveyor in the district in the 1870s found 'what he at first thought to be coal shale, but subsequently it was pronounced to be opossum guano'.[100] E. W. ('Ted') Perkins had found 'a piece of bitumen' at 'a blacksmith's shop at Ravensthorpe' in 1895 and had been obsessed by oil in the area since. He reported finding oil at Bremer Bay, 200 km from Kendenup, prior to the Great War 'but the outbreak of hostilities prevented its further investigation'.[101] Perkins teamed with Peter Martin, a German chemist, who was able to operate a small laboratory in a tent at key sites to analyse samples.[102] Martin, like Perkins, was adamant that there was oil in the area.

In 1921, C. J. became a founder shareholder in the South West Oil Company, based in Melbourne, with a capital of £5,000. Victor Courtney, the editor of *The Call,* accompanied C. J. to inspect one of the Perkins bores.[103] 'I never quite made up my mind about Martin', Courtney writes, 'but he was either scientifically a fool or personally something of a boomster...He showed us an amazing array of test tubes and in two or three a small quantity of fluid'. Martin invited the visitors to dip a splinter into fluid he claimed was from the bore, and to light it; it 'flared up instantly..."The oil is there", he announced emphatically. "We have discovered a great oil field."'[104] The Western Australian government gave no credence to the claims, and according to Rick Wilkinson's history of Australian oil exploration, 'Perkins and Martin were brought back to earth with a thump...This sort of farce did little to enhance the credibility of the fledgling oil industry'.[105] Yet rumours persisted, and indeed placed the rich deposits very close to Kendenup. While deepening a well on their property, the Ridge brothers, early Kendenup settlers and traders, discovered a dark greasy substance floating on the water, with a strong smell of gas and flammable bubbles.[106]

C. J. believed that 'if he mentioned oil' to American investors, 'it would look as if he were dragging a red herring across the trail to divert attention from other operations at Kendenup'.[107]

However, he confirms the rumours in *The Victories of Failure*, in relaying one of his in-depth conversations with Schwartz. 'My boy, the time has now come when America has decided to allow Australia to discover oil', says the American.

> You have oil in Australia in at least fourteen districts. Kendenup is one of them, and one of the biggest in the world. I speak from knowledge, not hearsay; but you can never locate it without American consent.

Schwartz told C. J. that McClelland wished to purchase exclusive rights to oil in Kendenup but 'you'll never find oil, until we are admitted to oil leases and to banking privileges'.[108] How the Americans would prevent the discovery of oil was not explained. McClelland, Schwartz and a solicitor, Higley, were signatories to a document agreeing to buy 275,000 Kendenup debentures; part of the agreement is to send 'oil-drilling parties' to Kendenup.[109]

On his departure from New York, on 14 September 1922, Schwartz handed C. J. 'a long sealed envelope' and asked him not to read it until the train had left. It was, C. J. would write, 'the most inspiring and helpful letter of his career'. It was for all intents and purposes a platonic love letter. It spoke of a 'true, firm, fine, happy and everlasting friendship' and told C. J.:

> Nature has been very kind, in fact more than kind to you, having blessed you with a personality which is winning, and which is convincing, a mind which is bordering upon genius – a versatility which is surprising and a body which you have not abused, and which can take a great deal of work or punishment.
>
> Were you to leave your own country and come here, I believe and feel very certain there are many things you could do which, from a standpoint of money-making, would pay you better than anything over there.[110]

The day after C. J. left, Schwartz wrote to J. J. Simons. The company had been 'disinclined', he said, to be associated with Kendenup because of the distance. But 'after getting to see something of C. J....I am compelled to admit that the personal equation entered very largely into the proposition...'.

> Of course, like everybody else, we are in business to make money, and we believe that Kendenup can, and will, do that for us. We believe that Kendenup as an agricultural proposition, is extraordinarily well set up, and with the new immigration which is soon to set in, based upon the arrangement which the Premier has made with England, Kendenup ought to profit very largely. A study showed that if there is any oil in Australia, it is in the Western State. I especially want to pay a tribute of respect to the Many-Sided Genius which I believe C. J. DeGaris to be. Whether it is reporting a cricket game, or writing by request for a New York paper on Australia, or whether it is in a matter of doing other necessary things, in all he shows a brilliancy, a dash, and a certain punch, as we call it here, that stamps him a man above the average. He made a very profound impression generally, and especially upon myself. I really count it a privilege to know him so well. I do not think the Australian public realises what an asset they have in C J....He is a dreamer, and it is men of his type and stamp that have done things as you well know. He is dreamy like Edison, dreamy like Ford, and dreamy like Columbus, and it is men of that type only who dare to dream things that the other fellow wasn't even thinking about...[111]

C. J. returned on the *Niagara,* leaving Vancouver on 22 September and disembarking in Sydney on 19 October. He found the press was much less interested in the fact that a solution had been found for Kendenup's crisis than it had been in its disastrous downfall. However, 'looking brown, and fit, and well', C. J. was reported by the ever-loyal *Call* as 'full of satisfaction at the events of the past few weeks, and full of optimism for the future'. He told the reporter the details of the Americans' deal, and also that, while the findings of the Grogan Royal Commission might have ruined everything, his prospective partners had not allowed it to 'shatter the faith of Americans in either Kendenup or myself'.

He also told the reporter from *The Call* about his letter from Schwartz. He regarded this 'as the greatest asset of my trip', and quoted the section that reinforced the value accorded him by his new friends – who believed he would be a brilliant business success in New York, the global centre of capitalism.[112]

To the settlers, he wrote:

> Words cannot even faintly convey to you my appreciation of your most wonderful loyalty to me ever since you linked your fate to Kendenup, including the period of my absence on this trip when your faith and confidence may possibly have been shaken. In the great days ahead you will be as proud of having exhibited that faith as I am (and always have been) of possessing it. Between us and with the help of our financiers we will lead Kendenup to its destined position as the example of successful closer settlement and mutual co-operation. I am prouder still of the wonderful Kendenup settlers, my dear personal friends whose hands I look forward to clasping very soon after this letter reaches you.[113]

From Sydney, he motored to Melbourne. It would be three weeks before C. J. arrived back in Western Australia, on Sunday 12 November. He was in Perth just long enough to be welcomed by the *West Australian*, but he was due at Kendenup for 'a welcome at half-past ten o'clock tonight, and I would not disappoint them for the world'. With 'a cheery wave of the hand' he departed. [114]

The five-hour trip from Perth was made by car. He was slightly early, and a rocket shot up to signal to those assembled at the hostel.[115] Twenty-five mounted men were waiting to escort him. Another rocket went up a mile from the hostel, and instantly an illuminated avenue appeared. He drove through this to the centre of festivities amidst electric lights and fireworks.[116] Over the portal of the hostel was displayed a brilliant sign declaring 'Welcome home to our chief'. Violet was the first to greet him, and many others crowded around with warm and hearty greetings. He gave a brief speech of thanks. C. J. writes of meeting Violet 'at the top of the steps...with a happy smile'. She had had her hair bobbed in the contemporary fashion, and the general consensus at Kendenup was that C. J. would dislike it; yet he praised her appearance.[117]

Monday, the following day, having been declared a public holiday, families gathered for a picnic. It rained. However, Kendenupites gathered under the sheds in the brickyard, toasted C. J. once more as the 'chief', and listened in awe as he spoke for an hour about the American arrangements. At the end, a unanimous vote of confidence mingled with thanks and cheers.[118] In the evening the Kendenup Kostume Koncert Komedy Kompany gave a celebration concert on the verandah of the dehydrator building, for an assembled audience on jarrah planks sitting atop benzene cases. Cheers were also given to Alfred Lloyd, the administrator during C. J.'s absence.[119]

'There is no happier settler on Kendenup just now than C. J. DeGaris,' wrote a *Mirror* journalist. 'In conformity with his pledge to live on Kendenup, C. J. has settled down in real earnest and is a live unit in every movement, grave or gay, likely to interest, profit or amuse the young settlement.'[120] C. J. wrote of going 'back to Kendenup, to find every moment of every day filled to overflowing, but glorious, work':

> Plenty of open air, frank discussions with settlers and their wives. Romps with the children at the school, and at their houses.
> The Xmas Tree and Xmas Sports were the best on record.
> The weeks flew by. The crops of potatoes and tomatoes were being harvested, and processed at the dehydrator. Payments

were promptly made, covering all crops 30 days from delivery, so that money was freely in circulation, and hope and confidence ran high.

Kendenup then, was assuredly, the place "Where Everybody Smiles".[121]

9

The alert, grey twinkling eyes of C. J. DeGaris

The American money didn't come.

The few months between late 1922 and early 1923 had been halcyon days for C. J. – he was perhaps the happiest he had ever been. He and Schwartz continued to correspond, and the oil experts were expected in mid-February.

Albert and Harry de Pledge's mother felt things were looking up financially for the Kendenup 'battlers' and ordered suits for both young men. 'As she was taking our measurements to send away to get made', Albert remembered many years later, 'our neighbour, Mr. Bill White, came to the house. Mother mentioned she was measuring us for a suit each. Mr. White said, "Perhaps you had better not send for the suits yet. DeGaris is broke and there will be no payment for produce"'.[1]

The first money to DeGaris (Kendenup) Co. had been due from R. J. McClelland and Co. on 15 February, and cables were being sent only a few days before that time. Then there was silence for two weeks, after which another cable was sent simply stating that McClelland did not intend to proceed. A cable came from Schwartz: 'Consider my firm gave you a raw, dirty deal'. He had, apparently, resigned 'as a protest against repudiation'.[2]

Melbourne, much less Kendenup, in 1923 was so far from New York, communication so slow and the law so patchy, it was extremely difficult to find out what had gone wrong. Gerald Beverley wrote to the *Murray Pioneer*: 'Why? Only the Americans appear to know, but the whole thing is incomprehensible'.

> That a reputable firm like McClellands Bank [sic] should go back on their written contract is unbelievable, for many reasons. That some underhand work against C. J.'s interests has been done is certain, but by whom? And Mr. Schwartz has upheld his personal honour by resigning from McClellands Bank as Vice-President...He is a MAN and if he ever comes to Kendenup he will receive a right royal welcome from those whom his associates refused to assist.

Nonetheless, Beverley – a C. J. colleague for a decade – was feeling resilient. 'If as some hard critics say', he continued, 'Kendenup has crumbled to ashes, then like the Phoenix she will arise from those same ashes and they will yet prove to be Ashes of Achievement'.[3] C. J. had learnt from 'private sources' that McClelland's firm had been 'internally disrupted' but Schwartz appears to have conveyed no explanation of this, and indeed his correspondence abruptly ceased at this point.[4]

The firm of R. J. McClelland wound up in March 1923 and McClelland became chairman of a new organisation, McClelland, Claggett Co.[5] Its one major project was a shopping centre in Elmira, New York. J. S. Schwartz disappeared as easily, it would seem, as he had appeared from nowhere to raise C. J.'s hopes and witness them dashed. Unless the Kendenup companies sued them – and they did not have the resources to do this – there would be no ramifications for the New Yorkers. C. J. theorises in *The Victories of Failure* that the discovery of new oil reserves in California meant that American capital had decided to keep a lid on Western Australian oil. This decade also marks the beginning of commercial oil extraction in the Middle East.

Feeling that the US's reputation was suffering, Perth's American Consular Agent, Udolpho Wolfe Burke, wrote to McClelland for an explanation. McClelland replied on 16 April 1923, with a dubious reason. Suggesting that Schwartz had taken negotiations too far with C. J. while McClelland was abroad, he said that nevertheless his firm 'concluded that if Mr. DeGaris's representations were correct and if he would do what he said he could do, we would go through with the situation'. He added:

> The contract was arranged with Mr. DeGaris covering the Kendenup development based on the representations made by him, which were to be substantiated by full information and data, such information as is always necessary before any business man will advance money for a situation of this kind. We didn't at that time have even a balance sheet nor have we since received one…The only things we have received to date are clippings of newspaper interviews – dinner cards and various publications – all interesting, but not particularly relevant to this subject. I quote from two of our cables which show the situation:

> "February 1, 1923 – very disappointed letters December gave no specific data oil contracts or Kendenup financial position. Expected complete auditor's statement giving assets and liabilities, all commitments, cash and stock appraisal, land not sold, amount due same, distribution of immigration, State relation dehydration company to Kendenup financial status. This data essential before giving further consideration." And again, on February 27…"Failure furnish authentic details necessary together with rumours received regarding unfortunate personal developments certain principals involved make it impossible to proceed."

In McClelland's view, C. J. also showed poor judgement in the 1922–23 period. He presumably meant the divorce from Rene. 'Mr. DeGaris,' McClelland continued, 'entered…into a personal scandal, reports of which reaching this country did not help his personal standing…'. In a second letter to Burke, McClelland declared: 'Nothing has happened in this situation for which he is not to blame. It is probably that the situation was such that he was helped by our attitude to delude himself into believing that business is done on oratory and hopes and enthusiasm created at banquets instead of on facts and figures'.[6] It should be remembered that, while this communication from McClelland thickens the plot, and arguably provides a rationale for McClelland's exit from the Kendenup arrangement, there is no proof that the cables quoted above were sent. It seems incomprehensible that, if they *were* sent, they were not replied to or requests accommodated, and that the DeGaris Kendenup companies decided providing the detail required was too hard. The contract with McClelland's was created over some weeks; all parties were in agreement; and professionally run organisations should not, and usually do not, enter into binding contracts hoping for more than they agree to.

C. J. assembled the settlers and discussed the situation with them. He and Simons left for Melbourne on Thursday 1 March, where he hoped to meet with 'certain capitalists'.[7] A week later, the company issued a statement to suggest that 'though no official communication has been received from the New York banking house, other information to hand indicates an internal rupture and absolute repudiation of their obligations'. C. J. added, promising 20 shillings in the pound – that is, the full sum of their investment – back to creditors.

> Whatever may happen to me, my creditors may rest assured that they will receive 20/ in the £, for the whole of the rest of my life will be devoted to this one purpose, and, living at Kendenup, I can devote my activities and earnings to the complete payment of every creditor, large or small.[8]

'If anybody suffers financially', he told *The Call,* 'I'm the man and I'm not worrying'. He added:

> I'm temporarily in charge at Kendenup by order of the trustees, and after everything is settled I'll still remain down there. I have had wonderful practical sympathy from creditors, friends and strangers, and I have been offered some lucrative positions. But I'm staying at Kendenup. It is my vision, my belief, and I'm seeing it through. That's all just now.

The Call's reporter added that with this, C. J. 'hurried away, smiling as sunnily as ever. C. J. DeGaris will never go under while he retains that smile'.[9]

As much as C. J. was resolute and prepared to invest the rest of his life in a principled plan to fix the problem, others had their futures to consider. As C. J. was returning from the USA, J. J. Simons had resigned his state parliamentary seat in part because of charges made against him. These included that he 'was in the pay of a foreign power...associated with [an] attempt at wage-cutting during the recent strike' and 'connected with a bogus enterprise in Kendenup'.[10] It was also asserted that he was making '£1,000 a year out of the Kendenup settlement, and changed his politics at the direction of Mr. C. J. DeGaris'.[11] An item in Simons' assiduously compiled Kendenup scrapbook records that the Kendenup 'settlers took the opportunity to resent the unwarranted attack on Kendenup laid by an opponent of Mr. J. J. Simons, M.L.A., at the East Perth election, and passed an enthusiastic and unanimous vote of confidence in Mr. Simons as a director of Kendenup'.[12] For his part, C. J. claimed that he had kept out of politics for twenty years – that is, his adult life – and 'abominated party politics, was not anti-Labor, most certainly was not pro-Mitchell, but he was pro-Australia, pro-Kendenup and therefore pro-Simons'. Premier Mitchell was, of course, one in the long line of dominoes who had put C. J. and Kendenup in their present situation. C. J. said that he considered Simons 'the biggest man in Western Australia to-day' and that, while he was not necessarily in concert with all of Simons' political views, he 'believed in his sincerity'. Simons, he said, was not making money from Kendenup, but had sacrificed an immediate salary 'to the settlers of Kendenup and took a chance of getting it back should the settlement prove a success'.[13] Simons could justifiably feel he had taken a principled step on behalf of Kendenup only to see its future disappear into the ether.

A letter from Simons to Frank Coote gives a searing insight into the decline in C. J.'s and Simons' relationship at the end of 1922 – and also a perspective on the way the men in C. J.'s life regarded Violet. Simons begins by explaining that he had recently seen C. J. twice, and that C. J. assisted Simons in the East Perth election, 'which as you know, I lost'. He then expresses desolate confusion at the idea that he may have fallen out of favour with the man he alternatingly calls 'Chief' and 'C. J.'. Coote has, apparently, written to Simons suggesting that C. J. is 'temporarily unsympathetic' towards him. Yet, Simons insists, C. J. had 'not given any sign or indication that I am out of favour'.

> I did say to him in perfect frankness, "It is peculiar that once Madam takes a set on any of your associates, it is the end of them." This phrase seemed to annoy him, but possibly he spared me the pain of a scene remembering that I was having a very stressful time in the election.

> I am deeply perplexed with the situation at Kendenup. My perplexities are added to by the implicit faith that C. J. has in Madam. Her words are accepted as divine inspiration, and I fear what the end will mean.

> I can say this unhesitatingly – I have been as intensely loyal to him as it has been possible to be. The result of the elections on Saturday was largely brought about by the bad odour with which Kendenup is surrounded. Honestly, I can say that 60%

of the platform talk and 50% of the literature, dealt with my association with Kendenup, as if the undertaking were an immoral enterprise. Kendenup was so much in the public mind, that the real issue was obscured...I am aware that Madam has been sowing the seeds of poison in the Chief's mind, and if they do germinate I know in my own heart that I have never done a thing to justify these insidious attempts against me.[14]

It is impossible to conclude that 'Madam' is anyone other than Violet. However, this is the one extant account that suggests her influence on C. J. was powerful, much less detrimental to his judgement.

Alfred Nicholas wrote to Simons commiserating: 'now that Kendenup has come to a dead end, and we have all been heavy losers over this venture, we cannot overlook the fact that you have been a tower of strength in a battle with the odds against us in trying to make this a practical success. We recognise the great loss sustained by you'.[15]

That Simons should surrender his political career for Kendenup was one irony, but there were more. Settlers had been lobbying for a school for eighteen months, and it opened with 130 pupils on 4 September 1922.[16] Up to 300 people attended its inauguration, not least to partake of the 'tempting eatables'. Ben Johnson photographed the future students and Alfred Lloyd 'with his hand on the Union Jack, and his countenance bespeaking intense pride and pleasure' officially opened the modern school building, announcing that it 'did justice...to Kendenup, and there was no possible doubt but that Kendenup warranted the building upon the steps of which he now stood'.[17]

The Kendenup branch of the Australian Natives Association, another of civilisation's markers that the settlers had long been hoping for, opened in March 1923. Chris Sandilands was the president, with C. J. one of the vice-presidents. General president T. H. Halse, presenting the ANA charter, said that while it was understood 'the district was for the time being under a cloud...

the enthusiasm of the large attendance present made it hard to realise that such was the case'.[18] Also too late, on 12 March 1923 – two weeks after the liquidation announcement – the local government body for Kendenup, Plantagenet Shire's roads board, tabled a plan for the Kendenup town site that it had received from Perth's most prominent modern town planning firm, Hope and Klem. It seems that C. J., enthused by the new injection of funds, had commissioned a 'real' town plan.[19]

Prospects and pursuits

No-one was being passive about their fates; indeed, they could not afford to be. The company had undertaken to guarantee crop purchases and prices, but the company was now in liquidation. The settlers were not the kind of people prone to useless hand-wringing and new ideas were being bandied about. There was a suggestion that Alfred Nicholas would return to Kendenup with a restructure proposal; the seventy soldier settlers of the area approached the federal government for financial help.[20] 'It is not a favour', they suggested in their telegram to Prime Minister Stanley Bruce, 'It is our right'.[21] Frank Coote, no longer employed by the company (there no longer was a company) but determined to remain a settler, reported that the 900 settlers on Kendenup were impoverished and indeed facing starvation; not only had their means of distribution failed, but a bad season had meant many had little to sell for the measly returns they were likely to get.[22] The federal government granted some relief for soldier settlers and the premier put forward £500; 'but what good is that?' asked the *Sunday Times*, 'there are 800 people on the settlement, and 12/6 each will not go far'.[23]

The *Albany Advertiser* reported that the Italian Consul had contacted C. J. with a scheme for placing a thousand Italian settlers with £1,000 apiece on Kendenup.[24] The accepted racial hierarchies of the 1920s meant that the prospect of Italian migrants would have been regarded with alarm by many Anglo-Australians, and this news would have been controversial; no more was said about this scheme. It might have been malicious rumour.

The needs of at least two groups had to be countenanced at Kendenup: the settlers and the debenture holders. Henry G. ('H. G.') McCutcheon, as representative of the debenture holders, visited the settlement in April.[25] H. G. was brother to the company's solicitor, Walter B. McCutcheon, also actively engaged in reconstruction; the McCutcheons were, incidentally, Methodists, with Wesley connections.[26] At a meeting with settlers H. G. made it plain that the debenture holders did not necessarily share the same commitment to Kendenup as those who lived there, and many with money invested in the settlement would feel ambivalent about the demise of the project. This, it was reported, was surprising to a number of Kendenupites.[27] McCutcheon offered a set of rates for produce for the next year, but these were refused by the settlers who wished to retain the higher rates of the old company promise.[28] This was not mere petulance. There was still considerable optimism for the long-term success of the settlement, and new options appeared all the time; there was a possibility, for instance, that a much more local market for Kendenup produce, at Katanning, might be developed.[29] There was also an ongoing attempt to force the federal government to aid the soldiers settled at Kendenup, thereby assisting the entire settlement. For their part, state and federal governments indulged in handballing responsibility back and forth, the kind of obfuscation Australian bureaucrats were only now getting good at.[30] Prime Minister Bruce, confronted with a deputation of returned servicemen with a list of demands including the fate of Kendenup's ex-soldiers, prevaricated in ways typical of this notoriously most ineffectual of prime ministers, promising to 'give consideration to their requests'.[31] Bruce was worried that, if he helped the soldier settlers, debenture holders would benefit ('So there we have it!' crowed the *Westralian Worker*).[32] He was also distancing himself from 'hysterical people' demonising the government's treatments of ex-soldiers; 'There were a lot of people who were inclined to "slobber" over the soldier as if he were a god or a genius', he observed. 'The soldier did not want that.'[33] C. J. also met with Bruce, who 'promised to help the settlers on the estate in conjunction with the State Government', which had of course already shown itself to be hostile.[34]

Smith's Weekly published a dismissive assessment of the entire enterprise. The *Westralian Worker* – at this time, under the editorship of John Curtin – responded. Its journalist 'T. H.' (if this was not the new Labor member for East Perth, Thomas Hughes, then many people would have assumed it to be) correctly surmised that the old Kendenup administration had failed, and the new was trying to apply greater cost savings. Both state and federal governments were looking on from the wings refusing to make any but the most petty of contributions. All was being done 'at the expense of the bottom dog' – that is, the settler. 'T. H.' spoiled his or her neat assessment of the situation by showing a meagre understanding of cause and effect: 'By the way, is it not about time that Grant Hervey, who was tarred and feathered for warning prospective investors against participation in Mr. DeGaris' scheme was bobbing up again?'[35] The *Mirror* reacted: 'Grant Hervey is referred to in an appreciative tone…This is just like Curtin…What has Curtin achieved?'[36] C. J. responded (to *Smith's* unsympathetic account, not to Curtin or the *Worker*, but the general sentiment could stand): 'Any damned fool can be a destructionist'.[37]

C. J. proposed a canning factory be set up at Kendenup by a syndicate; a new method of preservation would not only serve the settlers well but also allow a scenario by which the originally guaranteed prices might be achieved. He also suggested vesting 3,000 acres of land (at £10 an acre) in trust for the settlers' benefit.[38] Another idea was put forward by Frank Coote and two others (H. Andrews and A. Nelson), and was known as the 'Trinity' scheme. It purported that Kendenup was 'in a vastly better position than it has ever been', with recognition, infrastructure, and a large number of settlers. It was proposed that a new company – to be called the Greater Kendenup Development and Packing Company – would purchase all debentures at a lower price and issue an allotment to each block holder resident on Kendenup before November 1922, alongside a share for every £10 worth of land she or he held: a reward and an 'added interest... and a voice in the management of affairs'.[39] Dr William Maloney, Labor Member of the House of Representatives, visited Kendenup via the steamer *Esperance,* declaring that, 'nothing can prevent Kendenup's progress'. He had, he said, seen splendid houses and much cultivation; 'if, through the injustice of an American company' Kendenup did not advance swiftly, 'the governments should go to the extent of assisting the settlers'.[40]

'Have a raisin, they help you think'

Meanwhile, C. J. had additional considerations. *The Victories of Failure* ends with the collapse of Kendenup in the early days of 1923. The man at the heart of the enterprise is ruined, without any opportunity for renewal. He is resigned to becoming a humble servant of Kendenup, working alongside his fellow man for its eventual solvency. While there may be a certain satisfaction to stoicism, compared to the glory he imagined, the future looks bleak.

On returning to Kendenup following his American trip, C. J. claims, he has told Violet that, despite the temptations of travelling in high society amongst fair ladies, her picture by his bedside was an anchor and a balm. During his travels, he has come to realise that he is deeply in love with her. He proposes that, after 23 May when his divorce from Rene is complete, they should marry.

She refuses him, responding that his feelings are not welcomed, much less reciprocated. However, four months later, following the final collapse of all hope, she fickly turns. He writes that, on 1 April 1923:

That evening, when his head was buried in his hands, as he sat at his desk, as he pictured each ambition (so vivid six weeks ago), now withered and useless, he heard the door quietly open, and looked up...
She came to him, and put her arms around him, and said...
"Now that you are down and out; now that you are ruined, and will be the object of hate and suspicion; now that I can't be accused of wanting you for your position; NOW I KNOW that I want to marry you, and whenever you like, after 23rd May, if you still want me, and will marry me, I'll be your partner for better or worse...I love you, and didn't know how much until to-night."

Violet left Kendenup for Melbourne in May.[41] On Sunday 3 June, C. J. also left Kendenup, in body if not in spirit; he also travelled to Melbourne.[42] 'His departure from Kendenup', readers of the *Kalgoorlie Miner* were told, 'was by mutual agreement between the trustee and himself'.[43] He took with him Murray Bye, who had been manager of the Kendenup dehydrator and who had been prosecuted as one of the vigilante party who had tarred and feathered Hervey, though Bye denied involvement.[44] C. J. and Violet were 'quietly' married on 27 June at the St Kilda Methodist Church.[45] It would appear that Violet's parents did not attend; she was given away by Ray S. Mark, formerly of Kendenup, who had also come to Melbourne to work with C. J.[46] Mark and Bye were, or soon would be, technically Violet's employees.[47] No-one from C. J.'s family, including his daughters, was present. Violet's sisters, Wilga and Marjory, were bridesmaids. The DeGarises honeymooned at Warrnambool and were then to reside at the remarkable beachfront mansion of 'Shandon', South Beaconsfield Parade, St Kilda.[48]

Dulcie, Winnie and Vera were probably forbidden to attend by Rene. Between the wedding and October 1923 a conflict had arisen; Rene was denying C. J. access to his daughters, at which he stopped his regular payments to her. The following year, after

The DeGaris–Austin wedding, 27 June 1923. Ernie Bye and Jean Wenborn are the children; the adults are, left–right, Ewan Tate, Wilga Austin, C. J., Violet, Roy MacGregor, Marjorie Austin. *Table Talk,* 5 July 1923, p. 29.

payment of all monies owed and a promise to pay £12 a week, fortnightly visits resumed.[49]

The next phase of C. J.'s career beckoned and he embraced it with gusto, not least because it was a chance for salvation. This time he would be in city real estate, through a business run in Violet DeGaris' name. He had nothing. Violet 'personally' believed that C. J. was 'rather foolish to hand over his jewellery and other personal gifts to the trustee'.[50] An anonymous backer (*Smith's Weekly* claimed it was a Melbourne real estate developer, George Hume)[51] lent them £300 to begin a business[52] which also allowed them to obtain a mortgage on 5 Roslyn St, Hawthorn, in the eastern part of the middle-ring suburb.[53] C. J. would work for £16 a week. 'After living expenses were paid', he said, 'any remaining profit was to be devoted to the payment of old accounts'.[54] Violet's mother, Ellen, was to live at Roslyn Street, dubbed – jokily or otherwise – 'Camelot', and indeed the house was in her name.[55]

Anyone who hoped to make money fast in 1923 would have gone into subdivision sales, and in any case it was not very far removed from C. J.'s usual business. The lot sizes were smaller, the responsibility to the customer less pressing, the risks greater but the money came much faster and, when things were going well, it came in large quantities. Kendenup purchasers had been a mixture of buyers aspiring to work and live in the region, alongside those who were purchasing as speculators, intending to sell at a higher price when the settlement took off. C. J. and his investors had a long-term association with Kendenup. In Melbourne, most purchasers would be speculators, only a handful hoping for a block to become suburban pioneers.

The new field of town planning – albeit freely interpreted – was embraced by government and private enterprise as a way to guide and shape cities. Speculative subdivisions had to be resilient, and capitalists needed town planning to predict 'best practice'. C. J. was to write:

> Recent years, with municipalities adopting the best town-planning methods in subdivisional works, have seen stringent provisions applied to all new building areas, all of which have tended to reduce the number of houses per acre, thereby increasing the comfort and health of the resident population, and "spreading" the homes considerably.[56]

There were already a few well-known players in the field of urban real estate who had risen quickly to prominence. Thomas Michael Burke was, like C. J., renowned as a fine orator, and wrote hundreds of columns for Australian newspapers that suggested investment in the expansion of Australian cities. While C. J. was making his promotional films for Mildura and Kendenup, Burke created a short film called *8d a Day* promoting his Broadmeadows estate.

Burke's first splash came in 1919 with an extensive enterprise known as the Merrilands Estate, north of Reservoir, on the train line to Whittlesea. For this impressive development, he had engaged a surveyor–planner, Saxil Tuxen, who produced a fine blend of the pragmatic and the visionary. It sold well at a time when Melbournians, regrouping after the Great War, were suddenly able to see a peaceful and prosperous future. This and subsequent projects were sold door-to-door by Burke's team of salesmen via a 'system' of small regular payments.

Tuxen, Melbourne-born of Danish descent, was to have an extraordinarily successful 1920s and would design over thirty suburban estates in Melbourne (and one in Albury) during the 1920s, as well as serving as an active member of the Metropolitan Town Planning Commission. He would work with Walter and Marion Griffin on the Ranelagh estate between Frankston and Mornington on the Mornington Peninsula, and it is likely that they recommended him to C. J. – if his reputation didn't recommend itself.

Like most things related to C. J. in the first few years of the 1920s, the Melbourne Sub-Divisions (MSD) project was manic, if not frantic. A careful newspaper reader would have first heard of its existence in mid-August through the classified section of the *Argus,* where C. J. placed an advertisement hoping to lease a 'furnished house, St. Kilda, with garage, with or without tennis-court.'[57] He used his new company name rather than his own. C. J. and Violet had been married two weeks by this stage.[58]

The MSD's next appearance came two months later with the announcement of the 'City, Town & Country' golf links on '136 acres at Coburg' as created by 'Mr Dick Banks, Victoria's leading links architect'.[59] In November it was announced that 'Mr B. Deramore Denver, Managing Director of Golf in Australia, has accepted the appointment as General Manager of these links'.[60] There was to be a housing development adjoining the links, a concept most advertising did not make clear. The links may have been convenient to Melbourne – they were accessible by both tram, train and of course car – but they were also very close to the notorious Pentridge Prison. Two Pentridge prisoners had escaped in separate incidents in 1922.[61]

The MSD opened an office – or, more likely, found a representative – in Geelong, at Little Malop Street with a 'Geelong

Manager' in C. W. Ruttledge. 'Melbourne's beautiful seaside suburbs' were mentioned as a company specialty.[62] The Baloomba Estate at Black Rock, for instance, was sold on a ten per cent commission basis for an associate. Next, the MSD advertised, with an unreassuring imprecision, 'about 12 choice allotments' for sale at Anglesea,[63] followed by the Tuxen-designed 'Heart of Rosebud' estate of eighty-four lots, sold by Ray S. Mark in December 1923.[64]

Four hundred people attended an auction on Saturday 29 December, and sixty-five lots were sold of the eighty-four.[65] Just over a week later, the MSD was advertising 116 lots under the same estate name for private sale to speculators: 'By buying NOW your year of fortune will surely commence'.[66] C. J. had acquired four large land blocks he quickly subdivided and resold. The Heart of Rosebud Estate was on 150 acres that C. J. had put £3,000 deposit on, then paid off after selling less than a fifth of the land as individual allotments.[67]

Heart of Rosebud was advertised as 'the biggest and best Town-planned Estate along the Beach Fringe', with its health-giving properties accentuated in the form of the 'Rosebud Doctor', an idea presumably inspired by C. J.'s recent experience of the 'Fremantle Doctor' and its Albany variant.[68] C. J. was quoted in the Melbourne *Evening Sun* as referring to Rosebud as 'an ideal holiday settlement by Mr Taxie Tuxem'.[69] This was Saxil Tuxen, his name mangled by a cloth-eared reporter. C. J. chose to market Heart of Rosebud as a country retreat for a middle-class clientele with expendable income and aristocratic aspirations: the attractions included 'Superb fishing. Good Quail shooting'.[70]

By May, the company was advertising eight estates, all at Peninsula locations: Beach Reserve, Balcombe Heights, Balcombe Park and Ricketts Point all at Black Rock; Tramway Terminus and Balcombe Parade at Beaumaris; Mornington Heights; and Rye Heights, as well as Heart of Rosebud. The MSD wanted to be known as 'the Seaside Specialists'.[71] C. J. bought a Jewett car on instalments with a £50 deposit.[72]

'It almost reads like a romance,' said *Table Talk* in July 1924:

> Most people presumably know that C. J. DeGaris – who carried out the Mildura fruit advertising campaign and was the promoter of Kendenup – is the director of sales and general manager of the company, and thereby is unfolded a remarkable story. The Kendenup settlement in West Australia met with difficulties – the particulars are too well known to need repetition – and Mr. DeGaris, having assigned his personal estate to the creditors, set himself to work – his moral obligation being stronger than his legal obligation – to pay his personal creditors and Kendenup debenture-holders a full 20/- in the pound. And with the earnings which he has made in the sub-divisional business he has already paid off no less a sum than £42,354 – a gigantic task in itself, and in spite of the fact that many creditors offered to compromise on a lesser basis. Whatever profits are being made on the Melbourne Sub-Divisions Company's subdivisions are going to pay off Mr. DeGaris's indebtedness on his own account.[73]

C. J. had hoped to conduct MSD business anonymously because he had been 'threatened with being made insolvent' in Victoria, although the fact that the MSD was largely staffed by ex-Kendenupites (forty-five of them by early 1924) made secrecy difficult.[74] The MSD – its public voice almost certainly C. J. himself – began to promote C. J.'s loyalty to the Kendenup settlers as a reason to trust the man and his current business, despite the fact that the washup from recent upsets was ongoing.

Another commission

C. J. could, justifiably, feel as though he was being harassed by the West Australian government. In late October 1923 it was decided another royal commission would be held into Kendenup. This was initiated by Thomas Hughes, who claimed that C. J.'s activities long before Kendenup – at least as far back as the press tour of Sunraysia – were conceived to defraud small investors. Hughes also suggested that C. J. and his family had left Western Australia with others' money. Violet, Hughes claimed, had suspiciously recently come into £10,000 from a deceased aunt jokingly referred to in the family as 'Auntie Kendenup'.[75] This was not true. Whereas the Grogan Royal Commission was triggered by C. J.'s request for money for a going concern, the

Violet DeGaris, an unsourced clipping in the J. J. Simons papers, State Library of Western Australia.

new commission – to be headed by barrister and solicitor Ross McDonald – was an inquest. It was created with a view to:

1. Ascertaining whether there has been any (a) misrepresentation or fraudulent misrepresentation to the settlers or debenture holders; (b) criminal action on the part of any person or persons concerned.
2. Inquiring into any other relevant matters.[76]

McDonald 'had made a considerable reputation as a lawyer in commercial cases before the war', the Perth *Truth* told its readers. 'Since his return from active service he has continued to forge ahead.'[77]

Much of the commission's evidence would come from the interrogations of another 'C. J.': solicitor Cecil J. R. Le Mesurier. Like C. J., Le Mesurier's family came from Guernsey, via Ceylon; he arrived in Perth in 1904.[78] Though he was employed initially to represent one disgruntled settler, then all Kendenup settlers, Le Mesurier's hostility towards C. J. and the Kendenup scheme was not recently concocted. It dated back at least as far back as C. J.'s Colombo trip, when Le Mesurier wrote a letter to a Ceylonese grower, Mr Fuge, interested in purchasing a Kendenup orchard. Le Mesurier told Fuge that Kendenup was a bad investment to 'shortly be turned into more or less useless scrub'. Fuge bought anyway.[79]

The commission began on 23 November 1923. C. J.'s counsel, Arthur Haynes, announced that there would be forty-five witnesses to call.[80] On Monday, a scene-setting tableau was brought forth by John Burkett, Kendenup trustee, who mentioned the £75,000 of worthless shares C. J. held in the Kendenup company; as well as farming property C. J. owned at Capecup, near to Kendenup, 'taken over by Mr. Padbury under mortgage'. C. J.'s life insurance policies, for £25,000, had been assumed by a bank in Melbourne 'which was paying the premiums to keep the policies alive'.[81] C. J. was, for all intents and purposes, a pauper.[82]

At the beginning of 1924 Premier James Mitchell wrote to the federal government requesting a national, rather than state, royal commission, with McDonald as the commissioner. This, according to Mitchell, was the only way that McDonald could effectively call people from other states (principally, Victoria).[83] The federal government responded that there were 'legal difficulties in the way of the appointment of a Federal Commission' and suggested instead that the Victorian government be requested to make the appointment.[84] This was agreed to on 23 January.[85]

The royal commission dragged out until May, and those tied to its execution must surely have felt they were being subjected to meaningless repetition. Le Mesurier found few unhappy settlers with grievances against Kendenup or C. J., but those he did locate were vociferous. Haynes, however, countered them with many more who pronounced themselves if not satisfied with their fate in a post-Kendenup world, at least unwilling to blame the 'Chief'.

The press made much of the negative testimony of two women: Cherry Barrow and Mrs Thom. Cherry and William Barrow had come to Kendenup with their two children in 1921 buying 64 acres of land and two £100 debentures. Clearing the land cost more than the £3 per acre they were originally quoted, Cherry said, and while she felt that they would have ultimately succeeded as long as they were guaranteed a market, she claimed that she left with six shillings to her name: 'I don't think we got enough to pay for the seed'.[86] Ray Mark, his view perhaps coloured by the fact that he was now an MSD employee and a DeGaris family intimate, testified that he 'knew the Barrow family, who had taken up land at Kendenup...Barrow was rather a frail man, and Mrs Barrow had done most of the work on their block'. Mark did not recall Mrs Barrow claiming disadvantage, rather that she was thankful that company staff had given her special treatment.[87]

There is no doubt that the Kendenup settlers' grievances were genuine and their angst justified – many people lost everything. Mrs Thom's fuming rhetoric is still compelling. She had written more than once to Hughes; she did not testify directly, although she wrote that she 'wished she could be at every sitting of the commission and hear every word spoken by Mr. DeGaris and his backers on their Bible oath'. That she did not appear directly might indicate that she had a change of heart by the time the commission came to sit, though much of it also took place in distant Victoria, not Western Australia. 'She is a woman of intense moods', C. J. noted, 'and one of her delights is to be at a public meeting where her oratory is given full play'.[88] Her words from April 1923 were widely quoted in the press. Mrs Thom had told C. J. he was 'not playing a straight game'. She said that 'there were two Kendenups, the musical comedy Kendenup at the hostel, and the actual reality on the land':

> Useless girls and boys were running about with pens behind their ears when they were not dancing or motoring, or raving about C. J., while serious settlers who had come to work looked on with contempt.

She claimed that 'there were men as well as women who regarded Mr. DeGaris as a sort of fairy prince with an Aladdin's lamp'. Mrs Thom, C. J. responded, 'was one of those women with one idea on Monday, another on Wednesday, and the original idea back on Saturday. I have been the subject of her admiration and her derision'.[89] Mrs Thom, as far as Alfred Lloyd was concerned, 'was certainly an excitable body'.[90] C. J.'s, and Lloyd's, attempts to belittle Mrs Thom show how well she could sting.

Le Mesurier failed to demonstrate that C. J. or his associates had set out at Kendenup to deliberately defraud innocent settlers and speculators; his upset at the audacity of the man seemed to blind him to the irrationality of much of his own theory. C. J. could not (as Haynes pointed out) be both brilliant swindler *and* business disaster. Haynes had in his armoury the excellent point that C. J. was not required, under law, to repay any of the money lost at Kendenup but that he was undoubtedly making money through the MSD and sending it west.

McDonald issued his report in late July. He reserved judgement on the value of the Kendenup project, but found that there was no fraud on C. J.'s or the company's part.

> Mr. DeGaris, the managing director of the companies, who had assigned his personal estate to a trustee under the bankruptcy law, had failed to give the settlement the supervision demanded. Through his power to over-ride the other directors his direction of the companies was characterized by exaggerated and sometimes reckless publicity methods and lax financial control. The Development Company's working capital was exhausted by the end of the first year…He seriously over-estimated the strength of his personal financial resources as a support to the settlement…

McDonald also found that Kendenup's contract with McClelland and Co. was 'prima facie enforceable' and while McClelland and his associates 'may have legal grounds for their repudiation… they have not stated them'. Perhaps most importantly – and most damningly, though also a testament to C. J.'s infectious charisma and 'Kendenupitis' – McDonald stated:

> Settlers and debenture-holders were influenced to association themselves with Kendenup largely, if not decisively, by the personality of DeGaris, and what, according to his publicity literature, he had accomplished at Mildura and Pyap, and would accomplish at Kendenup. The collapse of the settlement was not so much due to Kendenup itself, but to failure of DeGaris to fulfil the personal role he assumed.[91]

C. J. was equivocal. 'I plead guilty to the charge of optimism and plead this cheerfully as an optimist should', he told the Perth *Mirror*, adding that his optimism was 'based on sincere Australianism which encouraged me to believe that a big State like Western Australia, requiring population and the opening up of its inland spaces, would appreciate and assist personal enterprise in settling with the right type of settler large areas that were lying dormant...'. He claimed he and Violet were 'the only people' to have 'done anything for the settlers in a practical way since the Kendenup failure', and noted that the MSD had been 'such a success' that they had been 'able to take back many Kendenup debentures at the full rate...'.

He added he had not given up on Kendenup: 'I am not yet 40 years of age. I still expect to prove to the public of Australia that Kendenup is all I have claimed for it...'.[92] He was less than six months away from a fateful night-time drive to Mentone.

10

'The Long Vision'

C. J. may have had cause to muse that there was 'no such thing as bad publicity' – a clichéd idea but a persistent one.[1] As he had done at Kendenup, C. J. pulled in favours from Walter Burley and Marion Mahony Griffin, innately generous people who were also likely to benefit from his success. Capitol House, in Swanston Street, Melbourne – with its extraordinary cinema, designed by Marion with a multicoloured ceiling reminiscent of stalactites – had ten floors of offices. The Griffins did not own the building but were apparently able to put in a good word for their associate.[2] C. J. arranged for his new venture to occupy the top floor, moving in even before the lifts were operating. He dubbed it the 'DeGaris floor: From where you can see all Melbourne'.[3]

C. J. had his office fitted with a dictaphone and other modern equipment; he would sit 'in his big chair and gave instructions with the speed of a machine gun'. The offices were redolent with 'sounds of incessant activity all day long'. The office table would always have four glass saucers of Mildura raisins, offered to visitors in the way most high-end businesses would offer cigarettes – these

C. J. at his desk, author collection.

were also available, as a second option. The reception rooms were fitted out with 'leathern armchairs'. A journalist wrote that:

> The polished maple and other Queensland decorative woods and the plate glass partitions made a splendid setting for the illustrated maps of subdivisional estates and on the counter in the public office were scenic views and literature setting out the advantages of investing in the subdivisional lands.[4]

The boldest and largest of real-estate organisations, such as T. M. Burke's, spoke with impressive majesty about the solidity of its enterprise: Burke encouraged his clients to ride the wave of prosperity, to get above the pack and turn their thrift and foresight into wealth for their family. C. J. clearly saw the value in grandeur, though the MSD's extraordinary emergence from nothing also required a believable narrative. The official line could easily be that the MSD existed primarily to rescue the Kendenup settlers (a noble cause no doubt), but C. J.'s desire to assuage his own guilt over the fate of farmer–settlers on the other side of the continent was, many suburban land buyers in mid-1920s Melbourne surely felt, hardly their concern. Let C. J. throw his *own* good money after bad: it need not be *their* money. So C. J. had to convince the people of Melbourne that he was neither a crook nor a bad businessman, that he was helping mop up the mistakes of Kendenup, and that the MSD was making massive amounts of money out of thin air quickly but was also entirely above board, and could not possibly replicate the problems that emerged at Kendenup. These ideas could not logically co-exist.

The MSD took out double-page spreads in major newspapers in the nation's largest cities to publicise the company itself and its staff. 'DeGaris floor' aside, it was important to show purchasers that the MSD was not a one-man operation, particularly important when the 'one man' had spearheaded a famously disastrous commercial concern that had been the subject of two royal commissions. True, C. J.'s picture was still bigger than all others, but he was shown as merely one of seventeen or so 'Reasons' for the company's success. They were men and women, mostly young and seemingly loyal, hard-working, and good humoured. They included Murray Bye, Fred Warnock, James Keogh and Ray Mark, all ex-Kendenupites, and Norman G. Forte, who had relocated from Albany. Mark and Warnock were developing regions just outside Melbourne: Mark at Rosebud, where he had gone so far as to become president of the Progress Association, and Warnock at Hurstbridge. Two of the Austin sisters were also represented – Marjorie, who had succeeded Violet as C. J.'s secretary, and Wilga. Violet, incidentally, did not appear in the advertising spread, although the company was officially hers. She gave birth to a daughter – her first and C. J.'s fourth – on 24 September. Adopting the 1920s trend for 'made-up' names, the couple chose to call their child Veema Vyzie DeGaris. Violet did not recover quickly from Veema's birth, and was ill for some months.

Newspaper reports on the MSD sometimes make it seem like a zany free-expression exercise, and it is a shame Mrs Thom, whose words had been so eloquent at the second royal commission, did not have the opportunity to critique it. The staff, it was said, were encouraged to explore their enthusiasms:

> one man, who was keen on afforestation, was allowed to select and plant ornamental trees on the streets and playgrounds on the company's sub-divisions. Another enthusiast in town planning drew attractive plans of garden cities. Surveyors, lawyers, forcible advertisement and booklet writers found happy employment for their respective talents in the superlative offices...[5]

Transport to estates by motor were an important element of an up-to-date business with sale items in faraway places. C. J. bought a single seater Vauxhall, a faster car than the Jewett, in order to save travel time. The Jewett became the Geelong office's car, and a Crossley was purchased 'for the Melbourne office'.[6] 'The commodore of the motor fleet', Melbourne *Herald* readers learnt, 'was an expert in conveying "the chief" and his clients to any estate at any hour of the day or night'.[7] This was to be important because, as impressive and delightful as the accommodations in Capitol House were, the Corio Garden Suburb at Geelong was to be the focus of the MSD for most of 1924.

C. J. had formed a syndicate with farm-equipment manufacturers Jelbart Brothers, initially from the western Victorian town of Merino then more recently Ballarat, and real estate agents Hendy, Leary and Co, to acquire and develop 700 acres inland from Corio Bay in November 1923. He commissioned a 2,600-lot new 'garden suburb' – closer to an industrial town than anything.[8] The suburb was designed by the Geelong architect I. G. Anderson in association with Arthur Stephenson, previously 'consulting planner' at the purpose-built colliery town of Yallourn, and the Melbourne architect Leighton Irwin. The *Australian Home Builder* put forward an eminently logical case:

As the people move out from the old, closely packed, colonial tenements of Geelong into this pre-arranged garden suburb the old city will expand over the congested residential areas near the heart of the city. Thus rebuilding the commercial city from within will be co-incident with the development of the garden suburb at Corio.[9]

When he had been trying to excite visitors and buyers about Kendenup – or even the 'Sunraysed settlements' – C. J. had to accommodate people who didn't necessary want to travel, but needed more than just descriptive text to make decisions about investment; so he used films, which were evocative, entertaining, modern and had a basis in reality. Geelong was different: enough potential investors lived nearby that he could bring the people to see it in person.

At Corio, according to one of the full-page advertisements placed in the *Herald*, 'industry and artistry, idealism and practicality, natural advantages and creative beauty are being expertly blended by scientific modern town-planning methods under the guidance of capable enthusiasts'.[10] A 'large canvas painting' was created of a perspective of the suburb and displayed at the MSD's Moorabool Street offices.[11] Shepparton's *Goulburn Valley Stock and Property Journal* was probably just reprinting MSD advertising copy when it told its readers that 'All the latest town planning methods are embodied in the outstanding venture, which is to provide Australia with its first real garden suburb in a healthy, attractive and prosperous centre'.[12] MSD agent Cedric Johnson – yet another C. J. – spent a week in August in Shepparton spruiking Corio, and the company arranged for locals to travel free to Geelong (probably on the 9 August) 'to inspect the site of the embryo town', in large cars operated by Trevaskis and Sons. The original intention had been to operate the excursion in a charabanc – an open bus – but travellers on the day might have been glad that Trevaskis was unable to provide one. The weather was perfect during the two-hour drive to Melbourne, but following the party's repast at the London Fish Café – a 'beautifully appointed dining salon' in Elizabeth Street – it rained heavily for the rest of the day.[13]

They were conveyed 50 km to Corio from Melbourne to be greeted by C. J. and 'other interested visitors' at the Corio Hall, purchased by the MSD, and all sat down to afternoon tea. Inspection of the estate in cars was then undertaken, and visitors saw the railway station and the 'half a dozen houses and a post office and store combined…already in the course of erection' and the ploughing and planting of recreation reserves. The group travelled to the beach, a major selling point of the estate under normal circumstances which 'could not be said to be looking at its best, owing to the incessant rain', and then to Geelong Grammar, adjacent to the northern boundary. The school was an established and prestigious amenity for the area, as well as a magnet for infrastructure – electricity and reticulated water – and these would be to the benefit of the new estate.[14]

The travellers were then conveyed to Geelong, where they dined with C. J. at the ABC, a local cafe, and then back to Melbourne where they were treated to a night at the Tivoli. Here the internationally famous Melbourne entertainer Albert Whelan was performing in his home city for the first time in twenty years.[15] Although most of the group returned to Shepparton the next morning, 'those who remained were specially invited to the Wattle Path Palais on St Kilda's Esplanade in the evening, where Joe Aaronson's famous orchestra was listened to by over a thousand coffee sippers under conditions never bettered in Australia'.[16] The Wattle Path had become a feature of 1920s Melbourne and its kauri dancefloor was advertised as the largest in the country.[17] Although this gratis entertainment was undoubtedly welcomed by the visitors, one might wonder how wise it was to give clients a chance to reflect on the contrast between Corio, primitive and undeveloped (and rainy) and the upbeat glamour of Melbourne nightlife. The fact that the following month a dozen Shepparton residents visited

Corio again to inspect blocks they had selected – whether on the 9 August trip or separately – suggests that the tactic was, in fact, highly effective.

The *Evening Sun*, for whom the MSD was a major advertiser, reported on an event taking place on 24 September that certainly topped the 'stunt' of bringing less than thirty Sheppartonians to Corio. The MSD chartered 'two special trains' to leave Melbourne at 1.30 pm and 2 pm on 24 September 'to afford country visitors now in Melbourne an opportunity to gauge the advantages and possibilities' of Corio. Visitors who needed information could obtain it from MSD staff, who would be in attendance 'distinguished by silk ribbon badges bearing the company's name'.

C. J. knew more than most people that newspapers, dazzled by advertising revenues, were rarely likely to damn a real-estate proposal and were often likely to praise it to the heavens. That said, Corio was a fine prospect, as long as the industry was substantial. The *Geelong Standard* was certainly effusive. Under the heading 'The Long Vision', it spruiked both Geelong, a city about to catch the upswing in Victoria's manufacturing fortunes, and C. J. DeGaris:

> Probably there are few men in the limelight of Victorian public life today more debated than Mr. C. J. DeGaris, and yesterday in this city there was no name more frequently heard. As the "chief optimist" of a company terming itself "constructive optimists", Mr. DeGaris yesterday carried to a successful conclusion one of the biggest advertising adventures with which this city has ever been associated, and through this venture the Victorian optimist taught many of the local pessimists a lesson of which they stand in need...The tour yesterday was an adventure in business psychology; it was still more an adventure in constructive citizenship, because it was an appeal to the imagination of the present to try and believe something of the possibilities of the future that the man who

planned the outing claims to see...Mr. DeGaris justly is entitled to his title of "chief optimist"...

As the Cape to Cairo route fired the imagination of Rhodes in other directions, as the trans-continental lines of Canada led to a new vision of the great prairies so will this first attempt in Australia to found a modern town-planning centre on scientific lines fire the imaginations of other parts. Corio as the success its promoters optimistically foresee will be the model for many another venture in this and other States.[18]

Well might the *Standard* wax lyrical about C. J.; it seems he was in negotiations to buy the paper.[19]

In one day, 1,075 people toured the Corio site. C. J. was described glowingly: 'hatless...in a leather motor coat' and radiating 'enthusiasm from those alert grey twinkling eyes'. He claimed for himself the title of 'the modern Batman'. Referring to the words with which John Batman reputedly founded Melbourne: 'this is the place for a village' – C. J. said 'this is the place not for a village, but for a garden suburb on the most advanced of town planning principles'.

He stressed the estate's best features, as he saw them: Geelong Grammar, Melbourne Road, the railway station and the bay. Corio's beach and foreshore were to receive the attention of Norman G. Forte, as the MSD's 'beautification expert'.[20] He told those assembled that the scheme 'met with the approval of the Town Planning Association, and he was sure it had a bright and prosperous future'.[21]

'I would like to come back in 100 years' time to this particular spot', announced Dr Frederick Moreton, founder of the Geelong Town Planning Association, 'I believe that in 100 years' time we will have 500,000 people in Geelong and that this suburb will extend to the You Yangs. We as town planners consider this suburb has been laid out on very excellent lines indeed. It has been approved by some of the best town planners in the

Corio's 'big day', Melbourne *Sun*, 22 September 1924.

world'.[22] Moreton was not a *professional* town planner – he was a medical doctor – but the plan for Corio Garden Suburb was definitely of a higher order. Cr J. R. Coxon, Mayor of Geelong West, also welcomed the visitors. Geelong, he said, was making great strides and 'Mr DeGaris was a great benefactor…boosting Geelong more than it had ever been boosted before…Geelong in the future would be a very large city, and almost to what Melbourne was now'.[23]

Welcoming the visitors at the station, C. J. insisted they would not be pestered by salespeople: 'The land was good enough to sell itself'.[24] 'They will have time', he said, 'to consider all the advantages and possibilities away from the influence of any interested in the new suburb. Then if they so desire they may make an application for a block'.[25]

Alongside the Jelbart Brothers factory, by which the company may well have been hoping to replicate H. V. McKay's success at Sunshine, other industries were committed to Corio. There was a steam car works, and a manufacturer of raisin products – raisin butter, raisin sauce, chutneys and cordial. Perhaps the most intriguing, and aligned with C. J.'s cultural interests, was the Phoenix Film Co., which had caused excitement that month on St Kilda beach by filming random women in pursuit of 'types suitable for use in… forthcoming productions'.[26]

The *Standard's* reportage gives us a wonderful sense of what must have been, for many, an exotic experience. Most notably it quoted a 'vivacious lady', visiting in the hope of finding somewhere to establish a grocer's shop, who told the reporter that 'They did us very well in the train…I got a small bottle of raisin butter, a packet of sultanas, a packet of cigarettes and a cigar! (All bore the motto 'Corio Garden Suburb.') It's not every day we get a train journey, a nice motor trip and a dinner at the end for nothing'. The report continues:

> Corio looked at its best yesterday, and the fair green fields, with the bay sparkling in the distance greatly appealed to

the metropolitan visitors, whose eyes were evidently tired of bricks and mortar. The double line of cars extended for nearly half a mile and formed a very fine sight. On return the visitors alighted at the Corio Hall, where afternoon tea was dispensed. Owing to the large crowd arriving at the hall almost simultaneously and its limited size, a section had to wait for some time outside the door before it could enter, but all were eventually served...

At five in the evening, once again two trains had been laid on to take the thousand visitors to Geelong where they were given another free dinner, which the MSD had arranged to pay for, 'at the leading hotels and cafes. The return to the capital was begun at 7.25 and 8 pm respectively, the interval after dinner being filled in with sightseeing'.[27]

The MSD Company, from its unadorned name up, was always modern. C. J. harnessed a new miracle – radio broadcasting – to help publicise Corio. Cedric Johnston arranged for C. J., in Corio, to speak to a crowd at the Shepparton Show in late October. He would be heard via a Parosovox receiving four-valve set, then through a loudspeaker. 'Good afternoon, ladies and gentlemen of Shepparton', came the salutation at 3.30 pm promptly (many onlookers, unused to hearing a voice without a person attached, responded: 'Good afternoon, Mr. DeGaris'). C. J. relayed a few choice facts about Corio, then handed over to George Jelbart, in the flesh, who spoke expansively about his company's decision to relocate to Geelong. The *Shepparton Advertiser*, reporting on this event, said that Jelbart was on hand to 'dispel some of the doubts which had existed as to the intentions of the firm', but was far too polite to say what these doubts might have been or how Jelbart responded to them.[28]

C. J.'s approach was never prescribed or obvious; he experimented with campaigns in imaginative ways. The blandest thing about his promotion of the Windulva estate was its name. C. J. had already considered the name of his and Rene's Mildura home for a subdivision in 1919; revisiting it was a throwback to a time that must have seemed much longer ago than a mere six years.[29] The estate – an enormous area 24 miles from Melbourne in the Croydon area – was, C. J. hoped, to be another MSD triumph. But awareness, once again, was everything, and in this instance there was no Jelbart Brothers or Phoenix Film Co. to capture the imagination. Instead, he was going to have to encourage his audience to whip up its own excitement about Melbourne's future. He launched a competition for the most imaginative use for Windulva. He tantalised his readership with its possibilities, making reference to the most modern developments of the day, perhaps even cocking a snook at Grant Hervey:

> Wonder what it could be used for? Too big for a park. Too small for a new state. Not quite big enough for a rival Federal Capital. Also too close to Melbourne. Bit large for a radio station. Or a golf course…Might make a racecourse. Yes, that's an idea. A racecourse. But there are plenty of racecourses now…[C. J.] said "It will be a most ambitious and unusual proposition."[30]

It was revealed ultimately that MSD was offering '£100 in cash for 250 word essays' to engage ordinary people imaginatively with their city's expansion:

> We know what we are going to do with "Windulva"
>
> But what would YOU do?
>
> So many Ideas Prevail as to the Purposes for which "The Mystery Sub-Division" Is to be used, that we would like to ascertain what you would do with it, if you owned it.[31]

The judges of the competition were E. Kennedy, the Melbourne *Sun's* real estate editor; G. H. Watkins, of the MSD, and Walter Burley Griffin. It seems likely that Griffin was also a shareholder in the MSD.[32] Harold Hansell, another voice from C. J.'s past, gave the 'poet-artist's viewpoint' on Windulva. He wrote:

> When I stood on the fairy green hills and watched the river winding like a ribbon of silver below – when I gazed across the lemon gums tipped with gold in the sunshine over towards the Ranges, up hill and down dale, miles and miles away on the one side, and out to the Christmas Hills on the other – peaceful, restful, quiet – I realised that I was gazing upon a little masterpiece from the Studio of Nature…WINDULVA IS THE LAND OF DREAMS COME TRUE…Nearly a million people are living within twenty miles of it – in ignorance of its beauty – All that I personally hope is that you will let them remain in ignorance – and leave it alone.[33]

Additional 'view-points' came from the MSD's sub-manager, James Keogh; surveyor and engineer L. H. Webber; and Forte, as the landscape gardener. Prospective buyers at Windulva, travelling in the area, might also be alerted to the potential of the 240 acre 'Seejay Estate', on the railway line.[34] Another, the 126-lot St Ruvia Estate, was located just north of one designed by the Griffins for the Rev Cheok Hong Cheong in 1921, and includes, touchingly, a small 'Veema Avenue'.[35]

In the midst of the Windulva and Corio campaigns, C. J. received a telegram at his office on the 'DeGaris floor' of Capitol House. It read: 'You are commanded by the Mystery Club to attend at Anzac House, 6 p.m. tonight, for dinner.' Always up for an adventure, he accepted the 'Mystery Club's' command, to find it a surprise party held by his staff at the MSD. All present congratulated him on the success of his first year of business under the MSD mantle. 'In characteristic phrases', it was reported, 'Mr. DeGaris acknowledged the unexpected tribute to himself, and demonstration of staff loyalty'.[36]

'I haven't got a bob'

Anyone keeping a close watch on DeGaris' affairs, and those of the MSD, would have seen the name of Joseph Woolf – a key member of the MSD board and the man C. J. would soon describe as his 'unworthy protégé' – appear an unusually high number of times in press reports of MSD activities. None of it was particularly happy news, either. Overextending his business into Melbourne's peripheries, C. J. had, somehow, come unstuck yet again.

An 'unexpected series' of financial disappointments had taken place, making it 'imperative to stop payments of cheques'. The company was 'saddled...with an overdraft of £9,500'.[37] The MSD was trying to flush its system with quick cash when it announced 'Two BIG Auction Sales' in the second half of December of land at the Heart of Rosebud (the amount of lots available unspecified) and another estate in Ringwood, the Best Part Estate, of sixty-nine lots ('without doubt the Gem of the Hillside suburbs').[38] On 11 November, less than three weeks after the triumphant Mystery Club dinner, C. J. was holding a meeting at the Melbourne Town Hall (a minute's walk from Capitol House) with the MSD's creditors.[39] The *Traralgon Record* noted that one of its residents, Gerald English, had been appointed to a committee to assist in running the company, 'which is a thoroughly go-ahead and up-to-date one.' It added:

> Perhaps there is no more experienced capable and optimistic person than C. J. DeGaris, and with an influential body assisting him, there is no telling to what heights the Company may rise. It is a good thing for Victoria as a whole that the big estates around Melbourne should be cut up and settled.[40]

These words almost sound like the interior monologue of a very nervous investor, which English almost certainly was at this time. The MSD was not going to simply devolve to an everyday real estate concern, however, much less peter out, and C. J. would not be C. J. if he was not ready to produce another extraordinary coup. Many creditors had no doubt come to the meeting expecting to suffer a considerable downturn in their fortunes and perhaps to lose everything in the collapse of a company set up almost entirely (at least from C. J.'s point of view) to mop up the mess of another company. The ace up C. J.'s sleeve was surely unexpected even by the most optimistic or fervent C. J. DeGaris supporter.

C. J. announced to the meeting that:

> Areas of land in our estates at Coburg and Windulva are among the four which we have under offer to Henry Ford. And I understand Mr. Grandjean, of the Canadian Ford Co., is going to discuss the matter with us when he arrives in Melbourne.

With these words, it was reported, C. J. 'convinced a big meeting of creditors that financial disaster could be averted by forming the company into a limited liability concern'. The creditors, who had come to hear that their money was irreparably lost, adopted his suggestion unanimously, and cheered C. J.

> The greater portion of the liabilities, he stated, was confined to less than 50 people; £6,000 was owing to 120 others. "Many of these", he continued, "have actually made money from the company and anything owing is profit. By December the company would have been more solid ground. But the biggest investors have sufficient faith to offer to cancel their profit, and accept a return of capital, plus interest."[41]

He admitted to the 200 men and women present that 'the business was too big for one man to carry' (a backhander to the sixteen other 'reasons' for the MSD's success so often touted by the MSD advertising throughout the year) but that he was understandably proud of what had been achieved. He claimed that the company 'could be quite easily reconstructed and show a profit of at least £325,000'. He suggested:

> A moratorium to curtain the amount of money required to carry on.
> The formation of a limited liability company with: -
> (a) Preference shares to subscribers of fresh capital
> (b) Ordinary shares to those with capital already invested in the business and creditors
> (c) Deferred shares in lieu of profits already accrued
>
> He suggested a board of directors of ten, and did not wish to be one of them. His own services could be retained or eliminated as the meeting desired; but he heartily wished to build these estates into the progressive suburbs which he knew they would become.[42]

'The size of the figures seem rather terrifying, when you remember the total value of the estates is £700,000', he told the meeting. As had been the case at Kendenup, C. J. was once again dangling a veiled threat of wider social calamity, without genuinely confronting the truth that the problem was, at least in part, of his own making. 'If this company is liquidated', he said, 'confidence in this land and land values generally will be destroyed'.[43] He came close to blaming those present for trusting him in the first place.

The meeting's chairman, the secretary of the Bank of Victoria, L. McNaughton, reminded those present that C. J. had been 'applying profits to paying debts previously incurred, and which he was under no responsibility to pay'.

> He has had previous troubles, but understand, that has got nothing to do with the Melbourne Subdivisions Company.
> Personally, I am perfectly satisfied to give him 12 months' run in the shape of a limited company. I'll get my money back, so will you. His only trouble has been that he was too optimistic…
> I am a secured creditor, and the moratorium extended by the secured creditors will allow the company to make enough

money to pay the unsecured as well. The secured creditors could foreclose, but they won't.[44]

'I haven't got a bob', C. J. told the meeting, when accused of funnelling profits due MSD investors to Kendenup. 'My home and everything else is mortgaged to try to keep the company afloat.' A board of ten men was appointed, and the meeting ended with cheers for C. J.[45]

The Rosebud auction was not, however, a success. C. J. was close to nervous collapse, and working up to 20 hours a day.[46] People he referred to as 'squealers', investors wanting special treatment, had been worrying him. Violet knew that he did not want to pass this worry on to her.[47] She reasoned her illness was probably why he had stopped discussing business matters with her. They decided to take a holiday, and on Christmas Eve travelled with Albert de Pledge, Violet's sisters, and some other MSD staff to their 'fair-sized' house in Rosebud[48] – C. J. may not have had a 'bob' but Violet had taken out mortgages on at least two properties through his machinations.

At Rosebud, C. J. spent a lot of time writing letters, though he also found time to go bathing. He asked de Pledge if he had any money put aside. De Pledge replied that any spare money he had he sent back to his family in Kendenup. C. J. travelled to Melbourne on Boxing Day to pick up Winnie, Dulcie and Vera, and bring them back to Rosebud for a few days; he also drove to the Roslyn Street house on 3 January to fetch some clothes for Violet and Veema.[49]

The holiday was due to end on 4 January. On Sunday, the 3rd, the holiday group had a sing song around the piano, and everyone went to bed around midnight. C. J. told de Pledge he might take the Packard to Melbourne the next morning, and asked him to check its condition, which he did by the bright moonlight. C. J. told Violet that he had some papers to take to the office early in the morning, and that he would not wake her when he left but he would return to drive her and Veema back to Hawthorn by 9 am.[50] She heard him leave the house at 3 am.[51]

The next morning she found his letters and his vow to drown himself at Mentone. Albert de Pledge recalled:

> I was standing in the backyard when the Austin girls called. I could see they were crying. "Albert there is a letter for you." It was from C. J. telling me I would understand and I would do as much as I could for Mrs. DeGaris helping them to get back to Melbourne. There was a five pound note enclosed...
>
> Mrs. DeGaris was very upset. She also had a letter from C. J. indicating what he was going to do. We all had his suicide in mind by this time...I helped Mrs. DeGaris and her sisters, all very upset, to get back to their home in Melbourne doing whatever I could, which was very little under the circumstances.[52]

The newspapers were, of course, ablaze that afternoon and the following morning – then, gradually, across the whole nation – with news of the last chapter in the extraordinary meteoric rise and catastrophic fall of the remarkable C. J. DeGaris. His fame and prominence, and his ability to capture the hearts and minds of thousands of men and women, to encourage them to follow him wherever he led them, was legion. It had ended with his personal life, and the ideals as described in his many letters to friends and family, as tabloid fodder. All signs pointed to a lonely and despairing man ending his life at an empty beach in Port Philip Bay.

11

Eight lost days

C. J. didn't die at Mentone.

At first, the possibility that his body was in the harbour was taken seriously by police and public alike. Crowds of people gathered on the beach in the days following his disappearance to help find it.[1] Sergeant Tennent commented that, sharks and sea lions notwithstanding, a body in the bay should be washed ashore with the northwest wind and tide. The water was shallow, and it was possible to walk 150 yards from the shore to anything deeper.[2]

On 7 January, a man called Roy Edwards was fishing in a dinghy with a companion near Albert Park Beach, when it capsized. Edwards resolved to swim for shore but disappeared. Much was made of this example amongst armchair experts discussing C. J.'s disappearance.[3] However, the search for C. J.'s body was abandoned two days after the alarm was raised, and instead Superintendent Potter had C. J.'s description circulated nationally.[4] He was now being regarded as a missing person, perhaps a man who had lost his mind. If he was not drowned at Mentone, though, where was he?

Suddenly he was everywhere and nowhere. It was emphatically stated by a passenger on a 'Trans' (trans-Australian) train that C. J. had travelled to Perth.[5] A friend of C. J.'s told detectives he saw him boarding the express for Sydney at Spencer Street on Monday night.[6] Dave Kingston, a local who claimed to know C. J., said he saw him walk from his car in the direction of Mentone. Kingston, who was out looking for his horse, said C. J. was fully dressed.[7] He could possibly have walked for half an hour from Mentone and caught the 5.39 pm train at Cheltenham – arriving at Flinders Street Station at 6.12 pm and catching a train to Sydney from Spencer Street Station.[8] The police, reviewing C. J.'s historical proclivity for incorporating aeroplanes into interstate travel, also theorised that after abandoning the Packard he 'boarded an aeroplane, in which he travelled as far as Albury', thence to Sydney by train.[9] Naturally, this would have entailed a great deal of plotting beforehand.

Alternatively, he may have dressed as a woman.[10] The Sydney *Daily Telegraph* suggested that C. J.:

> probably motored as far as Goulburn – a comparatively easy stage in such circumstances – and arriving there at midnight on Monday, caught the mail train from Cooma. That train travels through sleepy and not very conspicuous hours, and many opportunities would be afforded the "lady" to change "her" disguise.[11]

This theory was supported by those who said he had done so before, for fun: a 'well-known Bendigo singer' claimed that, in amateur theatricals, C. J. took delight in making up and that 'One of his popular parts was that of a girl'.[12] Jack Munro, the general manager of Stadiums Limited, remembered C. J. from the trip to America on the *Niagara* two years prior, telling the Sydney *Sun*:

> He appeared at a dance dressed as a woman. His make-up was extraordinarily good. As a matter of fact, no one on board

could detect the change, and everyone wondered who the woman was. Later, DeGaris purposefully gave himself away and the passengers who attended the dance were much amused at the way in which they had been duped.[13]

This talent, incidentally, was not noted publicly before C. J.'s disappearance. Perhaps it was a theory evolved on the fly.

A letter, sent by C. J. before he disappeared, arrived for the board at the MSD. It read, in part:

> My only excuse for the past eight weeks is that I have certainly been subnormal, or abnormal, and all this dated from the double strength of domestic illness, which at one time seemed hopeless, and my worried appearance caused by that illness being mistaken for financial worry. But for that illness in December I would have had the biggest and most genuine grouping of syndicated estates, each with a legitimated developmental policy, ever seen in Australia. At that time it was easy to get all the money we wanted and more, much more. But panic is more infectious than confidence, and a panic was begun through my domestic illness worry being mistaken for financial worry, and the idea soon spread that we were up against it, and one after another withdrew promised financial support until I allowed panic to grip me, too, and did things which I would gladly undo, if I could. So far as I know amongst our investors and creditors although there will be cases of heavy losses and hardships, I do not think there will be a single instance of ruin and simply in my weakness I got what I could to satisfy special cases which worried me. On every hand this instance of my weakness and futility is also sufficient evidence to me that I had become a menace to those of whom I think most, because it was always to them I turned.[14]

On Tuesday 6 January, the day following C. J.'s disappearance, there was a special MSD meeting at Capitol House 'conducted in private'.[15] Joseph Woolf was on holiday at Lorne, 150 km from Melbourne, and in his absence the 'round-table conference' decided not to issue C. J.'s four-page statement, which he had asked be made simultaneously available to all metropolitan newspapers.[16] Board member W. J. Morgan told the *Argus* 'We are like sheep without a shepherd, and we have not arrived at any decision'.[17] Whether their shepherd was Woolf or C. J. is unclear.

Woolf had to continually reassure investors and potential customers that all was well. To the Adelaide *Register*, he said:

> I have no idea whether Mr. C J DeGaris is dead or alive, but with all my heart I hope he is alive. If Mr. DeGaris had not lost his nerve he would have cleaned up a certain clear profit out of the company of £150,000 or £200,000. That profit will still be made for Mrs. DeGaris, and all investors in the company will make large profits, and buyers of blocks are thoroughly secured. Mr. DeGaris was a land expert without equal. All his purchases of estates were sound, and were completed before he broke down under nervous strain...Mr DeGaris was a genius, a man I admired and loved. He was straightforward and honest, and close examination of the affairs of the company shows that he has secured every one who invested or lent him money... He controlled 30 estates, and the administration of any one of them required a clever brain...Every man has his breaking strain, but we break in many different ways. He had an iron nerve and a big heart...[18]

He told the Melbourne *Herald* that to assume C. J. 'may be hiding is to presume that his mind is still keen and efficient, whereas all the evidence goes to show that his mind had reached its breaking point'.[19] Yet, he added, C. J. was correct in suggesting that his presence was a detriment to the business:

> If one could imagine some omniscient being who desired to serve DeGaris's best interests, and the interests of everybody

else, one would have to imagine the omniscient friend saying to DeGaris, "Your presence at this stage is making difficulties. You had better go away for a while..."[20]

To the Adelaide *Advertiser,* Woolf explained the way he saw C. J.'s state of mind. He used an ill-advised metaphor to discuss a man who may have just drowned:

> The whole position as I see it is this. If the strongest swimmer had 50 people hanging on to his arms and legs he would go under. Of course he would. But here you have the case of a man with not 50 but 500 people clinging on to him. He has a powerful mentality, but with the insistent calls of these 500 people that mentality has been prevented from functioning just as the limbs of a swimmer would be paralysed were a group of people all clinging wildly to them.[21]

Violet told the Sydney *Sun* that C. J.'s disappearance was 'like a thunderbolt'.[22] Many papers reported her angry words:

> I do not need any of the sympathy of the public. Whatever people say about my husband now, they cannot say any more than they have said. He is gone. I feel sure of that. All his clothes are here...The trouble is that with him everything was for other people and nothing for himself.[23]

The day that C. J. disappeared, Violet received a writ from the Melbourne *Sun* for unpaid advertising, totalling £1,100.[24] As if in response to this, C. J.'s letter to the MSD board from beyond his watery grave was prescient:

> I want to make it clear that Mrs. V. M. DeGaris has no knowledge of the ramifications or operations of the business. It is in her name, but in all things she has been under my domination and has acted exactly on my suggestions. Especially

is this so since 25th September (the date baby was born), when for 10 weeks she hovered between life and death, and is not even now fully recovered. Another thing is that there are no secret resources in her or my possession. This is one aspect of high finance in which I have most conspicuously failed. I have never put anything on one side for myself, wife or children, although I should have done, as it has been made plain to me that most people think I have.[25]

There were further demands on C. J. or his estate. On 22 December – that is, just prior to leaving for Rosebud – C. J. had exchanged £300 cash from a shareholder, the prosperous and well-known coachbuilder Charles Francis ('Frank') Northcott, for a cheque from his Mount Barker bank.[26] It would appear that there *were* adequate funds in the bank to cover the cheque, but the bank, for reasons unclear, failed to honour it. It was later suggested that Northcott went to the police at the urging of Meredith Roberts Green, another MSD shareholder.[27]

C. J. ceased being merely a curious case of a missing man who had lost his wits, and became a fugitive, suspected of making off with another man's money. A warrant was issued for his arrest, publicised not only by newspapers and police networks but on the new radio station 3LO; wireless broadcasting was less than a year old in Victoria but already making major changes in the way news became available.[28] The extraordinarily ramshackle diffusion of news in Australia in 1925 can be gleaned from one example: the Cairns *Northern Herald* first reported his suspected suicide at Mentone eight days after he had disappeared.[29]

The only guest at the Palace Hotel

The waterside suburb of Mortlake is 13 km from central Sydney. The Australian Gas and Light Company's gasworks kept it a suburb of working people; the smell drove away those who did not need to live nearby, but the works themselves employed 1,400 men.[30] In the early 1920s the Palace Hotel had changed licensee, from Lesser Opitz and his family to Frank White, and his.[31] When White took over the hotel licence from the Opitzes, he quickly moved to demolish the existing 'old-fashioned'[32] structure and erect a new one 180 m away.[33] In early 1925 the old hotel was still operating, the new one nearly built.

At 6.30 in the morning of Tuesday 6 January, a portly man in a white panama hat and dark 'goggles' (glasses) alighted from Mortlake tram terminus 'walking in a decidedly uncomfortable manner'.[34] It was the last place an American visitor would be likely to select for lodgings,[35] and Frank White said as much: his hotel was 'not good enough'.

'I have come here for peace and quietude', replied O. Young, 'and it will do me'.[36] Young was a journalist.[37] He was a widower, with a daughter living in Los Angeles.[38] A friend had recommended the place; he was in Australia to write articles for an American newspaper syndicate.[39]

He asked to be recommended a good car service – that is, a man to drive him on the days he was in town. White asked why he did not take the tram, and Young replied that he preferred a car for its versatility. 'I'm not conversant with the city', he said. 'Those goldarned things set you down anywhere. Now, if I get an auto it'll take me right to the place I want to go to'.[40]

White recommended a driver, Ernest W. Handley. Young had a list of tasks, written in pencil on a piece of scrap paper. They drove first to Parramatta Road, and at a mercer's he purchased a small boy's skull cap. Handley then drove him to Annandale post office, where he posted some letters.[41] They then proceeded to the city and Union Company's office in George Street to inquire about sailings.[42] Here, he told the booking clerk that he was Canadian, that his parents were British, and that he was planning on relocating to New Zealand – thus keeping his travels safely within the Empire.[43] He bought a second-class ticket. Whether this was his preference is uncertain; there may not have been any first-class tickets available because of recent strike action. Young then asked Handley to drive him to Elizabeth Street: 'I want to buy a typewriter'. He bought a Corona, then said: 'I want to see this city, so drive me home another way'.[44] That evening, the sound of the typewriter was heard from his hotel room, though he also typed on his balcony.

The Palace Hotel's Frank White had three sons: one also called Frank, as well as Alan and Ernie; they had a friend and neighbour, Hubert Solomon. The boys were probably in their early teenage years, or just approaching (Hubert was nearly 13).[45] They were intrigued by Young, the hotel's only guest, and he was friendly towards them, giving them books and telling them about America. They noticed that, when Young was typing on his balcony, he always faced the roadway, with an uninterrupted view of anyone approaching.[46] They also peeked through his keyhole, and noticed that he did not wear the oversize dark glasses indoors.[47]

The next day, Wednesday, Young asked Handley to pick him up at noon, and then requested he be driven to Burwood post office. Whatever he did there, it was very fast. On returning, he told Handley, 'I want you to get my rug and suitcase from the hotel and take them to the Union Company's wharf in Margaret-street. They are labelled "Mr. Leslie, berth 1, cabin 81, steerage"'.[48] On the same day, NSW police searched the *Sonoma*, bound from Sydney for San Francisco, just prior to her departure, in case C. J. was on board.[49]

Young spent freely, although he did not drink. He tipped the hotel's waitresses with half a crown under the plate, as well as five shillings to the cook.[50] He would always retire at sunset and rise at dawn.[51] However, he was keen to engage anyone who came into his orbit with a detailed account of his abiding interest, the eradication of prickly pear. He told White about his interest in this topic and 'the acquisition of suitable land in Queensland' to undertake his plan. He would be absorbed in articles on prickly pear whenever anyone entered his room. He claimed to have typed a letter to American friends expressing his belief that millions could be made by obtaining land currently rendered useless by this pest. He believed that the best solution was to clear land with tractors fitted with knives.[52] The cactus had value in pulp form, and he would start a business in America for this product, as well as the passionfruit he would replace it with.[53] Indeed, Young talked so much about prickly pear that White became suspicious, not of his identity but his intentions: 'I thought perhaps that at any time he would spring it on me to take up shares.'[54]

The DeGaris mystery was a cause célèbre, and Frank Jr, Alan, Ernie and Hubert were suspicious of Young's true identity. They showed White a newspaper photograph of C. J. upon which they had drawn dark glasses – there was a striking similarity.[55] White telephoned the Burwood police, and confided his suspicions.

Burwood constables Cameron and Parker were, admittedly, hampered by the fact that they had not been sent a description or a picture of C. J., though of course these were available in daily newspapers. One of the boys was sent instead to ask Young if he could inspect White's new car with his acquaintances – Cameron and Parker, in plain clothes. He did so, and quickly made friends with the men. Young told them he had been eight months in Australia, landing in Fremantle.[56] He made much of the subtle difference in terms used in the USA and Australia, such as the 'drug store' and the 'chemist'.[57] He professed ignorance of Australian slang, such as 'bosker', meaning 'wonderful'.[58]

The constables noted that Young had sandy hair streaked with grey, and that he was evidently trying to grow a moustache; while his hair was not black, his nascent moustache was. His large, smoked, black-rimmed spectacles hid his eyes: Constable Cameron determined their colour, blue, by standing alongside him and looking at him sideways.[59]

The constables were of the opinion that the man was in disguise, but that whoever he was, he was not C. J. DeGaris, and said as much to White when Young had left them. 'He did not walk with a free gait', said one, 'and there was obviously padding underneath his clothes. His fair gingery hair was all ruffled as if he had omitted to brush it before he left his bedroom'.[60] This was comedic police ineptitude which papers such as *Smith's Weekly* would find riotous. Even Senior Detective M. J. Davey, of Victorian Police, was to express disbelief at the merry dance on which he and his NSW colleagues had been led. 'It was like a paper chase', Davey said. 'He might as well have gone away in a distinctive uniform.'[61]

Later, Young asked White who his friends were, and White – cunningly – told him they were plainclothes detectives, who had visited on suspicion that he was C. J. DeGaris but had decided he could not be. 'I watched him closely as I said this', White said, 'and though there was no movement of his face I noticed that his chest heaved, indicating emotion under strong control. "I will have to ring up my car driver for the morning. This might cause a bit of delay. They might still think I am this guy, and I had better get away earlier." He was about to ring for the driver when the driver rang for him'.[62] Young told White that anyone who thought he was C. J. was making 'a big mistake. DeGaris is a little fellow; I'm fat'. Here he rubbed his chest and abdomen to make his point.[63] Observers estimated his weight at 14 stone (90 kg).[64]

Young left the Palace Hotel at 8.45 the next morning,[65] evading the police – who returned to the hotel – by a matter of minutes.[66] He asked Handley to drive to Strathfield post office, presumably to post more letters, and then requested to be driven around Parramatta Park to reach his ship, the *Maheno*, at 11.15 am. Handley's wife was a passenger in the car at this point. 'I wonder if the police still believe I am DeGaris', he mused, looking anxiously through the back of the car as though he imagined they might be followed.[67] He had his typewriter, his suitcase and the travelling rug, the last two labelled with the name 'Leslie'. He explained that Martin Leslie was a friend who would be travelling with him and he had arranged for the luggage to go under that name.[68] He explained to Handley that he might miss the boat altogether,[69] and told the driver to wait for him at a hotel in Erskine Street. He pointed it out, and Handley and his wife waited, but Young did not return.[70]

Young had written down a list of addresses, all but one of which he called at with Handley. The only one he did not visit was Mr and Mrs Mitchell's second-hand clothes shop at 139b Bathurst St, Sydney.[71] On the day after the *Maheno* sailed, a man in dark glasses, wearing a light suit, a diamond ring and a diamond in his tie visited the shop. He said he was a Canadian Jew looking for a family he could board with. He had been staying at the Metropole Hotel and found it to be like a prison, 'I cannot stand the Christian cooking', he told the proprietor. 'I want Jewish cooking.'[72]

The *Maheno*

The *Maheno* had been in service for twenty years, most of that time taking passengers between Australia and New Zealand, but also as a hospital ship and troop carrier in Europe in the Great War; she served at Gallipoli. The voyage from Sydney to Auckland would take four days, and it left on time at midday on Friday.

By this time police were concerned that C. J. DeGaris would be on the *Maheno*, attempting to leave Australia. However, there was also considerable suspicion that the evidence was too neat; that O. Young, with his American accent, prickly pear obsession and letter-writing enthusiasm, was overly obvious (if not obvious enough for the Burwood constables). The law moved slowly, and information and disinformation flowed freely. Many of C. J.'s associates, for instance, believed he could not operate a typewriter.[73] There was also much uncertainty about whether, like Young, C. J. had a full set of false teeth, or only partial.[74] C. J. had a full set of false teeth, probably at the urging of his sister Mary, who routinely recommended complete extraction for bodily health.

Young continued to be dissected in his absence, not least through the efforts of the White boys and Hubert Solomon.

After the police had examined his room and found very little, the boys found some keys on a string in a drawer. The eight keys had two tags, one stating: 'These keys are for the locks described below'.[75] The other tag bore the label 'C. J. DeGaris, east door'.[76] They also discovered some materials hidden under the linoleum. Torn up telegram forms bore the words 'Mrs' on one, 'de' on another, and 'Garis' on a third.[77] A brown wig was also found.[78] There was also a ten-inch-long braid of twisted hair, closely compressed, and frizzled at one end.[79] 'It is considered', Sydney's *Sunday Times* claimed, 'that DeGaris had used some of this stuff in the wig transformation of his hair. As he was disguised, the description was that of a man 52 years, 5ft 7in high, very stout, sallow complexion, thin hair parted in the middle'.[80] If anybody thought to wonder whether the boys had planted evidence, it was not publicly suggested. The staff at the MSD, when contacted, said there was no east door to Capitol House – but they were wrong; the entire building faces east.[81] In any case, the keys were not labelled 'Capitol House'. The boys, having done more than most to uncover C. J., opined as one: 'We wish he would come back'.[82]

Melbourne detective Superintendent Montague sent a wireless message to the *Maheno*.[83] Detective Watkins of Sydney police told the press, 'Emphatically he is DeGaris. There is no doubt about it.'[84] The *Maheno*, however, communicated to the *Herald*: 'Up to present can find no one answering description of the man you enquire for.'[85] At the same time, writs against Violet were coming thick and fast: one from the Bank of NSW was for £9,355.[86]

Similarly, while William 'Snowy' Brown, a forecabin-steward, immediately had suspicions of the passenger 'Martin Ernest Leslie',[87] some Melbourne detectives were of the opinion that this man might have been a friend of C. J.'s who was 'dragging a red herring across the trail'.[88] Nobody saw Leslie board the ship, and no-one knew what had happened to Young, whether they were the same person, or if one or the other or both of them was C. J. DeGaris.

Martin Leslie was 36 years old, a farmer and, like O. Young, a widower.[89] He shared a second-class cabin with three other men and did not, therefore, encounter any of the saloon passengers who knew C. J. DeGaris. He was popular with his fellow steerage passengers as a 'charming, entertaining fellow'.[90] Although he seemed worried and nervous, he entered into spirited conversation at meals. Like Young, Leslie had a thick accent; Leslie's was American, and he wore a huge pair of tortoiseshell-rimmed glasses, tinted dark brown. His hair was parted in the middle. If a steward entered the cabin suddenly, he would give a violent start then pass off the situation with a commonplace remark. Sometimes, when awakened for early morning tea, he would shout out, then ask the steward to repeat what he had said.

On second day of the voyage, Brown waited until Leslie was in the dining saloon and went to his cabin to examine his luggage. There, he found a pair of dilapidated pyjamas marked with the name DeGaris in ink. He reported on this to the chief steward, who advised the captain. The pyjamas were taken to the captain's cabin and carefully examined. Violet was told about the pyjamas and responded that C. J. 'had no pyjamas that bore his name, apart from old ones now used as dusters'.[91] Leslie's pyjamas were, however, 'dilapidated'; perhaps they had been retrieved from amongst the 'dusters'. Violet was adamant this was not the case, claiming that 'the fact that his name was on the pyjamas found in the cabin...makes me doubt the identity' of the man on the *Maheno*.[92]

C. J. never spoke publicly about his decision to publish Joseph Furphy's *Rigby's Romance,* but there is a feature of the book that might well have had a significant impact on its publisher. *Rigby's Romance* is a book about nothing. Rigby's own story as he sits round the campfire, failing to keep his appointment with Kate Vanderdecken, is however about something. The tale is of the marital and financial trials of one Fritz Wetterliebenschaff. Discovering that his marriage, which he had imagined would be a life of property ownership and other riches, is in fact exposing him to greater debt, Fritz loses his mind. When he comes back into reality he finds himself 'standing on the deck of a 'Frisco steamer, with a small portmanteau in his hand, whilst a peculiar sensation of coldness on his upper lip seemed to convey...that his moustache was amongst the sweepings of a barber's shop'. Fritz is attempting to flee the country under a fraudulent identity, pretending his German accent is Norwegian.[93]

Several jumps ahead of the hunt

> This morning Davey received by post, sent anonymously, a doggerel parody on "The Blue Bells of Scotland" entitled "C. J. D. G.".
>
> "Whoever composed the verses," remarked the detective, "exhibited a very perverted sense of humour. Such communications neither assist the police in their work, nor are they fair to a man against whom a serious allegation has been made."
>
> – *Riverine Herald*, 10 January 1925[94]

Once it became fair to assume that C. J. might not be dead after all, the parodies and lighthearted recaps came fast in the Australian media. The public was hungry for more of the story, and now that C. J. was apparently alive but incommunicado on the open sea, there was little to do but rake over the old tales. That said, Joseph Woolf seemed to have osmosed some of C. J.'s dramatic tendencies: he claimed the 'real secret of DeGaris's disappearance' was within the letter he wrote to the committee. They decided not to reveal or propagate this at their second meeting after his disappearance: 'it would not be wise to reveal it at present'.[95]

J. J. Simons was conspicuously silent on the subject of C. J., and *The Call* opined little on the latest disaster. Victor Courtney nevertheless published a tentative obituary on 9 January – just as the *Maheno* was leaving Sydney:

Had C. J. DeGaris interested himself in racehorses or poker-schools, he would have avoided the withering fire of criticism which has encompassed his end. If he had devoted his life to doing things for himself instead of endeavouring to help other people, the world would have left him alone, as it leaves all selfish people. DeGaris stands condemned of the heinous crime of trying to accomplish something. And that in Australia today seems almost the unforgiveable sin. [...]

"The goal was too far, and I fainted," wrote Adam Lindsay Gordon when worried by adversity, want and petty minds, he shot himself on St. Kilda Beach. Something the same may be written of DeGaris.

Let those who shot at DeGaris behind the hedge of privilege preen themselves on their victory...'[96]

The *Australian Worker* was much less sympathetic and indeed stooped to compare C. J. to Grant Hervey, suggesting that Hervey was a prophet without honour. 'It will be remembered', it claimed, 'that the equally theatrical Grant Hervey denounced DeGaris some time back – and was tarred and feathered in return'.[97]

Newcastle's *Morning Herald* was more equivocal, and like C. J. himself, suggested that strain and reach were the issue:

Described as a "live wire", he suddenly appeared as a champion of the raisin industry, and he taught us more about raisins than ever we had believed possible. He went raisin mad, and from raisins went to greater raisins – new settlements, new publicity methods, surely among the most daring ever conceived. This may be the secret of his undoing. His mind became inflated – he began to think on impossible lines.[98]

Smith's Weekly told a story suggesting a finicky, spoiled C. J., a man for whom luxury was not enough. The public had not seen this side of C. J. and indeed it probably did not exist. *Smith's* told of C. J. seeing a car, an 'Austin runabout' (whether this was a backhander against Violet is impossible to say, but that would not be beneath *Smith's*) in a city store and demanded it. However, it was already sold; C. J. insisted, and the buyer was persuaded to relinquish the car. C. J. paid, then returned it the next day. 'It was too small, his wife had decided'. He opted instead for a two-seater vehicle but he brought this back a few days later with a broken door. Paying for the repair and the difference, he purchased a much bigger car: a 'six-cylinder option'. He drove it away then, shortly afterwards, put it down as security on a new land purchase. 'There will always be a wide range in the public estimates of this man's character and ability', *Smith's* crowed. 'Fool or charlatan, which?'[99]

Elsewhere, those who still believed in C. J. remained staunch. One former employee was adamant that 'his wits are so keen that he is always bound to be several jumps ahead of the hunt'.[100] Violet remained loyal, telling the Sydney *Sunday Times*:

> I have never heard him say a cross word to anyone, living or dead. He always made excuses for his worst enemies and never had anything but a kind word for everyone. I hope he comes back to face the situation whatever it might be. I shall look after my husband's business and do all I can to bring it to a successful issue...I am torn between two fires, hoping for his safety and return, and thinking his mind is unbalanced and not knowing what he is doing or where he is.[101]

Curiously, she was also quoted as saying that 'if my husband does not return, it will not be my fault'.[102]

Radio communication between Sydney and the *Maheno* meant that when she anchored 'in the stream' for medical and customs reasons Auckland detectives were ready to board the ship, where Senior-Detective Ward found the man they were looking for leaning over the rail of the deck.[103]

'I believe you are DeGaris', said Ward.

'I never heard of DeGaris in my life', was the reply. 'My name is Leslie.'

'I am satisfied you are DeGaris, you will be arrested.'[104]

They took him downstairs, where he admitted he was C. J. DeGaris. He was then placed under arrest, and led down the gangway to the launch, pulling the brim of his Panama hat over his eyes. He was taken in a taxi to the police station from Kings Wharf. A name had been torn from inside his hat, and his pyjamas were nowhere to be seen – it was presumed he had thrown them overboard. In his typewriter case there was a bottle of prussic acid (hydrogen cyanide). The police would later claim he had written letters to Australian firms signed 'Leslie, en route to Honolulu'.[105]

When the news leaked out, the *New Zealand Herald* reported, the shock aboard the *Maheno* was immense. 'Among the women passengers, astonishment was even greater than that of the men. "Fancy that", said one lady, in a bewildered tone, "just fancy his being on board all the while. And after he had written all those letters about going to commit suicide"'.[106]

C. J.'s arrest in Auckland was such big news that a special run of the Melbourne *Sun* sold out.[107] The following day, Wednesday 14 January, he was in court. Hundreds of Aucklanders – new to the DeGaris myth, notwithstanding his visit in quite different circumstances two years prior – crowded into the court. Looking 'spic and span in a grey suit, and seemingly in excellent health, he smiled' when he was charged.[108]

He stated he had no intention of contesting deportation or seeking bail, but simply wished to return to Australia as quickly as possible. During others' discussion, he leaned against the dock railing, his arms folded. On leaving the court, photographers tried to take his picture: he shook his head and, still smiling, put his hands in front of his face.[109] He made the very unlikely claim that he did not know how he got on the *Maheno* and did not realise he was on it until he was at sea.[110] However, he was not being charged with travelling to New Zealand under a false name, and certainly any accomplices he may have had could relax: they would not be betrayed. In jail he was said to be 'passing his time not unpleasantly', waiting for a Melbourne detective to travel to Auckland to escort him home.[111] He sent a telegram to Violet:

> Northcott warrant executed New Zealand. Returning home first boat, defend. Terribly sorry all arrested developments. Newspapers will give particulars. Much upset because of strain. Retained Allan Moody, barrister. Consult Woolf. Love – Jack.[112]

Twenty-five years after Freud first wrote about parapraxis – a kind of forgetting that reveals one's real feelings – Violet made what might be considered a damning act against C. J. She left a bag of 'most private and important documents' for his forthcoming defence next to a post at Princes Bridge, when she got on a tram. She only noticed it missing when she got out at Auburn, half an hour later. Rushing back in a taxi she found the bag exactly where she left it.[113]

Most of the mysteries of O. Young and Martin Leslie were solved. But what of the Canadian Jew who visited the Mitchells after the *Maheno* had sailed, following Young's pencilled list of addresses? The Sydney police had a perfectly good explanation.

It was just 'one of those strange happenings which occur sometimes'.[114]

Infamy

Melbourne Sub-Divisions Company

Mr. DeGaris bought £700,000 worth of land, and raised £150,000 in the form of loans from so-called investors, promising a huge bonus in addition to the normal profit. Owing to the illness of his wife, his ordinary activity, both mental and physical, was partially paralysed, and a panic broke out among the investors that he was in financial difficulties.

Some time before Mr DeGaris disappeared, I sent a circular letter to all investors pointing out the necessity of raising an immediate sum of money, and asking them to safeguard their own interests by investing in shares for the carrying out of a scheme of reconstruction. Two issues of preference and ordinary shares, were notified, to produce £55,000 for the carrying on of the operations of the company.

Practically no response was received, each investor apparently taking it for granted that sufficient money would be forthcoming from the others.

> The only solution was Mr DeGaris' disappearance. With what I think was remarkable wisdom, he tried to gain the maximum of respect and sympathy. This would be created by the fact that he had had to drown himself owing to the lack of response to a business appeal.
>
> If the disappearance was more or less theatrical, it was still designed to achieve the same end. That it failed was owing to the fact that Mr Northcott took out a warrant for his arrest.[1]

Statements such as this early February missive from Joseph Woolf, as the company's chairman, show him desperately keen to maintain public confidence in the MSD. While it was solvent and profitable he could keep funds coming in, perhaps realise the riches estimated to result from MSD activity, and not scare Henry Ford away.

However, without C. J. making miraculous money and keeping all investors entertained, the shareholders could not maintain level heads. Meredith Green and Frank Northcott were not the only hostile shareholders: Leon Abrahams and Sol Lyons were additionally problematic. Banks, organisations and individuals were also pressing the MSD, and Violet, for moneys owed. Woolf prepared a draft prospectus proposing five types of share, labelled A to F, each according different rights and values.

The Abrahams family had substantial landholdings and shares in the entertainment industry; they were known as the 'Gun Abrahams' by dint of their ownership of the Small Arms Company. Lyons was a part of the Abrahams family by marriage.[2] Joseph Opas, another shareholder and committee member, was Joseph Woolf's nephew.[3] Early in 1924, with C. J.'s affairs in disarray, the Abrahams family had taken over the *Sunraysia Daily* and (according to *Truth*) installed Lyons 'to keep it afloat until a buyer could be found'.[4]

In the MSD collapse, Leon Abrahams had called on Woolf and demanded special 'B' class shares, threatening to 'smash the reconstruction scheme' if he did not receive them.[5] Woolf claimed he would sue Abrahams for £10,000 and that the money would then go to reconstruction. Many of the Abrahams men were very private people, a situation Woolf sought to exploit by suggesting that, if funds were not forthcoming to get Violet out of insolvency, 'all their private business would be published in *Truth*'.[6]

Woolf found Abrahams and Lyon controllable compared to Green and Northcott, who were outright wreckers. Woolf believed the men aspired to force collapse to gain MSD land at a cheaper price. They were explicitly discussed in the press as 'instrumental in having DeGaris arrested'.[7] Green did not deny this.[8] He claimed, however, to be in favour of reconstruction, and stated 'Mr Woolf says it is better for the scheme if DeGaris were to stay away, and I disagree. I say DeGaris should be brought back. I don't think that will affect the reconstruction scheme'.[9]

'All we want', said Woolf, 'is that DeGaris should not come back in custody, because this would have a bad effect on the reconstruction work'.[10] With this in mind, pressure was immense on Northcott to drop the charge against C. J.; Woolf claimed that the DeGaris incident had made the company 'the best advertised in the world' and that any loss of trust 'would be restored within a month'.[11] He needed C. J. to be seen as a man of honour, notwithstanding his disappearance, and was hoping to give him a job as a manager and expert advisor within the company. To massage C. J.'s image, Woolf's story of the burdens 'as heavy as millstones' on C. J. was calculated to make him seem superhuman for crashing through the impediments, rather than a fallen idol for succumbing to them.[12] *Truth* wondered whether C. J. would be met on his return by Woolf 'at the wharf with a brass band' and whether other MSD committee members would be 'the instrumentalists of that band?'[13]

In anticipation of poor publicity over shareholders' antagonisms to C. J. and each other, a meeting at the Melbourne Town Hall supper room was ticketed, with Woolf personally approving all applicants. Green was denied admission, as according to Woolf, 'it would not be wise to endanger your personal safety by allowing you admission to a meeting of those who consider their interests imperilled by your past attitude and actions towards the Reconstruction Committee'.[14] Woolf also denied admission to Northcott, Lyons and Abrahams, on the basis that he desired 'to avoid any upsetting influence at the meeting' by those who were 'endeavouring to "dynamite" the reconstruction scheme'.[15]

A Miss E. Downs was proposed as part of the new committee, but asked to be excused as she was ignorant of business affairs. She was then accused of taking notes and had the papers in her possession seized by Woolf. She wept for five minutes.[16] 'Those who had invested £150,000 in the company', Woolf announced, 'would be asked under the plan to contribute a proportion of the money required to carry on. Those who did not wish to contribute to the new company should relinquish their claims for the benefit of those who wished to stand by'.[17]

At the end of January, the Reconstruction Committee began to take on a confessional aspect, as motions passed that compelled shareholders to bear responsibility for past decisions: that if, for instance, 'a sympathetic response had been made to the appeal… for pro rata payments' C. J. would not have been 'forced to leave Melbourne', and that he did so 'for the purpose of leaving the committee unhampered by his presence'. Those present agreed to underwrite capital for reconstruction to £55,000.[18]

C. J. remained in the castle-like former barracks of the Mount Eden Gaol in Auckland, ostensibly passing time in a leisurely fashion, receiving visitors and catching up on his reading, although it is hard to imagine the prison was a pleasant place to reside. Much discussion was had in the press, and indeed behind closed doors at the MSD, about the contents of the letter C. J. had sent to Woolf and which apparently revealed 'the secret of his disappearance'.[19] At the end of January, Woolf released (at least part of) the letter to the press; the most controversial part of it was surely mention of the 'fiasco of the Rosebud sales'.[20]

Detective Davey left for New Zealand on the *Maheno* on 23 January to retrieve C. J.[21] They were to return on the *Marama*, the *Maheno*'s sister ship. On 7 February C. J. boarded the vessel two hours before it sailed, to avoid crowds.[22] Davey and C. J. were to develop some camaraderie on the journey. When the *Marama* was met at Sydney by massed reporters, NSW police's Inspector Mackey went aboard the vessel and stood in the dining room facing reporters, telling them he had not seen C. J. and was 'not particularly interested in his movements'. While he was distracting them, C. J. was bundled onto a waiting boat (some wharf labourers recognised him and 'gave him hearty cheers, and shouted words of encouragement') and taken to a train.[23] He and Davey travelled from Sydney to Albury, where they were met by MSD staff with documents to review(!). They then proceeded not to Spencer Street Station, where more journalists would amass, but to the suburban station of Essendon – and thence to police headquarters. It was 11 February, five weeks since he disappeared.[24]

When reporters could quiz him, C. J. could not help but peel back the curtain a little on the first week of his absence. It was like the director's commentary. He had not intended that Violet claim his life insurance, he said, at least 'until my body was found. I was in such a condition that I might have done anything'.[25] Handley, he told reporters, had been a 'good offsider' although he had 'some difficulty in understanding my Americanisms'. He had suspected that Constables Cameron and Parker, who had interviewed O. Young at White's request, were police, he said. 'I felt perfectly secure, and I think my disguise was perfect. I don't think my best friends would have known me.' He had gone into character: 'I was to all intents and purposes, in my own mind, Young. It sounds queer, but that is the way I felt'.[26] He also added that he had no intention of travelling beyond New Zealand (an unusual claim for a man who did not know what he was going to do) and that the 'pretty plain trail' he left had been deliberate: 'This reason I will disclose in good time.'[27] He also, however, contradicted this, claiming he had left the 'trail' from carelessness, 'because he was so upset'.²⁸

Returning to 'Camelot' on the Wednesday night, he spent a 'pleasant time' relating his experiences to his family. 'I told them much more than I have told the newspapers', he said, and in a perverse, almost macabre act he also 'dressed up in the disguise I adopted in Sydney. They all screamed with laughter'.²⁹ Surely at least some of the screaming, if screaming there was, was born of frustration and anguish, more than delight. Similarly, C. J. seemed to take a very cavalier attitude to the angst of his border collie, Prince, during his absence. 'This is the happiest dog in Australia, now', he told a journalist, 'he has been moping for the last five weeks'.³⁰

C. J., Violet, Veema and Prince, Adelaide *Mail*, 10 January 1925 p. 1.

Shortly after the *Marama* trip, another piece was added to the legend of C. J. DeGaris: that he had sold two blocks of land to Davey during the journey. At the same time as this idea was gaining currency, printed in a wide range of papers across the nation,[31] the Melbourne *Herald* quoted Davey saying, 'Coming down in the train yesterday, several jokes were passed, and DeGaris laughingly told a man that he had sold two blocks to me'.[32] The story was almost immediately discredited, but it was too good to not spread: such was the myth of C. J. and the desire, broadly speaking, to have him back. There was, indeed, a lot of good humour. C. J. visited the MSD offices on Friday, to talk to Woolf and staff. Papers noted a cavalier comment he made to the elevator operator at Capitol House, who asked him how he was. C. J. replied with a dad joke: 'Oh much the same as you. Having a few ups and downs'.[33]

Violet and Morgan attempted to meet with Northcott to persuade him to withdraw the warrant, but failing to achieve this, they went to Green instead. They offered him £600 but Green said that 'the matter had gone beyond that stage'.[34] However, on 18 February, Northcott's lawyer agreed to let the matter drop on payment of £300.[35] Northcott formally withdrew the charge on 6 March.[36] It was later revealed that C. J. *did* have adequate credit with the West Australian bank at the time he wrote the cheque, but that once he went missing, the bank refused to collaborate with the Criminal Investigation Branch and supply any further information. If there was more to this story (and there must surely have been) no-one was inclined to take it further at the time. Once C. J. paid his extradition expenses of £48 he would be a free man.[37] C. J. must have dwelt long and hard on the irony: had the West Australian bank not been so intransigent, he may well have made it to the USA, if indeed that was where he was headed.

As nominal head of the MSD, Violet might have taken heart from this news, although it was balanced by the claim of £10,456 against her – 'trading as the Melbourne Subdivisions Company' – which she owed to the *Sun* for advertising.

To rub salt in the wound, while it seemed Ford would come to Corio, it was likely that the MSD wasn't going to be there to gain advantage from it. Jelbarts, which had a controlling interest in the Garden Suburb land, was taking the attitude that the MSD had defaulted on its terms of purchase, and that Jelbarts had the right to sell directly to purchasers both existing and new. Woolf claimed that, while there might be some validity in the suggestion that the MSD had not furnished the promised money in time, Jelbarts had also arguably defaulted by failing to begin work on the factory it promised to build within a specified period.[38]

The investor Julius Solomon had promised to put up £5,000 to carry the company through reconstruction.[39] Soon, Woolf and Solomon were also at loggerheads. In April, they were in court, Woolf accusing Solomon of retaining a document – an annotated copy of one of the reconstruction proposals – Woolf had lent him. Woolf was of the opinion that Solomon believed he was now in a position to benefit financially from the demise of the MSD.

The case was struck out, but the MSD was left looking like more of a mess than ever, and was surely now far beyond death by a thousand cuts. Another meeting, on 8 April, saw 'warm' (that is, hostile) exchanges between Woolf and Green. An 'elderly shareholder' moved 'that Mr. Green be dumped out of the window'; Solomon declared the reconstruction scheme 'useless'; E. McGuinness, a member of the Reconstruction Committee, stated that had the MSD held Corio for another four months 'the profits would have totalled £1,000,000' and C. J. claimed that the meeting 'had clearly shown what had "driven him off his beam"'. Woolf resigned the chairmanship.[40] The MSD's sumptuous office furniture was auctioned off a fortnight later.[41]

The Victories of Failure
It is difficult to see precisely when C. J. made time to write his 'business romance', *The Victories of Failure*. He announced it on returning to Australia in early February; 'This book of mine

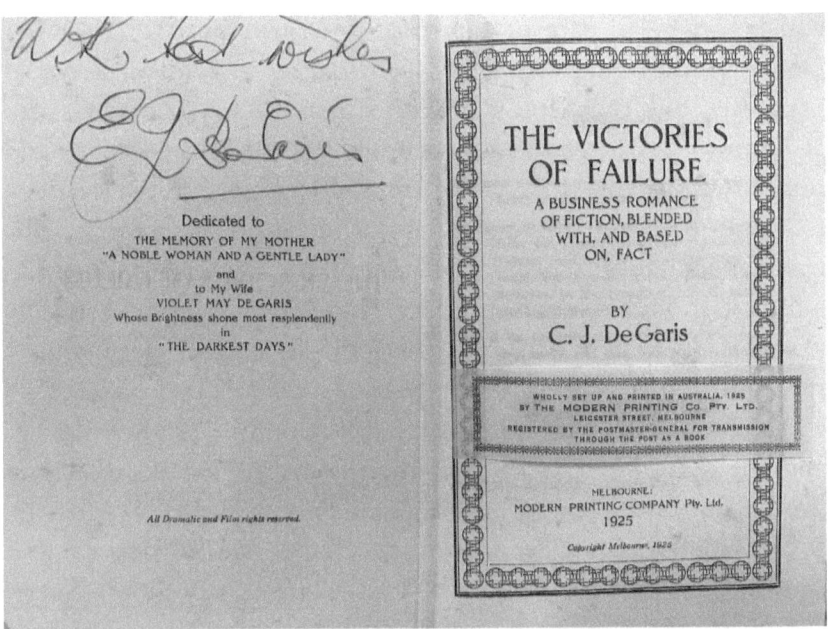

The Victories of Failure, with C. J.'s inscription. AUTHOR COPY.

will be wonderfully interesting.'[42] He claimed to have written it over the next ten weeks.[43] It was certainly complete by mid-May 1925.[44] Even if most of it was compiled from diaries, with a writing style that is unembellished, its 544 pages were a major undertaking – especially as C. J. had other distractions.

The book relates all the major events in C. J.'s life, with most names changed but almost all major figures easily matchable to real life. Its action ends on 2 April 1923, just before his departure from Kendenup and marriage to Violet. Anyone hoping to purchase it to read C. J.'s take on his 'suicide' – or how he escaped Melbourne for Sydney – would be disappointed. Though no mention of a sequel appears between its covers, a second book was promised elsewhere.[45] Indeed, the Adelaide *Mail* suggested there may have been *two* more books to follow.[46]

C. J. suggested that his life story would serve to pay off some debts, and he surely owed a sum to the Modern Printing Company, which had taken care of the more arduous aspects of the C. J. DeGaris Publishing House. It seems likely that his decision to make his book more frank about sex than most was, firstly, a stab at commercial success, and, secondly, to exonerate Violet (and himself) from any rumours of impropriety during his marriage to Rene. A reader might assume that if he was going to be this frank about (for instance) his affair with the mysterious Gertrude, he was probably being honest. The general public certainly knew it contained titillating passages, as almost every review mentioned this fact, usually purse-lipped. The Adelaide *News* was offended by C. J.'s 'continual harping on his "sex impulses"'[47] and the Adelaide *Observer* felt that 'many of the details given should not be there'.[48] *The Land's* reviewer, 'W. M. S.', felt the 'love passages of the story are crude to a painful degree' and showed the author as 'not gifted with fineness of fibre, decent reticence, or refinement of feeling'.[49] The Melbourne *Advocate* decried the book's 'silly, erotic rubbish'.[50] The *Daily Telegraph and North Murchison and Pilbara Gazette* was primly equivocal: 'The chief plan in the book is the introduction of his domestic affairs which, we think, would have been wisely left out. We suppose, however, the author wished to make a clean breast of everything hence the result'.[51]

Reviewers had other objections to the book, however – not least the perceived arrogance of its author. The *Murrumbidgee Irrigator* suggested that after C. J.'s 'stupid, crudely conceived "suicide stunt"' he would have 'sought the seclusion of the bush, rabbiting or following some other useful, if obscure, occupation, instead of foisting himself again on the public notice'.[52] The Sydney *Sunday Times* found it a 'pathetically petty, vainglorious, priggish holding of the mirror up to DeGaris by DeGaris'.[53] Melbourne's *Age* was withering:

> A reader in Italy may be pardoned for wondering why Australia has neglected the services of this budding Mussolini in setting the affairs of his country straight. Pierpont Morgan and Henry

Ford, should they read this book, will be thankful that the accident of birth has kept this rival out of the United States... it is doubtful that any book ever written contains so much egotism and self adulation.[54]

The most scathing, and funniest, response was the parody by Reg Moses ('Mo')[55] in *Smith's Weekly*, which made short work of a long tale. 'The Hashes of Achievement' is the story of 'Good Little Normie' [sic] who, at birth, steals the watch of the doctor who delivers him, then goes to school to exploit his fellow students, selling shares in trees for which all the branches are 'catapult prongs'. He then fakes suicide by strewing his old clothes over a railway line, a farewell note pinned to the hat, to enjoy 'the exquisite thrill of running over and killing my dead past at the level crossing'.[56]

C. J. had made certain to note that 'All dramatic and film rights' were reserved for his book,[57] a stipulation that some reviewers found risible. He did, however, tell journalists that he had been made a 'tempting offer' by a Sydney film concern 'to take the lead in a moving picture production', which featured at least in part his own life story.[58] *Smith's Weekly* was probably joking when it claimed that the film would be called *The Boomerang*.[59] Again, in late August, C. J. claimed that 'one of the biggest studios in America intended to film the story'.[60] In October, he told the Adelaide *News* that 'at the present moment' the book was 'being filmed in Los Angeles'.[61] There is no evidence that this happened.

Ridicule and fame

Mine tinkit pleece bin berry smart pfellows catchem DeGaris. Mine tinkit 'im get ten years, dut daz, no takem im long do ten years. 'Im plurry smart pfellow.

The *Uralla Times*' 'Binghi' represents a common comic trope of the 1920s, the Aboriginal commentator whose innocent pronouncements speak a greater truth than he realises. If you were infamous enough to be a part of Binghi's world, you were ubiquitous. C. J. found himself taking on a range of meanings.

Firstly, there was the idea of copycat suicides. Two weeks after C. J.'s disappearance, a 45-year-old butcher called Howard Harding, in love with a 'thin, tall woman' who had abandoned him, left a suicide note and disappeared.[62] The letter, 'expressing hopes that his body would not be found...is a very lengthy one, and is couched in pathetic terms a la DeGaris'.[63] Even six months later, Jack Douglas, a missing fisherman off the coast of Bunbury, was described as 'a second DeGaris episode'.[64]

Then, there were the absconders, such as Ernest Heiner of Queensland, 'a State that can lay claim to having a DeGaris all of its own'. Heiner had invested trustees' money in silver mines, and disappeared.[65]

But perhaps surprisingly – and if C. J. had a publicist, she or he would have taken heart from this – his 'brand' was still that of a 'go-getter'. Hence, businessman Gilbert Taylour, talking up the potential of the Melbourne suburb of Williamstown, took care to point out he was 'not a Henry Ford or a DeGaris but he had seen millions lost by failure to grasp opportunities'.[66] The Premier of Victoria, John Allan, suggested less than a month after C. J.'s return in custody, 'What is needed is a little more of the DeGaris spirit, so that we could get things done'.[67]

'It has been rather a unique experience', C. J. told the Adelaide *News*, 'to sit in railway carriages and hear yourself openly discussed. I often find staunch supporters and sometimes bitter antagonists I have never before seen'.[68]

In Melbourne, the DeGarises became even more of a 'celebrity couple', and found themselves associated with another cause célèbre. twenty-year-old Audrey Jacob's trial for murder was career-defining for her lawyer, Arthur Haynes. Jacob's fiancé had assaulted then abandoned her; she shot and killed him in front of hundreds of people at a dance in Perth. She was acquitted, and when she relocated to Melbourne to study art, Haynes introduced her (via letter) to C. J., who 'showed her some little kindnesses'.[69] Her account of the DeGarises' lifestyle is revealing. 'I went to Mr. and Mrs. DeGaris' home, and had parties galore' she told *Truth*. 'They gave me some wonderful times.'[70] She also claimed that when she 'was taken about by the DeGarises, a number of men wanted to marry me'.[71] For some, C. J. and Audrey Jacob had the same dark glamour. She disappeared quickly from the DeGarises' lives, marrying an American businessman and departing the country.

C. J. occasionally looked back at old interests. He felt that the ADFA, having risen briefly from slumber during his publicity campaign, was back in its pre-DeGaris slump. He urged it to 'Tell the world. Use again The Magic Wand of Publicity'. He claimed that, in October 1923, he had written to the association offering to buy its whole lexia crop 'at prices 1d per lb above the net results of that year, and in addition to spend £30,000 in publicity on lexias…The ADFA, in its wisdom (?) decided "the letter be not read".' Perhaps the ADFA had a more realistic sense of C. J.'s finances than he did.

He added: 'I am not after a job, being too busy at New Corio and Geelong to need to look elsewhere, but the industry can surely find some leader who will realise the needs and act upon his knowledge'.[72]

New Corio

He was, as he said, 'busy at New Corio'. Having used the MSD to generate at least partial reimbursement for Kendenup, C. J. now proposed a new scheme to assist those who had lost, or were in danger of losing, money through the MSD. Additionally – and satisfyingly for the man who had persuaded Ford to come to Geelong – it was a new chance to profit from that triumph. He offered MSD creditors the option to buy lots in a 1300 acre (526 hectare) new estate in the prime position between the Ford factory and Geelong Grammar.[73] *Truth* suggested that he would 'probably earn a Victoria Cross if there was ever one awarded for gallantry in business'.[74] C. J. would make £5 on every lot sold, and *Truth* was cautious: 'It looks to be a case of per-haps or per-we-don't think so'.[75] But by March 1926 C. J. could report to the MSD that 588 of the 663 lots at New Corio had been sold, at a profit of £11,139. He took pains to point out how visionary he had been:

> Huge developments involving many millions of pounds sterling at Altona, Laverton, Werribee, Little River, Corio, North Geelong and Geelong (all of these are on the Melbourne-Geelong railway line) are to take place within 12 months, each one of which will have a direct effect on New Corio and raise its value far beyond the 10/- per foot which cynical humorists laughed at so heartily only 10 months ago.[76]

During a visit to Loxton he told a journalist 'the success of the New Corio Estate subdivision is assured and he will be able to pay in full the £360,000 in liabilities he has assumed' from the MSD.[77] He published a small pamphlet, *As I See Geelong in 1935*, and it was typical boosterism. Geelong, he told readers, was already known as Australia's Bradford and Birmingham, and 'The Capital of the Western District'. Through Ford, it was about to become 'The Detroit of Australia' and in ten years 'The New York of Australia'.[78]

Indeed, his celebrity was such that people started to assume he was involved in every and any major enterprise. A syndicate purchased 10,000 acres at Little River, 30 km from Geelong and 50 km from Melbourne. It was rumoured that C. J. was involved.[79] Agent W. S. Keast said, however, he had never met C. J. 'and had no desire to do so'.[80] Quizzed about the plan, C. J. claimed confidential knowledge about the scheme, dropping in the information that he was 'engaged in developing brown coal resources between Altona and the You Yangs'.[81]

Here, perplexingly, Reginald Stoneham re-entered the picture. It must surely have been Stoneham who interested C. J. in the Federal Oil Syndicate Development Company, of which he was a major shareholder.[82] At a talk that C. J. and Violet attended, Stoneham spoke at length about the products obtainable from brown coal and the immense reserves at 'Lavertona'. The *Geelong Advertiser* reported that C. J. was one of a number of individuals present with 'interests in land on which bores have been sunk and tests made of the brown coal'.[83] Suddenly, C. J. was sensing fossil fuels everywhere he trod.

Back to Kendenup

"I intend to take a run across to Western Australia in a week or so, and shall look up the old spot Kendenup, and out of the ashes – Well, we will see", he concluded, with an expressive gesture of the hands.[84]

C. J. had, plainly, remained obsessed with Kendenup, and in 1924 he might well have wondered what reception he would get there. There were stories at the McDonald Royal Commission of settlers refusing to take gifts from C. J., in part from disappointment about the failure of the settlement, and also from resentment at his treatment of Rene. The 172 Kendenupites that remained had been tested – but they had cause for optimism in the longer term. The majority of settlers had received the title deeds to their farms as a gift from the DeGarises. They assumed debentures would revert to C. J.[85]

There were still some legal issues, largely at the instigation of Le Mesurier, the solicitor at the Macdonald Royal Commission. Le Mesurier was a terrier, famous for his long and mendacious trial speeches. Cherry Barrow claimed damages for fraudulent misrepresentation.[86] She was followed by her husband William. Both were struck out.[87] Charles Courtis brought a similar case.[88] In all, C. J. was successful.

On 27 November, C. J., Violet and Veema arrived in Kendenup to spend four days. C. J. claimed the visit was 'more or less philanthropic in character'.[89] He declared himself amazed at the 'rapid development of orchards and pastures'.[90] Of 31,000 fruit trees at Kendenup, he said, government experts could not find one weak tree.[91] But there was more:

> Mr DeGaris said that there was a movement on foot, the nature of which he could not divulge, which would probably re-act to the advantage of the settlers now at Kendenup and to the debenture holders. The value of a debenture was £20, but he expected that that figure would be materially increased as a result of his visit to the West.[92]

C. J. 'had a scheme for the benefit of the settlers', but the settlers themselves also had a proposal, which he consented to.[93] This probably included his return to an administrative role at Kendenup – as warm an embrace and 'hand-clasp' as he could ever imagine.

During C. J. and Violet's stay, an Australian Natives Association 'Children's night' was held at Lawson Hall. Two hundred people attended, half of them children. There were recitations and musical items, and 'an appropriate item given by Mr. DeGaris was received with thunderous applause especially from the children'. It was 'just like old times', with obvious absences – such as J. J. Simons, who had no place in the Kendenup picture in 1925.

Four months later, in March 1926, C. J., Violet and Veema set out once again for Kendenup. They were staying at the Perth Savoy when it was announced he would once again take an administrative role at the settlement. Kendenup debentures jumped in value.[94] The settlers would be enabled to request government assistance to increase their landholdings, which they felt was necessary.[95] C. J. was of the opinion that the original small farms would be adequate, at least for some, but in Kendenup matters he was diplomatic. Once again, the DeGarises were present at a dance at Kendenup Hall; once again both performed 'vocal items' as part of the entertainment. Violet gave toys and gifts to the Kendenup children.[96] C. J., incidentally, always refused to dance, even when Violet was insistent.[97]

In so many ways the world had changed, but in many ways it seemed that C. J.'s fortunes and forays were repeating in a loop. Whereas in 1923 it had been 'the Americans', now in 1926 it was 'a large Anglo-German concern' that was interested in establishing 'a certain enterprise' that would employ from 3,000 to 10,000 in the area. He insisted, nonetheless, that he did not wish to make any money from Kendenup himself.[98]

C. J. was no stranger to 'spin', but there were arguments that he had been right about Kendenup just as he had been right about Corio, and in both cases it was not a case of simple prediction but proactive enterprise on his part. Kendenup in 1926 was, admittedly, a much smaller project than had been envisaged, and its produce went way beyond the growing of fruit and vegetables: turkey and sheep farming were introduced by settlers. Additionally, 'Kendenup cream is the most important factor at the Albany butter factory', he told the Adelaide *News*, during a stopover en route to Melbourne from Western Australia. Nonetheless, tomatoes, beans, potatoes and peas grown there were 'insufficient to meet the demand created' and he saw Kendenup exporting between 90,000 and 120,000 cases of fruit a year.

He took the opportunity, too, to discuss New Corio. 'I have had the good fortune', he told the *News* reporter, 'to reduce the liabilities of £420,000 to an amount that is negligible…We are already reselling for original buyers at £3 2/6 a foot land which they bought at 50/-.'[99] 'Geelong', he had told the Perth *Daily News*, was 'rapidly becoming the third city in the Commonwealth', due to low state taxation and 'the few difficulties with labour troubles' but also the city's deep water bay facilities.[100]

Oil

If the 200 Kendenup settlers stubbornly stuck to their guns, so did C. J. He proved to be particularly unwilling to drop the question of oil at Kendenup. C. J. insisted the repudiation of the contract with McClelland was an outcome of oil fortunes around the world, and that Kendenup sat upon a sea of oil.[101]

Utilising Albert Black, an associate of Stoneham's and a 'Lavertona' brown coal expert, C. J. undertook further investigations into the possibility of oil reserves in the area. Kendenup possessed, C. J. told Perth *Truth,* a stagnant shallow pond 25ft in width producing vapours driving people from their houses and 'the fowls off their roosts'. This noxious phenomenon, incidentally, had been conspicuously absent from Kendenup advertising. Black placed an inverted tub over the water and collected a gas through a rubber tube, converting it into light oil. *Truth,* after visiting Kendenup and receiving the wisdom of government expert Gibb Maitland, was decidedly dubious, even more so when it discovered that Black was not, as it had been led to believe, a geologist but a chemist.[102] Of course, either discipline had value in this search, but the implication was obviously that whatever Black was collecting may have been flammable, but need not have been derived from oil. Another expert, government mineralogist E. S. Simpson, believed that Black's methods, reasoning and equipment were faulty and that he was 'mistaken in his determinations'.[103] *Smith's Weekly* revealed that Black had been employed by the Melbourne Tramway Company until 1920, 'a favourable position', it sniggered, 'for the study of oil on coursing and pony meetings'. It also ridiculed Black's six years of oil investigation in Tasmania and Victoria. This included the Great Southern Oil Company in which, it said, he was in cahoots with the architect B. Dunstan Reynolds, better known (in *Smith's* world, at least) for operating the Reynoldi spaghetti company.[104]

C. J. said he had been 'convinced' by Woodard in 1922 of the existence of oil at Kendenup, and once again put forth his opinion that American interests conspired to suppress oil production in Australia.[105] Added to this was the fact that C. J. had no particular reason to trust government experts, and in a statement released in June 1926 he reminded Western Australians of experts' unwillingness to vest any validity in 'the idea of gold existing in this state', and their insistence that there was no coal in Western Australia. In any case, he said, 'I am not going to be turned aside from my purpose to explore the possibilities fully even though the officials are so dogmatic in their negative pronouncements'.

'The oil has been stripped from a gas seepage', said C. J.

> It is a larger development than we have realised. Already we have received inquiries from two American sources. Evidence of the value of the gas shows that development can be self-supporting. The revenue from the stripped gas can pay for the sinking and boring.[106]

Arthur Haynes announced his intention to establish a joint enterprise with C. J. to develop an oil field, and thirty-eight Kendenup families accepted an invitation to share in oil wealth from the concern.[107] 'I am sure', C. J. said, 'all patriotic Western Australians…hope we will succeed, because the financial and industrial advantage to Western Australia would be beyond computation'.[108]

After C. J.'s Mentone and *Maheno* exploits, Albert de Pledge had found a job with a butcher in Melbourne's CBD. He remembered:

> I met him one day on the road. My butcher's van was parked outside a customer's shop when C. J. pulled in behind. As I walked towards him and the car, full of his family, his hand outstretched and gripped mine, a big grin all over his face. After some time and enquiries about Kendenup, he said "Keep in touch. I'll soon have something going and I'll have you back with me".

> Later he invited Thelma and I to spend an evening with them at their Hawthorn home...C. J. had now got interested in oil at Kendenup...where I understand he was doing some drilling... He invited me to stay a weekend with him and family at Mornington, a seaside resort. It was very enjoyable...[109]

C. J. had no need to pin all his hopes on oil discovery. He could very justifiably argue that Kendenup was a success as a farming community in any case; true, it had a quarter of the population in 1926 as it had in 1923, but it was a productive and even an innovative community, exactly as he would have hoped. While Corio might, arguably, be another one that got away, it was clear that his Corio Garden Suburb, now being remade as 'Grandjean Estate' after the Ford representative who chose Corio for the company's plant, was selling lots rapidly and increasing in value week by week. He was experiencing, demonstrably, achievement from ashes, and victories from failure.

13

'Fell down on a big job'

C. J. frequently said he did not want millions of pounds. His relatively humble Kendenup home in Hassell Avenue, and his willingness to 'make do' when necessary, suggested his real motivation was status, philanthropy or patriotism – probably all three. Perhaps he would have been happy to simply 'make a difference'. None of this explains his actions in 1926.

Many friends who had not seen C. J. for some time were pleasantly surprised in the first few months of the year 'when Mr DeGaris walked into their offices and paid in cash the full amount of debts owed before his insolvency. One such payment was for £1,000'.[1] He was not forthcoming about the source of his wealth but often talked about oil, telling a friend that there was between five and six million pounds 'in this latest venture of his'. His friend 'advised him to leave oil alone, or it would be the end of him but he would have none of my pessimism'.[2] The oil was, it was assumed by everyone, to be found in Kendenup. However, C. J. had also sent applications to the Lands Department to lease areas around Mornington, as well as nearby Bittern and Hastings.[3]

Ferdinand Nuske was interested in the manufacture of nitrogen from air and water. He founded the Nuskonia Land Company in September 1925, changing its name to Nuske Power, Fuel and Nitrogen early the following year. He anticipated building a nitrogen factory at Liverpool, NSW, which would employ 35,000. Like the Ford workers at Corio, these workers would need somewhere – preferably nearby – to live. 'It was this side of the proposition', *Truth* reported, 'that fascinated DeGaris, and his pet Closer Settlement Garden City vision'. Nuske's was, incidentally, an 'Anglo-German' business, and it is possible that at some point C. J. was anticipating location of a nitrogen factory at Kendenup.

C. J. was not financially settled or secure, but in his continual borrowing-from-Peter-to-pay-Paul fashion, he had a certain measure of stability. He did not want to miss out on this opportunity. He wrote to backers saying that, if they invested £500 with him by 7 March, he would pay it back to them on 10 July, then deliver the same amount in October, the same again in January the following year, and two further instalments in April and July 1927: that is, £2,000 for £500, over sixteen months.

It is easy to say that C. J. was crazy to propose this, but it is also apparent that he still, after all his notorious stunts and stumbles, could find people willing to part with funds. He wrote to his backers a few months later to say:

> The Sydney investment did not proceed as I was not satisfied with the quality and stability of the guarantee. Fortunately, however, I was able to arrange an exactly similar ratio of investment in another direction, the only difference being that the quarterly payments will commence on July 21 instead of July 10. On July 21, therefore, you will receive your quarterly instalment.

He then wrote that 'advices have just been received' that payments which were to be made on July 21 and October 21 would now be made on 'July 27, 1926 which will be to our mutual advantage'.

He added that

> our operations in the Kendenup district adjoining the Kendenup Estate during the last three days have completely and favourably set the seal of success on our operations there... Firstly, free mineral oil is not only a claim but a fact. Eight test bores proved it beyond doubt. The value of twenty acres is proved to be not less than £260,000 and the adjoining areas are even better.

He predicted reaping at least nine million pounds, having secured 'oil rights over thousands of acres of private land in the locality'. C. J. wrote:

> This unexpected outcome involves a complete change of plans, as it calls for a much larger purchase from our buyers who now require the greater oil rights on a much better basis for us, and much bigger cash payment which, however, incurs a fortnight's delay...Without fail there will be no delay on August 12.

'My name will be on the lips of everyone within a few days', C. J. told his barber in the second week of August.[4] He also made a phone call to *Truth*, which consistently had a different take on his operations than almost any other organ. 'I hear you are writing something about me', he said. 'Before you do, will you promise that you will let me know.'[5] They weren't planning anything, but they promised they would advise him if they did. He also telephoned Joseph Woolf, who he had not seen for some time, to tell him that he was 'being wonderfully successful' and 'making large sums of money out of sales in Geelong'.[6]

Truth was a scandal sheet, but Australia in the 1920s had a lot of scandals the papers 'of record' wouldn't touch. *Truth* certainly invested more in detailed reportage than many of its more staid competitors, and C. J., notably, gave it respect. *Truth* attempted to explain C. J.'s activities at this time by veiled references to

Shell Oil and a mysterious Dutch official. It claimed that an official connected with 'one of the richest – if not the richest oil corporation in the world' had arrived in Melbourne on the SS *Marella* from Java. Having heard rumours of oil in Western Australia, he got in touch with C. J. and made independent inquiries.[7] A major deal was to be transacted with international financiers; however, the promised funds did not arrive.[8] This, as *Truth* told it, was the final straw.[9]

Since April, C. J. and Violet had rented Dunoon, a house on The Esplanade in Mornington. It was a two-storey building which they had taken furnished.[10] C. J. was spending most of his time there – presumably in large part because of the Mornington Peninsula oil explorations – only occasionally returning to their new Hawthorn home at 1 Hawthorn Glen. On 16 August, a Monday, C. J. visited the local plumber, John Scott, to make an appointment 'about something very important'[11] for midday the next day. Scott had seen C. J. frequently during the preceding two months; in this instance, C. J. did not tell Scott what he wanted to see him about.[12]

C. J. stayed at Hawthorn Glen that night. He told Violet that 'some bank draft had not come through, and that there was some delay'.[13] He left the house at 7 am the next day, saying he was going to Ringwood and asking her to have an early lunch ready for him when he returned.[14]

Scott was five minutes early.[15] He found a note on the front door labelled: 'For noon, Tuesday. Memo. John H. Scott, instructions under mat'. There lay the horrifying message:

> Sorry to drag you into this; but you are a plumber, and a plumber is needed. There may be danger to anyone else. The gas must be cut off outside the house. The kitchen is closed, and full of gas, and you will find me there. The gas must be cut off, and the door opened carefully before entering. No matches must be used; you had better ring the police, also my wife, Hawthorn 2839. Poor girl, she has no idea I fell down on

a big job yesterday. Am paying the penalty to-day. Please see parcels under mat reach destination – C. J. DeGaris.

Scott entered the house. Spaces under the door, and vents, were blocked with rags. C. J. was lying on the table in the kitchen, his head on a tea cosy and his mouth close to the jet of a gas stove. Scott summoned the police – Constable R. F. Mason – and a doctor, I. T. Cameron.[16] Cameron found C. J.'s body still warm, but reasoned he had probably been dead since 11 am. Nevertheless, he tried artificial respiration for an hour.[17] C. J.'s body was taken to the Royal Hotel, then viewed by the coroner who gave order for burial.[18]

While dying, C. J. had torn pieces from a newspaper and written messages ranging from the practical – that his car was at a garage in Mornington[19] – to 'pathetic farewells' to Violet ('My darling Vi and Vee, god bless you. My end is getting nearer. It is a slow business. Fondest love, hugs and kisses – Daddy.') – to the almost clinical: 'This is a slow process, but it is very certain.'[20] He wrote a ten page letter to Violet 'describing the process of his dying method'.[21] Other notes were poignant, if strange: 'I don't know what I am doing. Forgive me. Take care of Jean and Betty.'[22] He also made certain to release his housekeeper from any suspicion: 'Mrs Ingamell knows nothing of my intentions. She only loyally delivered my messages and carried out my instructions, and must often have been puzzled herself.'[23] After writing these messages, he had clipped his gold pencil into his vest pocket.[24]

Truth told its readers that a black cat model on the mantelshelf of Dunoon's kitchen had been broken from its stand. On the cat's body was emblazoned, in gold letters, the symbols for pounds, shillings and pence, 'on the footpiece…were words expressing good luck'.[25]

As was the case with the Mentone episode, he had written many letters to friends and associates. Woolf said that his letter from C. J. showed him to be 'immensely despondent'.[26] The letter, as released to the press, read:

Dear Mr. Woolf – Waterloo, with a vengeance. The fruits of rigid secrecy, faithfully adhered to by me, have two hours ago, placed me in the position of being the subject of further threats, recriminations and actions which I've not the courage to face. And yet to-day I woke believing I had the greatest day's work of my life to accomplish, and the certainty of all debts paid and a big bank balance for me and mine. And yet – disaster.
This memo is only a word of good-bye. You have been a wonderful friend to me, and though I haven't called on you for about twenty weeks, I was looking forward to clasping your hand this week and to say "the Band can now play".
Best wishes and keen regrets.[27]

To Arthur Haynes, his Kendenup oil business partner, he wrote:

I've made a mess of things, through trying to carry through very big negotiations without your knowledge. This thing is so big it is worse than useless without me here to refute any contradictions. The value of the 640-acre Reward lease to sell is at least £1,000,000. The oil content of the sands alone from 27 to 40 feet is £9,000,000 gross, and when you bore more deeply there are millions more. Whether I stop, or those I leave behind or my creditors get any of it at all, depends, of course, on your generosity, as legally the lease is yours and as I won't be here to do my bit. Cheerio, Old Scout. Thanks for all your great help re: Kendenup and its many problems, Regards and best wishes for a great career, which you so well deserve.[28]

Haynes, it would be discovered soon afterwards, had insured C. J.'s life for £5,000.

Mary wrote to her sister Bessie on the 18 August:

Unlike you I am not surprised. I thought he had done it last time and thought tho he failed then to die, he might not so fail again. He never seemed to me to recover a truly normal aspect — his eyes kept a strange look...

I think "oil" interests helped to break him — he wrote so himself — but nothing but a long holiday last year could have saved him from his recurrent breakdown...

Papa has been hit financially as well as parentally — seriously I fear: when the funeral is over we will discuss matters...

I do not grieve for Jack — I think only a terrible unhappiness and ill health of mind can enable a physically strong man to take his own life. Vi said, as she looked at him — "a tortured soul at rest".[29]

14

'The essence of kindness'

The funeral of the late Mr. C. J. de Garis, whose body was found in a house at Mornington on Tuesday, took place yesterday afternoon at Brighton Cemetery. A large number of mourners attended, and the ceremony was witnessed also by a considerable gathering of curious onlookers. At the graveside Rev. C. E. Tregear conducted the service. In a brief address he said that Mr. de Garis had an extraordinary brain, wonderful vision, great courage and exceptional business knowledge. He was the essence of kindness, but unfortunately he had to fight against adversity.[1]

A man born to C. J. DeGaris' class and race in Australia in 1884 might have had a reasonable expectation to live at least till the mid-1950s or later. Had he lived to 80, he might have caught the Kennedy assassination and the beginnings of Beatlemania. Had he lived to 85, he would have seen the moon landing, which would surely have impressed the record-breaking aviator of 1919–20. Dying when he did, he missed the privations of the

Great Depression (which would have hit him and his businesses at least as hard as the Kendenup 'crash'); the rise and reign of Prime Minister Robert Menzies (a man who, in 1925 in his days as a lawyer, had appeared for a litigant against C. J. in a minor court case), and the Second World War.[2]

Instead, his descendants, his siblings, his father and the thousands of others – creditors, Kendenup settlers, business partners – had to go through those things *without* him, but *with* his sad, perhaps even shameful, legacy. When he boasted to the MSD's Reconstruction Committee that suicide was a brave act, he might also have reflected what it meant to have spent so much of one's life persuading so many people to trust in a man who then deliberately removes himself. The ramifications of his choices persist, arguably, to the present day.

For decades following his death, C. J. was an embarrassing anomaly, deliberately forgotten and rarely talked about. Versions of his story were occasionally dredged up for a page of historical

C. J.'s grave, Brighton Cemetery. AUTHOR PHOTO, 2005.

feature in a tabloid or a popular magazine, or – painfully, it would seem, for his surviving family – a chapter in Keith Dunstan's popular survey of Australian tall poppies, *Ratbags*. Many would imagine that, reading Dunstan's account of C. J.'s life, they knew the whole story. Certainly, Dunstan was accurate as far as he went, but the mere name of the book suggested its subjects were zanily inept.

In the early 1990s, the West Australian writer and broadcaster Bill Bunbury interviewed a small selection of people with connections to C. J. and Kendenup. The interviews were used in a radio documentary, *The Story of C. J. DeGaris*, and the tapes are now located in the State Library of Western Australia's Battye collection.

Bunbury came to his interviewees too late, and in the main they retold stories they'd read, or otherwise they couldn't remember enough of the 1920s to be properly informative. Albert de Pledge and Rica Erickson, who were teenagers in the 1920s and clearly still bright in the 1990s, are the notable exceptions, aside from family informants such as C. J.'s nephew Peter Sutcliffe who did not know him personally. Occasionally, Bunbury hit a mark: for instance, he asked one interviewee if C. J. was a Skase or Bond figure – and was politely shot down for the suggestion. Veema DeGaris, a toddler when her father died, was apparently terrified of even being recorded, and her interview is painful listening as a result.

The DeGaris family suffered, dismally, from C. J.'s death. Perhaps worst of all was his brother Alfred, who had been closely involved in many of the same enterprises as C. J. over time, though he had not been a part of the Kendenup experiment. On 13 October 1927 passengers in the Murray river steamer *Gem* saw a body in the river. It was found to be Alfred, in his pyjamas and dressing gown.[3] We can only assume that Alfred's suicide was linked to C. J.'s.

C. J.'s youngest brother, Lucas, better known as George, let his grief manifest in a very different way. Always prickly, and seemingly far more religious than even his father, George suffered breakdowns in the 1920s and was alienated from his wife and family by the end of the decade. He professed complete ignorance of its cause, yet the alienation was surely connected to his near total obsession with a personally devised new economic system of universal credit, and his decision to eschew paid work his entire life to advocate for it. Based around 'Wice currency', it was needlessly, indeed hopelessly, complex. George's biggest supporters in his endeavour were his sister Mary and father Elisha, who surely indulged him out of love rather than commitment to the cause. In his thousands of pages of baffling published writing, George only mentions C. J. in ways indicating complete indifference, yet, while George was undoubtedly strange, it is hard to imagine C. J.'s death wasn't an emotional disaster for an already disturbed man. George left an extensive and incomprehensible legacy. When he wrote to John Mackin of Mount Barker Junior High School, who had contacted him in 1961 looking for information about C. J., there was a slight tenderness behind the stiff formality. 'Currently, his name stands high with those who come within the orbit of his reputation', George wrote.[4]

How did C. J.'s death affect his children? Winnie, Dulcie, Vera and Veema had lives, of course, and all four married. An item from *Table Talk* in 1929 mentions not only that Dulcie had given a tea party in honour of a friend's marriage (Winnie was in attendance) but also that Rene had returned 'from a visit to her late husband's relatives in South Australia, where she had a happy holiday'.[5] Both girls appeared in an amateur pantomime of *Cinderella* at Her Majesty's, Ballarat in April 1931. Winnie was one of the 'solo dancers'.[6]

Those close to C. J. called him 'Jack'. Dulcie and Vera both married men called John, and Winnie married a man called Enoch – who everyone called 'Jack'. Vera married John Gibson Findlay in Ballarat in 1935,[7] and Dulcie was married to John Richard Henry of Maldon in 1936.[8] When she died in 1986 she was living in Rodbrough Crescent, Corio, part of the garden suburb commissioned by her father fifty-eight years before.[9]

Independent and fearless, according to her son Rick, Winnie worked for Kodak in London in the mid-30s, married an American from Florida – Enoch Doble – divorced him after eight years and worked and lived in New York, running 'social activities for the Columbia School of Journalism including the Pulitzer Prize Dinners'. Rick says she had 'very little to say' about her father, 'other than he flew planes, was a businessman, and committed suicide'. However, he adds, 'I had the feeling she was close to him and quite devastated when he died, especially by the way he died'.[10] Winnie, who resisted obtaining American citizenship until very late in life, died in 1979.

Rene and C. J.'s daughters knew their father well, but Veema had no memory of him at all. Her mother barely spoke of C. J., and all the information Veema had came from her aunts or, perhaps, her half-sisters. She did maintain a close relationship with Mary DeGaris for the rest of that formidable and remarkable lady's life, and their correspondence not only suggests a fond and enduring bond but also marks a connection to the DeGaris side of her family that Veema surely valued. Veema became an air hostess for TAA; touchingly, she added her flight record to C. J. and Briggs' logbook of flights from a quarter of a century earlier. This document is held in the National Library of Australia. Veema contracted polio in 1948 and was a paraplegic the rest of her life. She married, and later divorced, a pilot; the marriage foundered on his alcohol dependence. She devoted many of her later years to her prized – and prizewinning – cats.[11]

Both of C. J.'s wives appear to have been, not unnaturally, embittered by their DeGaris experience. One can only wonder at the life of Rene. Surely news of her disgrace carried to Ballarat, where she lived out the last thirty years of her life. The mention above of her visit to C. J.'s South Australian relatives is intriguing: it is heartening to see that some DeGarises continued to embrace her. Certainly in the twenty-first century few of us would feel she deserved the punishment she was dealt. Rick DeGaris Doble remembers his grandmother as a stern and humourless woman.

She 'came from Australia and lived with us for six months when I was about eight years old', he recalls. 'Everyone said that she was quite difficult including my mother.' One of Rene's nieces, Donnie, remembers her coming for afternoon tea in the early-to-mid 1960s with her sister Mollie (the 'Mary' who roller skated with C. J., Rene and Dulcie in Mildura in July 1912); she was a tall, well-dressed woman in hat and gloves who carried herself 'quite regally'. Donnie continues: 'I had never seen or met a woman quite so self-confident. She must have made quite an impression as I always picture her walking through the front door and being amazed at her presence/aura. Mollie paled in comparison and I always loved seeing Mollie arrive for a visit!'[12] Rene died in 1976, having outlived Violet by eight years.

Violet is even harder to understand. J. J. Simons called her 'Madam' and implied she interfered in C. J.'s affairs and friendships, but without the man she was married to for a scant three years she was, it would appear, a mess. The nominal head of the Melbourne Sub-Divisions Company clearly had no aptitude for business or money, as became plain when the MSD affairs were brought to light in the early 1930s. Between 1928 and 1931, Violet and Veema lived at Kendenup.[13] She was declared bankrupt in 1933 owing £255,387.[14] However, she had been under the impression that upon reaching adulthood, Veema was to be the sole beneficiary of C. J.'s will (she had read it soon after his death, she told the court in 1936, but had forgotten its contents: he had, she said, 'told her that he could not leave her anything because her estate was so involved').[15] She also endured for close to a decade under the illusion that all the DeGaris companies of which she might once have been a beneficiary were valueless when, to her surprise, DeGaris Kendenup W.A. Development Company started to pay dividends.[16] She and Veema moved to Sydney, presumably in the 1930s, and lived there for the rest of their lives. Violet was one of seven sisters: the others being Dorothy, Marge, Freda, Wilga, Mid and Aud; the sisters died in sequence of age, Violet in 1968.[17]

Let us deal, finally, with C. J.'s enemies. Ron Coote might not fall precisely into this category, and indeed C. J. categorically failed to make any pronouncement on this young man even at the time his cuckolding was revealed: blame fell almost exclusively on Rene. Yet Ron clearly took his infamy hard, in ways that saw others suffer. In 1925 he was prosecuted for stealing a horse, and two years later four people were injured when a car he was driving collided with a yellow cab at the corner of William and Hay streets, Perth.[18] Establishing equilibrium – and even becoming a successful tennis player – at the end of the decade, he would later become a popular musician and composer in Geraldton.[19] It is pleasing to close the curtain on him in 1949, as he plays his own composition, 'Caprice', to the Geraldton Music Lovers' Club at the High School.[20]

Grant Hervey lived only six years after C. J.; diabetes killed him in the Alfred Hospital, Melbourne in 1933. His life for that half-decade was typically rough, split between jail time (his extortion and blackmail activities continued) and the editing (apparently anonymously) of a racist scandal sheet, *Becket's Budget* (sample headline: 'Immigrants Given Jobs While Australian Girls Starve').[21] While in Goulburn prison, he completed what was, presumably, the historical novel originally begun to compete in C. J.'s literary competition. *The Eden of the Good* is an absurd version of nineteenth-century Australian history populated, even dictated, by Hervey's ancestors. It was published posthumously. I have not been able to establish what became of his wives or his son, Lincoln.

This leaves C. J.'s pride and joy, Kendenup, which at time of writing is celebrating its centenary. Kendenup was, in many senses, a gamble, and it would be a mistake to ascribe its rise and fall as merely a part of DeGaris' own narrative; apart from anything else, for C. J. to look upon Kendenup's failure to become a new Mildura as his tragedy alone is to deny the serious impact it had on settlers who had paid higher prices for their land on the basis of a guaranteed market for their produce.[22] Those who stayed on at Kendenup and chose to continue to work the land without the protections of the DeGaris companies were tenacious. They also suffered: 'Children went barefoot to school in ragged clothes and some didn't have enough money for soap', Joan Allen, the daughter of hostel manager Fred Allen, relates in *Kendenup Stories*.[23]

While Kendenup itself has sustained as a community, it is on a much smaller scale than any of DeGaris' publicity predicted: Mount Barker is certainly *not* its suburb. Over decades, the infrastructure installed by the Company was removed. The dehydrator, which had been used as a house for some time, was demolished in the late 1940s – in an age of building material shortages, its component materials were of greater value in other structures.[24] When I first visited Kendenup in 2002 I was regaled with stories of local farmers who had demolished old buildings in the area as 'nuisances'. The main street, however, still retains a sense of the optimism of the original settlers, and the Lawson Hall is a noble building that continues to be used by the community. The brick house that C. J. built for himself, Rene and their children, remains.

It should be remembered that, although C. J. paid a large amount of money towards 'rescuing' Kendenup settlers, he did so through the Melbourne Sub-Divisions Company which bought, subdivided and quickly resold land on the city's fringe to investors and speculators. This is entirely above board and legal, as is the use of 'booster' language to describe what the land in question would be worth, materially or qualitatively, in the future. Some of the land C. J. 'boosted', like the New Corio estate, remains undeveloped: a 'zombie subdivision'.[25] Parts of Windulva became the comfortable far-eastern suburb of Wonga Park. Corio, for reasons more closely aligned to the decline of manufacturing in Australia than anything to do with its inherent value or design, is at time of writing one of Victoria's most disadvantaged suburbs. The point remains that many of the MSD customers were unlikely to have made much money from their purchases, and possibly lost heavily. Real estate speculation of this nature was exploitative.

A man of his time?

There is value, when trying to understand a man like C. J. DeGaris, in setting him against the cultural developments of the early twentieth century in western civilisation. I am intrigued by the question of how much of a genuinely 'modern' man C. J. was — where he fits in the twentieth century, as we understand it in the twenty-first, a hundred years after he was most active. C. J. had no inkling of Hitler, of course; he would have been aware of Mussolini, just transitioning from democratic prime minister to fascist dictator, and indeed one review of *The Victories of Failure* jokingly compared him to the Italian leader. C. J. was there at the very beginning of wireless in Australia, and even dabbled in broadcasting himself; he would surely have spent some time listening to 3AR and 3LO in Melbourne, or 6WF in Perth, all established in 1924. Of course, he would only have understood television theoretically and would never have witnessed a 'talking picture' as we understand it — the *Jazz Singer* was released in the USA the year after he died. He was on the cusp of a lot of things, and denied himself the chance to take them further.

This matters because — as you have seen in this book — DeGaris was perennially engaged; always up to date and ready to embrace any and every new movement. His interest in all and every method of media and culture, whether it served his immediate purposes or just signified progress, was palpable. He made much of his record-breaking flights, and the successes of 'his' publishing house authors; he seemed highly invested in the future, both his and his country's. Notwithstanding the impulsive aspect of many suicide attempts, this to me is the greatest mystery of C. J.'s decision to die.

Australia, like every nation, has a small and select coterie of entrepreneur heroes, almost all men, who rose to prominence as movers and shakers in business, often particularly land development or media (or both), almost always pursuing financial success for its own benefit. Such individuals will, naturally, have their critics and their defenders; Alan Bond and Christopher Skase will certainly come to mind for readers of a particular generation, but individuals like Twiggy Forrest and Gina Rinehart can also fit roughly into the category. Rupert Murdoch and Kerry Packer (and their fathers, and their children) are also arguably similar in many respects. 'Having a go' is an Australian cliché, and while those Australians lucky enough to find themselves in the wide band of middle-class waged existence are content to dwell a relatively stress-free life there, there is an expectation – the USA has its own, far more fervently held cultural attitude – that people with a good head for finances and an eye for markets are to be admired for their bravery and vision.

It would be dangerously ahistorical to try to categorise, or for that matter pathologise these people, or even to try to typify their motives or their values. Anyone who reads my account of C. J.'s life, however, and then goes on to peruse Paul Barry's forensic *The Rise and Fall of Alan Bond* would start to feel party to a particular stream of anthropological investigation: habits and attitudes of the Australian millionaire. In late 1974, Bond's business was in turmoil, but he was eager to reassure the public that his key project, Yanchep north of Perth, was 'bang on budget, and selling faster than any real estate development in Western Australia', but that also 'more capital was on its way from overseas, from a source he couldn't name'. Simultaneously he was threatening and cajoling the banks he owed money to – almost blackmailing them into supporting him, as an America's Cup participant and therefore a national hero – and lobbying both state and federal government to prop him up.[26] Bond was lucky; he did not have an enemy like Hervey to light the touchpaper underneath him, and – unlike C. J. – he had the extraordinary cache of a ridiculously decadent international boat race to run to in an era of emergent nationalism that far outdid C. J.'s Empire-era patriotism. That both were active in Western Australia is possibly not as relevant as it might initially seem, as C. J. was really a Victorian operating in the west with a largely Victorian backing. Nevertheless, Bond's chutzpah is not unlike C. J.'s. Both men, fifty years apart, wandered into the business landscape, attracted investors large and small, and then, when problems became endemic, appealed to government to help them resolve the issues they had created – for the good of the people, particularly the 'little people', involved.

Similarly, many passages in Tom Prior's book on Christopher Skase have an eerie resonance. Prior quotes, for instance, the *Sun Herald's* Gerald Carringon on Skase:

> He kept moving on all the time. Borrow, borrow, borrow, build, build, build. If he had stopped borrowing and building for a year or two, he might have been all right. If he had stopped to consolidate, he would have had much more success. He might even have survived.[27]

It is also notable that Skase's publicists, like C. J. at Corio sixty years before, were eager to grab the mantle of a modern Batman: he tells us they 'paraphrased John Batman in Port Philip Bay a century and a half before to announce: "This is the place for a resort."'[28] It is also notable that, like Bond and C. J., Skase claimed incapacitation to escape the consequences of his ambition.

Was C. J. an early version of a Bond or Skase 'type'? Firstly, it needs to be remembered that he was small beer even in the thinking of the time and, while obsessed by success and failure, he clearly did not prioritise business above all else. His greatest project was Kendenup, an idea for which he might, indeed, have stood to make a lot of money, but which was more important for him as a model settlement in 'unconquered' territory, demonstrating the value and purpose of new technology and individual investment. The most important thing to C. J. – as is clear from his memoir and his public pronouncements, right up to the last – was how C. J. looked. Was he a decent, popular, 'straight' (as in 'honourable') man? Was he fit to lead?

Psychohistory is a largely discredited field in the early twenty-first century. That said, what might tell us more about C. J. and his later equivalents (to the degree there are any) is not the desire to pursue a vision and create or claim an empire, but the ways in which so many Australians were persuaded to follow.

C. J. often appealed to venality; his message was that investors would come away from his endeavours (particularly his speculative projects) with a spectacular return on investment. Perhaps his most extraordinary achievement is that, once bitten, his investors did not seem to learn from the experience. The story is full of people who, after losing money, are persuaded to either invest more or at least to relinquish salvaging their investment in the short term, for the promise of greater rewards in a 'reconstructed' project. The MSD reconstruction story – when C. J. seemingly saves the day with the announcement of Ford's entré into Corio – feels not only like a crowd applauding because their money is safe, but also because the *narrative* is perpetuating, indeed even escalating. 'This is a twist in the tale!' they seem to be saying, 'Whatever will happen next?' Similarly, the story that C. J., disgraced, under arrest, returning from New Zealand, sold two parcels of land to a detective, was the kind of story people wanted (and still want) to believe. It should be truer than it is.

Clearly, C. J. also wanted to be loved by many: *F. F. F.* is the perfect example of this, as much as he dressed it up as a project created to satisfy a personal dare that an Australian musical comedy could be as good as an import. It is hard to imagine a twenty-first century comparison, but Alan Bond's obsession with sailing and the America's Cup was, perhaps, a similarly patriotic ambition that had precisely no relation to his daily job, but which provided a talking point about the man and his drive.

Max Weber's conception of charismatic leadership concerns a figure who will perform a range of 'miracles' (for those who do not believe in magic or religion, perhaps these might be propelled by luck and chance). C. J. was already living something of a charmed life before his publicity campaign for the ADFA propelled him to national fame. He appeared to generate enormous wealth out of thin air – although in truth, a range of circumstances from government policy, high production, the wealth of his family business and other random variables were responsible. While *F. F. F.* and the literary competition were not exactly smash successes, they suggested a man who could turn his hand to a diverse range of accomplishments. Kendenup – the vision and the optimistic outlook – appealed strongly to people who expected a reward for the privations of war, who wanted to share in the prosperity and also the creation of the new nation, and who were ready to embrace the notion of a wealthy and productive regional Australia without sacrificing a social or a community life. Consciously and unconsciously, C. J. fit all the criteria: here was a man who could be leader, visionary but also friend. He had a brand you could trust, and trusting him felt good.

Australians no doubt see themselves as more cynical today, but in truth, we often vote with our wallets, follow trends, and use our money to support our ideals. However bizarre C. J.'s actions might appear to be, and his investors naïve, in the twenty-first century many of us are at least as cavalier or foolish with our wealth and our lives. Indeed, just as we surround ourselves with material goods that seem to define us, our financial choices are as emotionally driven. C. J. was energetic and modern, quick-witted and unflappable. When fate knocked him down, he bounced back up, and most likely he would do it humming one of Reginald Stoneham's jaunty songs, or mouthing some tailored quip or retooled quote.

The Rev Charles Tregear, who had married C. J. and Violet three years before, also presided over his funeral. Of course, Tregear spoke at C. J.'s funeral for the consolation of the living, not in sober assessment of C. J.'s life and career. Yet however much we might wish to frame the actions of men who take it upon themselves to improve the world – as egotistical or intrusive, for instance – we should perhaps consider that C. J.'s oldest and longest-lasting model was his father. Elisha was a businessman with a religious impulse to improve the earthly lot of the people.

C. J. took up many of his father's attitudes and ideas, possibly too eagerly and definitely too recklessly. Triangulate C. J.'s beliefs, ideas and expectations, and we might find a man with a mission to improve his industry, and thereby his nation, both for individuals close to him and by example. Tregear did, then, sum up some (not all) of the diverse elements of this unusual person:

> Today we are laying to rest the body of no ordinary man. I will alter that and say that he was a most extraordinary man, a man with brains, wonderful vision, courage, and business ability: but behind it all he was a kindly and good man. I have known Mr. DeGaris for many years, and I have never known him to do an unkind or unfair act. We all know what Mr. DeGaris' intentions were. Every man would have been paid to the utmost penny had he lived and had God given him the strength to do the wonderful work that he was capable of doing: but to the strongest man there comes a test that he cannot survive.

There is also no little value in adding an assessment from another quarter. The *Truth* – in its different capital-city versions – was C. J.'s jester, cajoling, browbeating and worrying at him throughout the 1920s. In 1925, after his discovery on the *Maheno*, *Truth* published something approximating an obituary, of a reputation and a career rather than of a man; the assumption was that C. J. could not 'come back' from the shame of his sham suicide. Its review is the best assessment of his appeal:

> DeGaris! He was as well known as the Post Office, and his name was inseparable from big, solid, influential advertising which shouted prosperity, financial reliability in every line. He looked a giant, and people took him at his face value. He had very little difficulty in getting Kendenup started. He was a magnificent salesman, and he was an inspired organizer. He began to do things right from the jump, and people took to

him straight away. They had seen plenty of giants who fizzled out in a shower of unfulfilled promises, but he was a man who actually did things, and let them see before they bought...

But, as the margin 'twixt genius and madness is but the breadth of a hair, so the difference between success and failure is but a hairline.[29]

Notes

Chapter 1: 'The pleasantest and surest death'

1. 'Mr. C. J. DeGaris', Melbourne *Argus*, 6 January 1925, p. 11; 'DeGaris Missing', *Sun News-Pictorial*, 6 January 1925, p. 3.
2. 'Mystery Deepens', *Sun News-Pictorial*, 7 January 1925, p. 3.
3. 'Under the Clock', Shepparton *Advertiser*, 8 January 1925, p. 8.
4. 'Mr. C. J. DeGaris', Melbourne *Argus*, 6 January 1925, p. 11.
5. 'Easiest Way', Sydney *Sun*, 6 January 1925, p. 7.
6. 'DeGaris figures in mystery', Sydney *Evening News*, 5 January 1925, p. 5; 'A snapshot of C. J. DeGaris…', *Buffalo Times*, 5 November 1922, p. 27.
7. 'DeGaris figures in mystery'. The name 'Alice Austin' was reported in the *Evening News*, but this is possibly an error; there was no Alice amongst the Austin family close to C. J. or Violet.
8. 'Mystery Deepens'.
9. 'Mystery Deepens'. This item misquotes the song as it was published, substituting 'Arconda' for 'Golconda'. I have used the published version here but, of course, 'Arconda' may well have been in the original.
10. 'Will end it all', *Maitland Daily Mercury*, 6 January 1925, p. 2.
11. 'DeGaris figures in mystery'.
12. 'No trace', *Sun News-Pictorial*, 8 January 1925, p. 3.
13. 'DeGaris's stunt suicide', *Smith's Weekly*, 10 January 1925, p. 13.
14. A. de Pledge, interviewed by B. Bunbury, 17 May 1991, in Battye Oral History collection; transcription in J. Burcham, et al. (eds), *Kendenup Stories*, publisher not identified, Kendenup, 2017, p. 49.
15. 'Where is Mr DeGaris?', Melbourne *Herald*, 7 January 1925, p. 1.
16. 'Easiest Way'.
17. 'Mystery Deepens'.
18. 'Mystery Deepens'.
19. 'DeGaris Missing', *Sun News-Pictorial*, 6 January 1925, p. 3.
20. 'Mr. C. J. DeGaris', Melbourne *Argus*, 6 January 1925, p. 11.
21. 'DeGaris Mystery', *Sydney Morning Herald*, 7 January 1925, p. 14.
22. 'Last of DeGaris', *New Zealand Herald*, 6 February 1925, p. 7.
23. 'Moonooloo!', *Sun News-Pictorial*, 6 January 1925, p. 3
24. 'The DeGaris Mystery', *Age*, 7 January 1925, p. 9.
25. de Pledge, *Kendenup Stories*, p. 50.
26. 'Kendenup Commission', Perth *Daily News*, 8 February 1924, p. 4.

27 'Mr. Johnson, a dentist, has stated that his dog barked loudly at 5 a. m., the hour at which Mr. DeGaris is said to have disappeared. A little later Mr. Johnson heard another dog bark excitedly in an adjoining paddock.' 'The DeGaris Mystery', Adelaide *Advertiser*, 7 January 1925, p. 13.
28 C. J. DeGaris, *The Victories of Failure*, Modern Publishing Co, Melbourne, 1925, p. 358.
29 de Pledge, *Kendenup Stories*, p. 50.
30 'Warrant Out', *Sun News-Pictorial*, 9 January 1925, p. 3.

Chapter 2: 'As many sides as the Kohinoor'
1 'Mr E. C. DeGaris: an irrigationist of the early eighties', *Sarnia Topics*, 16 April 1919, p. 8.
2 'Mr E. C. DeGaris: an irrigationist of the early eighties'.
3 'A Patriarch Comes to Perth', *The Call*, 20 August 1920, p. 7.
4 'A memento at 93', undated item in E. C. DeGaris papers MS 7076.
5 DeGaris, *Victories of Failure*, p. 8.
6 DeGaris, *Victories of Failure*, p. 9.
7 'Mr. Elisha Clement DeGaris', *Cyclopedia of Victoria*, vol. 3, p. 276.
8 H. A. Overend, 'The Church and the Community', in C. Irving Benson (ed.), *A Century of Victorian Methodism Melbourne*, Spectator Publishing Co., 1935, pp. 280–8.
9 Ruth Lee, *Woman War Doctor*, Australian Scholarly Publishing, Kew, 2014, p. 4.
10 Ruth Lee and David Nichols, 'Life…the manifestation of a purpose', *Journal of the Royal Australian Historical Society*, June 2006, p. 49.
11 DeGaris, *Victories of Failure*, p. 1.
12 DeGaris, *Victories of Failure*, pp. 1–2.
13 DeGaris, *Victories of Failure*, p. 16.
14 M. C. DeGaris, quoted in R. L. Lee, *Woman War Doctor: The Life of Mary DeGaris*, Australian Scholarly Publishing, Kew, 2014, p. 14; DeGaris, *Victories of Failure*, pp. 14–15.
15 'Mr. Elisha Clement DeGaris', *Cyclopedia of Victoria*, vol. 3, p. 276.
16 J. C. Lawton, 'Notes on the Circuits', in C. I. Benson (ed.), *A Century of Victorian Methodism*, Melbourne, Spectator Publishing Co., 1935, pp. 403–95.
17 E. C. DeGaris, letter to 'Jack', 21 February 1921, in L. G. DeGaris papers, National Library of Australia (NLA) MS2303 box 41.
18 'Mr E. C. DeGaris: an irrigationist of the early eighties', p. 8.
19 DeGaris, *Victories of Failure*, p. 11.
20 E. C. DeGaris, letter to 'Jack'.
21 'Mr E. C. DeGaris: an irrigationist of the early eighties'.
22 E. C. DeGaris, letter to 'Jack', 21 February 1921, in NLA MS2303 box 41.
23 E. C. DeGaris, letter to 'Jack', 21 February 1921, in NLA MS2303 box 41.
24 'Central Irrigation League', Melbourne *Argus*, 14 October 1884.

25 E. C. DeGaris, papers MS 7085, *Prospectus of the Associated Australian Yeomanry Ltd*, 1891.
26 E. C. DeGaris, papers MS 7075, sales figures dated 11 March – 13 May 1924.
27 'Mr. Elisha Clement DeGaris', *Cyclopedia of Victoria*, vol. 3, p. 276.
28 E. C. DeGaris, papers MS 7085, *Prospectus of the Associated Australian Yeomanry Ltd*, 1891.
29 'Mr E. C. DeGaris: an irrigationist of the early eighties'.
30 'Mr. Elisha Clement DeGaris', *Cyclopedia of Victoria*, vol. 3, p. 276.
31 E. C. DeGaris, 'Rainfall needed', notes in E. C. DeGaris papers MS 7077 on back of envelope dated 14 February 1907.
32 K. A. Ferris, 'History and Development of the Dried Fruits Industry in Australia', State Library of Victoria (SLV), p. 1; K. Voullaire, *Mildura Irrigation Settlement: the Early Years*, Sunraysia Daily, Mildura, 1985, p. 9.
33 'The Federal Elections', *Mildura Cultivator*, 5 January 1901, p. 2.
34 Voullaire, *Mildura Irrigation Settlement*, p. 15.
35 'Wanderer', 'With the Chaffey Brothers', *The Chronicle*, cutting dated 12 April 1890, in E. C. DeGaris papers MS7080 box 407, scrapbook labelled 'Book of Securities'; 'Interview with Mrs Beth Coldicutt by Carolyn Rasmussen, 12 October 1992'.
36 E. C. DeGaris, letter to 'Jack', 21 February 1921, in NLA MS2303 box 41.
37 'Mr E. C. DeGaris: an irrigationist of the early eighties', p. 9.
38 'To the electors of Yarra', 11 January 1910, typescript p. 2, in E. C. DeGaris papers, SLV MS 7085.
39 'The Fusion Candidate for Yarra', *Wagga Worker*, 17 March 1910, p. 15.
40 K. A. Ferris, 'History and Development of the Dried Fruits Industry in Australia', Melbourne, Victoria Dried Fruits Board, 1966, p. 1.
41 Chaffey Brothers Limited, *The Australian Irrigation Colonies' Director's report*, Mildura, 1890.
42 'Irrigation: The Chaffey Colonies on the Murray', *Daily Telegraph*, 30 December 1989, cutting in scrapbook labelled 'Book of Securities' in E. C. DeGaris papers, SLV MS7080 box 407.
43 DeGaris, *Victories of Failure*, p. 12.
44 DeGaris, *Victories of Failure*, p. 4.
45 DeGaris, *Victories of Failure*, p. 20.
46 DeGaris, *Victories of Failure*, p. 20.
47 DeGaris, *Victories of Failure*, p. 6.
48 DeGaris, *Victories of Failure*, p. 3.
49 DeGaris, *Victories of Failure*, p. 23.
50 DeGaris, *Victories of Failure*, p. 6.

Chapter 3: 'Smile with your eyes', 1898–1910
1 DeGaris, *Victories of Failure*, p. 29.
2 DeGaris, *Victories of Failure*, p. 29.

3   DeGaris, *Victories of Failure*, p. 30.
4   DeGaris, *Victories of Failure*, p. 32.
5   DeGaris, *Victories of Failure*, p. 32.
6   DeGaris, *Victories of Failure*, p. 89.
7   DeGaris, *Victories of Failure*, p. 38.
8   DeGaris, *Victories of Failure*, p. 42.
9   DeGaris, *Victories of Failure*, p. 51.
10 DeGaris, *Victories of Failure*, p. 56.
11 DeGaris, *Victories of Failure*, p. 66.
12 C. J. DeGaris, letter to E. DeGaris, 17 April 1899, in possession of Kathy Hancock.
13 C. J. DeGaris, letter to E. DeGaris, 21 August 1899, in possession of Kathy Hancock.
14 C. J. DeGaris, letter to E. DeGaris, 12 April 1899, in possession of Kathy Hancock.
15 DeGaris, *Victories of Failure*, p. 80.
16 'From Lord Roberts to J. C. DeGaris', *Mildura Cultivator*, 10 November 1900, p. 7.
17 DeGaris, *Victories of Failure*, p. 51.
18 'General News', *Mildura Cultivator*, 30 March 1901, p. 3.
19 For instance, 'Methodists vs Presbyterians', *Mildura Cultivator*, 31 May 1902, p. 8.
20 'Football', *Mildura Cultivator*, 21 June 1902, p. 10.
21 'Editorial', *Age*, 22 May 1869, p. 2.
22 A. Lapthorne, *Mildura Calling*, 3rd edition, Mildura Gallery Society, Mildura, 1965, p. 30. 'ADFA' is an acronym shared since 1986 with the Australian Defence Force Academy; the organisation now prefers DFA.
23 'A Trip to the Old Country', Hamilton *Spectator*, 18 March 1902, p. 4.
24 DeGaris, *Victories of Failure*, p. 90.
25 DeGaris, *Victories of Failure*, p. 91.
26 'Local News', *Mildura Cultivator*, 14 November 1891, p. 2.
27 DeGaris, *Victories of Failure*, p. 92.
28 DeGaris, *Victories of Failure*, p. 96.
29 DeGaris, *Victories of Failure*, p. 91.
30 See for instance A. Hunt, 'The Great Masturbation Panic and the Discourses of Moral Regulation in Nineteenth- and Early Twentieth-Century Britain', *Journal of the History of Sexuality*, vol. 8, no. 4, 1998, pp. 575–615.
31 DeGaris, *Victories of Failure*, p. 91.
32 DeGaris, *Victories of Failure*, p. 92.
33 R. L. Lee *Woman War Doctor* pp. 26–8 *passim*.
34 'Local News', *Mildura Cultivator*, 9 August 1902, p. 10.
35 'Local News', *Mildura Cultivator*, 18 October 1902, p. 7.

36 Presumably this was a very different type of 'racy' from what we might conventionally expect, notwithstanding the term is archaic today. 'An Australian Across the Sea', *Mildura Cultivator*, 22 November 1902, p. 10.
37 K. DeGaris, *DeGaris: In Australia since 1854*, Ken DeGaris, Struan, 1991, p. 53.
38 'Mildura Musical and Elocutionary Competition', Adelaide *Chronicle*, 26 September 1903, pp. 13–14.
39 DeGaris, *Victories of Failure*, p. 112.
40 'Mildura Musical and Elocutionary Competition'.
41 'South Street Competitions', Ballarat *Star*, 5 October 1905, p. 1.
42 M. Hartwell, 'Sim's Little Girl', Vermont *Watchman and State Journal*, 30 July 1873, p. 4.
43 In the present century we grapple with the meaning and purpose of the 'coon song'. They are, of course, an American invention, but white Australians took to them with gusto. Written to be sung in a particular patois, often by white performers in blackface, they were typically comedic or sentimental, and presented African-Americans as childish, foolish and backward. A quick online survey of Australian newspapers sees the genre first mentioned in 1893, when 'Little Liza Loves You' was performed at the Gaiety Theatre, Brisbane; and the last at the Molloy Tennis Club Social, held north of Cairns, Queensland in 1954. In 1907, George Hall, musical conductor for J. C. Williamson, acknowledged the popularity of the 'coon song' but suggested the Australian disposition was for 'something more musicianly'. ('Australia's Taste in Music', Melbourne *Punch*, 14 February 1907, p. 29). C. J.'s inability to carry a tune probably did not matter when it came to performing a 'coon song'.
44 Untitled item dated 23/10/99 in scrapbook labelled 'Book of Securities', E. C. DeGaris papers, State Library of Victoria, MS7080 box 407.
45 Anon, 'Mr. Elisha Clement DeGaris', J. Smith, *Cyclopedia of Victoria*, v. III, Cyclopedia Company of Victoria, Melbourne, 1903, p. 276.
46 'Welcoming Ode to the Railway', *Mildura Cultivator*, 13 July 1901, p. 2.
47 'Carnegie Free Library', Melbourne *Age*, 18 January 1907, p. 6. A war memorial clock tower would be added in 1922, see A. Lapthorne, *Mildura Calling*, p. 41.
48 'Local News', *Mildura Cultivator*, 12 May 1906, p. 6.
49 'A Generous Millionaire', Adelaide *Express and Telegraph*, 3 August 1906, p. 4.
50 'Table Talk', Orange *Leader*, 4 August 1906, p. 2.
51 'Local News', *Mildura Cultivator*, 12 October 1907, p. 7.
52 'Gift from Mr Carnegie', Melbourne *Argus*, 16 October 1907, p. 6.
53 C. J. DeGaris, letter to M. DeGaris, 3 August 1907, in possession of K. Hancock.
54 DeGaris, *Victories of Failure*, p. iii.
55 'Wedding', *Mildura Cultivator*, 2 October 1907, p. 3; see also *Australasian*, 9 November 1907, p. 64.
56 Information courtesy Harold Corbould, personal communication, July 2019.

57 DeGaris, *Victories of Failure*, p. 117.
58 DeGaris, *Victories of Failure*, p. 121.
59 DeGaris, *Victories of Failure*, p. 131.
60 'Local News', *Mildura Cultivator*, 7 October 1905, p. 7. Etna had not erupted since 1669, but unbeknownst to all, it would erupt again in 1928.
61 'Wedding', *Mildura Cultivator*, 27 January 1906, p. 10.
62 DeGaris, *Victories of Failure*, p. 122.
63 DeGaris, *Victories of Failure*, p. 132.
64 DeGaris, *Victories of Failure*, p. 137.
65 DeGaris, *Victories of Failure*, p. 142.
66 DeGaris, *Victories of Failure*, p. 143.
67 C. J. DeGaris, letter to M. DeGaris, 3 August 1907, in possession of K. Hancock.
68 C. J. DeGaris, letter to M. DeGaris, 9 August 1908, in possession of K. Hancock.

Chapter 4: Establishing an empire, 1913–20

1 'Sporting Items', *Mildura Cultivator*, 23 April 1913, p. 9.
2 'Lawn Tennis', *Mildura Cultivator*, 17 May 1913, p. 11.
3 'Provincial Tennis Championship', *Mildura Cultivator*, 26 November 1913, p. 10.
4 'Mildura District Hospital', *Mildura Cultivator*, 20 December 1913, p. 5.
5 'Local News', *Mildura Cultivator*, 7 May 1913, p. 7.
6 'First Mildura Irrigation Trust', *Mildura Cultivator*, 19 March 1913, p. 8.
7 'Mildura Growers' Progress Association', *Mildura Cultivator*, 30 August 1913, p. 7.
8 'Mildura Caledonian Society', *Mildura Cultivator*, 23 July 1913, p. 5.
9 'Mildura District Hospital', *Mildura Cultivator*, 19 July 1913, p. 5.
10 C. J. DeGaris, letter to M. DeGaris, 18 July 1912, in possession of K. Hancock.
11 I am grateful to Hal Corbould for uncovering archival material – a postcard and an autograph book – that reveal Marianne, known for much of her life as Molly, was commonly known as Mary around 1910. That this may have been to avoid confusion with Mary DeGaris is my own surmise.
12 'Great Clearing Sale!', *Mildura Cultivator*, 29 April 1899, p. 4.
13 'Local News', *Mildura Cultivator*, 14 April 1909, p. 7.
14 'Olympia', *Mildura Cultivator*, 13 November 1912, p. 7.
15 C. J. DeGaris, letter to M. DeGaris, 18 July 1912, in possession of K. Hancock.
16 C. J. DeGaris, letter to M. DeGaris, 3 August 1907, in possession K Hancock.
17 'The Founder of Mildura', *Age*, 5 June 1926, p. 16.
18 'Early Closing Movement', *Mildura Telegraph and Darling and Lower Murray Advocate*, 18 July 1916, p. 2.

19 'Fast Motor Run', *Mildura Telegraph and Darling and Lower Murray Advocate*, 6 February 1914, p. 4.
20 'Mildura Musical and Elocutionary Competitions', *Mildura Cultivator*, 22 October 1910, p. 8.
21 'Social Letter', *Mildura Cultivator*, 27 July 1912, p. 12.
22 DeGaris, *Victories of Failure*, p. 108.
23 'Rowing Club Concert', *Mildura Cultivator*, 19 March 1910, p. 8.
24 'Concert at Irymple', *Mildura Cultivator*, 13 September 1911, p. 9.
25 'Obituary', *Riverina Recorder*, 3 October 1923, p. 2.
26 'Country News', Melbourne *Argus*, 28 September 1923, p. 18, records her death. 'Mildura', *Age*, 28 September 1923, p. 12, notes she was 40.
27 'Mildura Tennis Association', *Mildura Cultivator*, 20 September 1913, p. 11.
28 'Local News', *Mildura Cultivator*, 15 January 1913, p. 10.
29 A. Lapthorne, *Mildura Calling*, p. 31.
30 'Advt', *Mildura Cultivator*, 22 January 1913, p. 8.
31 'Local News', *Mildura Cultivator*, 14 December 1912, p. 11.
32 S. Blayde, 'Notes and Comments', *Mildura Cultivator*, 17 October 1914, p. 4.
33 DeGaris, *Victories of Failure*, p. 185.
34 DeGaris, *Victories of Failure*, p. 188.
35 'News of the River', *Murray Pioneer and Australian River Record*, 11 July 1913, p. 5.
36 'The Country', Adelaide *Advertiser*, 14 August 1913, p. 12.
37 'Pyap's New Manager', *Murray Pioneer and Australian River Record*, 4 June 1914, p. 4.
38 'Legion of Frontiersmen', *Mildura Cultivator*, 1 March 1913, p. 5.
39 'Round the Packing-Houses', *Mildura Cultivator*, 25 January 1913, p. 4.
40 'Patriotic meeting', *Mildura Cultivator*, 12 August 1914, p. 8.
41 'For the Empire', *Mildura Telegraph and Darling and Lower Murray Advocate*, 14 August 1914, p. 4.
42 'Patriotic meeting'.
43 'For the Empire'.
44 'Patriotic meeting'.
45 C. J. DeGaris, 'Belgian Relief Fund', *Mildura Cultivator*, 27 February 1915, p. 7.
46 'Mildura Shire Council', *Mildura Telegraph and Darling and Lower Murray Advocate*, 4 December 1914, p. 2.
47 'Australian Dried Fruits Association', *Mildura Cultivator*, 13 February 1915, p. 6.
48 'Local News', *Mildura Cultivator*, 14 November 1914, p. 10.
49 E. C. DeGaris, letter to M. DeGaris, 10 September 1914, in possession K. Hancock.
50 'Ambition Run Mad', *Mildura Telegraph and Lower Murray Advocate*, 9 April 1915, p. 2.

51 C. J. DeGaris, *Ambition Run Mad, or Whom the Gods Destroy: A Military Drama*, Murray Pioneer Printing Office, n.d.
52 C. J. DeGaris, *Ambition Run Mad*, National Archives of Australia, A1336, 3670, p. 10.
53 'The Shire Elections', *Mildura Cultivator*, 30 August 1902, p. 7.
54 'Returned Soldiers Welcomed', *Mildura Telegraph and Lower Murray Advocate*, 8 August 1916, p. 3.
55 'Russian Refugees' Fund', *Mildura Telegraph and Darling and Lower Murray Advocate*, 15 August 1916, p. 2.
56 DeGaris, *Victories of Failure*, p. 219.
57 'Anti-Conscription Meeting', *Mildura Telegraph and Darling and Lower Murray Advocate*, 24 October 1916, p. 2.
58 'Returned Soldiers Welcomed'.
59 R. L. Lee, *Woman War Doctor*, p. 73.
60 'The War Loan', *Mildura Telegraph and Darling and Lower Murray Advocate*, 28 July 1916, p. 2.
61 DeGaris, *Victories of Failure*, p. 228.
62 'University Extension Centre', *Mildura Telegraph and Darling and Lower Murray Advocate*, 13 October 1916, p. 3.
63 C. J. DeGaris, *Repatriation: A Gigantic Problem, a Practical Scheme*, C. J. DeGaris, Melbourne, 1917(?), p. 3.
64 DeGaris, *Repatriation*, p. 2.
65 DeGaris, *Repatriation*, p. 5.
66 DeGaris, *Repatriation*, p. 6.
67 DeGaris, *Repatriation*, p. 8.
68 Lapthorne, *Mildura Calling*, p. 35.
69 'Hospital entertainment', *Ouyen Mail*, 12 September 1917, p. 5.
70 'Grand Concert', *Ouyen Mail*, 5 September 1917 p. 4. I have calculated Violet's age from the fact that her funeral notice ('Violet May DeGaris', *Sydney Morning Herald*, 23 September 1968, p. 27) puts her at 72 in 1968.
71 'Social Letter', *Mildura Cultivator*, 29 November 1919, p. 3.
72 DeGaris, *Victories of Failure*, p. 351.
73 DeGaris, *Victories of Failure*, p. 385.
74 'Penelope', 'Social Letter', *Mildura Cultivator*, 30 September 1916, p. 12.
75 'Local News', Mildura *Cultivator*, 23 September 1916, p. 9.
76 During their divorce proceedings in late 1922, C. J. was asked whether her affair with Ronald Coote that year was 'the only occasion you have had trouble with your wife?' to which C. J. replied, 'Yes, of this nature'. 'DeGaris' Discovery', Perth *Truth*, 2 December 1922, p. 8.
77 E. C. DeGaris, letter to W. B. Chaffey, 14 June 1918, in possession K. Hancock.
78 C. J. DeGaris, letter to B. DeGaris, 23 June 1919, in possession K. Hancock.
79 E. C. DeGaris, letter to children, 15 July 1918, in possession K. Hancock.

80 '"The Australian" Interviews C. J. DeGaris', Perth *Australian*, 9 January 1920, p. 5.
81 DeGaris, *Victories of Failure*, p. 344.
82 "Stralia's Sun-Raysed Sensation', Angaston *Leader*, 27 March 1919, p. 4.
83 'Kendenup Salaries', Melbourne *Argus*, 8 March 1924, p. 17.
84 'Circulation of *Topics*', *Sarnia Topics*, vol. 4 no. 1, 19 February 1919, p. 1.
85 'Circulation of *Topics*'.
86 'Australian Dried Fruits Association', Adelaide *Express and Telegraph*, 23 April 1902, p. 3.
87 C. J. DeGaris, letter to M. C. DeGaris, 12 December 1913, in possession K. Hancock.
88 DeGaris, *Victories of Failure*, p. 244.
89 DeGaris, *Victories of Failure*, pp. 248–9.
90 DeGaris, *Victories of Failure*, p. 250.
91 'A.D.F.A. Annual Conference', *Murray Pioneer and Australian River Record*, 1 November 1918, p. 3.
92 'Australian Dried Fruits Association', *Mildura Cultivator*, 2 November 1918, p. 13.
93 'Sun-Raysed Stunts', Hobart *World*, 31 July 1920, p. 3.
94 'Sun-Raysed Fruits', Adelaide *Advertiser*, 14 December 1918, p. 11.
95 'Social Letter', *Mildura Cultivator*, 30 November 1918, p. 12.
96 'Local News', *Mildura Cultivator*, 15 February 1919, p. 10.
97 'Farm and Garden', *Murray Pioneer and Australian River Record*, 24 October 1919, p. 2.
98 'River Murray Problems', Adelaide *Observer*, 31 May 1919, p. 4.
99 'Farm and Garden'.
100 'Farm and Garden'.
101 'The Eternal Why', *Smith's Weekly*, 12 July 1919, p. 4.
102 'Australian Dried Fruits', *Daily Commercial News and Shipping List*, 16 July 1919, p. 11.
103 'Good Little Normey', Rockhampton *Morning Bulletin*, 18 January 1919, p. 3.
104 'Harry Julius: the one Australian who draws for the cinema', *The Triad*, 10 July 1916, p. 10.
105 'Economy as a Food', *Farmer's Advocate*, 7 February 1919, p. 2; 'Publicity Director at Work', *Murray Pioneer and Australian River Record*, 7 February 1919, p. 3.
106 'Publicity Buildings', *Mildura Cultivator*, 22 March 1919, p. 6.
107 'Publicity Buildings'.
108 'The Little Normey', *Sunday Times*, 7 September 1919, p. 14.
109 'Local News', *Mildura Cultivator*, 31 March 1920, p. 8.
110 'The Normey and Molly Duologues', Peterborough *Times and Northern Advertiser*, 13 February 1920, p. 4.
111 'Fruits Industry and City Campaign', *Mildura Cultivator*, 28 June 1919, p. 5.

NOTES TO CHAPTER 4

112 '"The Australian" Interviews C. J. DeGaris', Perth *Australian*, 9 January 1920, p. 5.
113 'Australian Dried Fruits', Adelaide *Register*, 4 May 1920, p. 9.
114 'Farm and Garden', *Murray Pioneer and Australian River Record*, 24 October 1919, p. 2.
115 'The A.D.F.A. Tea Room', Prahran *Telegraph*, 17 May 1919, p. 6.
116 'Popularising "Sun-Raysed" Fruits in Melbourne', Angaston *Leader*, 6 June 1919, p. 3.
117 'Farm and Garden'.
118 DeGaris, *Victories of Failure*, p. 297.
119 'River Murray Problems'.
120 'Farm and Garden', *Murray Pioneer and Australian River Record*, 24 October 1919, p. 2.
121 'A Poet with a Pistol', Brisbane *Truth*, 19 November 1905, p. 3.
122 'Grant Hervey', Brisbane *Truth*, 27 June 1915, p. 6.
123 She died (as Margaret M. Kearney) in 1935 aged 63 or 64. 'Who's Who and What's What', Australian *Worker*, 1 May 1935, p. 14; 'Lady Journalist's Death', Kyogle *Examiner*, 10 May 1935, p. 7.
124 'Odds and Ends', Lismore *Northern Star*, 31 January 1900, p. 5.
125 'Society Gossip', Adelaide *Critic*, 5 July 1902, p. 26.
126 G. Hervey, 'Steerage to the West', 21 December 1902, p. 12.
127 'A Literary Star', Perth *Sunday Times*, 14 December 1902, p. 4.
128 G. Hervey, 'The Inky W. A.', Wagga *Worker*, 20 February 1904, p. 7.
129 'Peeps at People', Perth *Sunday Times*, 4 June 1905, p. 13.
130 'Grant Hervey', Brisbane *Truth*, 27 June 1915, p. 6.
131 'Melbourne', Bendigo *Advertiser*, 23 March 1901, p. 5.
132 'Shooting Sensation', Melbourne *Herald*, 24 November 1905, p. 6.
133 'A Poet with a Pistol'.
134 'Theatre Royal', *Table Talk*, 2 November 1905, p. 17.
135 'A Poet with a Pistol'.
136 'Shooting Sensation'.
137 'Shooting Sensation'.
138 'Shooting Sensation'.
139 'Shooting Sensation'.
140 'Shooting Sensation'.
141 'Shooting Affray in Melbourne', *Sydney Morning Herald*, 10 November 1905, p. 8; 'Hervey-Baker Case', Boulder *Evening Star*, 24 November 1905, p. 3.
142 'Shooting Sensation'.
143 'Victoria', *Sydney Morning Herald*, 25 November 1905, p. 13.
144 'Hervey Shooting Case', Adelaide *Advertiser*, 15 December 1905, p. 7.
145 'Decentralisation Movement', *Age*, 11 April 1910, p. 11.
146 'Railway Extension', Portland *Guardian*, 24 April 1912, p. 3.
147 'The People's Party', *Casterton News*, 9 January 1911, p. 3.

148 J. Brett, *The Enigmatic Mr. Deakin*, Text, Melbourne, 2017, p. 407.
149 G. Hervey, 'How "Liberals" Flout the Law', *Labor Call*, 28 August 1913, p. 2.
150 G. Hervey, 'The Inky W. A.'.
151 'Libel action', Portland *Guardian*, 1 May 1912, p. 2; 'Actions for Libel', *Horsham Times*, 30 April 1912, p. 5.
152 Editorial, Casterton *News*, 21 March 1912, p. 2; 'Visit of the Railway Commissioners', Casterton *News*, 28 March 1912, p. 4.
153 'A Sportsman and a Man', Mount Gambier *Border Watch*, 3 January 1912, p. 1.
154 'Withdrawal of Mr Grant Hervey', Hamilton *Spectator*, 14 June 1912, p. 6.
155 'Adam Lindsay Gordon', Penshurst *Free Press*, 6 July 1912, p. 2.
156 'A Sportsman and a Man'.
157 'Grant Hervey', Melbourne *Truth*, 9 January 1915, p. 6.
158 'Friendless and Alone', Adelaide *Register*, 1 January 1915, p. 9.
159 'Grant Hervey', Melbourne *Truth*, 9 January 1915, p. 6.
160 'Journalist Charged', Sydney *Daily Telegraph*, 19 December 1914, p. 15; 'Grant Hervey convicted', Hamilton *Spectator*, 5 February 1915, p. 4.
161 'Grant Hervey', Melbourne *Truth*, 9 January 1915, p. 6.
162 'Friendless and Alone'.
163 'Grant Hervey', *Age*, 31 December 1914, p. 4.
164 M. Cannon, *That Damned Democrat: John Norton, an Australian Populist 1858–1916*, Melbourne University Press, Carlton, 1981, p. 42.
165 'Grant Hervey', Brisbane *Truth*, 27 June 1915, p. 6.
166 'A Startling Charge', Hobart *Mercury*, 30 December 1914, p. 5.
167 M. Cannon, *That Damned Democrat*, p. 42.
168 M. Cannon, *That Damned Democrat*, p. 30.
169 'Grant Hervey Sentenced', Melbourne *Truth*, 13 February 1915, p. 6.
170 'Grant Hervey', Brisbane *Truth*, 27 June 1915, p. 6. We will, of course, never know the full truth of this scenario. I have taken the attitude that if it quacked like a duck it was one. However, the situation may be more complicated than it appears. Jefferys and Josephs may have sent the initial telegram as a joke; Hervey may have then seen an opportunity to use the situation to persecute Gazzard and the Casterton *News*. Hervey did suggest Norton had double-crossed him, which might arguably indicate at very least that Norton had encouraged Hervey to embark on an affair with Ada, only to then – for reasons of 'madness' or otherwise – change his mind and deny all involvement. The incessant quacking, however, is difficult to ignore.
171 G. Hervey, 'Consider the Lilies', Melbourne *Socialist*, 20 September 1918, p. 3.
172 'Grant Hervey on Gaol Life', Hobart *World*, 4 August 1919, p. 3.
173 DeGaris, *Victories of Failure*, p. 298.
174 'The Boobs of Mildura', *Smiths Weekly*, 16 August 1919, p. 1.
175 DeGaris, *Victories of Failure*, p. 301.
176 'Greater Mildura', *Mildura Cultivator*, 6 August 1919, p. 10.
177 'The Boobs of Mildura', p. 2.

178 'Greater Mildura'.
179 G. M. Harvey, 'Wanted – A Goethals for Mildura and 5000', *Mildura Cultivator*, 10 September 1919, p. 10.
180 DeGaris, *Victories of Failure*, p. 299.
181 G. Hall, 'In DeGaris' Employ', in L. Milborn (ed.), *Mildura Police Station: The First 100 Years: Addendum and Corrigendum*, Les Milborn, Mildura, 1996, p. 167.
182 DeGaris, *Victories of Failure*, p. 304.
183 'Sun-Raysed Fruits', Perth *Sunday Times*, 7 December 1919, p. 3.
184 ''Stralia's Sun-Raysed Sensation'.
185 'A.D.F.A. Conference', *Murray Pioneer and Australian River Record*, 31 October 1919, p. 3.
186 'A.D.F.A. Publicity Methods', *Mildura Cultivator*, 15 May 1920, p. 4.
187 'A.D.F.A. Publicity Methods', p. 4.
188 'A.D.F.A. Publicity Methods', p. 7.

Chapter 5: 'The Aussie Glide'
1 'Dip-Tin', 'Sun-Raysed Column', Burra *Record*, 12 May 1920, p. 3.
2 'The "Name": One "Conscientious" Objector', *Sarnia Topics*, vol. 3, no. 12, 22 January 1919, p. 3.
3 DeGaris, *Victories of Failure*, p. 342.
4 DeGaris, *Victories of Failure*, p. 343.
5 DeGaris, *Victories of Failure*, p. 344.
6 '"Sun-Raysed" A Word Wide Known', Perth *Daily News*, 5 January 1920, p. 6.
7 'A Picnic on the Sands', *Murray Pioneer and Australian River Record*, 5 March 1920, p. 5.
8 DeGaris, *Victories of Failure*, p. 344.
9 DeGaris, *Victories of Failure*, p. 346.
10 F. Van Straten, 'The Riddle of "FFF", A Forgotten Australian Musical Comedy', *Australasian Music Research*, no. 6, 2002, pp. 105–19.
11 'Social Letter', *Mildura Cultivator*, 29 May 1920, p. 12.
12 DeGaris, *Victories of Failure*, p. 316.
13 DeGaris, *Victories of Failure*, p. 349.
14 'Scientific Painless Dentistry', Horsham *Times*, 25 June 1920, p. 5.
15 'C. J. DeGaris flies home', *Mildura Cultivator*, 26 June 1920, p. 7.
16 'Personal Items', *The Bulletin*, 1 July 1920, p. 14.
17 'All About the Town', *Everyone's*, 14 July 1920, p. 5.
18 S. Blayde, 'Some Fly', *Mildura Cultivator*, 3 July 1920, p. 13.
19 'Combined staffs pay tribute to "C. J. D."', *Mildura Cultivator*, 3 July 1920, p. 13
20 'Man and Machine of Many Records', Melbourne *Herald*, 24 January 1921, p. 2.

NOTES TO CHAPTER 5

21 'Mildura to Sydney', *Tweed Daily*, 7 July 1920, p. 3.
22 'Aeroplane Flights', Kalgoorlie *Miner*, 10 July 1920, p. 4.
23 'F. F. F.', Adelaide *Advertiser*, 30 August 1920, p. 8.
24 'F. F. F.', *Mildura Cultivator*, 1 September 1920, p. 2.
25 'DeGaris! The man who put the sun in Sun-Raysed', *The Call*, 24 September 1920 p. 2.
26 DeGaris, *Victories of Failure*, p. 384.
27 'F. F. F.', Melbourne *Age*, 8 October 1920, p. 12.
28 'F. F. F.', Adelaide *Daily Herald*, 6 September 1920, p. 2.
29 'H.R.H. The Prince of Wales', *Bunbury Herald and Blackwood Express*, 23 July 1920, p. 7.
30 'Local News', *Mildura Cultivator*, 14 August 1920, p. 10.
31 'The Prince's Mail', Adelaide *Express and Telegraph*, 18 August 1920, p. 2.
32 'The Prince of Wales', Broken Hill *Barrier Miner*, 19 August 1920, p. 4.
33 'Prince's Mails Received on Thursday', Mildura *Cultivator*, 21 August 1920, p. 10.
34 'DeGaris! The man who put the sun in Sun-Raysed'.
35 'DeGaris! The man who put the sun in Sun-Raysed'.
36 C. J. DeGaris, 'The Golden West', *Murray Pioneer and Australian River Record*, 6 February 1920, p. 2.
37 'Obituary Notices', Adelaide *Observer*, 28 May 1927 p. 43. This is the source that suggests Claffey's first name was John.
38 'Kendenup Inquiry', Perth *Daily News*, 22 February 1924, p. 5. The land agent's name is here reported as 'Clabby' but more commonly in accounts from the time it is 'Claffey'. Claffey ultimately refused to pay Taylor more than £50, a considerable amount for contact with a man like C. J., who would not have been difficult to approach.
39 F. W. Rowe, 'The Standard Gold Mining Company Ltd. of Kendenup', typescript dated July 1965, in State Library of Western Australia, SLWAPR14528/STA.
40 'Kendenup Sold', Albany *Advertiser*, 21 August 1920, p. 3.
41 'Titus Salt', 'Purchase of Kendenup', *Albany Dispatch*, 26 February 1920, p. 1.
42 'Mr. D. T. Edmunds Dead', Adelaide *Mail*, 26 September 1925, p. 5.
43 W. Grogan, *Report of the Royal Commission appointed to inquire into and report upon the establishment of the Settlement at Kendenup*, Government Printer, Perth, 1922, p. 4.
44 'Good News for W.A.', Perth *Australian*, 20 August 1920, p. 4.
45 'Citizens or Sheep?', Kendenup *Index*, August 1921, p. 1.
46 'Did You Know Your Country Was as Big as This?', Melbourne *Evening Sun*, 6 May 1924, p. 2.
47 'Come to Kendenup' *Graphic*, 20 October 1921, in J. J. Simons' scrapbook, J. J. Simons papers, State Library of Western Australia, MN3065.
48 'C J DeGaris, "Kendenup"', Kendenup *Index*, July 1921, p. 1.

49 'Kendenup Chirps', Kendenup *Index*, June 1921, p. 16.
50 'United States of Australia', Melbourne *Evening Sun*, 1 February 1924, p. 3.
51 V. Courtney, *The Life Story of J. J. Simons, Founder of the Young Australia League*, Young Australia League Inc., Sydney, 1961, p. vii.
52 Courtney, *The Life Story of J. J. Simons*, p. vii.
53 Courtney, *The Life Story of J. J. Simons*, p. 29.
54 'Mr. J. J. Simons', Sydney *Sunday Times*, 13 November 1927, p. 4.
55 Courtney, *The Life Story of J. J. Simons*, p. 31.
56 'Mildura's Hustler', Perth *Daily News*, 21 September 1920, p. 7.
57 'DeGaris! The man who put the sun in Sun-Raysed'.
58 In his interview with Bill Bunbury, C. J.'s nephew Peter Sutcliffe remembers spending hours poring over C. J.'s diaries, which his mother Wilga, C. J.'s sister-in-law, had kept in her shed. B. Bunbury, 'Interview with Peter Sutcliffe and Arthur Webb', 1991, State Library of Western Australia Oral History Collection, OH2636/12.
59 DeGaris, *Victories of Failure*, p. 370.
60 DeGaris, *Victories of Failure*, p. 385.
61 DeGaris, *Victories of Failure*, p. 385.
62 'Kendenup Commission', *West Australian*, 28 May 1924, p. 7.
63 'Kendenup Chirps', Kendenup *Index*, June 1921, pp. 15–16.
64 'Newspaper sends special investigator to Kendenup', Melbourne *Argus*, 20 January 1921, p. 8.
65 '£35 an Acre Land for £10 at KENDENUP, W. A.', *Australian Business*, March 1921, p. 36.
66 'Kendenup (Western Australia) Land Now for Sale', Melbourne *Argus*, 13 January 1921, p. 4.
67 'Kendenup Chirps', Kendenup *Index*, May 1922, p. 12.
68 DeGaris, *Victories of Failure*, p. 389. Beverley is called 'Mr. Gerard' in this account. It seems likely that the trip took place on 22 September 1920 ('Mildura's Hustler').
69 DeGaris, *Victories of Failure*, p. 390. Frank Coote is called 'Curry'.
70 DeGaris, *Victories of Failure*, p. 392.
71 DeGaris, *Victories of Failure*, p. 397.
72 'Newspaper sends special investigator to Kendenup'.
73 'Local News', *Mildura Cultivator*, 31 May 1913, p. 10.
74 'King's Theatre', *Table Talk*, 14 October 1920, p. 14.
75 'King's Theatre – F. F. F.', *Age*, 11 October 1920, p. 8.
76 'F. F. F.' *Mildura Cultivator*, 1 September 1920, p. 2.
77 DeGaris, *Victories of Failure*, p. 408.
78 F. Van Straten, 'The Riddle of "FFF"', p. 112.
79 DeGaris, *Victories of Failure*, pp. 361–2.
80 'A.D.F.A. Publicity Methods,' p. 4.

81 DeGaris, *Victories of Failure*, pp. 406. For no apparent reason, the *Victories of Failure* puts the publication of the first issue at 15 October (p. 405).
82 'Personal', Wagga Wagga *Daily Advertiser*, 8 June 1923, p. 2.
83 'Launching of the Country Party', *The Farmer and Settler*, 11 July 1913, p. 4.
84 'Death of Journalist', *Riverine Herald*, 10 September 1947, p. 4.
85 'Sunraysia Daily', *Murray Pioneer and Australian River Record*, 18 June 1920, p. 8.
86 'New Journalistic Venture', Launceston *Examiner*, 5 October 1920, p. 12.
87 DeGaris, *Victories of Failure*, pp. 415–16.

Chapter 6: The establishment of Australian literature, 1920

1 C. J. DeGaris, '£550 Cash' (advertisement), Melbourne *Argus*, 27 December 1919, p. 6.
2 R. Lee and D. Nichols, '"Life...the manifestation of a purpose". The uses of memoir in the writings of Mildura's DeGaris siblings', *Journal of the Royal Australian Historical Society*, vol. 92, no. 1, 2006, pp. 46–63.
3 M. Dugan, 'C. J. DeGaris as publisher', *Biblionews*, 1970, pp. 18–19.
4 R. Nile and D. Walker, 'The Mystery of the Missing Bestseller', in M. Lyons and J. Arnold (eds), *A History of the Book in Australia 1891–1945: A National Culture in a Colonised Market*, University of Queensland Press, St Lucia, 2001, p. 241.
5 C. J. DeGaris, in Harold Hansell, *The Arising of Jimmie Munro*, C. J. DeGaris Publishing House, Melbourne, 1920, p. i.
6 DeGaris, in Hansell, *Jimmie Munro*, p. i.
7 Hansell, *Jimmie Munro*, p. 1.
8 Hansell, *Jimmie Munro*, p. 2.
9 Hansell, *Jimmie Munro*, p. 4.
10 Hansell, *Jimmie Munro*, p. 6.
11 Hansell, *Jimmie Munro*, p. 10.
12 Hansell, *Jimmie Munro*, p. 8.
13 Hansell, *Jimmie Munro*, p. iii.
14 Hansell, *Jimmie Munro*, p. 12.
15 C. J. DeGaris, 'Enter: the Prince and the Publisher', in Harold Hansell, *The Everlastin' Ballads*, C. J. DeGaris Publishing House, Melbourne, 1920, p. 13.
16 'Missing Ballads', Melbourne *Advocate*, 5 August 1920, p. 11. Fans of ephemera will be interested to know that there were two war-hero Halseys, an American and a Briton. This was *not* the Admiral Halsey made famous by Paul and Linda McCartney in their 1972 hit song 'Uncle Albert/Admiral Halsey'.
17 Editorial, *Burra Record*, 3 November 1920, p. 2.
18 'Review', *Critic*, 3 November 1920, p. 9.
19 'The Everlastin' Ballads', *Coffs Harbour Advocate*, 3 November 1920, p. 2.
20 'Verse and Raisins', Sydney *Sun*, 7 November 1920, p. 19.
21 'Athanaeum Hall', Melbourne *Age*, 9 April 1921, p. 20.
22 'Athanaeum – Miss Winifred Moverley', Melbourne *Age*, 18 April 1921, p. 8.

23 'Broadcast Programmes', *West Australian*, 31 October 1925, p. 9; 'Anzac Observance', *Glenelg Guardian*, 22 April 1931, p. 1.
24 C. J. DeGaris, '£550 Cash'.
25 'Donalbain', 'The Prize Novel that Isn't'; DeGaris, *Victories of Failure*, p. 355.
26 'Victorian's Book Accepted', Melbourne *Age*, 30 May 1933, p. 6.
27 G. Hervey, 'Why I Scrapped C. J. DeGaris', *Murray Pioneer and Australian River Record*, 20 July 1923, p. 22.
28 'A Mildura Playwright', *Murray Pioneer and Australian River Record*, 24 September 1920, p. 5.
29 'News and Notes', *The Bookfellow*, 15 February 1921, p. 5. The original misspells this name as 'Wolla Miranda'.
30 'The Ashes of Achievement', *Murray Pioneer and Australian River Record*, 13 January 1922, p. 14; 'Social Letter', *Mildura Cultivator*, 18 September 1920, p. 12.
31 While there is no direct evidence of Russell attending Wesley, a review claims he has sketched the school's headmaster expertly ('New Books', Port Pirie *Recorder*, 23 December 1920, p. 3). His obituary indicates he was born in 1886; while DeGaris was two years older, he attended Wesley as a slightly more mature student after working in the family business during the 1890s Depression ('Frank Russell Dead', *Dalby Herald*, 28 December 1934, p. 3). Frank A. Russell, 'A Misapprehension Corrected', *Mildura Cultivator*, 11 September 1920, p. 7.
32 'Donalbain'.
33 Victor Courtney, 'When DeGaris slept!', *The Call*, 31 December 1920, p. 2.
34 Frank A. Russell, *The Ashes of Achievement*, C. J. DeGaris Publishing House, Melbourne, 1920, p. 111.
35 Russell, *Ashes of Achievement*, p. 191.
36 Russell, *Ashes of Achievement*, p. 311.
37 Russell, *Ashes of Achievement*, p. 349.
38 'Book Review', *W. A. Record*, 1 January 1921, p. 5.
39 'An Australian Prize Novel', *Sydney Morning Herald*, 18 December 1920, p. 8.
40 'Book Reviews: "The Ashes of Achievement"', Launceston *Daily Telegraph*, 22 December 1920, p. 5.
41 DeGaris, *Victories of Failure*, p. 31.
42 'The Skirts of Opportunity', *Mildura Cultivator*, 29 September 1920, p. 7.
43 'In the World of Music and Drama', Sydney *Mail*, 27 October 1920, p. 10; 'A Mildura Playwright'.
44 'An Australian Novel', *Queenslander*, 18 June 1921, p. 3.
45 J. M. Walsh, *The Lost Valley*, C. J. DeGaris Publishing House, Melbourne, 1921, p. 14.
46 Walsh, *The Lost Valley*, p. 22.
47 Walsh, *The Lost Valley*, p. 165.
48 'Australian Novel Competition', Melbourne *Advocate*, 13 January 1921, p. 11.

49 'Australian Prize Story', Brisbane *Daily Mail*, 19 May 1921, p. 6.
50 H. V. Evatt, *William Holman: Australian Labour Leader* Angus and Robertson, 1940 (abridged edition 1954, 1979), p. 97.
51 'Mrs Holman Dead', *Sydney Morning Herald*, 6 April 1949, p. 7.
52 Marion Mahony Griffin, *Magic of America*, copy held in Monash University Library, pp. 69–71.
53 See Marion Miller Knowles, 'The Ladies' Letter', *Advocate*, 3 March 1921, p. 28 establishing Holman's connection to the *Australasian* and 'A. K.', 'A Township Problem', *Australasian*, 7 August 1897, p. 29 ('A. K.' may well stand for 'Ada Kidgell').
54 Ada A. Holman, *Sport of the Gods*, C. J. DeGaris Publishing House, Melbourne, 1921, pp. 118, 86.
55 Holman, *Sport of the Gods*, p. 33.
56 Holman, *Sport of the Gods*, p. 24.
57 Holman, *Sport of the Gods*, p. 132.
58 Holman, *Sport of the Gods*, p. 89.
59 Holman, *Sport of the Gods*, p. 180.
60 Holman, *Sport of the Gods*, p. 299.
61 'Sport of the Gods', *Barrier Miner*, 21 October 1922, p. 6. 'Bagnio' is a coy term for 'brothel'.
62 Tom Collins (Joseph Furphy), *Rigby's Romance*, C. J. DeGaris Publishing House, Melbourne, 1921, p. 93.
63 'New Fiction', *Sydney Morning Herald*, 12 November 1921, p. 8.
64 C. J. DeGaris (ed.), *'Sun-Raysed' Children's Fairy Story Book*, F. W. Niven & Co., Melbourne, 1919.
65 'Death of Mr. J. J. Morris', Melbourne *Argus*, 21 January 1920, p. 14; 'Child killed by motor car', Melbourne *Argus*, 29 April 1921, p. 5.
66 Ethel Jackson Morris, *The White Butterfly and Other Fairy Tales*, C. J. DeGaris Publishing House, Melbourne, 1921, p. 33.
67 Morris, *The White Butterfly*, p. 45.
68 Morris, *The White Butterfly*, pp. 89–97.
69 Morris, *The White Butterfly*, p. 96.
70 Morris, *The White Butterfly*, p. 81.
71 'Social and Personal', Gawler *Bunyip*, 16 January 1925, p. 4; 'Mordecai MacCobber', *Riverina Recorder*, 17 February 1926, p. 3.
72 'Ladies' Letter', *Table Talk*, 27 April 1922, p. 32; 'Family Notices', Brisbane *Courier*, 21 April 1922, p. 6; 'G. H. S.', *Facing the Inevitable*, C. J. DeGaris Publishing House, Melbourne, 1921, p. 21.
73 C. J. DeGaris in 'G. H. S.', *Facing the Inevitable*, p. 9.
74 'The One Thing Certain', *Western Mail*, 23 February 1922, p. 39; 'His Last Care', Rockhampton *Morning Bulletin*, 23 June 1922, p. 13.
75 'G. H. S.', *Facing the Inevitable*, p. 18.

76 J. Kauffman, *The Sunraysia Wonder Book; The seventeen pearls in a necklace of surprises: the seventeen sunraysed settlements of Australia*, C. J. DeGaris Publishing House, Melbourne, for the Australian Dried Fruits Association, 1921, p. 11.
77 Kauffman, *The Sunraysia Wonder Book*, p. 9.
78 Kauffman, *The Sunraysia Wonder Book*, p. 9.
79 Kauffman, *The Sunraysia Wonder Book*, p. 7.
80 'Mr. Theodore Pelloe Farewelled', *Mildura Telegraph and Darling and Lower Murray Advocate*, 10 November 1916, p. 3.
81 'The Queen of Sport', *Mildura Cultivator*, 7 October 1916, p. 7.
82 E. H. Pelloe, 'Mountaineering in W. A.', Perth *Sunday Times*, 23 October 1921, p. 17.
83 'A Patriarch comes to Perth: To Found town at Kendenup'.
84 E. H. Pelloe, *Wildflowers of Western Australia*, C. J. DeGaris Publishing House, Melbourne, 1920, p. 18.
85 Pelloe, *Wildflowers of Western Australia*, pp. 45, 66.
86 DeGaris, *Victories of Failure*, p. 410; Dunstan, *Ratbags*, p. 253; 'Real estate', *West Australian*, 27 January 1921, p. 8; 'Real Estate', Melbourne *Herald*, 13 April 1921, p. 5.
87 'DeGaris Mystery', *Sydney Morning Herald*, 7 January 1925, p. 14.

Chapter 7: My town Kendenup, where everybody smiles
1 'American Lady Calls in', Kendenup *Index*, 24 October 1921, p. 2.
2 'Many Buildings Being Erected on Townsite', Kendenup *Index*, September 1921, p. 12.
3 'Building is Brisk', Kendenup *Index*, June 1921, p. 4.
4 'Many Buildings Being Erected on Townsite'.
5 'Building is brisk'.
6 'American Lady Calls In'.
7 Grogan, *Report of the Royal Commission appointed to inquire into and report upon the establishment of the Settlement at Kendenup*, Government Printer, Perth, 1922, p. 4.
8 'Series of Welcomes', Kendenup *Index*, 20 December 1921, p. 6.
9 'Railway Heads', Kendenup *Index*, June 1921, p. 5.
10 'DeGaris' Discovery'.
11 'Land sale success at Kendenup', Melbourne *Argus*, 10 January 1921, p. 8.
12 'What the Settlers are Doing', Kendenup *Index*, June 1921, p. 9.
13 'Kendenup Chirps', Kendenup *Index*, July 1921, p. 15.
14 'Kendenup Chirps', Kendenup *Index*, August 1921, p. 16.
15 J. J. Simons, 'Slumpless Kendenup', Kendenup *Index*, July 1921, p. 11.
16 'Chief Interviewed', Kendenup *Index*, June 1922, pp. 6–7.
17 'American Lady Calls In'.
18 'Mr. C. J. DeGaris's Arrival', Kendenup *Index*, June 1921, p. 13.

19 'Mr. Frank J. Pennifold', *Weekly Times*, 21 August 1920, p. 49; 'Talk of the Week', *Table Talk*, 13 January 1921, p. 5.
20 'Affairs of C. J. DeGaris', Melbourne *Argus*, 11 March 1924, p. 14.
21 'Kendenup's Last King', Kendenup *Index*, 26 July 1922, p. 4
22 'Tile machine coming', Kendenup *Index*, June 1921, p. 6.
23 'Kendenup Chirps', Kendenup *Index*, May 1922, p. 11.
24 'Our new building', *The Boomerang*, 28 February 1922, p. 2; 'The League's New Home', *The Boomerang*, 31 March 1922, pp. 2–3.
25 'Tile Machine Coming'.
26 'Kendenup Chirps', Kendenup *Index*, June 1921, p. 16.
27 'Buy Land in Kendenup!', *Age*, 9 February 1921, p. 11.
28 'Local and General News', Albany *Advertiser*, 5 January 1921, p. 2.
29 'Building Fund Activities', *The Boomerang*, July 1921, p. 11.
30 K. O'Malley, diary entry 21 November 1921, in King O'Malley papers, National Library of Australia, MS 460, box 13, items 7366–7411.
31 'The Great East-West Flight', Melbourne *Age*, 5 December 1920, p. 19.
32 'Brisbane–Melbourne One Day Flight', *S.A. Wheelman*, 25 January 1921, p. 18.
33 'To Satisfy Kendenup Investors', Perth *Sunday Times*, 24 April 1921, p. 2.
34 Untitled item, Kendenup *Index*, June 1921, p. 12.
35 'A Practical Farmer', 'To the Editor', *West Australian*, 13 January 1922, p. 2.
36 'Kendenup', Kendenup *Index*, July 1921, p. 1.
37 'What the Settlers are Doing: Gleanings from the Blocks', Kendenup *Index*, 25 November 1921, p. 3.
38 'Our Settlers' Association', Kendenup *Index*, 24 October 1921, p. 8.
39 de Pledge, *Kendenup Stories*, p. 46.
40 'What the Settlers are Doing: Gleanings from the Blocks', Kendenup *Index*, 28 January 1922, p. 3.
41 'What the Settlers are Doing: Gleanings from the Blocks', Kendenup *Index*, July 1921, p. 8; 'What the Settlers are Doing: Gleanings from the Blocks', Kendenup *Index*, 28 January 1922, p. 2.
42 'What the Settlers are Doing: Gleanings from the Blocks', Kendenup *Index*, June 1921, p. 8.
43 'What the Settlers are Doing: Gleanings from the Blocks', Kendenup *Index*, 25 November 1921, p. 3; 'The Coming of Kendenup', Perth *Sunday Times*, 2 January 1921, p. 1; de Pledge, *Kendenup Stories*, p. 17; 'A Model Orchard', *Albany Advertiser*, 28 April 1917, p. 3.
44 'What the Settlers are Doing: Gleanings from the Blocks', Kendenup *Index*, 25 November 1921, p. 2.
45 'The Guides of the Settlers', Perth *Daily News*, 5 October 1921, p. 7.
46 'What the Settlers are Doing: Gleanings from the Blocks', Kendenup *Index*, June 1921, p. 9.

NOTES TO CHAPTER 7

47 'Kendenup Chirps', Kendenup *Index*, August 1921, p. 15. There is a slight possibility that it may have been another child born within a few weeks of this one, who was named 'Kendenup'. In any case this first name does not seem to have been used later in life. Further research can be carried out in July 2021, when 'Kendenup Cooper's' birth certificate will be available from the Western Australian Registry.
48 'What the Settlers are Doing: Gleanings from the Blocks', Kendenup *Index*, June 1921, p. 8.
49 'What the Settlers are Doing: Gleanings from the Blocks', Kendenup *Index*, 25 November 1921, pp. 2–3.
50 'Our Settlers' Association'.
51 'What the Settlers are Doing: Gleanings from the Blocks', Kendenup *Index*, July 1921, pp. 8–9; 'What the Settlers are Doing: Gleanings from the Blocks' Kendenup *Index*, 20 December 1921, p. 10.
52 'What the Settlers are Doing: Gleanings from the Blocks', Kendenup *Index*, June 1921, p. 10.
53 'What the Settlers are Doing: Gleanings from the Blocks', Kendenup *Index*, 28 January 1922, p. 2.
54 'What the Settlers are Doing: Gleanings from the Blocks', Kendenup *Index*, June 1921, p. 9.
55 'What the Settlers are Doing: Gleanings from the Blocks', Kendenup *Index*, June 1921, p. 5, 9; 'What the Settlers are Doing: Gleanings from the Blocks', Kendenup *Index*, 24 October 1921, p. 5.
56 'What the Settlers are Doing: Gleanings from the Blocks', Kendenup *Index*, June 1921, p. 9; 'Doings at Kendenup', Katanning *Southern Districts Advocate*, 23 May 1921, p. 1; 'Publications Received', Adelaide *Advertiser*, 26 July 1902, p. 9.
57 'Kendenup DeGaris', *The Call*, 29 July 1921, p. 2.
58 'Mr. DeGaris Returns from Colombo', Perth *Daily News*, 10 September 1921, p. 9
59 H. D'Arcy-Evans, 'Kendenup Life', Kendenup *Index*, June 1922, p. 5.
60 'The Glut Slayer', Kendenup *Index*, June 1921, p. 2.
61 'The Glut Slayer'.
62 'Kendenup Chirps', Kendenup *Index*, June 1921, p. 16.
63 'One of our Weekends', Kendenup *Index*, June 1921, p. 6.
64 'Chief Interviewed'.
65 'Concert at Kendenup', Kendenup *Index*, 28 January 1922, p. 6.
66 'Kendenup Chirps', Kendenup *Index*, June 1921, p. 16.
67 'One of Our Week-Ends'.
68 Grogan, *Report of the Royal Commission*, p. 12.

Chapter 8: A big smash, 1921–23

1. DeGaris, *Victories of Failure*, p. 443.
2. 'News from the Seat of War', *North Eastern Ensign*, 30 March 1900, p. 3.
3. 'Who Backed Hervey?', *The Call*, 28 October 1921, p. 2.
4. DeGaris, *Victories of Failure*, p. 443.
5. 'The Gentle Art of Kicking the Dead', Mildura and Merbein *Sun*, 24 September 1921, p. 1.
6. DeGaris, *Victories of Failure*, p. 446.
7. 'Hervey Before Court', Melbourne *Herald*, 25 November 1921, p. 10.
8. G. Hervey, 'Is Capitalism Immoral?', 22 September 1926, National Archives of Australia, item 15430.
9. Untitled, Mildura and Merbein *Sun*, 13 October 1921, p. 7.
10. G. Hervey, 'An Open Letter' Mildura and Merbein *Sun*, 17 September 1921, p. 6.
11. 'On his knees!', Perth *Daily News*, 1 March 1924, p. 10.
12. 'Tarred and Feathered', Sydney *Sun*, 25 December 1921, p. 10.
13. T. Clarke, *My Northcliffe Diary*, Victor Gollancz, London, 1931, p. 36 *passim*.
14. Northcliffe, quoted in Clarke, *My Northcliffe Diary*, pp. 219–20.
15. 'An Invitation to the Murray Valley', Adelaide *Register*, 9 September 1921, p. 7
16. 'To Lord Northcliffe', Melbourne *Argus*, 24 September 1921, p. 8.
17. 'This is Lord Northcliffe's Message to Mildura', Melbourne *Argus*, 1 October 1921, p. 6.
18. 'The Death-Day of Sunraysia Daily', Mildura and Merbein *Sun*, 13 October 1921, p. 7.
19. DeGaris, *Victories of Failure*, p. 456.
20. 'Mr. C. J. DeGaris', *Graphic*, 27 October 1921, in J. J.Simons' Scrapbook; '£1,000 Reward', Melbourne *Herald*, 24 October 1921, p. 6.
21. 'Mr. C. J. DeGaris: Statements Refuted', Melbourne *Argus*, 25 October 1921, p. 6.
22. 'On his knees!'.
23. 'Tarred and Feathered', Sydney *Sun*, 25 December 1921, p. 10; 'Grant Hervey', *Riverina Recorder*, 2 November 1921, p. 4.
24. 'Testimonial from Grant Hervey', 1 December 1921, National Archives of Australia, item 9932.
25. G. Hervey (1921), quoted in 'Personal Reminscences', Port Pirire *Recorder*, 18 July 1931, p. 3.
26. 'Hervey Before Court'.
27. Charles Brown-Parker was said to be the instigator, the others being John Ludlow, Etienne Kelson, Robert Veale (not to be confused with Veall), Claude Coe, Murray Bye, Gifford Hall, William Hickey, William Walker, Sydney Martin, Jock Mallock and Henry Sutton. Only a few of these men were well-known in DeGaris organisations, chiefly Bye and Hall. How the American-born Brown-Parker was involved in the melee is a mystery,

although he did have Tivoli connections, with a 'ball-punching' act 'to a musical setting'. ('Athlete's Illness', Sydney *Sun*, 14 April 1942, p. 10).
28 'Tarred and Feathered', Sydney *Sun*, 25 December 1921, p. 10.
29 'Tar and Feathers', *Western Argus*, 20 December 1921, p. 12; 'Tar and Feathers Case', Orange *Leader*, 19 December 1921, p. 6.
30 'Alleged Assault', *Cairns Post*, 17 December 1921, p. 2.
31 It is possible that C. J. organised the attack at arm's length. Chris Wallace Crabbe's father Ken, who worked on the *Sunraysia Daily* at this time, told him that the perpetrators were 'set onto Hervey by DeGaris', and also claimed to have been part of the throng. Personal communication, 17 August 2007.
32 G. M. Hervey, 'From Sydney to the Golden Mile', *New Age*, 12 January 1922, pp. 130–1.
33 DeGaris, *Victories of Failure*, p. 494.
34 DeGaris, *Victories of Failure*, p. 440.
35 'Kendenup Estate', *Daily News*, 12 January 1922, in J. J. Simons' scrapbook.
36 'Public Service Appeal', *West Australian*, 12 May 1921, p. 6.
37 'Kendenup Royal Commission', Katanning *Great Southern Herald*, 12 August 1922, p. 2.
38 'Kendenup Summed Up', *The Call*, 11 August 1922, in J. J. Simons' scrapbook.
39 C. J. DeGaris, letter dated 22 April 1922, reprinted in Kendenup *Index* compile, 1983.
40 DeGaris, *Victories of Failure*, p. 489.
41 'Kendenup Finances', Melbourne *Argus*, 29 February 1924, p. 6.
42 'Kenenup Affairs', Melbourne *Argus*, 12 March 1924, p. 17.
43 'About the Commission', Kendenup *Index*, August 1922, p. 6.
44 'About the Commission', p. 5.
45 'Music and Song', Kendenup *Index*, 28 February 1922, p. 11.
46 'DeGaris' Discovery'.
47 'DeGaris Divorce Case', Melbourne *Argus*, 24 November 1922, p. 10; 'DeGaris Divorce', Melbourne *Argus*, 1 June 1923, p. 14. See also 'C. J. DeGaris Sued', Melbourne *Argus*, 17 April 1924, p. 10.
48 DeGaris, *Victories of Failure*, p. 501.
49 DeGaris, *Victories of Failure*, p. 498.
50 'Farewell Function', Kendenup *Index*, June 1922, p. 7.
51 'Staff Personnel', Kendenup *Index*, 20 November 1922, p. 5.
52 'Farewell to Mrs. DeGaris', Kendenup *Index*, 19 December 1922, p. 7.
53 'Kendenup Inquiry', Geelong *Standard*, 7 March 1924, p. 12.
54 'Kendenup Inquiry', Geelong *Standard*, 7 March 1924, p. 12.
55 DeGaris, *Victories of Failure*, p. 503.
56 'Mr. C. J. DeGaris', Perth *Daily News*, 10 May 1922, p. 2.
57 'Needs, Wants, Happiness', *Eudora Weekly News*, 11 May 1916, p. 1.
58 'Personal', *Eudora Weekly News*, 24 January 1918, p. 3.

59 '$200,000 of Eastern Capital Added to the Gillette Safety Tire Co. To Finance Industry', Eau Claire *Leader-Telegram*, 21 November 1916, p. 3.
60 'Financing Kendenup', Perth *Daily News*, 13 May 1922, p. 17; 'Kendenup/American Aid', *West Australian*, 13 May 1922, p. 9.
61 'Kendenup Finance', Melbourne *Argus*, 29 February 1924, p. 6.
62 'Financing Kendenup', Perth *Daily News*.
63 'Kendenup/American Aid'.
64 'Financing Kendenup', Perth *Daily News*.
65 'Kendenup/American Aid'.
66 'Financing Kendenup', Perth *Daily News*.
67 'Financing Kendenup', Perth *Daily News*.
68 'Kendenup/American Aid'.
69 Francis James Coote examined by William Grogan, 1 June 1922, Grogan, *Kendenup Royal Commission appointed to inquire into and report upon the establishment of the Settlement at Kendenup*, Government Printer, Perth, 1922, p. 45.
70 'About the Commission', Kendenup *Index*, August 1922, p. 6.
71 'Settlers' Meeting: Chief's parting words', Kendenup *Index*, June 1922, p. 2.
72 'Kendenup Finance', Melbourne *Argus*, 29 February 1924, p. 6.
73 'Obituary: Mr. E. R. Peacock', Melbourne *Argus*, 5 September 1932, p. 6.
74 Reprinted in 'A Knocker and a Booster', Kendenup *Index*, June 1922, p. 3.
75 'A Knocker and a Booster'.
76 'Kendenup Notes', Albany *Despatch*, 13 July 1922, in J. J. Simons' scrapbook.
77 'Kendenup Notes', *Albany Despatch*.
78 'Kendenup Notes', *Albany Despatch*.
79 Untitled item, Kendenup *Index*, 26 July 1922, p. 11.
80 'Fruit Industry', *Auckland Star*, 26 June 1922, in J. J. Simons' scrapbook.
81 Possibly 'Escadero'? 'Atascadero' is in 'Kendenup is saved!', *The Call*, 20 October 1922, p. 2.
82 'Kendenup', *West Australian*, 28 December 1923, p. 6.
83 DeGaris, *Victories of Failure*, pp. 507–8.
84 DeGaris, *Victories of Failure*, p. 505.
85 DeGaris, *Victories of Failure*, p. 515.
86 The *New York Times* version of this article does not appear in the currently available edition of this paper, however it was reprinted as C. J. DeGaris, '"Americanizing Australia" with Our Slang and Our Movies' in the *St Louis Globe-Democrat*, 27 August 1922, p. 15, and as 'Aussies and Yanks', *Kendenup Index*, 23 October 1922, pp. 2–3.
87 'Aussies and Yanks'.
88 'Kendenup. Mr DeGaris Returns', *West*, 13 November 1922, p. 8.
89 DeGaris, *Victories of Failure*, p. 506.
90 'Australia has a unique settlement', *The Pennsylvania Register*, n. d., in J. J. Simons' scrapbook.

NOTES TO CHAPTER 8

91 'McClelland Forms New Firm', *New York Herald*, 27 September 1919, p. 16.
92 R. J. McClelland, 'Expansion of Electric Power Supply Urged by Expert', *New York Tribune*, 21 October 1918, p. 10.
93 'Finance Expert to Talk to Baptist Men's Club', *Brooklyn Standard Union*, 11 March 1922, p. 4.
94 'Pittsburgh Park Bank Closes when Bank Discovers Institution's Funds are Short', *Taylor Daily Press*, 13 February 1919, p. 1.
95 'Pittsburgh Bank Closed', *Wall Street Journal*, 14 February 1919, p. 10; 'Pittsburgh Bank Closes Doors', Carlisle *Sentinel*, 13 February 1919, p. 4.
96 DeGaris, *Victories of Failure*, p. 517.
97 'Kendenup is saved!'
98 DeGaris, *Victories of Failure*, p. 498.
99 'Kendenup Finance'.
100 'Oil Boring at Bremer Bay', *Age*, 19 August 1921, p. 9.
101 'Oil Exploitation', Albany *Despatch*, 2 February 1920, p. 3.
102 'Bremer Oil Prospects', Albany *Advertiser*, 14 September 1921, p. 3.
103 V. Courtney, *All I May Tell: A Journalist's Story*, Shakespeare Head Press, London, 1956, p. 199.
104 Courtney, *All I May Tell*, p. 200.
105 R. Wilkinson, *Where God Never Trod: Australia's Oil Explorers Across Two Centuries*, David Ell Press, Balmain, 1991, p. 35.
106 'Oil Reported at Kendenup', *Herald*, 28 November 1922, in J. J. Simons' scrapbook.
107 'Kendenup', *West Australian*, 13 November 1922, p. 8.
108 DeGaris, *Victories of Failure*, pp. 518–9.
109 DeGaris, *Victories of Failure*, p. 520.
110 DeGaris, *Victories of Failure*, p. 526.
111 'Kendenup Commission', Perth *Daily News*, 8 February 1924, p. 4.
112 'Kendenup is Saved!'
113 'Latest from Chief', Kendenup *Index*, 23 October 1922, p. 11.
114 'Kendenup. Mr DeGaris Returns'.
115 'Happy Kendenup', *Sunraysia Daily*, 28 November 1922, p. 12.
116 'Happy Kendenup'.
117 DeGaris, *Victories of Failure*, pp. 533–4.
118 'Mr C. J. DeGaris', *Western Mail*, 23 November 1922, in J. J. Simons' scrapbook.
119 'General News', Adelaide *Register*, 25 November 1922, in J. J. Simons' scrapbook; 'Happy Kendenup'.
120 'Kendenup! Kendenup! Home of Western Australia's Most Progressive Settlement', *Mirror*, 21 January 1923, in J. J. Simons' scrapbook.
121 DeGaris, *Victories of Failure*, pp. 536–7.

Chapter 9: The alert, grey twinkling eyes of C. J. DeGaris

1. de Pledge, *Kendenup Stories*, p. 47.
2. 'Kendenup Commission', Perth *Daily News*, 8 February 1924, p. 4.
3. 'A Letter from Kendenup', *Murray Pioneer and Australian River Record*, 23 March 1923, p. 18.
4. 'Kendenup to Wind Up', Melbourne *Herald*, 9 March 1923, p. 1; 'Kendenup: "Black Repudiation"', Warwick *Daily News*, 16 March 1923, p. 6.
5. 'Good News for the Public', Elmira *Star-Gazette*, 25 October 1923, p. 21.
6. 'Kendenup Collapse', Perth *Sunday Times*, 4 March 1923, p. 1.
7. Editorial, Albany *Despatch*, 5 March 1923, p. 2.
8. 'Kendenup to liquidate', Melbourne *Herald*, 7 March 1923, p. 8.
9. 'Lost Eighty Thousand', *The Call*, 16 March 1923, p. 2.
10. 'Shall the People Rule?', *The Call*, 17 November 1922, p. 2.
11. 'A Western Politician', *Table Talk*, 30 November 1922, p. 10.
12. 'General News', Adelaide *Register*, 25 November 1922, in J. J. Simons' scrapbook.
13. 'Mr. Simons and Kendenup', *West Australian*, 18 November 1922, p. 12.
14. J. J. Simons, letter to Frank J. Coote, 21 November 1922, in J. J. Simons' scrapbook. In the original, the last use of 'Madam' is not capitalised.
15. 'Kendenup', *West Australian*, 28 December 1923, p. 6.
16. 'Schooldays at last!', Kendenup *Index*, 30 September 1922, pp. 6–7.
17. 'Kendenup notes', Albany *Despatch*, 7 September 1922, in J. J. Simons' scrapbook.
18. 'Australian Natives Association', *West Australian*, 24 March 1923, p. 11.
19. 'Plantagenet Road Board', Albany *Despatch*, 12 March 1923, p. 4.
20. 'The Future of Kendenup', *Albany Advertiser*, 17 March 1923, p. 3.
21. 'Kenden – Up the Pole', Brisbane *Daily Standard*, 19 March 1923, p. 6.
22. 'Kendenup settlers', Perth *Daily News*, 23 March 1923, p. 3.
23. 'The Kendenup Calamity', Perth *Sunday Times*, 25 March 1923, p. 7.
24. 'Debenture Holders', *Albany Advertiser*, 28 March 1923, p. 3.
25. 'Mt. Barker Notes', *Albany Advertiser*, 14 April 1923, p. 3.
26. 'Kendenup', *Beverley Times*, 21 April 1923, p. 2; 'Obituary', Melbourne *Argus*, 24 May 1934, p. 8.
27. 'Kendenup', *Beverley Times*, 14 April 1923, p. 2.
28. 'The Kendenup Scheme', Perth *Sunday Times*, 15 April 1923, p. 1.
29. 'Personal', Katanning *Great Southern Herald*, 14 April 1923, p. 3.
30. 'Kendenup Situation', *Albany Advertiser*, 18 April 1923, p. 3.
31. 'Yesterday's deputations', Perth *Sunday Times*, 6 May 1923, p. 3.
32. 'R. S. L. and Prime Minister', Albany *Despatch*, 7 May 1923, p. 2; 'Apt notes and pertinent quotes', *Westralian Worker*, 11 May 1923, p. 7.
33. 'Returned Soldiers', Hobart *Mercury*, 7 May 1923, p. 3.
34. 'Kendenup', Albany *Despatch*, 7 May 1923, p. 2.

35 'T. M.', 'Kendenup and Mr. J. J. Simons', *Westralian Worker*, 20 April 1923, p. 4.
36 'The Wobbly "Worker"', Perth *Mirror*, 21 April 1923, p. 2.
37 'Well-deserved rap to "Smith's"', Perth *Australian*, 20 April 1923, p. 4.
38 'Kendenup Affairs', Katanning *Great Southern Herald*, 28 April 1923, p. 2.
39 'Another Proposal', Albany *Despatch*, 10 May 1923, p. 3.
40 'Praise for Kendenup', *West Australian*, 18 May 1923, p. 8.
41 'DeGaris's Affairs', Melbourne *Herald*, 12 March 1924, p. 7.
42 'Kendenup Settlement', *West Australian*, 8 June 1923, p. 8.
43 'Kendenup Settlers', *Kalgoorlie Miner*, 8 June 1923, p. 5.
44 'Kendenup Inquiry', *West Australian*, 21 February 1924, p. 9.
45 'DeGaris – Austin', *Table Talk*, 5 July 1923, p. 29.
46 'Kendenup Inquiry', Perth *Daily News*, 23 February 1924, p. 10.
47 'The Kendenup Commission', Adelaide *Advertiser*, 23 February 1924, p. 16.
48 'DeGaris – Austin'.
49 'New DeGaris', Melbourne *Herald*, 6 March 1924, p. 5.
50 'DeGaris's Affairs'.
51 'Why "Smith's" exposed DeGaris', *Smith's Weekly*, 17 January 1925, p. 11.
52 'Kendenup Inquiry', *West Australian*, 21 February 1924, p. 9.
53 'DeGaris's Affairs'. They also owned, soon after, 369 Auburn Road, just around the corner. The present author grew up two minutes' walk from these homes, fifty years later.
54 'Kendenup', *West Australian*, 13 March 1924, p. 9.
55 'DeGaris puts it up to *Smith's Weekly*', Katanning *Great Southern Leader*, 15 May 1925, p. 5. It is not clear why Clarence Austin was not living with his wife at this time. He died in 1936 in Sydney. 'Deaths', Melbourne *Argus*, 20 November 1936, p. 1.
56 C. J. DeGaris, *As I See Geelong in 1935*, C. J. DeGaris, Hawthorn, 1925, p. 4.
57 'Wanted', Melbourne *Argus*, 13 August 1923, p. 3.
58 'Kendenup Inquiry: Mrs DeGaris gives evidence', *Geelong Advertiser*, 13 March 1924, p. 2.
59 'Preliminary Announcement', Melbourne *Herald*, 13 October 1923, p. 10.
60 'City Town and Country Golf Links Coburg', Melbourne *Sporting Globe*, 28 November 1923, p. 7.
61 'Escapes from Pentridge', Melbourne *Argus*, 5 August 1922, p. 20.
62 'Melbourne Subdivisions Coy', Geelong *Advertiser*, 22 October 1923, p. 4.
63 'Anglesea', *Argus*, 8 December 1923, p. 32.
64 'The Wealth in the "Heart of Rosebud"', Melbourne *Argus*, 8 December 1923, p. 29; 'Heart of Rosebud', Melbourne *Herald*, 17 December 1923, p. 8.
65 'Seaside Auction', Melbourne *Herald*, 2 January 1924, p. 10.
66 'Let Us Help You to Start the New Year Profitably!', *Table Talk*, 10 January 1924, p. 30.
67 'The Kendenup Inquiry', *Ballarat Star*, 4 March 1924, p. 6.

68 'Heart of Rosebud Estate' plan, in 'Rosebud' box, Coghill and Houghton papers, Melbourne University Archives. There is also a full-page advertisement for this estate in the *Evening Sun*, 14 December 1923, p. 13. Both estate map and advertisement credit the design to Saxil Tuxen.
69 'New Suburbs Planned', *Evening Sun*, 7 December 1923, p. 11. DeGaris may have been referring to Tuxen affectionately: other sources suggest 'Tux' as Tuxen's nickname.
70 'Heart of Rosebud', *Evening Sun*, 14 December 1923, p. 13.
71 'Plain Facts', Melbourne *Herald*, 7 May 1924, p. 15.
72 'High Finance', *Ballarat Star*, 4 March 1924, p. 6.
73 'Talk of the Week', *Table Talk*, 17 July 1924, p. 13.
74 'Kendenup', *Sydney Morning Herald*, 4 March 1924, p. 9.
75 *Hansard*, Western Australia, 19 September 1923, pp. 760–8.
76 'Kendenup Commission', *West Australian*, 20 October 1923, p. 13.
77 'The Political Pow-Wow', Perth *Truth*, 27 October 1923, p. 4.
78 'Mostly Personal', *Western Mail*, 17 December 1931, p. 7.
79 'The Kendenup Company', *Kalgoorlie Miner*, 5 March 1924, p. 3.
80 'Here and There', *Mullewa Mail*, 29 November 1923, p. 2.
81 'The Kendenup Enquiry', Adelaide *Register*, 27 November 1923, p. 9.
82 'Kendenup Affairs', Melbourne *Argus*, 27 November 1923, p. 9.
83 'Local and General News', *Albany Advertiser*, 9 January 1924, p. 3.
84 'Kendenup Commission', *Kalgoorlie Miner*, 22 January 1923, p. 3.
85 'Investigation in Victoria', Adelaide *Register*, 24 January 1924, p. 12.
86 'Kendenup', *Western Mail*, 17 January 1924, p. 16.
87 'The Kendenup Failure', Geelong *Standard*, 23 February 1924, p. 12.
88 'Two Kendenups', Melbourne *Argus*, 7 March 1924, p. 6.
89 'Two Kendenups'.
90 'Kendenup', Perth *West Australian*, 14 March 1924, p. 9.
91 'Kendenup', Hobart *Mercury*, 25 July 1924, p. 2.
92 'What DeGaris says', Perth *Mirror*, 26 July 1924, p. 1.

Chapter 10: 'The Long Vision'
1 'Douglass speaks of the Illinois "insect"', Nashville *Brown County Democrat*, 24 November 1921, p. 1.
2 S. M. Lyons, *Telling the World about the Abrahams Millionaires*, Sol Lyons, St Kilda, 1928, p. 12.
3 'Here are the Reasons of the Success...', Melbourne *Sun News Pictorial*, 7 October 1924, pp. 22–3.
4 'At Capitol House', Melbourne *Herald*, 6 January 1925, p. 6.
5 'DeGaris Staff', Melbourne *Herald*, 7 January 1925, p. 5.
6 'High Finance'.
7 'DeGaris Staff'.
8 'Land Purchase at North Shore', Geelong *Advertiser*, 23 November 1923, p. 2.

9 'Corio – A Garden City', *Australian Home Builder*, 15 July 1924, p. 66.
10 Untitled item, Melbourne *Herald*, 16 August 1924, p. 25.
11 'Industrial Progress', Geelong *Advertiser*, 2 February 1924, p. 4.
12 'Geelong's Garden Suburb', *Goulburn Valley Stock and Property Journal*, 13 August 1924, p. 6.
13 'Advertising', Melbourne *Herald*, 20 September 1917, p. 9.
14 'A Trip to Corio', *Goulburn Valley Stock and Property Journal*, 14 August 1924, p. 9.
15 'Melbourne', *Everyone's*, 20 August 1924, p. 30; 'Tivoli Theatre – Albert Whelan', *Age*, 18 August 1924, p. 11.
16 'A Trip to Corio'.
17 Wattle Path Palais de Danse & Café Ltd: Esplanade St Kilda, Monash Collections Online.
18 'The Long Vision', Geelong *Standard*, 25 September 1924, p. 10.
19 'DeGaris's Stunt Suicide', *Smith's Weekly*, 10 January 1925, p. 13.
20 'Here are the Reasons of [sic] the Success of the Melbourne Subdivisions Co', Sydney *Sunday Times*, 12 October 1924, p. 20.
21 'Corio Garden Suburb: A Favourable Impression', Geelong *Standard*, 25 September 1924, p. 14.
22 'Corio Garden Suburb: A Favourable Impression'.
23 'Corio Garden Suburb: A Favourable Impression'.
24 'Corio Garden Suburb: A Favourable Impression'.
25 'Corio Development', Geelong *Standard*, September 1924, p. 14.
26 'Melbourne-Made Movies', Melbourne *Herald*, 29 September 1923, p. 3. The Phoenix film company seems likely to have been a fly-by-night operation.
27 'Corio Garden Suburb: A Favourable Impression'.
28 'Shepparton Show', *Shepparton Advertiser*, 23 October 1924, p. 3.
29 'This night week at "Windulva"...', *Mildura Cultivator*, 27 November 1918, p. 11; 'E. DeGaris & Co. Pty Ltd', *Mildura Cultivator*, 17 April 1920, p. 3.
30 '975- - 24/Mystery Numbers', *Evening Sun*, 19 September 1924, p. 11.
31 Untitled Item, *Evening Sun*, 25 October 1924, p. 14.
32 There was a 'Mr. Griffin' present at an MSD reconstruction meeting of shareholders on 11 February 1925; he did not hold any official position, but seconded a motion ('Pricking the Degaris Bubble').
33 H. Hansell, 'The Poet-Artist's View-point' in 'There is No Mystery', Melbourne *Sun News-Pictorial*, 21 October 1924, p. 11.
34 'The DeGaris Land Campaign', Melbourne *Herald*, 14 January 1925, p. 12.
35 'Land Selling Schemes', Perth *Daily News*, 14 January 1925, p. 5. Detail on MSD estates is hard to ascertain. Veema Ave's documentation at Landata, however, definitively establishes this small street as part of the St. Ruvia Estate (LP15972).
36 'Surprised', *Table Talk*, 23 October 1924, p. 39.
37 'Melbourne Subdivisions', *Albany Advertiser*, 3 December 1924, p. 3.

38   'Two BIG Auction Sales', *Table Talk*, 13 November 1924, p. 33.
39   'C. J. DeGaris', *Lenora Miner*, 22 November 1924, p. 3; 'Creditors' Meeting', Melbourne *Herald*, 5 January 1925, p. 5.
40   'Melbourne Subdivisions Co', *Traralgon Record*, 25 November 1924, p. 2.
41   'Melbourne Subdivisions', *Albany Advertiser*, 3 December 1924, p. 3. That the Canadian Ford company was involved in establishing the Australian operation was a quirk of the British Empire which, apart from anything else, shows the difficulty Australians had dealing directly with American business in the early 1920s. This was the problem C. J. faced in bringing his New York investors to account.
42   'Melbourne Subdivisions', *Albany Advertiser*.
43   'Melbourne Subdivisions', *Albany Advertiser*.
44   'Melbourne Subdivisions', *Albany Advertiser*.
45   'Melbourne Subdivisions', *Albany Advertiser*.
46   'Mr. C. J. DeGaris', Melbourne *Argus*, 6 January 1925, p. 11.
47   'Degaris Missing', Perth *Daily News*, 5 January 1925, p. 8.
48   de Pledge, *Kendenup Stories*, p. 49; 'Mr. C. J. DeGaris', Melbourne *Argus*, 6 January 1925, p. 11.
49   'Mrs DeGaris's Full Statement', Melbourne *Herald*, 6 January 1925, p. 1.
50   'Mr. C. J. DeGaris', Melbourne *Argus*, 6 January 1925, p. 11.
51   'The Degaris Mystery', Melbourne *Herald*, 5 January 1925, p. 3.
52   de Pledge, *Kendenup Stories*, p. 50.

Chapter 11: Eight lost days
1   'Search for Degaris', Riverine *Herald*, 7 January 1925, p. 2.
2   'No Traces of Body', Brisbane *Telegraph*, 6 January 1925, p. 5.
3   'Where is Mr DeGaris?', Melbourne *Herald*, 7 January 1925, p. 1; 'Where is DeGaris?', Perth Mirror, 10 January 1925, p. 1; 'No Light on Mystery', Sydney Sun, 7 January 1925, p. 9. Edwards' body was found the following Wednesday near the women's baths at St. Kilda. 'Albert Park Drowning', Melbourne Argus, 12 January 1925, p. 14.
4   'Mentality Sapped', Brisbane *Telegraph*, 7 January 1925, p. 9.
5   'C. J. DeGaris', *South Western Times*, 13 January 1925, p. 4.
6   'Dead or Alive?', Adelaide *News*, 7 January 1925, p. 1; 'DeGaris Mystery', Sydney *Evening News*, 7 January 1925, p. 5.
7   'Seen Leaving Car', *Newcastle Sun*, 9 January 1925, p. 5. 'Fully dressed', Sydney Sun, 9 January 1925, p. 7. There was a suggestion in the Melbourne Herald that Kingston himself vanished after making the statement, however this is unclear as it does not mention Kingston by name and claims that the man who found C. J.'s Packard had disappeared, yet the car was found by Swann, from Rosebud. See 'Mentone Man Vanishes', Melbourne *Herald*, 15 January 1925, p. 16.
8   'Mystery of DeGaris', Melbourne *Herald*, 10 January 1925, p. 6.

NOTES TO CHAPTER II

9   'Suit of Pyjamas', Sydney *Evening News*, 12 January 1925, p. 7.
10 'The Missing C. J. Degaris', *Age*, 8 January 1925, p. 9.
11 'DeGaris is on board the *Maheno* bound for Auckland', Sydney *Daily Telegraph*, 12 January 1925, p. 1.
12 'Heavy Borrowings', Sydney *Sun*, 11 January 1925, p. 2.
13 'Disguised as woman', Sydney *Sun*, 12 January 1925, p. 7.
14 'Mentality Sapped', Brisbane *Telegraph*, 7 January 1925, p. 9.
15 'The DeGaris mystery', Melbourne *Age*, 7 January 1925, p. 9.
16 The board was W. J. Morgan, Julius Solomons, H. French. E. McGuinness, M. R. Green, Joseph Henry Opas, Gerald English, J. P. Keogh and Leo Levi, company solicitor. 'Investors Meet', Melbourne *Age*, 7 January 1925, p. 9.
17 'Melbourne Subdivisions', Melbourne *Argus*, 7 January 1925, p. 11.
18 'An Administrative Genius', Adelaide *Register*, 8 January 1925, p. 7.
19 'Warrant for Arrest of DeGaris', Melbourne *Herald*, 8 January 1925, p. 1.
20 'Warrant for Arrest of Degaris'.
21 'Faith in DeGaris', Adelaide *Advertiser*, 12 January 1925, p. 9.
22 'Easiest Way'.
23 'Dead or Alive?', Adelaide *News*, 7 January 1925, p. 1.
24 'Last Minute News', Melbourne *Herald*, 6 January 1925, p. 7.
25 'Mr. C. J. DeGaris', Melbourne *Argus*, 7 January 1925, p. 11.
26 'Warrant for Arrest of Degaris'; 'Where is DeGaris?', Perth *Mirror*, 10 January 1925, p. 1.
27 'DeGaris's letter', Sydney *Sun*, 28 January 1925, p. 14.
28 'DeGaris Mystery', *Riverine Herald*, 10 January 1925, p. 2.
29 'DeGaris passes!', *Cairns Northern Herald*, 14 January 1925, p. 20.
30 'Licensing Application', *Cumberland Argus and Fruitgrowers Advocate*, 24 October 1923, p. 2.
31 'New year's greetings', *Hebrew Standard of Australasia*, 17 September 1920, p. 7.
32 'The DeGaris sensation', Melbourne *Age*, 10 January 1925, p. 15.
33 'Quarter Sessions Appeal', *Sydney Morning Herald*, 17 January 1924, p. 6.
34 'Mystery no longer', Sydney *Sunday Times*, 11 January 1925, p. 1.
35 'DeGaris mystery', Adelaide *Register*, 10 January 1925, p. 8.
36 'Mystery no longer', Sydney *Sunday Times*, 11 January 1925, p. 1.
37 'Who was he?', Brisbane *Daily Mail*, 10 January 1925, p. 7; the Sydney *Evening News* reported the man's name as 'O'Young', which seems unlikely. 'DeGaris?', Sydney *Evening News*, 9 January 1925, p. 7.
38 'Mystery man on *Maheno* wears pyjamas branded DeGaris', Sydney *Truth*, 11 January 1925, p. 11.
39 'DeGaris?'; 'Who was he?'
40 'Mystery man on *Maheno* wears pyjamas branded DeGaris'.
41 'Mystery no longer'.
42 'Off to New Zealand', Brisbane *Daily Mail*, 10 January 1925, p. 7.
43 'Mystery no longer'.

NOTES TO CHAPTER 11

44 'Mystery no longer'.
45 Information on Hubert's age gleaned from family trees at http://www.whaitefamily.com.
46 'Caught by boys', Melbourne *Herald*, 14 January 1925, p. 5.
47 'Mystery no longer'.
48 'Mystery no longer'.
49 'Mystery of C. J. DeGaris', Melbourne *Herald*, 10 January 1925, p. 6.
50 'Mystery man', Newcastle *Sun*, 10 January 1925, p. 1; 'The DeGaris sensation', Melbourne *Age*, 10 January 1925, p. 15.
51 'Who was he?'; 'The DeGaris sensation', Melbourne *Age*, 10 January 1925, p. 15.
52 'Where is DeGaris?', Perth *Mirror*, 10 January 1925, p. 1.
53 'Where is DeGaris?'.
54 'Was he decoy?', Melbourne *Herald*, 10 January 1925, p. 3.
55 'Mysterious "Mr. Young"', Perth *Sunday Times*, 11 January 1925, p. 1; 'Caught by boys'.
56 'DeGaris mystery', Brisbane *Telegraph*, 10 January 1925, p. 8.
57 'DeGaris mystery'.
58 'Mystery man on *Maheno* wears pyjamas branded DeGaris'.
59 'DeGaris', *Sydney Morning Herald*, 10 January 1925, p. 15.
60 'DeGaris mystery'.
61 'Wire from DeGaris', Melbourne *Herald*, 13 January 1925, p. 1.
62 'Was he decoy?'
63 'Mystery no longer'.
64 'The DeGaris mystery', Geraldton *Guardian*, 10 January 1925, p. 3.
65 'Was he decoy?'
66 'Is he alive?', Brisbane *Courier*, 10 January 1925, p. 7.
67 'DeGaris mystery'.
68 'DeGaris mystery'.
69 'Mystery man', Newcastle *Sun*, 10 January 1925, p. 1.
70 'Mystery man on *Maheno* wears pyjamas branded DeGaris'.
71 'Mystery of DeGaris'; 'A buyer of left-off clothing', *Sydney Morning Herald*, 26 May 1925, p. 7.
72 'Strange Visits', Sydney *Evening News*, 12 January 1925, p. 7.
73 'DeGaris no typist', Sydney *Sun*, 10 January 1925, p. 4.
74 'The DeGaris sensation', Melbourne *Age*, 10 January 1925, p. 15; 'False teeth', Melbourne *Herald*, 10 January 1925, p. 1.
75 'The DeGaris sensation'.
76 'DeGaris no typist'.
77 'The DeGaris sensation'; 'DeGaris Mystery', Brisbane *Telegraph*, 10 January 1925, p. 8. Interviewed in the *Weekly Times* the following month, C. J. said he was at a loss to understand the telegram form. Perhaps the police, or the

NOTES TO CHAPTER II

boy detectives, planted some evidence of what they knew to be true. 'DeGaris back', *Weekly Times*, 14 February 1925, p. 9.
78 'DeGaris mystery', Adelaide *Register*, 10 January 1925, p. 8.
79 'The DeGaris sensation'.
80 'Mystery no longer'.
81 '"DeGaris no typist"'.
82 'Caught by boys'.
83 'Seen on Monday', Brisbane *Daily Mail*, 10 January 1925, p. 7.
84 'Is he alive?'
85 '£9,355 writ against Mrs DeGaris', Melbourne *Herald*, 10 January 1925, p. 1.
86 '£9,355 writ'.
87 'DeGaris arrested', Sydney *Evening News*, 13 January 1925, p. 7.
88 'Arrest of DeGaris', New Zealand *Herald*, 14 January 1925, p. 11.
89 'Mystery no longer'.
90 'DeGaris arrested at Auckland', Sydney *Daily Telegraph*, 14 January 1925, p. 1.
91 'Arrest of DeGaris'.
92 'His handwriting', Sydney *Evening News*, 13 January 1925, p. 7.
93 *Rigby's Romance*, p. 159.
94 'DeGaris Mystery', *Riverine Herald*, 10 January 1925, p. 2.
95 '"Beneficial" Absence', Brisbane *Telegraph*, 13 January 1925, p. 3.
96 V. Courtney, 'C. J. DeGaris', *The Call*, 9 January 1925, p. 9.
97 'Men and other things', *Australian Worker*, 7 January 1925, p. 1.
98 'DeGaris', *Newcastle Morning Herald and Miners' Advocate*, 10 January 1925, p. 5.
99 'DeGaris's Stunt Suicide'.
100 'Victorian Opinions', Perth *Sunday Times*, 11 January 1925, p. 1.
101 'He is Mental', Sydney *Sunday Times*, 11 January 1925, p. 7.
102 'He is Mental'.
103 'DeGaris arrested'.
104 'DeGaris returning', Sydney *Sun*, 5 February 1925, p. 10.
105 'DeGaris returning'.
106 'Arrest of DeGaris', *New Zealand Herald*.
107 'No Prima Facie Charge', Newcastle *Sun*, 14 January 1925, p. 5.
108 'DeGaris smiles when charged', Melbourne *Herald*, 14 January 1925, p. 1.
109 'DeGaris smiles when charged'.
110 'Advertising hoax?', Brisbane *Daily Standard*, 14 January 1925, p. 5.
111 'Happy in Gaol', *Tweed Daily*, 19 January 1925, p. 2.
112 'DeGaris Smiles', Adelaide *News*, 14 January 1925, p. 11. Original has 'descen' for 'defend'.
113 'The DeGaris Case', Adelaide *Advertiser*, 16 January 1925, p. 9.
114 'Second Mystery Man', Melbourne *Herald*, 13 January 1925, p. 4.

Chapter 12: Infamy

1. 'Why DeGaris decamped', *Singleton Argus*, 10 February 1925, p. 4.
2. This book is not the forum for unpicking the multiple and various intrigues of the Abrahams family – or this branch of it – in the 1920s and '30s, though it is a fascinating story. In 1927, mimicking C. J.'s attempts to flee Australia, Lyons arranged for Emanuel Abrahams to escape to England, and his tax liabilities, under a fake name, 'John Barlow'. ('Story of Alleged Bribing of Federal Official', Melbourne *Herald*, 16 November 1927, p. 1; 'Bribes for a Passport', Sydney *Daily Telegraph*, 17 November 1927, p. 2). It was presumably a complete coincidence that Opas later made his name uncovering a fraud perpetrated by *another* (genuine) Barlow, Alexander, the following decade. (See for instance 'Bretherton Estate', Melbourne *Argus*, 15 July 1938, p. 6; also P. Opas, *Our Father Which Art*, unpublished memoir, 1988 in State Library of Victoria.)
3. P. Opas, *Our Father Which Art*, unpublished memoir, 1988, in State Library of Victoria, 'Attachment "C"'. Opas does not acknowledge the Woolf connection to the Opas family anywhere but in his family tree. His great-aunt Isabel, or Bella, married Woolf in 1896 (see 'Family Notices', Melbourne *Argus*, 18 January 1896, p. 1). Perhaps it is more curious that, despite quoting a 1954 article from the *Argus* in full (G. Williams, 'Crook detector Joe helps you', Melbourne *Argus*, 23 April 1954, p. 4) which mentions Opas' opinion of C. J. – '25 years ahead of his time' – Philip Opas does not otherwise discuss, or even acknowledge, his father's connection to C. J. or the MSD, jumping from the mid-1920s to the mid-1930s with aplomb.
4. 'Secret History of the Day', *Smith's Weekly*, 16 February 1924, p. 11.
5. 'Melbourne Sub-Divisions Mess', Sydney *Truth*, 19 April 1925, p. 9. See also 'Pricking the DeGaris Bubble', Perth *Truth*, 14 February 1925, p. 7. This article is described as originally appearing in the Melbourne *Truth*, but is not evident in the currently available run of the Melbourne edition.
6. 'Pricking the DeGaris Bubble'.
7. 'DeGaris's letter', Sydney *Sun*, 28 January 1925, p. 14.
8. 'DeGaris's cable to wife', Melbourne *Herald*, 14 January 1925, p. 1.
9. 'DeGaris's cable to wife'.
10. 'Security for DeGaris', Sydney *Sun*, 23 January 1925, p. 9.
11. 'Melbourne Sub-divisions', Melbourne *Herald*, 14 January 1925, p. 5.
12. 'What was in letter?', Burnie *Advocate*, 20 January 1925, p. 5.
13. 'Pricking the DeGaris Bubble'.
14. 'DeGaris Case', Melbourne *Herald*, 26 January 1925, p. 1.
15. 'Secret Meeting', Melbourne *Herald*, 24 January 1925, p. 11.
16. 'Pricking the DeGaris Bubble'.
17. 'Meeting of Creditors', Melbourne *Argus*, 15 January 1925, p. 9.
18. 'Melbourne Subdivision', Melbourne *Argus*, 29 January 1925, p. 10.
19. 'What was in letter?'

NOTES TO CHAPTER 12

20 'DeGaris's letter'.
21 'Detective Davey Leaves', Sydney *Sun*, 23 January 1925, p. 9.
22 '"I can answer charge" says C. J. DeGaris', Perth *Mirror*, 7 February 1925, p. 1.
23 'Hide and Seek', Brisbane *Daily Standard*, 11 February 1925, p. 5.
24 'DeGaris returns', Adelaide *News*, 11 February 1925, p. 1.
25 'C. J. DeGaris in Melbourne', Adelaide *Advertiser*, 12 February 1925, p. 12.
26 'DeGaris Back', Melbourne *Herald*, 11 February 1925, p. 1. Original does not capitalise 'Young'; that C. J. is talking about 'O. Young', not youth, is my interpretation.
27 'Melbourne News', *Portland Guardian*, 12 February 1925, p. 2; 'C. J. DeGaris in Melbourne'.
28 'So Upset', Grafton *Daily Examiner*, 12 February 1925, p. 5.
29 'DeGaris tries his disguise', Melbourne *Herald*, 12 February 1925, p. 5.
30 'DeGaris talks like a book & will write one', Perth *Truth*, 28 February 1928, p. 8.
31 'Melbourne News', *Portland Guardian*, 12 February 1925, p. 2; 'C. J. DeGaris in Melbourne'; 'DeGaris returns', Melbourne *Argus*, 12 February 1925, p. 12.
32 'DeGaris and the detective', Melbourne *Herald*, 12 February 1925, p. 5.
33 'DeGaris visits M.S.D.', Melbourne *Herald*, 13 February 1925, p. 7.
34 'The Warrant', Sydney *Sun*, 14 January 1925, p. 15.
35 'DeGaris in court', Brisbane *Telegraph*, 18 February 1925, p. 2.
36 'DeGaris free', Hobart *News*, 6 March 1925, p. 1.
37 'DeGaris Set Free', Melbourne *Age*, 7 March 1925, p. 19.
38 'Tangled titles', Adelaide *Mail*, 21 February 1925, p. 3.
39 'The DeGaris case', Melbourne *Herald*, 15 January 1925, p. 16.
40 'Melbourne Subdivision', Melbourne *Argus*, 8 April 1925, p. 16.
41 'Melbourne Subdivision Co.', Melbourne *Argus*, 25 April 1925, p. 29.
42 'DeGaris in Sydney', Broken Hill *Barrier Miner*, 11 February 1925, p. 1; 'DeGaris's Escape', Brisbane *Daily Mail*, 12 February 1925, p. 7.
43 'Mr C. J. DeGaris', *Murray Pioneer and Australian River Record*, 4 July 1925, p. 9.
44 'The Victories of Failure', *Murray Pioneer and Australian River Record*, 15 May 1925, p. 9.
45 'A New Life Story', Melbourne *Herald*, 3 June 1925, p. 4.
46 'More Frenzied Finance', *Adelaide Mail*, 13 June 1925, p. 2.
47 'Victories of Failure', Adelaide *News*, 6 June 1925, p. 4.
48 'A Book of Revelations', Adelaide *Observer*, 13 June 1925, p. 59.
49 'New Books Received', *Land*, 26 June 1925, p. 2.
50 'A Rocket that Fell Heavily', Melbourne *Advocate*, 11 June 1925, p. 3.
51 'The Victories of Failure', *Daily Telegraph and North Murchison and Pilbara Gazette*, 21 August 1925, p. 5.
52 '"Mr. Rogers" DeGaris', *Murrumbidgee Irrigator*, 23 June 1925, p. 1.
53 'The Victories of Failure', Sydney *Sunday Times*, 14 June 1925, p. 7.
54 'New Books', Melbourne *Age*, 13 June 1925, p. 4.

NOTES TO CHAPTER 12

55 'Obituary', *Labor Daily*, 4 April 1936, p. 6. Moses is not to be confused with Roy Rene.
56 'Mo', 'The Hashes of Achievement', *Smith's Weekly*, 13 June 1925, p. 9.
57 DeGaris, *Victories of Failure*, p. ii.
58 'Film Idol', *Portland Guardian*, 6 April 1925, p. 2.
59 'DeGaris writing a book about it', *Smith's Weekly*, 4 April 1925, p. 9.
60 'DeGaris Again', Sydney *Sunday Times*, 30 August 1925, p. 1.
61 'DeGaris in Adelaide', Adelaide *News*, 10 October 1925, p. 5.
62 'A mysterious disappearance', Adelaide *Advertiser*, 21 January 1925, p. 9.
63 'Is it a Hoax?', Burnie *Advocate*, 20 January 1925, p. 5.
64 'A Missing Fisherman', *South Western Times*, 1 June 1926, p. 2.
65 'Fickle Fate's Pendulum', Sydney *Truth*, 1 February 1925, p. 15.
66 'Wealthy Williamstown', *Williamstown Chronicle*, 13 June 1925, p. 2.
67 '"Getting Things Done"', Melbourne *Argus*, 24 February 1925, p. 11.
68 'DeGaris in Adelaide'.
69 'Audrey Jacob tells truth about Tacke', *Smith's Weekly*, 30 January 1926, p. 11.
70 'Audrey Jacobs' Own Story', Sydney *Truth*, 31 January 1926, p. 11.
71 'Audrey herself tells her story to *Truth*', Perth *Truth*, 30 January 1926, p. 5.
72 'The Fruit Industry's Needs', *Murray Pioneer and Australian River Record*, 13 June 1925, p. 6.
73 'DeGaris' New Scheme', *Kalgoorlie Miner*, 10 July 1925, p. 4.
74 'Trying a "Come-back"', Perth *Truth*, 6 June 1925, p. 4.
75 'Trying a "Come-back"'.
76 'Romance of Land Dealing', *Geelong Advertiser*, 9 March 1926, p. 5.
77 'Mr C. J. DeGaris', *Murray Pioneer and Australian River Record*, 4 July 1925, p. 9.
78 C. J. DeGaris *As I See Geelong in 1935*, C. J. DeGaris, Hawthorn 1925 p. 3.
79 'Linking Geelong with Melbourne', *Geelong Advertiser*, 6 February 1926, p. 8.
80 'Werribee – and the Little River Land Deal', *Werribee Shire Banner*, 18 February 1926, p. 6.
81 'Sewerage Farm Purchases', *Geelong Advertiser*, 4 March 1926, p. 1.
82 'Mining Notices', Melbourne *Argus*, 1 March 1923, p. 1.
83 'Future of Brown Coal', *Geelong Advertiser*, 17 March 1926, p. 7.
84 'DeGaris in Adelaide'.
85 'Kendenup's Future', *Swan Express*, 30 October 1925, p. 5.
86 'The Kendenup Estate', Adelaide *Chronicle*, 28 February 1925, p. 49.
87 'Kendenup Again', Perth *Daily News*, 29 April 1926, p. 5.
88 'Struck Out', Perth *Daily News*, 9 April 1926, p. 7.
89 'The DeGaris Settlements', *Toowoomba Chronicle and Darling Downs Gazette*, 9 January 1926, p. 6.
90 'Mr. DeGaris Revisits Kendenup', Albany *Advertiser*, 5 December 1925, p. 3.
91 'Kendenup Group', Perth *Sunday Times*, 20 December 1925, p. 10.
92 'Kendenup Again', Adelaide *News*, 19 November 1925, p. 6.
93 '"Smiling Kendenup"', Perth *Daily News*, 5 December 1925, p. 7.

94 'DeGaris Here', Perth *Daily News*, 24 March 1926, p. 3.
95 'Country News', *West Australian*, 8 December 1925, p. 4.
96 'A Little Bird Says', Perth *Call*, 16 April 1926, p. 2.
97 V. DeGaris, interviewed by B. Bunbury.
98 'The Future of Kendenup'.
99 'Mr. DeGaris Satisfied', Adelaide *News*, 17 April 1926, p. 1.
100 'Kendenup', Perth *Daily News*, 28 April 1926, p. 4.
101 'The Future of Kendenup'.
102 'What's the Strength of C. J.'s oil find?', Perth *Truth*, 22 May 1926, p. 5.
103 'Kendenup Oil Myth', *West Australian*, 10 June 1926, p. 10.
104 'De Garis' Very Latest', *Smith's Weekly*, 5 June 1926, p. 3. I have not been able to find evidence this company exists, and I suspect it may be an in-joke.
105 'Mr. DeGaris says there is oil at Kendenup', Melbourne *Herald*, 24 May 1926, p. 4.
106 'Oil at Kendenup', *Albany Advertiser*, 26 May 1926, p. 3.
107 'What's the Strength of C. J.'s oil find?'.
108 '"Kendenup Oil"', *West Australian*, 14 June 1926, p. 10.
109 de Pledge, *Kendenup Stories*, p. 15.

Chapter 13: 'Fell down on a big job'
1 'Millions in Oil', Adelaide *News*, 18 August 1926, p. 1.
2 'Misfire', Sydney *Sun*, 18 August 1926, p. 9.
3 'Mr. C. J. DeGaris found dead', Melbourne *Argus*, 18 August 1926, p. 21.
4 'Millions in Oil'.
5 'Read this remarkable story of DeGaris' final frenzied flutter in finance', Melbourne *Truth*, 21 August 1926, p. 6.
6 'Suicide of C. J. Degaris', *Weekly Times*, 21 August 1926, p. 10.
7 'A message of ill omen', Sydney *Truth*, 29 August 1926, p. 16.
8 'Read this remarkable story of DeGaris' final frenzied flutter in finance'.
9 *Truth* talks of a mysterious Dutch stranger, recently arrived in Melbourne on the SS *Morella*, who went up 'quietly to the Rev. C. Tregear and say, "thank you, sir, for the wonderful way you spoke of our friend", and, with tears in his eyes, he was seen to look again at the grave, and depart by the side gate of the Brighton Cemetery, where a Yellow was waiting to take him back to the city. Inside the taxi was much baggage, and after the door was shut, orders were given to "Drive to Spencer-Street station."
No one has seen the Dutchman since then.' ('A message of ill omen').
10 'Mr. C. J. DeGaris found dead'.
11 'Suicide', Sydney *Sun*, 24 August 1926, p. 11.
12 'Death of DeGaris', Brisbane *Telegraph*, 25 August 1926, p. 12.
13 'Suicide' Sydney *Sun*, 24 August 1926, p. 11.
14 'Death of DeGaris'.
15 'Suicide', Sydney *Sun*, 24 August 1926, p. 11.

16 'Mr. C. J. DeGaris found dead'.
17 'Death of DeGaris'.
18 'Mr. C. J. DeGaris found dead'.
19 'Mr. C. J. DeGaris found dead'.
20 'Read this remarkable story of DeGaris' final frenzied flutter in finance'.
21 'Read this remarkable story of DeGaris' final frenzied flutter in finance'.
22 'Death of DeGaris'.
23 'Read this remarkable story of DeGaris' final frenzied flutter in finance'.
24 'The Ashes of DeGaris' Achievements', Sydney *Truth*, 22 August 1926, p. 1.
25 'The Ashes of DeGaris' Achievements'.
26 'Millions in Oil'.
27 'Suicide of C. J. DeGaris', Melbourne *Age*, 19 August 1926, p. 10.
28 'DeGaris's letter'.
29 M. DeGaris, letter to Bessie DeGaris, 18 August 1926 in possession of Kathy Hancock, also reproduced in Lee, *Woman War Doctor*, p. 116.

Chapter 14: 'The essence of kindness'
1 'Funeral of Mr. C. J. DeGaris', Melbourne *Age*, 20 August 1926, p. 11.
2 'Financing DeGaris', Brisbane *Telegraph*, 6 October 1925, p. 20. Of course there is an unknowable possibility that, had C. J. remained alive, his continued presence on Earth would have altered events as they played out after his death.
3 'Found Drowned. Mr. A. E. DeGaris', *Sydney Morning Herald*, 14 October 1927, p. 11. The *Gem* is now known as the *Pyap*, and on permanent display in Swan Hill.
4 L. G. DeGaris, letter to J. Mackin, 27 July 1961, in L. G. DeGaris papers, National Library of Australia, MS2303.
5 'Ballarat Chatter', *Table Talk*, 14 February 1929, p. 59.
6 '"Cinderella" at Ballarat', Melbourne *Herald*, 21 April 1931, p. 15.
7 'Social Gossip', Melbourne *Herald*, 4 June 1935, p. 12.
8 'Family Notices', Melbourne *Argus*, 22 April 1936, p. 16.
9 'Law notices', Melbourne *Age*, 12 February 1986, p. 60.
10 Rick Doble, personal communication, 16 February 2020.
11 In the interview she undertook with Bill Bunbury, Veema claims that in the early 1930s – before she was ten – she was supporting her family by singing on the radio. There is no other verification of this notion, but of course she may well have performed under a pseudonym.
12 D. Corbould, personal communication, 8 August 2019.
13 'How Debts were Made', Kyogle *Examiner*, 27 April 1934, p. 3.
14 'Will of C. J. DeGaris comes before court', Melbourne *Herald*, 17 November 1936, p. 8; 'DeGaris Estate', *Sydney Morning Herald*, 18 November 1936, p. 13.
15 'In the Law Courts', Melbourne *Age*, 18 November 1936, p. 14.

16 'Will of C. J. DeGaris comes before court', Melbourne *Herald*, 17 November 1936, p. 8.
17 Funeral notice, *Sydney Morning Herald*, 23 September 1968, p. 27.
18 'Illegal use of a horse', Carnarvon *Northern Times*, 23 October 1925, p. 2; 'Local Happenings', Perth *Sunday Times*, 26 June 1927, p. 17.
19 Geraldton *Guardian*, 23 July 1949, p. 5.
20 'Local and General', Geraldton *Guardian*, 17 September 1949, p. 2.
21 'Why Women Go On the Streets', *Beckett's Budget*, 2 August 1929, p. 6.
22 de Pledge, *Kendenup Stories*, p. 48.
23 J. Allen in *Kendenup Stories*, p. 70.
24 'Demolition of Dehydrator Building', Albany *Advertiser*, 22 November 1948, p. 6.
25 See V. Kolankiewicz, D. Nichols, E. Taylor, N. Phelps, 'Tracing the "Zombification" of Undeveloped Estates in Greater Melbourne and its Outlying Regions', State of Australian Cities Conference (SOAC19), Perth, WA.
26 P. Barry, *The Rise and Fall of Alan Bond*, ABC/Bantam, Sydney, 1990, pp. 72–4.
27 T. Prior, *Christopher Skase: Beyond the Mirage*, Wilkinson Books, Melbourne 1994, p. 105.
28 Prior, *Christopher Skase*, p. 137.
29 'The Decline of Degaris', Perth *Truth*, 17 January 1925, p. 1.

Bibliography

Archival and unpublished sources

B. Bunbury, interviews for *The Story of C. J. DeGaris*, 1991, including 'Interview with Peter Sutcliffe and Arthur Webb', 1991, OH2636/12; 'Interview with Veema DeGaris, Charles Moore and Albert Smith', OH2636/1; 'Interview with Albert De Pledge', OH2636/3; and others. State Library of Western Australia Oral History Collection.

Cairns, D. C., *A History of Kendenup: a resume of the growth and development from the first explorers to the present time*, c. 1965, State Library of Western Australia,

Coghill and Houghton papers, Melbourne University Archives.

DeGaris Kendenup (WA) Development Company Records, 1893–1992, in State Library of Western Australia, ACC5008A.

E. C. DeGaris papers, State Library of Victoria, MS7080.

F. W. Rowe, 'The Standard Gold Mining Company Ltd. of Kendenup', typescript dated July 1965, in Kendenup Collection, State Library of Western Australia, SLWAPR14528/STA.

Hancock, Kathy, private collection of DeGaris family letters.

G. Hervey, 'Is Capitalism Immoral?', 22 September 1926, National Archives of Australia, item 15430.

Interview with Mrs Beth Coldicutt by Carolyn Rasmussen, 12 October 1992, courtesy Carolyn Rasmussen and Ruth Lee.

J. J. Simons papers, State Library of Western Australia, ACC8919A.

K. A. Ferris, 'History and Development of the Dried Fruits Industry in Australia', State Library of Victoria.

L. G. DeGaris papers, National Library of Australia, MS2303.

King O'Malley papers, National Library of Australia, box 13, items 7366–7411, MS 460.

Marion Mahony Griffin, *Magic of America*, copy held in Monash University Library.

P. Opas, *Our Father Which Art*, unpublished memoir, 1988, State Library of Victoria.

Stephens, R. *Kendenup 1840-1940*, State Library of Western Australia, 994.12/KEN.

'Testimonial from Grant Hervey', 1 December 1921, item 9932, National Archives of Australia.

Wattle Path Palais de Danse & Café Ltd: Esplanade St Kilda, Monash Collections Online.

Personal communications
Corbould, D., personal communication, 8 August 2019.
Corbould, H., personal communication, 8 August 2019.
Doble, Rick DeGaris, personal communication, February 2020.
Paul Sutcliffe, personal communication, December 2019.
Wallace Crabbe, C., personal communication, 17 August 2007.

Journal articles
Dugan, M., 'C. J. DeGaris as publisher', *Biblionews*, 1970, pp. 18–19.
Hervey, G. M., 'From Sydney to the Golden Mile', *New Age*, 12 January 1922, pp. 130–1.
Hunt, A., 'The Great Masturbation Panic and the Discourses of Moral Regulation in Nineteenth- and Early Twentieth-Century Britain', *Journal of the History of Sexuality*, vol. 8, no. 4, 1998, pp. 575–615.
Lee, R. and Nichols, D., 'Life… the manifestation of a purpose', *Journal of the Royal Australian Historical Society*, June 2006, p. 49.
Van Straten, F., 'The Riddle of "FFF", A Forgotten Australian Musical Comedy', *Australasian Music Research*, no. 6, 2002, pp. 105–19.

Books
Barry, P., *The Rise and Fall of Alan Bond*, ABC/Bantam, Sydney, 1990.
Brett, J., *The Enigmatic Mr. Deakin*, Text, Melbourne, 2017, p. 407.
Burcham, J., et al (eds), *Kendenup Stories*, publisher not identified, Kendenup, 2017.
Cannon, M., *That Damned Democrat: John Norton, an Australian Populist 1858-1916*, Melbourne University Press, Carlton, 1981.
Chaffey Brothers Limited, *The Australian Irrigation Colonies' Director's report*, Mildura, 1890.
Clarke, T., *My Northcliffe Diary*, Victor Gollancz, London, 1931.
Collins, T., *Rigby's Romance*, C. J. DeGaris Publishing House, Melbourne, 1921.
Courtney, V., *All I May Tell: A Journalist's Story*, Shakespeare Head Press, London, 1956.
Courtney, V., *The Life Story of J. J. Simons, Founder of the Young Australia League*, Young Australia League Inc., Sydney, 1961.
DeGaris, C. J., *Ambition Run Mad, or Whom the Gods Destroy: A Military Drama*, Murray Pioneer Printing Office, n.d.
DeGaris, C. J., *As I See Geelong in 1935*, C. J. DeGaris, Hawthorn, 1925.

BIBLIOGRAPHY

DeGaris, C. J., *Repatriation: A Gigantic Problem, a Practical Scheme*, C. J. DeGaris, Melbourne, 1917(?).

DeGaris, C. J. (ed.), *'Sun-Raysed' Children's Fairy Story Book*, F. W. Niven & Co., Melbourne, 1919.

DeGaris, C. J., *The Victories of Failure*, Modern Publishing Co, Melbourne, 1925.

DeGaris, K., *DeGaris: In Australia since 1854*, Ken DeGaris, Struan, 1991.

Evatt, H. V., *William Holman: Australian Labour Leader*, Angus and Robertson, 1940 (abridged edition 1954, 1979).

G. H. S., *Facing the Inevitable*, C. J. DeGaris Publishing House, Melbourne, 1921.

Grogan, W., *Report of the Royal Commission appointed to inquire into and report upon the establishment of the Settlement at Kendenup*, Government Printer, Perth, 1922.

Hansell, H., *The Arising of Jimmie Munro*, C. J. DeGaris Publishing House, Melbourne, 1920.

Hansell, H., *The Everlastin' Ballads*, C. J. DeGaris Publishing House, Melbourne, 1920.

Holman, A. A., *Sport of the Gods*, C. J. DeGaris Publishing House, Melbourne, 1921.

Kauffman, J., *The Sunraysia Wonder Book; The seventeen pearls in a necklace of surprises: the seventeen sunraysed settlements of Australia*, C. J. DeGaris Publishing House for The Australian Dried Fruits Association, 1921.

Lee, R. L., *Woman War Doctor: The Life of Mary DeGaris*, Australian Scholarly Publishing, Kew, 2014.

Lyons, M. and Arnold, J. (eds), *A History of the Book in Australia 1891-1945: A National Culture in a Colonised Market*, University of Queensland Press, St Lucia, 2001.

Lyons, S. M., *Telling the World about the Abrahams Millionaires*, Sol Lyons, St Kilda, 1928.

Morris, E. J., *The White Butterfly and Other Fairy Tales*, C. J. DeGaris Publishing House, Melbourne, 1921.

Pelloe, E. H., *Wildflowers of Western Australia*, C. J. DeGaris Publishing House, Melbourne, 1920.

Prior, T., *Christopher Skase: Beyond the Mirage*, Wilkinson Books, Melbourne, 1994.

Russell, F. A., *The Ashes of Achievement*, C. J. DeGaris Publishing House, Melbourne, 1920.

Voullaire, K., *Mildura Irrigation Settlement: the Early Years*, Sunraysia Daily, Mildura, 1985.

Walsh, J. M., *The Lost Valley*, C. J. DeGaris Publishing House, Melbourne, 1921.

Wilkinson, R., *Where God Never Trod: Australia's Oil Explorers Across Two Centuries*, David Ell Press, Balmain, 1991.

Book chapters

Hall, G., 'In DeGaris' Employ', in L. Milborn (ed.), *Mildura Police Station: The First 100 Years: Addendum and Corrigendum*, Les Milborn, Mildura, 1996, p. 167.

J. C. Lawton, 'Notes on the Circuits', in C. I. Benson (ed.), *A Century of Victorian Methodism*, Melbourne, Spectator Publishing Co., 1935, pp. 403–95.

'Mr. Elisha Clement DeGaris', *Cyclopedia of Victoria*, vol. III, p. 276.

H. A. Overend, 'The Church and the Community', in C. Irving Benson (ed.), *A Century of Victorian Methodism* Melbourne, Spectator Publishing Co., 1935, pp. 280–8.

Newspaper articles

'$200,000 of Eastern Capital Added to the Gillette Safety Tire Co. To Finance Industry', Eau Claire *Leader-Telegram*, 21 November 1916, p. 3.

'£1, 000 Reward', Melbourne *Herald*, 24 October 1921, p. 6.

'£35 an Acre Land for £10 at KENDENUP, W. A.', *Australian Business*, March 1921, p. 36.

'£9,355 writ against Mrs DeGaris', Melbourne *Herald*, 10 January 1925, p. 1.

'975- - 24/Mystery Numbers', *Evening Sun*, 19 September 1924, p.11.

'A Book of Revelations', Adelaide *Observer*, 13 June 1925, p. 59.

'A buyer of left-off clothing', *Sydney Morning Herald*, 26 May 1925, p. 7.

'A Generous Millionaire', Adelaide *Express and Telegraph*, 3 August 1906, p. 4.

'A Knocker and a Booster', Kendenup *Index*, June 1922, p. 3.

'A Letter from Kendenup', *Murray Pioneer and Australian River Record*, 23 March 1923, p. 18.

'A Literary Star', Perth *Sunday Times*, 14 December 1902, p. 4.

'A Little Bird Says', Perth *Call*, 16 April 1926, p. 2.

'A message of ill omen', Sydney *Truth*, 29 August 1926, p. 16.

'A Mildura Playwright', *Murray Pioneer and Australian River Record*, 24 September 1920, p. 5.

'A Missing Fisherman', *South Western Times*, 1 June 1926, p. 2.

'A Model Orchard', *Albany Advertiser*, 28 April 1917, p. 3.

'A mysterious disappearance', Adelaide *Advertiser*, 21 January 1925, p. 9.

'A New Life Story', Melbourne *Herald*, 3 June 1925, p. 4.

'A Patriarch Comes to Perth', *The Call*, 20 August 1920, p. 7.
'A Picnic on the Sands', *Murray Pioneer and Australian River Record*, 5 March 1920, p. 5.
'A Poet with a Pistol', Brisbane *Truth*, 19 November 1905, p. 3.
'A Practical Farmer', 'To the Editor', *West Australian*, 13 January 1922, p. 2.
'A Rocket that Fell Heavily', Melbourne *Advocate*, 11 June 1925, p. 3.
'A snapshot of C. J. DeGaris...', *Buffalo Times*, 5 November 1922, p. 27.
'A Sportsman and a Man', Mount Gambier *Border Watch*, 3 January 1912, p. 1.
'A Startling Charge', Hobart *Mercury*, 30 December 1914, p. 5.
'A Trip to Corio', *Goulburn Valley Stock and Property Journal*, 14 August 1924, p. 9.
'A Trip to the Old Country', Hamilton *Spectator*, 18 March 1902, p. 4.
'A Western Politician', *Table Talk*, 30 November 1922, p. 10.
"About the Commission', Kendenup *Index*, August 1922, p. 5.
'Adam Lindsay Gordon', Penshurst *Free Press*, 6 July 1912, p. 2.
A.D.F.A. Annual Conference', *Murray Pioneer and Australian River Record*, 1 November 1918, p. 3.
'A.D.F.A. Conference', *Murray Pioneer and Australian River Record*, 31 October 1919, p. 3.
'A.D.F.A. Publicity Methods', *Mildura Cultivator*, 15 May 1920, p. 4.
'Advertising hoax?', Brisbane *Daily Standard*, 14 January 1925, p. 5.
'Advertising', Melbourne *Herald*, 20 September 1917, p. 9.
'Advt.', *Mildura Cultivator*, 22 January 1913, p. 8.
'Aeroplane Flights', Kalgoorlie *Miner*, 10 July 1920, p. 4.
'Affairs of C. J. DeGaris', Melbourne *Argus*, 11 March 1924, p. 14.
'A.K.', 'A Township Problem', *Australasian*, 7 August 1897, p. 29.
'Albert Park Drowning', Melbourne *Argus*, 12 January 1925, p. 14.
'All About the Town', *Everyone's*, 14 July 1920, p. 5.
'Alleged Assault', *Cairns Post*, 17 December 1921, p. 2.
'Ambition Run Mad', *Mildura Telegraph and Lower Murray Advocate*, 9 April 1915, p. 2.
'American Lady Calls in', Kendenup *Index*, 24 October 1921, p. 2.
'An Administrative Genius', Adelaide *Register*, 8 January 1925, p. 7.
'An Australian Across the Sea', *Mildura Cultivator*, 22 November 1902, p. 10.
'An Australian Novel', *Queenslander*, 18 June 1921, p. 3.
'An Australian Prize Novel', *Sydney Morning Herald*, 18 December 1920, p. 8.
'An Invitation to the Murray Valley', Adelaide *Register*, 9 September 1921, p. 7.
'Anglesea', Melbourne *Argus*, 8 December 1923, p. 32.

BIBLIOGRAPHY

'Another Proposal', Albany *Despatch*, 10 May 1923, p. 3.
'Anti-Conscription Meeting', *Mildura Telegraph and Darling and Lower Murray Advocate*, 24 October 1916, p. 2.
'Anzac Observance', *Glenelg Guardian*, 22 April 1931, p. 1.
'Apt notes and pertinent quotes', *Westralian Worker*, 11 May 1923, p. 7.
'Arrest of DeGaris', *New Zealand Herald*, 14 January 1925, p. 11.
'At Capitol House', Melbourne *Herald*, 6 January 1925, p. 6.
'Athanaeum – Miss Winifred Moverley', Melbourne *Age*, 18 April 1921, p. 8.
'Athanaeum Hall', Melbourne *Age*, 9 April 1921, p. 20.
'Athlete's Illness', Sydney *Sun*, 14 April 1942, p. 10.
'Audrey herself tells her story to *Truth*', Perth *Truth*, 30 January 1926, p. 5.
'Audrey Jacob tells truth about Tacke', *Smith's Weekly*, 30 January 1926, p. 11.
'Audrey Jacobs' Own Story', Sydney *Truth*, 31 January 1926, p. 11.
'Australia has a unique settlement', *The Pennsylvania Register*, undated, in Simons' scrapbook.
'Australian Dried Fruits Association', *Mildura Cultivator*, 13 February 1915, p. 6.
'Australian Dried Fruits Association', *Mildura Cultivator*, 2 November 1918, p. 13.
'Australian Dried Fruits Association', Adelaide *Express and Telegraph*, 23 April 1902, p. 3.
'Australian Dried Fruits', Adelaide *Register*, 4 May 1920, p. 9.
'Australian Dried Fruits', *Daily Commercial News and Shipping List*, 16 July 1919, p. 11.
'Australian Natives Association', *West Australian*, 24 March 1923, p. 11.
'Australian Novel Competition', Melbourne *Advocate*, 13 January 1921, p. 11.
'Australian Prize Story', Brisbane *Daily Mail*, 19 May 1921, p. 6.
'Australia's Taste in Music', Melbourne *Punch*, 14 February 1907, p. 29.
'Ballarat Chatter', *Table Talk*, 14 February 1929, p. 59.
'"Beneficial" Absence', Brisbane *Telegraph*, 13 January 1925, p. 3.
'Book Review', *W. A. Record*, 1 January 1921, p. 5.
'Book Reviews: "The Ashes of Achievement"', Launceston *Daily Telegraph*, 22 December 1920, p. 5
'Bremer Oil Prospects', Albany *Advertiser*, 14 September 1921, p. 3.
'Bretherton Estate', Melbourne *Argus*, 15 July 1938, p. 6.
'Bribes for a Passport', Sydney *Daily Telegraph*, 17 November 1927, p. 2.
'Brisbane-Melbourne One Day Flight', *S.A. Wheelman*, 25 January 1921, p. 18.

'Broadcast Programmes', *West Australian*, 31 October 1925, p. 9.
'Building Fund Activities', *The Boomerang*, July 1921, p. 11.
'Building is Brisk', Kendenup *Index*, June 1921, p. 4.
'Buy Land in Kendenup!', Melbourne *Age*, 9 February 1921, p. 11.
'C J DeGaris, "Kendenup"', Kendenup *Index*, July 1921, p. 1.
'C. J. DeGaris flies home', *Mildura Cultivator*, 26 June 1920, p. 7.
'C. J. DeGaris in Melbourne', Adelaide *Advertiser*, 12 February 1925, p. 12.
'C. J. DeGaris Sued', Melbourne *Argus* 17 April 1924, p. 10.
'C. J. DeGaris', *Lenora Miner*, 22 November 1924, p. 3; 'Creditors' Meeting', Melbourne *Herald*, 5 January 1925, p. 5.
'C. J. DeGaris', *South Western Times*, 13 January 1925, p. 4.
'Carnegie Free Library', Melbourne *Age*, 18 January 1907, p. 6.
'Caught by boys', Melbourne *Herald*, 14 January 1925, p. 5.
'Central Irrigation League', Melbourne *Argus*, 14 October 1884.
'Chief Interviewed', Kendenup *Index*, June 1922, pp. 6–7.
'Child killed by motor car', Melbourne *Argus*, 29 April 1921, p. 5.
'"Cinderella" at Ballarat', Melbourne *Herald*, 21 April 1931, p. 15.
'Circulation of "Topics"', *Sarnia Topics*, vol. 4, no. 1, 19 February 1919, p. 1.
'Citizens or Sheep?', Kendenup *Index*, August 1921, p. 1.
'City Town and Country Golf Links Coburg', Melbourne *Sporting Globe*, 28 November 1923, p. 7.
'Combined staffs pay tribute to "C. J. D."', *Mildura Cultivator*, 3 July 1920, p. 13.
'Come to Kendenup', *Graphic*, 20 October 1921, in J. J. Simons' scrapbook, J. J. Simons papers, State Library of Western Australia, MN3065.
'Concert at Irymple', *Mildura Cultivator*, 13 September 1911, p. 9.
'Concert at Kendenup', Kendenup *Index*, 28 January 1922, p. 6.
'Corio – A Garden City', *Australian Home Builder*, 15 July 1924, p. 66.
'Corio Development', Geelong *Standard*, September 1924, p. 14.
'Corio Garden Suburb: A Favourable Impression', Geelong *Standard*, 25 September 1924, p. 14.
'Country News', Melbourne *Argus*, 28 September 1923, p. 18.
'Country News', *West Australian*, 8 December 1925, p. 4.
'De Garis' Very Latest', *Smith's Weekly*, 5 June 1926, p. 3.
'Dead or Alive?', Adelaide *News*, 7 January 1925, p. 1.
'Death of DeGaris', Brisbane *Telegraph*, 25 August 1926, p. 12.
'Death of Journalist', *Riverine Herald*, 10 September 1947, p. 4.
'Death of Mr. J J Morris', Melbourne *Argus*, 21 January 1920, p. 14.
'Deaths', Melbourne *Argus*, 20 November 1936, p. 1.
'Debenture Holders', *Albany Advertiser*, 28 March 1923, p. 3.
'Decentralisation Movement', Melbourne *Age*, 11 April 1910, p. 11.

'DeGaris Again', Sydney *Sunday Times*, 30 August 1925, p. 1.
'DeGaris and the detective', Melbourne *Herald*, 12 February 1925, p. 5.
'DeGaris arrested at Auckland', Sydney *Daily Telegraph*, 14 January 1925, p. 1.
'DeGaris arrested', Sydney *Evening News*, 13 January 1925, p. 7.
'DeGaris – Austin', *Table Talk*, 5 July 1923, p. 29.
'DeGaris Back', Melbourne *Herald*, 11 February 1925, p. 1.
'DeGaris back', *Weekly Times*, 14 February 1925, p. 9.
'DeGaris Case', Melbourne *Herald*, 26 January 1925, p. 1.
'DeGaris Divorce', Melbourne *Argus*, 1 June 1923, p. 14.
'DeGaris Divorce Case', Melbourne *Argus*, 24 November 1922, p. 10
'DeGaris Estate', *Sydney Morning Herald*, 18 November 1936, p. 13.
'DeGaris figures in mystery', Sydney *Evening News*, 5 January 1925, p. 5.
'DeGaris free', Hobart *News*, 6 March 1925, p. 1.
'DeGaris Here', Perth *Daily News*, 24 March 1926, p. 3.
'DeGaris in Adelaide', Adelaide *News*, 10 October 1925, p. 5.
'DeGaris in court', Brisbane *Telegraph*, 18 February 1925, p. 2.
'DeGaris in Sydney', Broken Hill *Barrier Miner*, 11 February 1925, p. 1.
'DeGaris is on board the *Maheno* bound for Auckland', Sydney *Daily Telegraph*, 12 January 1925, p. 1.
'Degaris Missing', Perth *Daily News*, 5 January 1925, p. 8.
'DeGaris Missing', *Sun News-Pictorial*, 6 January 1925, p. 3.
'DeGaris mystery', Adelaide *Register*, 10 January 1925, p. 8.
'DeGaris Mystery', Brisbane *Telegraph*, 10 January 1925, p. 8.
'DeGaris Mystery', Riverine *Herald*, 10 January 1925, p. 2.
'DeGaris Mystery', Sydney *Evening News*, 7 January 1925, p. 5.
'DeGaris Mystery', *Sydney Morning Herald*, 7 January 1925, p. 14.
'"DeGaris no typist"', Sydney *Sun*, 10 January 1925, p. 4.
'DeGaris passes!', Cairns *Northern Herald*, 14 January 1925, p. 20.
'DeGaris puts it up to *Smith's Weekly*', Katanning *Great Southern Leader*, 15 May 1925, p. 5.
'DeGaris returning', Sydney *Sun*, 5 February 1925, p. 10.
'DeGaris returns', Adelaide *News*, 11 February 1925, p. 1.
'DeGaris returns', Melbourne *Argus*, 12 February 1925, p. 12.
'DeGaris Set Free', Melbourne *Age*, 7 March 1925, p. 19.
'DeGaris smiles when charged', Melbourne *Herald*, 14 January 1925, p. 1.
'DeGaris Smiles', Adelaide *News*, 14 January 1925, p. 11.
'DeGaris Staff', Melbourne *Herald*, 7 January 1925, p. 5.
'DeGaris talks like a book & will write one', Perth *Truth*, 28 February 1928, p. 8.
'DeGaris tries his disguise', Melbourne *Herald*, 12 February 1925, p. 5.

'DeGaris visits M.S.D.', Melbourne *Herald*, 13 February 1925, p. 7.
'DeGaris writing a book about it', *Smith's Weekly*, 4 April 1925, p. 9.
'DeGaris! The man who put the sun in Sun-Raysed', *The Call*, 24 September 1920, p. 2.
'DeGaris! The man who put the sun in Sun-Raysed'.
'DeGaris?', Sydney *Evening News*, 9 January 1925, p. 7.
'DeGaris' Discovery', Perth *Truth*, 2 December 1922, p. 8.
'DeGaris' New Scheme', *Kalgoorlie Miner*, 10 July 1925, p. 4.
'DeGaris', *Newcastle Morning Herald and Miners' Advocate*, 10 January 1925, p. 5.
'DeGaris', *Sydney Morning Herald*, 10 January 1925, p. 15.
'DeGaris's Affairs', Melbourne *Herald*, 12 March 1924, p. 7.
'DeGaris's cable to wife', Melbourne *Herald*, 14 January 1925, p. 1.
'DeGaris's Escape', Brisbane *Daily Mail*, 12 February 1925, p. 7.
'DeGaris's letter', Sydney *Sun*, 28 January 1925, p. 14.
'DeGaris's Letters', *Nambucca and Bellinger News*, 3 September 1926, p. 6.
'DeGaris's Stunt Suicide', *Smith's Weekly*, 10 January 1925, p. 13.
'Demolition of Dehydrator Building', Albany *Advertiser*, 22 November 1948, p. 6.
'Detective Davey Leaves', Sydney *Sun*, 23 January 1925, p. 9.
'Did You Know Your Country Was as Big as This?', Melbourne *Evening Sun*, 6 May 1924, p. 2.
'Dip-Tin', 'Sun-Raysed Column', Burra *Record*, 12 May 1920, p. 3.
'Disguised as woman', Sydney *Sun*, 12 January 1925, p. 7.
'Doings at Kendenup', Katanning *Southern Districts Advocate*, 23 May 1921, p. 1.
'Douglass speaks of the Illinois "insect"', Nashville *Brown County Democrat*, 24 November 1921, p. 1.
'E. DeGaris & Co. Pty Ltd', *Mildura Cultivator*, 17 April 1920, p. 3.
'Early Closing Movement', *Mildura Telegraph and Darling and Lower Murray Advocate*, 18 July 1916, p. 2.
'Easiest Way', Sydney *Sun*, 6 January 1925, p. 7.
'Economy as a Food', *Farmer's Advocate*, 7 February 1919, p. 2.
'Publicity Director at Work', *Murray Pioneer and Australian River Record*, 7 February 1919, p. 3.
'Editorial', Melbourne *Age*, 22 May 1869, p. 2.
'Escapes from Pentridge', Melbourne *Argus*, 5 August 1922, p. 20.
'F. F. F.', *Mildura Cultivator*, 1 September 1920, p. 2.
'F. F. F.', Adelaide *Advertiser*, 30 August 1920, p. 8.
'F. F. F.', Adelaide *Daily Herald*, 6 September 1920, p. 2.
'F. F. F.', Melbourne *Age*, 8 October 1920, p. 12.

'F. F. F.', *Mildura Cultivator*, 1 September 1920, p. 2.
'Faith in DeGaris', Adelaide *Advertiser*, 12 January 1925, p. 9.
'False teeth', Melbourne *Herald*, 10 January 1925, p. 1.
'Family Notices', Brisbane *Courier*, 21 April 1922, p. 6.
'Family Notices', Melbourne *Argus*, 18 January 1896, p. 1.
'Family Notices', Melbourne *Argus*, 22 April 1936, p. 16.
'Farewell Function', Kendenup *Index*, June 1922, p. 7.
'Farewell to Mrs. DeGaris', Kendenup *Index*, 19 December 1922, p. 7.
'Farm and Garden', *Murray Pioneer and Australian River Record*, 24 October 1919, p. 2.
'Fast Motor Run', *Mildura Telegraph and Darling and Lower Murray Advocate*, 6 February 1914, p. 4.
'Fickle Fate's Pendulum', Sydney *Truth*, 1 February 1925, p. 15.
'Film Idol', *Portland Guardian*, 6 April 1925, p. 2.
'Finance Expert to Talk to Baptist Men's Club', *Brooklyn Standard Union*, 11 March 1922, p. 4.
'Financing DeGaris', Brisbane *Telegraph*, 6 October 1925, p. 20.
'Financing Kendenup', Perth *Daily News*, 13 May 1922, p. 17.
'First Mildura Irrigation Trust', *Mildura Cultivator*, 19 March 1913, p. 8.
'Football', *Mildura Cultivator*, 21 June 1902, p. 10.
'For the Empire', *Mildura Telegraph and Darling and Lower Murray Advocate*, 14 August 1914, p. 4.
'Found Drowned. Mr. A. E. DeGaris', *Sydney Morning Herald*, 14 October 1927, p. 11.
'Frank Russell Dead', *Dalby Herald*, 28 December 1934, p. 3.
'Friendless and Alone', Adelaide *Register*, 1 January 1915, p. 9.
'From Lord Roberts to J. C. DeGaris', *Mildura Cultivator*, 10 November 1900, p. 7.
'Fruit Industry', *Auckland Star*, 26 June 1922, in Simons' scrapbook.
'Fruits Industry and City Campaign', *Mildura Cultivator*, 28 June 1919, p. 5.
'Fully dressed', Sydney *Sun*, 9 January 1925, p. 7.
'Funeral of Mr. C. J. DeGaris', Melbourne *Age*, 20 August 1926, p. 11.
'Future of Brown Coal', *Geelong Advertiser*, 17 March 1926, p. 7.
'Geelong's Garden Suburb', *Goulburn Valley Stock and Property Journal*, 13 August 1924, p. 6.
'General News', Adelaide *Register*, 25 November 1922, in Simons' scrapbook.
'General News', *Mildura Cultivator*, 30 March 1901, p. 3.
'General News', Adelaide *Register*, 25 November 1922, in Simons' scrapbook.
'"Getting Things Done"', Melbourne *Argus*, 24 February 1925, p. 11.

'Gift from Mr Carnegie', Melbourne *Argus*, 16 October 1907, p. 6.
'Good Little Normey', Rockhampton *Morning Bulletin*, 18 January 1919, p. 3.
'Good News for the Public', Elmira *Star-Gazette*, 25 October 1923, p. 21.
'Good News for W.A.', Perth *Australian*, 20 August 1920, p. 4.
'Grand Concert', Ouyen *Mail*, 5 September 1917, p. 4.
'Grant Hervey', Brisbane *Truth*, 27 June 1915, p. 6.
'Grant Hervey', Melbourne *Age*, 31 December 1914, p. 4.
'Grant Hervey', Melbourne *Truth*, 9 January 1915, p. 6.
'Grant Hervey convicted', Hamilton *Spectator*, 5 February 1915, p. 4.
'Grant Hervey on Gaol Life', Hobart *World*, 4 August 1919, p. 3.
'Grant Hervey Sentenced', Melbourne *Truth*, 13 February 1915, p. 6.
'Great Clearing Sale!', *Mildura Cultivator*, 29 April 1899, p. 4.
'Greater Mildura', *Mildura Cultivator*, 6 August 1919, p. 10.
'H.R.H. The Prince of Wales', *Bunbury Herald and Blackwood Express*, 23 July 1920, p. 7.
'Happy in Gaol', *Tweed Daily*, 19 January 1925, p. 2.
'Happy Kendenup', '*Sunraysia Daily*', 28 November 1922, p. 5.
'Harry Julius: the one Australian who draws for the cinema', *The Triad*, 10 July 1916, p. 10.
'He is Mental', Sydney *Sunday Times*, 11 January 1925, p. 7.
'Heart of Rosebud', *Evening Sun*, 14 December 1923, p. 13.
'Heart of Rosebud', Melbourne *Herald*, 17 December 1923, p. 8.
'Heavy Borrowings', Sydney *Sun*, 11 January 1925, p. 2.
'Here and There', Mullewa *Mail*, 29 November 1923, p. 2.
'Here are the Reasons of the Success...', Sydney *Sunday Times*, 12 October 1924, p. 20.
'Here are the Reasons of the Success...', Melbourne *Sun News Pictorial*, 7 October 1924, pp. 22–3.
'Hervey Before Court', Melbourne *Herald*, 25 November 1921, p. 10.
'Hervey Shooting Case', Adelaide *Advertiser*, 15 December 1905, p. 7.
'Hervey-Baker Case', Boulder *Evening Star*, 24 November 1905, p. 3.
'Hide and Seek', Brisbane *Daily Standard*, 11 February 1925, p. 5.
'High Finance', *Ballarat Star*, 4 March 1924, p. 6.
'His handwriting', Sydney *Evening News*, 13 January 1925, p. 7.
'His Last Care', Rockhampton *Morning Bulletin*, 23 June 1922, p. 13.
'Hospital entertainment', *Ouyen Mail*, 12 September 1917, p. 5.
'How Debts were Made', Kyogle *Examiner*, 27 April 1934, p. 3.
'"I can answer charge" says C. J. DeGaris', Perth *Mirror*, 7 February 1925, p. 1.
'Illegal use of a horse', Carnarvon *Northern Times*, 23 October 1925, p. 2.

BIBLIOGRAPHY

'In the Law Courts', Melbourne *Age*, 18 November 1936, p. 14.
'In the World of Music and Drama', Sydney *Mail*, 27 October 1920, p. 10.
'Industrial Progress', Geelong *Advertiser*, 2 February 1924, p. 4.
'Investigation in Victoria', Adelaide *Register*, 24 January 1924, p. 12.
'Investors Meet', Melbourne *Age*, 7 January 1925, p. 9.
'Irrigation: The Chaffey Colonies on the Murray', *Daily Telegraph*,
    30 December 1889, cutting in scrapbook labelled 'Book of Securities'
    in E. C. DeGaris papers, State Library of Victoria, MS7080, box 407.
'Is he alive?', Brisbane *Courier*, 10 January 1925, p. 7.
'Is it a Hoax?', Burnie *Advocate*, 20 January 1925, p. 5.
'Journalist Charged', Sydney *Daily Telegraph*, 19 December 1914, p. 15.
'Kenden – Up the Pole', Brisbane *Daily Standard*, 19 March 1923, p. 6.
'Kendenup (Western Australia) Land Now for Sale', Melbourne *Argus*,
    13 January 1921, p. 4.
'Kendenup Affairs', Katanning *Great Southern Herald*, 28 April 1923, p. 2.
'Kendenup Affairs', Melbourne *Argus*, 27 November 1923, p. 9.
'Kendenup Again', Adelaide *News*, 19 November 1925, p. 6.
'Kendenup Again', Perth *Daily News*, 29 April 1926, p. 5.
'Kendenup/American Aid, *West Australian*, 13 May 1922, p. 9.
'Kendenup Chirps', Kendenup *Index*, August 1921, p. 15.
'Kendenup Chirps', Kendenup *Index*, August 1921, p. 16.
'Kendenup Chirps', Kendenup *Index*, July 1921, p. 15.
'Kendenup Chirps', Kendenup *Index*, June 1921, pp. 15–16.
'Kendenup Chirps', Kendenup *Index*, May 1922, p. 11–12.
'Kendenup Collapse', Perth *Sunday Times*, 4 March 1923, p. 1.
'Kendenup Commission', *West Australian*, 28 May 1924, p. 7.
'Kendenup Commission', *Kalgoorlie Miner*, 22 January 1923, p. 3.
'Kendenup Commission', Perth *Daily News*, 8 February 1924, p. 4.
'Kendenup Commission', *West Australian*, 20 October 1923, p. 13.
'Kendenup DeGaris', *The Call*, 29 July 1921, p. 2.
'Kendenup Estate', *Daily News*, 12 January 1922, in Simons' scrapbook.
'Kendenup Finances', Melbourne *Argus*, 29 February 1924, p. 6.
'Kendenup Group', Perth *Sunday Times*, 20 December 1925, p. 10.
'Kendenup Inquiry: Mrs DeGaris gives evidence', *Geelong Advertiser*,
    13 March 1924, p. 2.
'Kendenup Inquiry', Geelong *Standard*, 7 March 1924, p. 5.
'Kendenup Inquiry', Perth *Daily News*, 22 February 1924, p. 5.
'Kendenup Inquiry', Perth *Daily News*, 23 February 1924, p. 10.
'Kendenup Inquiry', *West Australian*, 21 February 1924, p. 9.
'Kendenup is saved!', *The Call*, 20 October 1922, p. 2.
'Kendenup Notes', Albany *Despatch*, 13 July 1922, in Simons' scrapbook.

'Kendenup notes', Albany *Despatch*, 7 September 1922, in Simons' scrapbook.
'"Kendenup Oil"', *West Australian*, 14 June 1926, p. 10.
'Kendenup Oil Myth', *West Australian*, 10 June 1926, p. 10.
'Kendenup Royal Commission', Katanning *Great Southern Herald*, 12 August 1922, p. 2.
'Kendenup Salaries', Melbourne *Argus*, 8 March 1924, p. 17.
'Kendenup Settlement', *West Australian*, 8 June 1923, p. 8.
'Kendenup Settlers', *Kalgoorlie Miner*, 8 June 1923, p. 5.
'Kendenup settlers', Perth *Daily News*, 23 March 1923, p. 3.
'Kendenup Situation', Albany *Advertiser*, 18 April 1923, p. 3.
'Kendenup Sold', Albany *Advertiser*, 21 August 1920, p. 3.
'Kendenup Summed Up', *The Call*, 11 August 1922, in Simons' scrapbook.
'Kendenup to liquidate', Melbourne *Herald*, 7 March 1923, p. 8.
'Kendenup to Wind Up', Melbourne *Herald*, 9 March 1923, p. 1
'Kendenup: "Black Repudiation"', Warwick *Daily News*, 16 March 1923, p. 6.
'Kendenup! Kendenup! Home of Western Australia's Most Progressive Settlement', *Mirror*, 21 January 1923, in Simons' scrapbook.
'Kendenup. Mr DeGaris Returns.', *'West'*, 13 November 1922, p. 8.
'Kendenup', Albany *Despatch*, 7 May 1923, p. 2.
'Kendenup', *Beverley Times*, 14 April 1923, p. 2.
'Kendenup', *Beverley Times*, 21 April 1923, p. 2.
'Kendenup', Hobart *Mercury*, 25 July 1924, p. 2.
'Kendenup', Kendenup *Index*, July 1921, p. 1.
'Kendenup', Perth *Daily News*, 28 April 1926, p. 4.
'Kendenup', Perth *West Australian*, 14 March 1924, p. 9.
'Kendenup', *Sydney Morning Herald*, 4 March 1924, p. 9.
'Kendenup', *West Australian*, 28 December 1923, p. 6.
'Kendenup', *West Australian*, 13 March 1924, p. 9.
'Kendenup', *West Australian*, 13 November 1922, p. 8.
'Kendenup', *West Australian*, 28 December 1923, p. 6.
'Kendenup', *Western Mail*, 17 January 1924, p. 16.
'Kendenup's Future', *Swan Express*, 30 October 1925, p. 5.
'Kendenup's Last King', Kendenup *Index*, 26 July 1922, p. 4.
'Kenenup Affairs', Melbourne *Argus*, 12 March 1924, p. 17.
'King's Theatre – F. F. F.', Melbourne *Age*, 11 October 1920, p. 8.
'King's Theatre', *Table Talk*, 14 October 1920, p. 14.
'Ladies' Letter', *Table Talk*, 27 April 1922, p. 32.
'Lady Journalist's Death', Kyogle *Examiner*, 10 May 1935, p. 7.

'Land Purchase at North Shore', Geelong *Advertiser*, 23 November 1923, p. 2.
'Land sale success at Kendenup', Melbourne *Argus*, 10 January 1921, p. 8.
'Land Selling Schemes', Perth *Daily News*, 14 January 1925, p. 5.
'Last Minute News', Melbourne *Herald*, 6 January 1925, p. 7.
'Last of DeGaris', *New Zealand Herald*, 6 February 1925, p. 7.
'Latest from Chief', Kendenup *Index*, 23 October 1922, p. 11.
'Launching of the Country Party', *The Farmer and Settler*, 11 July 1913, p. 4.
'Law notices', Melbourne *Age*, 12 February 1986, p. 60.
'Lawn Tennis', *Mildura Cultivator*, 17 May 1913, p. 11.
'Legion of Frontiersmen', *Mildura Cultivator*, 1 March 1913, p. 5.
'Let Us Help You to Start the New Year Profitably!', *Table Talk*, 10 January 1924, p. 30.
'Libel action', Portland *Guardian*, 1 May 1912, p. 2; 'Actions for Libel', *Horsham Times*, 30 April 1912, p. 5.
'Licensing Application', *Cumberland Argus and Fruitgrowers Advocate*, 24 October 1923, p. 2.
'Linking Geelong with Melbourne', *Geelong Advertiser*, 6 February 1926, p. 8.
'Local and General News', Albany *Advertiser*, 5 January 1921, p. 2.
'Local and General News', Albany *Advertiser*, 9 January 1924, p. 3.
'Local and General', Geraldton *Guardian*, 17 September 1949, p. 2.
'Local Happenings', Perth *Sunday Times*, 26 June 1927, p. 17.
'Local News', *Mildura Cultivator*, 18 October 1902, p. 7.
'Local News', *Mildura Cultivator*, 9 August 1902, p. 10.
'Local News', *Mildura Cultivator*, 12 October 1907, p. 7.
'Local News', *Mildura Cultivator*, 12 May 1906, p. 6.
'Local News', *Mildura Cultivator*, 14 April 1909, p. 7.
'Local News', *Mildura Cultivator*, 14 August 1920, p. 10.
'Local News', *Mildura Cultivator*, 14 December 1912, p. 11.
'Local News', *Mildura Cultivator*, 14 November 1891, p. 2.
'Local News', *Mildura Cultivator*, 15 February 1919, p. 10.
'Local News', *Mildura Cultivator*, 15 January 1913, p. 10.
'Local News', *Mildura Cultivator*, 14 November 1914, p. 10.
'Local News', *Mildura Cultivator*, 23 September 1916, p. 9.
'Local News', *Mildura Cultivator*, 31 March 1920, p. 8.
'Local News', *Mildura Cultivator*, 31 May 1913, p. 10.
'Local News', *Mildura Cultivator*, 7 May 1913, p. 7.
'Local News', *Mildura Cultivator*, 7 October 1905, p. 7.
'Lost Eighty Thousand', *The Call*, 16 March 1923, p. 2.

'Man and Machine of Many Records', Melbourne *Herald*, 24 January 1921, p. 2.
'Many Buildings Being Erected on Townsite', Kendenup *Index*, September 1921, p. 12.
'McClelland Forms New Firm', *New York Herald*, 27 September 1919, p. 16.
'Meeting of Creditors', Melbourne *Argus*, 15 January 1925, p. 9.
'Melbourne News', *Portland Guardian*, 12 February 1925, p. 2; 'C. J. DeGaris in Melbourne', Adelaide *Advertiser*, 12 February 1925, p. 12.
'Melbourne News', *Portland Guardian*, 12 February 1925, p. 2.
'Melbourne Sub-Divisions Mess', Sydney *Truth*, 19 April 1925, p. 9.
'Melbourne Sub-divisions', Melbourne *Herald*, 14 January 1925, p. 5.
'Melbourne Subdivision Co.', Melbourne *Argus*, 25 April 1925, p. 29.
'Melbourne Subdivision', Melbourne *Argus*, 29 January 1925, p. 10.
'Melbourne Subdivision', Melbourne *Argus*, 8 April 1925, p. 16.
'Melbourne Subdivisions Co', *Traralgon Record*, 25 November 1924, p. 2.
'Melbourne Subdivisions Coy', Geelong *Advertiser*, 22 October 1923, p. 4.
'Melbourne Subdivisions', Albany *Advertiser*, 3 December 1924, p. 3.
'Melbourne Subdivisions', Melbourne *Argus*, 7 January 1925, p. 11.
'Melbourne-Made Movies', Melbourne *Herald*, 29 September 1923, p. 3.
'Melbourne', Bendigo *Advertiser*, 23 March 1901, p. 5.
'Melbourne', *Everyone's*, 20 August 1924, p. 30.
'Men and other things', *Australian Worker*, 7 January 1925, p. 1.
'Mentality Sapped', Brisbane *Telegraph*, 7 January 1925, p. 9.
'Mentone Man Vanishes', Melbourne *Herald*, 15 January 1925, p. 16.
'Methodists vs Presbyterians', *Mildura Cultivator*, 31 May 1902, p. 8.
'Mildura Caledonian Society', *Mildura Cultivator*, 23 July 1913, p. 5.
'Mildura District Hospital', *Mildura Cultivator*, 19 July 1913, p. 5.
'Mildura District Hospital', *Mildura Cultivator*, 20 December 1913, p. 5.
'Mildura Growers' Progress Association', *Mildura Cultivator*, 30 August 1913, p. 7.
'Mildura Musical and Elocutionary Competition', Adelaide *Chronicle*, 26 September 1903, pp. 13–14.
'Mildura Musical and Elocutionary Competitions', *Mildura Cultivator*, 22 October 1910, p. 8.
'Mildura Shire Council', *Mildura Telegraph and Darling and Lower Murray Advocate*, 4 December 1914, p. 2.
'Mildura Tennis Association', *Mildura Cultivator*, 20 September 1913, p. 11.
'Mildura to Sydney', *Tweed Daily*, 7 July 1920, p. 3.
'Mildura', Melbourne *Age*, 28 September 1923, p. 12.
'Mildura's Hustler', Perth *Daily News*, 21 September 1920, p. 7.
'Millions in Oil', Adelaide *News*, 18 August 1926, p. 1.

'Mining Notices', Melbourne *Argus*, 1 March 1923, p. 1.
'Misfire', Sydney *Sun*, 18 August 1926, p. 9.
'Missing Ballads', Melbourne *Advocate*, 5 August 1920, p. 11.
'Moonooloo!', *Sun News-Pictorial*, 6 January 1925, p. 3
'"Mordecai MacCobber"', *Riverina Recorder*, 17 February 1926, p. 3.
'More Frenzied Finance', *Adelaide Mail*, 13 June 1925, p. 2.
'Mostly Personal', *Western Mail*, 17 December 1931, p. 7.
'Mr C. J. DeGaris', *Western Mail*, 23 November 1922, in Simons' scrapbook.
'Mr C. J. DeGaris', *Murray Pioneer and Australian River Record*, 4 July 1925, p. 9.
'Mr E. C. DeGaris: an irrigationist of the early eighties', *Sarnia Topics*, 16 April 1919, p. 8.
'Mr. C. J. DeGaris found dead', Melbourne *Argus*, 18 August 1926, p. 21.
'Mr. C. J. DeGaris', Melbourne *Argus*, 6 January 1925, p. 11.
'Mr. C. J. DeGaris', *Graphic*, 27 October 1921, in Simons' scrapbook.
'Mr. C. J. DeGaris', Melbourne *Argus*, 7 January 1925, p. 11.
'Mr. C. J. DeGaris', Perth *Daily News*, 10 May 1922, p. 2.
'Mr. C. J. DeGaris's Arrival', Kendenup *Index*, June 1921, p. 13.
'Mr. D. T. Edmunds Dead', Adelaide *Mail*, 26 September 1925, p. 5.
'Mr. DeGaris Returns from Colombo', Perth *Daily News*, 10 September 1921, p. 9.
'Mr. DeGaris Revisits Kendenup', Albany *Advertiser*, 5 December 1925, p. 3.
'Mr. DeGaris Satisfied', Adelaide *News*, 17 April 1926, p. 1.
'Mr. DeGaris says there is oil at Kendenup', Melbourne *Herald*, 24 May 1926, p. 4.
'Mr. Frank J. Pennifold', *Weekly Times*, 21 August 1920, p. 49; 'Talk of the Week', *Table Talk*, 13 January 1921, p. 5.
'Mr. J. J. Simons', Sydney *Sunday Times*, 13 November 1927, p. 4.
'"Mr. Rogers" DeGaris', *Murrumbidgee Irrigator*, 23 June 1925, p. 1.
'Mr. Simons and Kendenup', *West Australian*, 18 November 1922, p. 12.
'Mr. Theodore Pelloe Farewelled', *Mildura Telegraph and Darling and Lower Murray Advocate*, 10 November 1916, p. 3.
'Mrs DeGaris's Full Statement', Melbourne *Herald*, 6 January 1925, p. 1.
'Mrs Holman Dead', *Sydney Morning Herald*, 6 April 1949, p. 7.
'Mt. Barker Notes', *Albany Advertiser*, 14 April 1923, p. 3.
'Music and Song', Kendenup *Index*, 28 February 1922, p. 11.
'Mysterious "Mr. Young"', Perth *Sunday Times*, 11 January 1925, p. 1.
'Mystery Deepens', *Sun News-Pictorial*, 7 January 1925, p. 3.
'Mystery man on "Maheno" wears pyjamas branded DeGaris', Sydney *Truth*, 11 January 1925, p. 11.
'Mystery man', Newcastle *Sun*, 10 January 1925, p. 1.

'Mystery no longer', Sydney *Sunday Times*, 11 January 1925, p. 1.
'Mystery of C. J. DeGaris', Melbourne *Herald*, 10 January 1925, p. 6.
'Mystery of DeGaris', Melbourne *Herald*, 10 January 1925, p. 6.
'Needs, Wants, Happiness', *Eudora Weekly News*, 11 May 1916, p. 1.
'New Books Received', *Land*, 26 June 1925, p. 2.
'New Books', Port Pirie *Recorder*, 23 December 1920, p. 3.
'New Books', Melbourne *Age*, 13 June 1925, p. 4.
'New DeGaris', Melbourne *Herald*, 6 March 1924, p. 5.
'New Fiction', *Sydney Morning Herald*, 12 November 1921, p. 8.
'New Journalistic Venture', Launceston *Examiner*, 5 October 1920, p. 12.
'New Suburbs Planned', *Evening Sun*, 7 December 1923, p. 11.
'New year's greetings', *Hebrew Standard of Australasia*, 17 September 1920, p. 7.
'News and Notes', *The Bookfellow*, 15 February 1921, p. 5.
'News from the Seat of War', *North Eastern Ensign*, 30 March 1900, p. 3.
'News of the River', *Murray Pioneer and Australian River Record*, 11 July 1913, p. 5.
'Newspaper sends special investigator to Kendenup', Melbourne *Argus*, 20 January 1921, p. 8.
'No Light on Mystery', Sydney *Sun*, 7 January 1925, p. 9.
'No Prima Facie Charge', Newcastle *Sun*, 14 January 1925, p. 5.
'No trace', *Sun News-Pictorial*, 8 January 1925, p. 3.
'No Traces of Body', Brisbane *Telegraph*, 6 January 1925, p. 5.
'Obituary', Melbourne *Argus*, 24 May 1934, p. 8.
'Obituary Notices', Adelaide *Observer*, 28 May 1927, p. 43.
'Obituary: Mr. E. R. Peacock', Melbourne *Argus*, 5 September 1932, p. 6.
'Obituary', *Labor Daily*, 4 April 1936, p. 6.
'Obituary', *Riverina Recorder*, 3 October 1923, p. 2.
'Odds and Ends', Lismore *Northern Star*, 31 January 1900, p. 5.
'Off to New Zealand', Brisbane *Daily Mail*, 10 January 1925, p. 7.
'Oil at Kendenup', *Albany Advertiser*, 26 May 1926, p. 3.
'Oil Boring at Bremer Bay', Melbourne *Age*, 19 August 1921, p. 9.
'Oil Exploitation', Albany *Despatch*, 2 February 1920, p. 3.
'Oil Reported at Kendenup', *Herald*, 28 November 1922, in Simons' scrapbook.
'Olympia', *Mildura Cultivator*, 13 November 1912, p. 7.
'On his knees!', Perth *Daily News*, 1 March 1924, p. 10.
'One of our Weekends', Kendenup *Index*, June 1921, p. 6.
'Our new building', *The Boomerang*, 28 February 1922, p. 2.
'Our Settlers' Association', Kendenup *Index*, 24 October 1921, p. 8.
'Patriotic meeting', *Mildura Cultivator*, 12 August 1914, p. 8.

'Peeps at People', Perth *Sunday Times*, 4 June 1905, p. 13.
'Personal Items', *The Bulletin*, 1 July 1920, p. 14.
'Personal', Wagga Wagga *Daily Advertiser*, 8 June 1923, p. 2.
'Personal', *Eudora Weekly News*, 24 January 1918, p. 3.
'Personal', Katanning *Great Southern Herald*, 14 April 1923, p. 3.
'Pittsburgh Bank Closed', *Wall Street Journal*, 14 February 1919, p. 10.
'Pittsburgh Bank Closes Doors', Carlisle *Sentinel*, 13 February 1919, p. 4.
'Pittsburgh Park Bank Closes when Bank Discovers Institution's Funds are Short', *Taylor Daily Press*, 13 February 1919, p. 1.
'Plain Facts', Melbourne *Herald*, 7 May 1924, p. 15.
'Plantagenet Road Board', Albany *Despatch*, 12 March 1923, p. 4.
'Popularising "Sun-Raysed" Fruits in Melbourne', Angaston *Leader*, 6 June 1919, p. 3.
'Praise for Kendenup', *West Australian*, 18 May 1923, p. 8.
'Preliminary Announcement', Melbourne *Herald*, 13 October 1923, p. 10.
'Pricking the DeGaris Bubble', Perth *Truth*, 14 February 1925, p. 7.
'Prince's Mails Received on Thursday', Mildura *Cultivator*, 21 August 1920, p. 10.
'Provincial Tennis Championship', *Mildura Cultivator*, 26 November 1913, p. 10.
'Public Service Appeal', *West Australian*, 12 May 1921, p. 6.
'Publications Received', Adelaide *Advertiser*, 26 July 1902, p. 9.
'Publicity Buildings', *Mildura Cultivator*, 22 March 1919, p. 6.
'Pyap's New Manager', *Murray Pioneer and Australian River Record*, 4 June 1914, p. 4.
'Quarter Sessions Appeal', *Sydney Morning Herald*, 17 January 1924, p. 6.
'R. S. L. and Prime Minister', Albany *Despatch*, 7 May 1923, p. 2.
'Railway Extension', Portland *Guardian*, 24 April 1912, p. 3.
'Railway Heads', Kendenup *Index*, June 1921, p. 5.
'Read this remarkable story of DeGaris' final frenzied flutter in finance', Melbourne *Truth*, 21 August 1926, p. 6.
'Real Estate', Melbourne *Herald*, 13 April 1921, p. 5.
'Real estate', *West Australian*, 27 January 1921, p. 8.
'Returned Soldiers Welcomed', *Mildura Telegraph and Lower Murray Advocate*, 8 August 1916, p. 3.
'Returned Soldiers', Hobart *Mercury*, 7 May 1923, p. 3.
'Review', *Critic*, 3 November 1920, p. 9.
'River Murray Problems', Adelaide *Observer*, 31 May 1919, p. 4.
'Romance of Land Dealing', *Geelong Advertiser*, 9 March 1926, p. 5.
'Round the Packing-Houses', *Mildura Cultivator*, 25 January 1913, p. 4.
'Rowing Club Concert', *Mildura Cultivator*, 19 March 1910, p. 8.

BIBLIOGRAPHY

'Russian Refugees' Fund', *Mildura Telegraph and Darling and Lower Murray Advocate*, 15 August 1916, p. 2.
'Schooldays at last!', Kendenup *Index*, 30 September 1922, pp. 6–7.
'Scientific Painless Dentistry', Horsham *Times*, 25 June 1920, p. 5.
'Search for Degaris', Riverine *Herald*, 7 January 1925, p. 2.
'Seaside Auction', Melbourne *Herald*, 2 January 1924, p. 10.
'Second Mystery Man', Melbourne *Herald*, 13 January 1925, p. 4.
'Secret History of the Day', *Smith's Weekly*, 16 February 1924, p. 11.
'Secret Meeting', Melbourne *Herald*, 24 January 1925, p. 11.
'Security for DeGaris', Sydney *Sun*, 23 January 1925, p. 9.
'Seen Leaving Car', Newcastle *Sun*, 9 January 1925, p. 5.
'Seen on Monday', Brisbane *Daily Mail*, 10 January 1925, p. 7.
'Series of Welcomes', Kendenup *Index*, 20 December 1921, p. 6.
'Settlers' Meeting: Chief's parting words', Kendenup *Index*, June 1922, p. 2.
'Sewerage Farm Purchases', *Geelong Advertiser*, 4 March 1926, p. 1.
'Shall the People Rule?', *The Call*, 17 November 1922, p. 2.
'Shepparton Show', *Shepparton Advertiser*, 23 October 1924, p. 3.
'Shooting Affray in Melbourne', *Sydney Morning Herald*, 10 November 1905, p. 8.
'Shooting Sensation', Melbourne *Herald*, 24 November 1905, p. 6.
'"Smiling Kendenup"', Perth *Daily News*, 5 December 1925, p. 7.
'So Upset', Grafton *Daily Examiner*, 12 February 1925, p. 5.
'Social and Personal', Gawler *Bunyip*, 16 January 1925, p. 4.
'Social Gossip', Melbourne *Herald*, 4 June 1935, p. 12.
'Social Letter', *Mildura Cultivator*, 29 November 1919, p. 3.
'Social Letter', *Mildura Cultivator*, 29 May 1920, p. 12.
'Social Letter', *Mildura Cultivator*, 18 September 1920, p. 12.
'Social Letter', *Mildura Cultivator*, 27 July 1912, p. 12.
'Social Letter', *Mildura Cultivator*, 30 November 1918, p. 12.
'Society Gossip', Adelaide *Critic*, 5 July 1902, p. 26.
'South Street Competitions', Ballarat *Star*, 5 October 1905, p. 1.
'Sport of the Gods', *Barrier Miner*, 21 October 1922, p. 6.
'Sporting Items', *Mildura Cultivator*, 23 April 1913, p. 9.
'Staff Personnel', Kendenup *Index*, 20 November 1922, p. 5.
'Story of Alleged Bribing of Federal Official', Melbourne *Herald*, 16 November 1927, p. 1.
'"Stralia's Sun-Raysed Sensation"', Angaston *Leader*, 27 March 1919, p. 4.
'Strange Visits', Sydney *Evening News*, 12 January 1925, p. 7.
'Struck Out', Perth *Daily News*, 9 April 1926, p. 7.
'Suicide of C. J. DeGaris', Melbourne *Age*, 19 August 1926, p. 10.
'Suicide of C. J. Degaris', *Weekly Times*, 21 August 1926, p. 10.

'Suicide' Sydney *Sun*, 24 August 1926, p. 11.
'Suit of Pyjamas', Sydney *Evening News*, 12 January 1925, p. 7.
'"Sun-Raysed" A Word Wide Known', Perth *Daily News*, 5 January 1920, p. 6.
'Sun-Raysed Fruits', Adelaide *Advertiser*, 14 December 1918, p. 11.
'Sun-Raysed Fruits', Perth *Sunday Times*, 7 December 1919, p. 3.
'Sun-Raysed Stunts', Hobart *World*, 31 July 1920, p. 3.
'Sunraysia Daily', *Murray Pioneer and Australian River Record*, 18 June 1920, p. 8.
'Surprised', *Table Talk*, 23 October 1924, p. 39.
'Table Talk', Orange *Leader*, 4 August 1906, p. 2.
'Talk of the Week', *Table Talk*, 17 July 1924, p. 13.
'Tangled titles', Adelaide *Mail*, 21 February 1925, p. 3.
'Tar and Feathers Case', Orange *Leader*, 19 December 1921, p. 6.
'Tar and Feathers', *Western Argus*, 20 December 1921, p. 12.
'Tarred and Feathered', Sydney *Sun*, 25 December 1921, p. 10.
'Grant Hervey', *Riverina Recorder*, 2 November 1921, p. 4.
'Tarred and Feathered', Sydney *Sun*, 25 December 1921, p. 10.
'The "Name": One "Conscientious" Objector', *Sarnia Topics*, vol 3, no. 12, 22 January 1919, p. 3.
'The A.D.F.A. Tea Room', Prahran *Telegraph*, 17 May 1919, p. 6.
'"The Ashes of Achievement"', *Murray Pioneer and Australian River Record*, 13 January 1922, p. 14.
'The Ashes of DeGaris' Achievements', Sydney *Truth*, 22 August 1926, p. 1.
'"The Australian" Interviews C. J. DeGaris', Perth *Australian*, 9 January 1920, p. 5.
'The Boobs of Mildura', *Smiths Weekly*, 16 August 1919, p. 1.
'The Coming of Kendenup', Perth *Sunday Times*, 2 January 1921, p. 1.
'The Country' Adelaide *Advertiser*, 14 August 1913, p. 12.
'The Death-Day of Sunraysia Daily', Mildura and Merbein *Sun*, 13 October 1921, p. 7.
'The DeGaris Case', Adelaide *Advertiser*, 16 January 1925, p. 9.
'The DeGaris case', Melbourne *Herald*, 15 January 1925, p. 16.
'The DeGaris Land Campaign', Melbourne *Herald* 14 January 1925, p. 12.
'The DeGaris Mystery', Adelaide *Advertiser*, 7 January 1925, p. 13.
'The DeGaris Mystery', Melbourne *Age*, 7 January 1925, p. 9.
'The DeGaris mystery', Geraldton *Guardian*, 10 January 1925, p. 3.
'The Degaris Mystery', Melbourne *Herald*, 5 January 1925, p. 3.
'The DeGaris sensation', Melbourne *Age*, 10 January 1925, p. 15.
'The DeGaris Settlements', *Toowoomba Chronicle and Darling Downs Gazette*, 9 January 1926, p. 6.

'The Eternal Why', *Smith's Weekly*, 12 July 1919, p. 4.
'The Everlastin' Ballads', *Coffs Harbour Advocate*, 3 November 1920, p. 2.
'The Federal Elections. Mr Henry Williams in the Wimmera. Federal Capital site the main plank.', *Mildura Cultivator*, 5 January 1901, p. 2.
'The Founder of Mildura', Melbourne *Age*, 5 June 1926, p. 16.
'The Fruit Industry's Needs', *Murray Pioneer and Australian River Record*, 13 June 1925, p. 6.
'The Fusion Candidate for Yarra', Wagga *Worker*, 17 March 1910, p. 15.
'The Future of Kendenup', Adelaide *Advertiser*, 1 April 1926, p. 18.
'The Future of Kendenup', *Albany Advertiser*, 17 March 1923, p. 3.
'The Gentle Art of Kicking the Dead', Mildura and Merbein *Sun*, 24 September 1921, p. 1.
'The Glut Slayer', Kendenup *Index*, June 1921, p. 2.
'The Great East-West Flight', 5 December 1920, p. 19.
'The Guides of the Settlers', Perth *Daily News*, 5 October 1921, p. 7.
'The Kendenup Calamity', Perth *Sunday Times*, 25 March 1923, p. 7.
'The Kendenup Commission', Adelaide *Advertiser*, 23 February 1924, p. 16.
'The Kendenup Company', *Kalgoorlie Miner*, 5 March 1924, p. 3.
'The Kendenup Enquiry', Adelaide *Register*, 27 November 1923, p. 9.
'The Kendenup Estate', Adelaide *Chronicle*, 28 February 1925, p. 49.
'The Kendenup Failure', Geelong *Standard*, 23 February 1924, p. 12.
'The Kendenup Inquiry', *Ballarat Star*, 4 March 1924, p. 6.
'The Kendenup Scheme', Perth *Sunday Times*, 15 April 1923, p. 1.
'The League's New Home', *The Boomerang*, 31 March 1922, pp. 2–3.
'The Little Normey', *Sunday Times*, 7 September 1919, p. 14.
'The Long Vision', Geelong *Standard*, 25 September 1924, p. 10.
'The Missing C. J. Degaris', Melbourne *Age*, 8 January 1925, p. 9.
'The Normey and Molly Duologues', Peterborough *Times and Northern Advertiser*, 13 February 1920, p. 4.
'The One Thing Certain', *Western Mail*, 23 February 1922, p. 39.
'The People's Party', *Casterton News*, 9 January 1911, p. 3.
'The Political Pow-Wow', Perth *Truth*, 27 October 1923, p. 4.
'The Prince of Wales', Broken Hill *Barrier Miner*, 19 August 1920, p. 4.
'The Prince's Mail', Adelaide *Express and Telegraph*, 18 August 1920, p. 2.
'The Queen of Sport', *Mildura Cultivator*, 7 October 1916, p. 7.
'The Shire Elections', *Mildura Cultivator*, 30 August 1902, p. 7.
'The Skirts of Opportunity', *Mildura Cultivator*, 29 September 1920 p. 7.
'The Victories of Failure', *Daily Telegraph and North Murchison and Pilbara Gazette*, 21 August 1925, p. 5.
'The Victories of Failure', *Murray Pioneer and Australian River Record*, 15 May 1925, p. 9.

'The Victories of Failure', Sydney *Sunday Times*, 14 June 1925, p. 7.
'The War Loan', *Mildura Telegraph and Darling and Lower Murray Advocate*, 28 July 1916, p. 2.
'The Warrant', Sydney *Sun*, 14 January 1925, p. 15.
'The Wealth in the "Heart of Rosebud"', Melbourne *Argus*, 8 December 1923, p. 29.
'The Wobbly "Worker"', Perth *Mirror*, 21 April 1923, p. 2.
'Theatre Royal', *Table Talk*, 2 November 1905, p. 17.
'This is Lord Northcliffe's Message to Mildura', Melbourne *Argus*, 1 October 1921, p 6.
'This night week at "Windulva"...', *Mildura Cultivator*, 27 November 1918, p. 11.
'Tile machine coming', Kendenup *Index*, June 1921, p. 6.
'Tivoli Theatre – Albert Whelan', Melbourne *Age*, 18 August 1924, p. 11.
'To Lord Northcliffe', Melbourne *Argus*, 24 September 1921, p. 8.
'To Satisfy Kendenup Investors', Perth *Sunday Times*, 24 April 1921, p. 2.
'To the electors of Yarra', 11 January 1910, typescript p. 2, E. C. DeGaris papers, State Library of Victoria, MS 7085.
'Trying a "Come-back"', Perth *Truth*, 6 June 1925, p. 4.
'Two Assault Charges', Melbourne *Herald*, 10 April 1926, p. 22.
'Two BIG Auction Sales', *Table Talk*, 13 November 1924, p. 33.
'Two Kendenups', Melbourne *Argus*, 7 March 1924, p. 6.
'Under the Clock', Shepparton *Advertiser*, 8 January 1925, p. 8.
'United States of Australia', Melbourne *Evening Sun*, 1 February 1924, p. 3.
'University Extension Centre', *Mildura Telegraph and Darling and Lower Murray Advocate*, 13 October 1916, p. 3.
'Verse and Raisins', Sydney *Sun*, 7 November 1920, p. 19.
'Victoria', *Sydney Morning Herald*, 25 November 1905, p. 13.
'Victorian Opinions', Perth *Sunday Times*, 11 January 1925, p. 1.
'Victorian's Book Accepted', Melbourne *Age*, 30 May 1933, p. 6.
'Victories of Failure', Adelaide *News*, 6 June 1925, p. 4.
'Visit of the Railway Commissioners', Casterton *News*, 28 March 1912, p. 4.
'Wanted', Melbourne *Argus*, 13 August 1923, p. 3.
'Warrant for Arrest of DeGaris', Melbourne *Herald*, 8 January 1925, p. 1.
'Warrant Out', *Sun News-Pictorial*, 9 January 1925, p. 3.
'Was he decoy?', Melbourne *Herald*, 10 January 1925, p. 3.
'Wealthy Williamstown', *Williamstown Chronicle*, 13 June 1925, p. 2.
'Wedding', *Mildura Cultivator* 2 October 1907, p. 3.
'Wedding', *Mildura Cultivator*, 27 January 1906, p. 10.
'Welcoming Ode to the Railway', *Mildura Cultivator*, 13 July 1901, p. 2.
'Well-deserved rap to "Smith's"', Perth *Australian*, 20 April 1923, p. 4.

'Werribee – and the Little River Land Deal', *Werribee Shire Banner*, 18 February 1926, p. 6.
'What DeGaris says', Perth *Mirror*, 26 July 1924, p. 1.
'What the Settlers are Doing: Gleanings from the Blocks', Kendenup *Index*, June 1921, pp. 5–9.
'What the Settlers are Doing: Gleanings from the Blocks', Kendenup *Index*, June 1921, p. 8.
'What the Settlers are Doing: Gleanings from the Blocks', Kendenup *Index*, June 1921, p. 9.
'What the Settlers are Doing: Gleanings from the Blocks', Kendenup *Index*, June 1921, p. 10.
'What the Settlers are Doing: Gleanings from the Blocks', Kendenup *Index*, July 1921, p. 8.
'What the Settlers are Doing: Gleanings from the Blocks', Kendenup *Index*, July 1921, pp. 8–9.
'What the Settlers are Doing: Gleanings from the Blocks', Kendenup *Index*, 24 October 1921, p. 5.
'What the Settlers are Doing: Gleanings from the Blocks', Kendenup *Index*, 25 November 1921, p. 2.
'What the Settlers are Doing: Gleanings from the Blocks', Kendenup *Index*, 25 November 1921, pp. 2–3.
'What the Settlers are Doing: Gleanings from the Blocks', Kendenup *Index*, 25 November 1921, p. 3.
'What the Settlers are Doing: Gleanings from the Blocks', Kendenup *Index*, 20 December 1921, p. 10.
'What the Settlers are Doing: Gleanings from the Blocks', Kendenup *Index*, 28 January 1922, p. 2.
'What the Settlers are Doing: Gleanings from the Blocks', Kendenup *Index*, 28 January 1922, p. 3.
'What was in letter?', Burnie *Advocate*, 20 January 1925, p. 5.
'What's the Strength of C. J.'s oil find?', Perth *Truth*, 22 May 1926, p. 5.
'Where is DeGaris?', Perth *Mirror*, 10 January 1925, p. 1.
'Where is Mr DeGaris?', Melbourne *Herald*, 7 January 1925, p. 1.
'Who Backed Hervey?', *The Call*, 28 October 1921, p. 2.
'Who was he?', Brisbane *Daily Mail*, 10 January 1925, p. 7.
'Who's Who and What's What', Australian *Worker*, 1 May 1935, p. 14
'Why "Smith's" exposed DeGaris', *Smith's Weekly*, 17 January 1925, p. 11.
'Why DeGaris decamped', *Singleton Argus*, 10 February 1925, p. 4.
'Why Women Go On the Streets', *Beckett's Budget*, 2 August 1929, p. 6.
'Will end it all', *Maitland Daily Mercury*, 6 January 1925, p. 2.

BIBLIOGRAPHY

'Will of C. J. DeGaris comes before court', Melbourne *Herald*, 17 November 1936, p. 8.
'Wire from DeGaris', Melbourne *Herald*, 13 January 1925, p. 1.
'Withdrawal of Mr Grant Hervey', Hamilton *Spectator*, 14 June 1912, p. 6.
'Yesterday's deputations', Perth *Sunday Times*, 6 May 1923, p. 3.
'Local News', *Mildura Cultivator*, 14 November 1914, p. 10.
'Latest from Chief', Kendenup *Index*, 23 October 1922, p. 11.
Editorial, Casterton *News*, 21 March 1912, p. 2.
Editorial, Albany *Despatch*, 5 March 1923, p. 2.
Editorial, *Burra Record*, 3 November 1920, p. 2.
Funeral Notice, *Sydney Morning Herald*, 23 September 1968, p. 27.
Untitled item, *Evening Sun*, 14 December 1923, p. 13.
Untitled Item, *Evening Sun*, 25 October 1924, p. 14.
Untitled item, Kendenup *Index*, 26 July 1922, p. 11.
Untitled item, Kendenup *Index*, June 1921, p. 12.
Untitled item, Melbourne *Herald*, 16 August 1924, p. 25.
Untitled, Mildura and Merbein *Sun*, 13 October 1921, p. 7.
Blayde, S., 'Notes and Comments', *Mildura Cultivator*, 17 October 1914, p. 4.
Blayde, S., 'Some Fly', *Mildura Cultivator*, 3 July 1920, p. 13.
Courtney, V., 'C. J. DeGaris', *The Call*, 9 January 1925, p. 9.
Courtney, V., 'When DeGaris slept!' *The Call*, 31 December 1920, p. 2.
D'Arcy-Evans, H., 'Kendenup Life', Kendenup *Index*, June 1922, p. 5.
DeGaris, C. J., '"Americanizing Australia"' with Our Slang and Our Movies', *St Louis Globe-Democrat*, 27 August 1922, p. 15.
DeGaris, C. J., '£550 Cash' (advertisement), Melbourne *Argus*, 27 December 1919, p. 6.
DeGaris, C. J., 'Belgian Relief Fund', *Mildura Cultivator*, 27 February 1915, p. 7.
DeGaris, C. J., 'The Golden West', *Murray Pioneer and Australian River Record*, 6 February 1920, p. 2.
DeGaris, C. J., letter to M. C. DeGaris, 12 December 1913, in possession K. Hancock.
Hansell, H., 'The Poet-Artist's View-point', in 'There is No Mystery', Melbourne *Sun News-Pictorial*, 21 October 1924, p. 11.
Hartwell, M. 'Sim's Little Girl', Vermont *Watchman and State Journal*, 30 July 1873, p. 4.
Harvey, G. M. (aka Hervey, G.), 'Wanted – A Goethals for Mildura and 5000', *Mildura Cultivator*, 10 September 1919, p. 10.
Hervey, G., 'Consider the Lilies', Melbourne *Socialist*, 20 September 1918, p. 3.

Hervey, G., 'An Open Letter', Mildura and Merbein *Sun*, 17 September 1921, p. 6.
Hervey, G., 'How "Liberals" Flout the Law', *Labor Call*, 28 August 1913, p. 2.
Hervey, G., 'Steerage to the West', 21 December 1902, p. 12.
Hervey, G., 'The Inky W. A.', Wagga *Worker*, 20 February 1904, p. 7.
Hervey, G., 'Why I Scrapped C. J. DeGaris', *Murray Pioneer and Australian River Record*, 20 July 1923, p. 1, p. 22.
Hervey, G., quoted in 'Personal Reminscences', Port Pirire *Recorder*, 18 July 1931, p. 3.
Knowles, M. M., 'The Ladies' Letter', *Advocate* 3 March 1921, p. 28.
McClelland, R. J., 'Expansion of Electric Power Supply Urged by Expert', *New York Tribune*, 21 October 1918, p. 10.
'Mo', 'The Hashes of Achievement', *Smith's Weekly*, 13 June 1925, p. 9.
Pelloe, E. H., 'Mountaineering in W. A.', Perth *Sunday Times*, 23 October 1921, p. 17.
'Penelope', 'Social Letter', *Mildura Cultivator*, 30 September 1916, p. 12.
Russell, F. A., 'A Misapprehension Corrected', *Mildura Cultivator* 11 September 1920, p. 7.
Simons, J. J., 'Slumpless Kendenup', Kendenup *Index*, July 1921, p. 11.
'T.M.', 'Kendenup and Mr. J. J. Simons', *Westralian Worker*, 20 April 1923, p. 4.
'Titus Salt', 'Purchase of Kendenup', *Albany Dispatch*, 26 February 1920, p. 1.
'Wanderer', 'With the Chaffey Brothers', *The Chronicle* cutting dated 12 April 1890 in E. C. DeGaris papers, MS7080, box 407, scrapbook labelled 'Book of Securities'.
Williams, G., 'Crook detector Joe helps you', Melbourne *Argus*, 23 April 1954, p. 4.

Acknowledgements

This book is the product of close to twenty-five years of abiding interest in C. J. DeGaris, who I discovered while trawling issues of Melbourne's *Star* newspaper in preliminary research for my PhD thesis in late 1996. I have, since that time, visited all the sites of C. J.'s triumphs and turmoil, from Mildura to Mentone, to Mortlake, to Mornington and a few other places in-between – including Pyap (once) and Kendenup (twice). I have also had the privilege to meet and speak with many fascinating and generous people, including the late and greatly missed Rica Erickson, the only person I have had the privilege to meet who actually knew C. J. DeGaris.

Since 'finding' C. J. and tracing his 1925 disappearance at Mentone, I have been lucky enough to be associated with projects allowing me to marginally pursue my interest in the man and his career alongside a host of parallel 'main games' as my own academic career progressed. My PhD thesis, which was specifically on Australian town plans and planners of the interwar period, was supervised by the brilliant and generous Renate Howe and Bill Logan at Deakin University between 1996 and 2001. In 2007, I was employed at the University of Melbourne in the Faculty of Architecture, Building and Planning initially to work on a project with Hannah Lewi, Julie Willis, Kate Darian-Smith and Philip Goad: all have been spectacular mentors, collaborators and colleagues since that time. That project, *Healthy Bodies, Healthy Minds*, gave rise to the book *Community: Building Modern Australia*, and in my fieldwork I was able to find a few moments to visit Pyap, Mildura, Loxton and other key 'C. J.' places. That position at Melbourne morphed into an ongoing academic role, and the commitment to research in 'ABP' has meant that further C. J. forays and research publications have been encouraged and, in small but important ways, funded. This has included three C. J.-oriented papers at various Australasian Urban History, Planning History (UHPH) conferences – a conference series which has been crucial to my development as an urban and planning historian. The UHPH was the brainchild of Professor Robert Freestone, who has been an invaluable friend and mentor to me about a month longer than I've been following the DeGaris trail.

I was fortunate to make contact, very early in my career (at the 2001 UHPH conference, as it happens) with Professor Andrea Gaynor, an inspirational academic and a generous colleague, who many years later set me on the path to UWA Publishing, the obvious spiritual home for this book, and the remarkable Terri-ann White, who ran that remarkable operation for many years and worked alongside the redoubtable Eleanor Hurt, Nicole van Kan and Kate Pickard. I am greatly appreciative of funding from the Staples Committee which assisted the publication of this book.

In the practical day-to-day, friends and colleagues have been encouraging, supportive and patient with me as I struggled through and was, of course, more of a bore than usual while writing and researching this account. I would like to mention Rabia Azad, Annabel Bleach, Stefanie Bollmann, Louise Brooks (who undertook important research for me at an early stage when I was still at Deakin University, through a small seeding fund), Angela Canavan, Michelle M. Cannane (genealogist extraordinaire), Laura Carroll (always a wise advisor), Hal Corbould, Kathryn Davidson (who is pragmatic, level-headed and hilarious); Annalisa Giudici, Maddi, Mark and Sarah DeGaris; Rick DeGaris Doble; Jenny Gregory, Ian Henry, Kathy Hancock, Nicola Hodgkinson, Ariele Hoffman, Roy Jones, Effie Karageorgos, Amanda Kerley, Victoria Kolankiewicz, the brilliant Ruth Lee, whose willingness to share knowledge of Mary DeGaris and other DeGaris highways, byways and present-day contacts has always been appreciated; James Lesh, Ann Maudsley, Alex McDermott, Glenn Miller, Jane Miller, Briony Neilson, Michael Nichols, Estella Qin, Iris Reynolds, Mia, John, Rosemary and Kerstin Schoen (who accommodated my Kendenup obsession with good humour), John Selwood, Sue Smith, the redoubtable and remarkable Paul Sutcliffe; Elizabeth Taylor, Matthew Tonts, Catherine Townsend, Samantha Trafford, David Walker, Chris Wallace Crabbe, Leanne Watmuff and

Carmelina Zappia. I would also like to thank all members of the 'Lost Kendenup' Facebook page and the editors of *Kendenup Stories*. I absolutely know that I will be ashamed to have missed some extremely key people – forgetfulness being, apparently, the curse of the Nicholses.

Additionally, I would like to acknowledge the sharp and resourceful librarians at the University of Melbourne's Leighton Irwin library, easily the best built environment library in Australia, and named for a man who, incidentally, worked for C. J. on one major project. I am also very grateful the staff at the Battye Library at the State Library of Western Australia, the State Library of Victoria and of course the National Library of Australia. These great libraries, much like university presses, are a resource and a service without which the nation's intellectual and cultural development, shaky as it often seems, would comprehensively wither and die.

David Nichols, Parkville 2020.

Index

Page numbers in italics indicate a photograph

Abrahams family 238; Leon Abrahams 238, 239, 240
Adelaide 80, 82–5, 90; Adelaide Fruit Conference 56; *Advertiser* (Adelaide) 223
Age (Melbourne) 246
Albany, W. A. 90, 92, 95, 123, 137, 203; *Advertiser* 184; butter factory 253; 'Albany doctor' 95, 192; Albany Highway 126, 129
Albert Park Beach 219
Albury, NSW 191, 220, 241
Alexander, Robert 36
Alfred Hospital 271
All Among the Fairies (book) 114
Allan, John 248
Allen, Fred 133, 272
Allen, Joan 272
Alphington, Vic. 16
'Altiora Peto' (Maggie Sullivan) 65
Altona, Vic 250
Ambition Run Mad (play) 48, 49, 51, 78
America's Cup 274
American Civil War 71
Americanism 168
Americanisms 93, 241
Anderson, I. G. 204
Andrews, H. 186
Angaston *Leader* 55
Anglesea, Vic 192
Anglo-Indian settlers 91, 134
Annandale, NSW 225
Anzac 49, 50
Argus (Melbourne) 150, 222
Argus (public figure) 166–7
Arising of Jimmie Munro, The 102–103, 115, 119
Arlen, Michael J. 152
Ashes of Achievement, The 102, 107–9, 112; use of phrase 178

Aspro 96
Associated Australian Yeomanry 17
Atascadero, California 167
Auckland, NZ 167, 234, 236
'Auntie Kendenup' 194
'Aussie Glide, The' (song) 79
Austin family 53
Austin, 'Mid' 270
Austin, Alice 2
Austin, Audrey ('Aud') 270
Austin, Dorothy 270
Austin, Ellen 189
Austin, Freda 270
Austin, Marjorie ('Marge') 137, 188–9, 203, 270
Austin, Violet (see De Garis, Violet)
Austin, Wilga 188, 203, 270
Austral Tennis Club 40
Australian (Perth) 63
Australian Catholic Federation 110
Australian Dried Fruits Association (ADFA) 29, 55–8, 60–3, 71–3, 78, 80, 89, 103, 123, 143, 153–4, 249, 276
Australian Gas and Light Company 224
Australian Home Builder 204
Australian Irrigation Colonies on the River Murray ('Red Book') 18
Australian Irrigationist 16
Australian Natives Association 183, 252
Australian Worker 233
Australians Yet (book) 70

Baker, Carlotta 66
Baker, Kate 112
Baker, Walter (Alfred Sadler) 66–7
Bakersfield, California 167
Balaclava, Vic 149
Balcombe Heights Estate 192
Balcombe Parade Estate 192
Balcombe Park Estate 192
Ballarat, Vic. 32, 161, 204, 269; Her Majesty's Theatre 268

Baloomba Estate 192
Bank of NSW 230
Bank of Victoria 216
Banks, Dick 191
Baptist Church 169
Baptist Men's Club 170
Barnett, W. H. 133
Barrett-Leonard vineyard 89
Barrier Miner 112
Barrow family 133; Cherry 196, 251; William 251
Barry, Paul 274
Batman, John 208, 275
Baxter, J. 162, 163
Bayonet (Melbourne) 99
Beach Reserve Estate 192
Beach Road, Mentone 1, 9
Beatlemania 265
Beaumaris, Vic 192; Pier, 10
Becket's Budget 271
Belgian settlers 91
Belgium 47
Belloc, Hilaire 152
Belmont Racecourse 129
Bendigo, Vic (see also Sandhurst) 33, 220
Berri, S. A. 88
Bessant, H. J. 133
Best Part Estate 214
Betting Book, The 66
Beverley, Gerald 45, 96, 126, 178
'Binghi' 247
Bishop Moorehouse 16
Bittern, Vic 257
Black Cat 44
Black Rock, Vic 191
Black, Albert 254
Bladwell, L. 99
Bland Holt company 66
Blayde, Steele see Hall, Gifford
Bloomfield, Sir Geoffrey (fictional character) 42
Boake, Barcroft 93
Boggabri, N. S. W. 121
Bond, Alan 267, 274, 275, 276
Bond, Sergeant 129
Bookfellow 107
Booty, Fred 66
Boulder, W. A. 121, 134

Boulton and Paul (aeroplane) 82
Bowring family 39; Doris 42
Branxholme, Vic 67
Brass and Cymbals (book) 107
Bremer Bay, W. A. 171
Briggs, Frank 81, 83, 88, 128, 269
Brighton, Vic: Beach 149; Cemetery 265; Police Court 151
British Empire 168
British settlers 91
Broomehill. W. A. 134
Brown, William 'Snowy' 230
Bruce, Stanley 184–6
Buffalo Times 2
Bulletin (Sydney) 99, 107
Bunbury, Bill 267
Buncle, Elizabeth see DeGaris, Elizabeth
Burke, T. M. 189, 191, 202
Burke, Udolpho Wolfe 179
Burkett, John 195
Burns, Rev. J. A. 53
Burra Record 106
Burwood, NSW 226
Butterick 70
Button, Cecil 133
Bye, Ernie *189*
Bye, Murray 188, 203

'C. J. DeGaris Publishing House, The' 102, 115, 117, 246
Cairns *Northern Herald* 224
Cairns Post 152
Calcutta 83
Caldwell, E. 133
California 163; replicated in Western Australia 168; oil reserves 178
Call, The (Perth) 88, 93, 108, 144, 156, 173–4, 181, 232
Camelot' (home) 189, 242
Cameron family 39
Cameron, Constable 227, 241
Cameron, Dr. 40
Cameron, Dr. I. T.
Cameron, Harcourt 133
Cameron, Kendenup 133
Cameron, R. G. 133
Campbell, Jean 107
Canadian Ford Co. 215, 258, 276
Capecup Estate 118, 195

INDEX

Capitol House, Melbourne 201, 213–14, 221, 230, 243
Carnavon Times 99
Carnegie, Andrew 33
Carr, Archbishop 42
Carrington, Gerald 275
Carstairs, Jimmy (fictional character) 109
Casterton, Vic 64, 68, 73
Cater family 39; W. Rupert 40
Catherwood, Mary Hartwell 32
Central Irrigation League of Victoria 16
Ceylon 84, 134, 143, 160, 168, 195 see also Colombo
Chaffey Agricultural College 20
Chaffey Lawns', Kendenup 95
Chaffey, George 18–20, 71, 95, 117
Chaffey, William 18–19, 39, 41, 53, 71, 95, 117
Cheltenham, Vic. 220
Cheong, Rev. Cheok Hong 213
Chester, Sergeant 88
China 90
Cinderella 268
City Mutual Assurance Co. 162
City, Town and Country Golf Links, Coburg, Vic 191, 215
Claffey, John 89
Clare, S. A. 93
Clement's Tonic 151
Cochrane, George see Hervey, Grant Madison
Coffs Harbour Advocate 106
Collins, Hugh D. (fictional character) 80
Colombo, Sri Lanka 195
Cook, Mrs 166
Cooma, NSW 220
Coon songs' 32, 43
Coote, Frank 96, 118, 126, 128, 138, 160, 164, 182, 184, 186
Coote, Ronald 138, 159–61, 271
Corbould family 39; Bean 35, 36; Charles 35; Clara 35, 35; Clarence 35
Corbould, Donnie 270
Corbould, Harold 35, 35, 97
Corbould, Marianne (also known as 'Mary', 'Molly' or 'Mollie') 35, 35, 40, 270
Corbould, Rene see DeGaris, Rene
Corbould, Robert Rutter 35

Corio, Vic 206, 272; Bay 204; Garden Suburb 4, 204–11, *209,* 213, 244, 256, 258, 268, 275 see also New Corio
Corona (typewriter) 226
Country Party 91, 98
Courtis, Charles 251
Courtney, Victor 108, 171, 232
Couttie family 39
Coxon, J. R. 210
Craig, Harry 68
Crisp, Harold 148
Critic (Adelaide) 106
Crossley (automobile) 204
Crouch and Wilson 12
Crowe, Anne 70, 144
Croydon, Vic 212
Cureton, Stephen 18, 147
Curlwaa, N. S. W. 60, 86
Curtin, John 186

Daily Commercial News 61
Daily Mail (Brisbane) 116
Daily News (Perth) 162–3, 253
Daily Telegraph 20
Daily Telegraph and North Murchison and Pilbara Gazette 246
Dance, William 149
Davey family 39
Davey, Miss 52
Davey, Senior Detective M. J. 228, 232, 241, 243
De Havilland (aeroplane) 86
de Pledge, Albert 4, 8, 134, 177–217, 218, 255, 267
de Pledge, Harry 177
de Pledge, T. 133
de Pledge, Thelma 255
Deakin Avenue, Mildura 61, 143
Deakin, Alfred 18, 39, 154
Debonaire, Lord (fictional character) 48
Decentralisation 67, 98
DeGaris (Kendenup) Pty Ltd 133, 159, 180, 270
DeGaris, Alfred 22, 31, 32, 35, 40, 267
DeGaris, Clement John ('C.J.')
acting 42, 43, 53, 118; American approach of 55; Australian affiliation 54; aviation 81–4, 86–7, 128, 129, *130;* 220; birth 13; boxing 28;

351

INDEX

charisma 99, 122, 198, 276; cycling 28; death 261; diminutive stature 21, 23, 26, 28, 145, *146*; divorce 160–1; disappearance 219; dressed as a woman 220–1; driving experience 44, 217; early work experience 21; education 25–7; films 60, 129, 190, 247; funeral 265; impact of death 267–9; imprisoned 240; insurance salesman 29; legacy 266; literary competition 78; lyricist 79, 84; marriage (to Rene Corbould) 34–5, 37, 41, 78, 94, 97, 159–60, 181, 251 (to Violet Austin) 161, 188, *189*, 191, 270; modernism 101, 277; nationalism 49; near death in infancy 15; new states movement 91–2; playwright, 48 passim, 79–80, 84; politics 181; pronunciation of name 'DeGaris' xi; publicity experience 57–63, 71. 73, 74; published author 102, 245, 246; publisher 102 passim; radio broadcaster 211, 273; Rechabite membership 41; recitation by 32, 42, 52; relationship with Violet Austin before marriage 159; religion 13; repatriation 51–52, 91; salesmanship 29; schooling 27 passim; sexual experience 30, 36; singing voice 31–2; spiritualism rumours 154; suicidal thoughts 4, 7, 74, 260, 278; tennis prowess 40, 43;
typing abilities 229; use of name 'C. J.' xi; war opinions 47, 49–50
DeGaris, Dulcie Estelle 4, 38, 41, 58, 126, 188, 217, 268
DeGaris, Elisha 10–13, 15–20, *22,* 23, 25–6, 28, 31, 33, 50, 53–4, 90, 102, 277
DeGaris, Elizabeth (Bessie) 14, *22,* 31, 36, 54, 262
DeGaris, Elizabeth 13, *22,* 23, 25–6, 31, 50, 53, 55
DeGaris, Ken 31
DeGaris, Lilian (Lily) *22,* 31, 35
DeGaris, Lucas 12, 28
DeGaris, Lucas George ('George') *22,* 31–2, 102, 267–8
DeGaris, Mary Clementina ('Clemmie')
14, *22,* 27, 30–1, 34, 40, 56, 102, 229, 262, 269
DeGaris, Rene (nee Corbould) 35, *35,* 36, 41, 43, 45, 47, 49, 50, 53, 55, 94–7, 123, 126, 134, 137–8, 159–61, 180, 187–8, 211, 246, 251, 268–70, 272
DeGaris, Veema Vyzie 4, 203, 217, *242,* 252, 261, 267–72
DeGaris, Vera Elizabeth 4, *35,* 45, 58, 126, 188, 217, 268
DeGaris, Violet; 'Vi' (nee Austin) 4, 8–9, 53, 63, 81, 94, 96–7, 137–8, 145, 159, 161, 175, 182–3, 187–9, *189,* 191, 194, *194,* 199, 203, 217, 223, 230–1, 234, 236, 238–9, 241, *242,* 243, 245–6, 251–3, 260–1, 263, 269–70
DeGaris, Winifred Rene (Winnie) Winnie 4, 41, 58, 188, 217, 268
Delineator, The 71
Denmark (nation) 165
Denver, B. Deramore 191
Department of Agriculture (W.A.) 156
Desailly family 39
Dewdrop Danby (book) 103
Diggers' Gazette, The 99
Dimboola, Vic 67
'Dip-Tin' 77
Dispatch (Albany newspaper) 166
Doble, Enoch 269
Doble, Rick DeGaris 269
Don Quixote of the Saltbush, A (serial) 147
'Donalbain' 107
Douglas, Clifford 152
Douglas, Jack 248
Downs, E. 240
Doyle, Arthur Conan 42
'Drifted Apart' 42
Duff, D. E. 121
Dugan, Michael 102
'Dunoon' (home) 260–261
Dunstan, Keith 267
Durham Ox, Vic 15

E. DeGaris & Co. 126
Early Closing Movement 42
East Burwood, Melbourne 133
East Perth, W. A. 182
Echuca, Vic 18
Eden of the Good, An (book) 147, 271

INDEX

Edmunds, Daniel 90, 121
Edward VII, 29
Edward VIII 86
Edwards, Roy 219
8d a Day (film) 189
Electric Bond and Share Company 169
Elizabeth St, Melbourne 206
Elizabeth St, Sydney 226
Elmira, New Jersey 178
English, Gerald 214
Erickson, Rica nee Sandilands 267
Erskine St, Sydney 229
Esperance (ship) 187
Esplanade, St Kilda 206
Essendon, Vic. 241
Etiwanda, California 18
Evatt, H. V. 110
Evening Sun (Melbourne) 91, 207
Everlastin' Ballads, The 102, 104–6, 108
Everybody's Magazine 70–1
Examiner (Launceston) 99

F. F. F. (musical) 3, 8, 79–81, 84–6, 89, 93, 97–8, 276
Facing the Inevitable 102, 116
Farmer and Settler (Sydney) 98, 99
Federalist (Launceston) 98
Fellows, Rev. S. B. 138
Fennel 42, 43
Ferguson, Fitzwilliam (fictional character) 80, 81, 86
Field, M. J. (fictional character) 108
Filippo (fictional character) 42, 43
Findlay, John Gibson 268
Fine Art Society 114
Fisher Unwin 109
Flentje, Rev. F. 35
Ford, Henry 215, 238, 244, 246, 248–9
Forrest, Twiggy 274
Forte, Norman G. 203, 208, 213
Franklin (ship) 86
Frankston, Vic 191
Fremantle, W. A. 227; 'Fremantle Doctor' 192
Fresno, Ca. 167
Freud, Sigmund 236
Froitzer, Lieutenant (fictional character) 48
Fuge, Mr. 195

Furphy, Joseph 102, 112, 231
Fusion Party 19

'G. H. S.' (George Henry Shoebridge) 102, 116
Garden of Girls' (song) 97, 138
Gazzard, Edward 69
Geddes, Grace 138
Geelong 110, 191, 207, 210, 250, 253; *Advertiser* (newspaper) 251; Grammar 28, 206, 208, 250; *Standard* (newspaper) 207, 210; Town Planning Association 208
Gem (steamer) 267
Geraldton, W. A. 271; Music Lovers' Club 271
Giannina (fictional character) 43
Gilchrist, A. 99
Gillette Safety Tire Company 162
Gillies, Margaret (fictional character) 108
Glasson, Elsie 35
Glenelg, Vic 67
Glenferrie, Vic 4
God, My Neighbour and Myself (book) 134
'Good Little Normey' 61–3, 77, 101, 104, 247
Goolibah (fictional location) 111
Gordon, Abraham Samuel 115–16
Gordon, Adam Lindsay 68, 233
Gotham National Bank 162
Goulburn Prison 271
Goulburn Valley Stock and Property Journal 205
Grand Coffee Palace, Mildura 20
Grandjean Estate 256
Grandjean, Mr. 215
Great Depression 266
Great War (First World War) 45, 52, 58, 83, 86, 91, 143, 148, 169, 171, 191, 229
Greater Kendenup Development and Packing Company 187
Greater Mildura 72
Green, Meredith Roberts 224, 238–40, 243–4
Griffin, Marion Mahony 110, 124, 127, 201, 213
Griffin, Walter Burley 110, 127, 201, 212, 213

INDEX

Grogan Royal Commission 155, 157–8, 164, 170, 194
Grogan, William 155–6, 174 see also Grogan Royal Commission
'Groom's Story, The' 42
Guernsey 50, 53, 195
Gun Abrahams' see Abrahams family

Hall, Gifford ('Steele Blayde') 44–5, 72, 82
Halse, T. H. 183
Halsey, Admiral 106
Handley, Ernest W. 225–6, 228
Hansell, Harold 102, 104–6, 117, 213
Harden, NSW 83
Harding, Howard 248
Harmsworth, Alfred see Northcliffe, Lord
Harris, Liza 152
Harvey, G. Madison' (see also Hervey, Grant Madison) 70–2
Hassell Ave, Kendenup 126, 257
Hassell family 89–90, 96
Hassell homestead 130–1, 135
Hastings, Flo (fictional character) 80
Hastings, Vic 257
Hawaii 84
Hawkes family 39
Hawthorn Glen, Hawthorn 260
Hawthorn, Vic. 189, 255
Hay, NSW 83
Haynes, Arthur 195–6, 248, 253, 262
Heart of Rosebud Estate 4, 192, 214, 217, 240
Heiner, Ernest 248
Hendy, Leary and Co. 204
Henry, John Richard 268
Henty, Frank 99
Herald (Adelaide) 86
Herald (Melbourne) 204
Herschell, Charles 60
Hertsman, Captain (fictional character) 48
Hervey, Grant Madison (George Cochrane; see also 'Harvey, G. Madison') 64, *64,* 65–70, 72, 73, 78, 86, 92–4, 107, 141, 144–5, 147–54, 158, 186, 188, 233, 271, 274
Hitler, Adolf 273

Hollick family 39; Mrs Percy 53; P. T. 40
Holman, Ada A. 102, 107, 110
Holman, William 110, 128
Hope and Klem 184
Hotham, Vic. (North Melbourne) 13
Howard, Detective 67
Howard, Sergeant 128
Hudson's Cafeteria (Mildura) 83
Hughes, Thomas 186, 193–4, 196
Hughes, William ('Billy') 71, 83, 86
Hull, F. H. 134
Hume, George 189
Hurstbridge, Vic. 203

In Mulga Town (book) 107
'In Nineteen-Hundred and Ninety-Nine' 137–8;
Index (Kendenup) 121, 124, *125*
Iredale, Mr. 47
Irrigation Act (Vic) 17
Irrigation 13, 15–20, 51, 56, 71, 91, 95, 99, 117, 147–8, 167
Irwin, Leighton 204
Italian migration to Kendenup 184–5

Jacob, Audrey 248–9
'James, Gertrude' (fictional character) 36, 246
Japan 84, 90
Java 260
Jeffries, Charles 69
Jelbart Brothers 204, 210–12; Jelbart, George 22
Jerome, Jerome K. 42
Jewett (automobile) 192, 204
Johnson, Ben 90, 183
Johnson, Cedric 205, 211
Josephs, Michael 69
Joy, Tommy 44
JP Morgan Chase 162
Julius, Harry 61
Junee, NSW 83

Kalgoorlie, W. A. 121; *Argus* (newspaper) 66; *Miner* (newspaper) 188
Katanning, W. A. 185
Kauffman, John 102, 117
Keast, W. S. 250

INDEX

Kendall, Henry 93
Kendenup, W. A. 2, 8–10, 89–91, 93–7, 99, 118–19, 121–4, 126–8, 129–2, 138, 141, 149–50, 153–5, 157, 159–90, 193–9, 201, 203, 205, 216–17, 245, 249, 251–9, 262, 266–7, 270–2, 275, 277–8; Development Company 121–2, 126, 129, 131–3, 137, 150; Hall 253; Kostume Koncert Komedy Kompany (KKKKK) 133, 137, 166, 175; Packing Company 132; Progress Association 137; Settlers' Association 133; *Kendenup Stories* 272
Kennedy, E. 212
Kennedy, John F. 265
Keogh, James 4, 203, 213
Kerang, Vic 15
Kew, Vic 25
Kimber, Ivo (fictional character) 111–12
King's Theatre, Melbourne 97
Kingston, Dave 220
Kipling, Rudyard 43
Knitlock 127
Kyabram, Vic. 133

La Varre, Marie 81
Labor Party 110
Labour or Gold? (book) 102
Lady Gwendoline (fictional character) 42
Land, The 246
Lands Department, Victoria 257
Langtree Avenue, Mildura 44
Lapthorne, Alice 52
'Lasca' 52
Laverton, Vic 250
Lawson Hall, Kendenup 252, 272
Lawson, Henry 93
Le Mesurier, Cecil J. R. ('C. J.') 195–6, 251
Lee, John Pascoe (fictional character) 108
Lee, Philip (fictional character) 108
Legge, James 147
Legion of Frontiersmen 45–6
Lennox Road Baptist Church, Brooklyn 170
Leslie, Martin Ernest (fictional character) 226, 230–1, 236
Levien, Mrs Harold 53
Levy, Goody (fictional character) 68

Lexia 60
Liberal Party 19, 67–8
Little Malop St, Geelong 191
Little River, Vic 250
Little, William 68
Liverpool, NSW 258
Lloyd, Alfred E. 45, 83, 127, 175, 183, 197
Lockwood, Florence 144, 150
London Fish Café, Melbourne 206
Long, Arthur 81
Los Angeles, Ca. 167, 225
Lost Valley, The 102, 109–10, 114
Love, Minnie 81, 84
Lyons, Sol 238, 240

Macartney, E. H. B. 123
MacGregor, Roy *189*
Mackey, Inspector 241
Mackin, John 268
Madden, John 33–34
'Magic Call – Coee, The' (song) 79
Maheno (ship) 228–32, 234–5, 255, 278
Mail (Adelaide newspaper) 245
Mail (Sydney newspaper) 109
Maitland, Gibb 254
Maldon, Vic 268
Mallee 42
Maloney, Dr. William 187
Mann, Mr. (WA politician) 155
Mapeson, Cecil Eucalyptus 'Euky' (fictional character) 111
Marama (ship) 241, 243
Marella (ship) 260
Margaret River 118
Mark, Ray S. 188, 192, 196, 203
Marle, E. R. 138
Martin, Peter 171
Mascot (airport) 84
Mason, Constable R. F. 261
'Masturbation panic' 30
McArthur, Justice 151
McColl, Hugh 15
McCutcheon, Henry ('H. G.') 185
McCutcheon, Walter B. 185
McDonald Royal Commission 195, 251
McDonald, Ross 195 see also McDonald Royal Commission
McIntosh, Hugh D. 80–1, 96–7

355

INDEX

McKay, H. V. 210
McLelland, Claggett Co. 178
McLelland, Ross ('R. J.') 169, 172, 179–80 see also R. J. M. McLelland and Co.; McLelland, Claggett Co.
McNaughton, L. 216
Melbourne Sub-divisions Company (MSD) 4, 7–8, 191–3, 196–7, 199, 202–8, 211–17, 221, 223–4, 230, 238–41, 243–4, 249–50, 266, 270, 272, 276
Melbourne, Vic. 27; Town Hall 214, 239; Tramway Company 254
Mentone, Vic. 1, 9, 10, 219, 220, 224, 255, 261
Menzies, Robert 266
Merbein 60; *Merbein Irrigationist* 98
Merrilands Estate 189
Methodist Ladies College, Vic 25
Metropolitan Town Planning Commission (Melbourne) 191
Mexican settlers 91
Middle East oil extraction 179
Midgely, Richard 40
Mildura, Vic. 9, 13, 18–19, 26, 28–30, 32, 39, 43, 64, 70, 72, 75, 88, 90, 94–5, 98, 131, 138; Agricultural High School 40; Airfield 152; Caledonian Society 40; Council Chamber 71 *Cultivator* (newspaper) 28, 33, 43–4, 46–7, 52, 58, 82, 84, 98, 107; District Hospital 40; Lawn Tennis Association 40; Mildura Memorial State a.k.a. Soldiers Memorial State 70, 92; Musical and Elocutionary Competitions 31, 42; Railway League 33; Rowing Club 42; Shire Council 33; Shire Hall 31, 35, 41–2, 50, 53, 109; *Telegraph and Lower Murray Advocate* (newspaper) 48, 98
Mildura-Ouyen Concert Party 52, 138
Milson's Point 69
Milthorpe, NSW 134
Mirror (newspaper, Perth) 175, 186, 198
Mitchell, James 126, 181, 196
Modern Printing Company 245
Molly Sandwich' 61–2, 77
Monash, John 126
Montague, Superintendent 230

Moody, Allan 236
Moonooloo' (song) 3, 8
Moorabool St, Geelong 205
Moore, Maggie 81
Mordant, Grace' (fictional character) 36, 37
Mordecai MacCobber (book) 115
Moreton, Frederick Dr. 208, 210
Morgan, Pierpont 246
Morgan, W. J. 222, 243
Morgold, Joseph (fictional character) 81
Morning Herald (Newcastle newspaper) 233
Mornington Peninsula 191, 260
Mornington, Vic 191, 260–1
Morris, Ethel Jackson 102, 114
Mortlake, NSW 224–5
Morton Efficiency Dehydrator 135–8, 272
Moses, Reg ('Mo') 247
Mount Barker, W. A. 96, 123, 131–3, 135, 224, 272; Junior High School 268
Mount Eden Gaol, Auckland 240
Mount Gambier, S. A. 68, 69
Moverley, Winifred 106
MSD see Melbourne Subdivisions Company
Mt Etna 36
Mundaring Weir 74
Munro, Jack 220
Murdoch, Rupert 274
Murphy, Fred 129
Murray Bridge, S. A. 82
Murray Moon' (song) 84, 98, 138
Murray Pioneer 48–60, 79, 109, 178
Murray River 18
Murrumbidgee Irrigator 246
Mussolini, Benito 246, 273
Mutt and Jeff' (comic strip) 145, *146*
Mystery Club' 213

Naldera (ship) 164
Naracoorte, S.A. 12, 29
National Electric Light Association 169
National Review 68
Neild, Hazel (fictional character) 147
Nelson, A. 186
Nelson, W. L. 166

INDEX

New Age (London) 68, 152
New Corio Estate 249, 250, 253, 272
New England (N.S.W.) 92
New York 108, 174; *New York Times* 167–8
New Zealand 225, 235, 241
New' Theatre Royal, Melbourne 66
News (Adelaide newspaper) 246, 247–8, 253
News (Casterton newspaper) 67
Niagara (ship) 165, 167, 173, 220
Niagara Daily Spotlight (newspaper) 167
Nicholas, Alfred 96–7, 165, 183, 184
Ninth Street Church, Mildura 36
Niven, F. W. 114
North Geelong, Vic 250
North Melbourne 13
Northcliffe, Lord (Alfred Harmsworth) 147–8
Northcott, Charles Francis ('Frank') 224, 238–40, 243
Norton, Ada 69
Norton, John 69–70, 72
Nuske Power, Fuel and Nitrogen 258
Nuske, Ferdinand 258
Nuskonia Land Company 258

O'Connor, C. Y. 74
O'Malley, King 128
Observer (Adelaide) 246
Oil exploration at Kendenup 170–2, 178, 254, 259, 263
Olympia Hall and Cinema 41–3, 54, 59, 83
Omrah Estate 133
Onkaparinga, S.A. 88
Ontario, California 18
Opas, Joseph 238
Opitz, Lesser 225
Orange, NSW 33
Osterley (ship) 134
Ouyen, Vic. 150; *Mail* (newspaper) 52

Packard (automobile) 1, 2, 9, 64, 217, 220
Packer, Kerry 274
Padbury, Mr. 195
Page, Earle 91
Palace Hotel, Mortlake 225, 228

Palace Hotel, Perth 121
Parker, Constable 227, 241
Parosovox address system 211
Parramatta Park 228
Parramatta Road, Sydney 225
Partridge, W. F. 99
Paterson, Banjo 93
Paulson 74
Peace Conference 83
Peacock, Ernest 165
Peggs, R. W. 134
Pelloe family 39; Emily 102, 118, 129; Theodore 118
Pennifold, Frank 126
Pennsylvania Register 168
People's Party 67
Perdriau rubber company 84
Perkins, E. W. ('Ted') 171
Perth, W. A. 78, 89, 220
Pestonjee Bomangee 12
Phillips, Ern 134
Phoenix Film Co. 210, 212
Pieries rapae 115
Pinggali (fictional character) 147
Plantagenet Shire 184
Plum-Street Brethren, The (book) 103
Port Elliot 82
Portland, Vic 67, 70–1
Potter, Superintendent 219
Pound, Ezra 152
Poyitt, Gertrude see 'Wolla Miranda'
Presbyterian Ladies' College 107
Prickly pear 226, 229
Prince (dog) 242, *242*
Prince of Wales 86, 93, 105
Prince of Wales theatre (Adelaide) 84
Princes Bridge, Melbourne 236
Princetown College (Calcutta) 134
Prior, Tom 275
Proposing' (song) 85, 98
Provincial Tennis Championship 40
Pugsley, S. J. 41, 44
Puritan, Stephen (fictional character) 147
Pyap Hall *45*
Pyap, S.A. 9, 42, 44–5, 82, 90, 95, 131, 150

Qualbert, King 126
Queen of Sport 118

Queen Street, Melbourne 66
Queenslander 109

R. J. M. McLelland and Co. 169, 177–8, 198, 254
Ranelagh Estate 191
Ratbags 267
Ravensthorpe, W.A. 171
Renmark, S.A. 18, 29, 42, 88, 148
Repatriation: A Giant Problem, a Practical Scheme 51
Reservoir, Vic 189
Reynoldi spaghetti company 254
Reynolds, B. Dunstan 254
Ridge Brothers 121, 171
Rigby's Romance (book) 102, 112, *113*, 117, 231
Rinehart, Gina 274
Ringwood, Vic. 260
Rise and Fall of Alan Bond, The (book) 274
Riverina (N. S. W.) 92
Riverina Recorder 115
Robinson family 134
Rollerskating 41
Rosebud, Vic. 1, 5, 203, 224, 240
Roseneath (house) 58
Roslyn St, Hawthorn 189, 217
Rowe, Fred 134
Rowe, Gertrude 134
Royal Melbourne Show 86
Russell (automobile) 42, 44
Russell, Frank A. 102, 107, 148
Russell, Howard 147
Ruttledge, C. W. 192
Rye Heights Estate 192

Sadler, Alfred see Walter Baker
San Francisco, Ca. 167, 226
Sandhurst, Vic (see also Bendigo) 15
Sandilands family 134; Chris 183
Sarnia Ave, Mildura 144, 148, 150
Sarnia Motor Garage 55
Sarnia Packing Pty Ltd 55, 83
Sarnia Topics 55, 124
Savoy Hotel, Perth 163, 252
Scadden, Jack 129
Schmidt 74
Schwartz, J. S. 8, 169–74, 177–8

Schwarz, J. S. see J. S. Schwartz
Scott, John H. 260
Second World War 266
Seedy, Simon (nom-de-plume of Elisha DeGaris) 16
Seejay Estate 213
Shandon' (home) 188
Shell Oil 260
Shepparton 133, 205–7; *Advertiser* (newspaper) 211; Show 211
Shoebridge, George Henry see 'G. H. S.'
Simons, Joseph ('J. J.') 8, 92, 123, 126, 128–9, 133, 135, 156, 167, 173, 180–3, 232, 252, 270
Simpson, E. S. 254
'Sims' Little Girl' 32, 36
6WF (radio station) 273
Skase, Christopher 267, 274–5
Skirts of Opportunity, The (play) 109
Small Arms Company 238
Smith, E. J. 121
Smith's Weekly 61, 72, 186, 189, 228, 233–4, 247, 254
Snowdrift (horse) 129
Social credit 152
Solomon Islands 138
Solomon, Hubert 226–7
Solomon, Julius 244
Sopwith (aeroplane) 88
Sourland (fictional character) 27
South African War 80, 143
South Street talent competition 36
South West Oil Company 171
Spanish Flu 58
Spectator (Perth) 66
Spencer Street Station 220, 241
Sport of the Gods (book) 102, 107, 110
Sportsman and a Man, A (play) 68
Sri Lanka see Ceylon
St Georges Terrace, Perth 121
St Kilda, Vic 15, 68, 123, 188, 191, 210; Methodist Church 188
St Ruvia Estate 213
St. Peters College, Adelaide 12
Standard Gold Mining Company Ltd of Kendenup 90
State Manufacturers Trust Co. 162
'Steele Blayde' see Hall, Gifford
'Steerage to the West' 65

Stephens, Harry J. 98, 145, 147, 149
Stephenson, Arthur 204
Steyne, Hugh 81, 84, 97, 130
Stoneham, Reginald 8, 79, 80, 81, 84, 138, 251, 254, 277
Story of C. J. DeGaris, The (documentary) 267
Subiaco, W. A. 134
Such is Life (book) 112
Sullivan, Maggie 65
Sun (Melbourne newspaper) 212, 223, 235, 243
Sun (Mildura and Merbein newspaper) 143, 144, 145, 148, 149, 152
Sun (Sydney newspaper) 106
Sun Herald (Sydney newspaper) 275
Sun-Maid Raisin 57
Sun-Raysed (aeroplane)
Sun-Raysed Café, Melbourne 63
Sun-Raysed Children's Fairy Story Book 62, 114
Sun-Raysed Film, The 60
Sun-Raysed Fruit 58, 59
'Sun-Raysed settlements' 86, 91, 205
'Sun-Raysed Waltz, The' 8, 80, 89
Sunday Times (Perth) 62, 65, 118, 158, 184
Sunday Times (Sydney) 230, 234, 246
Sunkist Orange 57
Sunraysia 58, 117, 129, 143, 147
Sunraysia Daily (newspaper) 98, 111, 149, 238
Sunraysia Wonder Book 102, 119
Sutcliffe, Peter 267
Sutton family 39
Sutton, Susie 43
Swann, Mr 9
Swartz, J. S. see J. S. Schwartz
Swarz, J. B. see J. S. Schwartz
Swedish settlers 91
Sydney 111, 241–2
Sydney Morning Herald 108

'T.H.' see Hughes, Thomas
TAA 269
Table Talk 97, 193, 268
Tagore, Rabindranath 43
Tasmania 254
Tate, Ewan *189*

Tate, Mr 166
Taylor, Harold 89
Taylour, Gilbert 248
Ten Weeks in Wonderful America (unpublished book) 167
Tennent, Sergeant 219
The Jazz Singer (film) 273
Theodore (horse) 37
Thom, Mrs. 196, 204
Thompson, Colin 49–50
Thompson, Jack (fictional character) 48
Thompson, Rene (fictional character) 48
Thomson brothers 44, 49
3AR (radio station) 273
3LO (radio station) 224, 273
Tivoli theatre (Melbourne) 81, 206
Town Planning Association of NSW 110
Tragowel Plains Irrigation Trust 17
Tramway Terminus Estate 192
Traralgon Record 214
Tregear, Rev. C. E. 265, 277–8
Trevaskis and Sons 205
Truth (national newspaper) 69, 239, 250, 258, 261, 278
Truth (Perth newspaper) 164, 254
Tuxen, Saxil 189, 192

Union Company 225–6
'United States of Australia' 92
University of Melbourne 31
'Upon the Road to Glory' 106
Upper Swan Valley, W. A. 89
Uralla Times 247
Urban Trust Water Tower, Mildura 62

Van Straten, Frank 80
Vancouver, Canada 167
Vanderdecken, Kate (fictional character) 112, 231
Vane, Sutton 66
Vauxhall (automobile) 204
Veall, George 143, 148, 150
Veema Ave, Croydon 213
Victoria Park, W. A. 134
Victoria, colony of 11
Victorian Employer's Federation 67

INDEX

Victories of Failure, The (book) 34, 73, 94, 109, 145, 153–4, 160–2, 169–70, 172, 178, 187, 244, *245*, 273
Violet Town, Vic 143

W. A. Record 108
Wagga *Worker* 65
Wahgunyah (home), 1
Walker, Mr. (WA politician) 155
Wallace-Crabbe, Ken 99, 156
Walsh, J. M. 102, 107
Walsh, T. P. 110
Wannon 68
War Cry (Melbourne) 98
Ward, Freda Dudley 86
Ward, Senior-Detective 234
Warnock, Fred 203
Warragul, Vic 149
Warrnambool, Vic 188
Watkins, Detective 230
Watkins, G. H. 212
Watmuff family 39
Wattle Path Palais, St Kilda 206
Webber, L. H. 213
Weber, Max 276
Wedderburn 82
Wenborn, Jean *189*
Wentworth, NSW 18
Werribee, Vic 18, 250
Wesley College 9, 26, 27, 185
West Australian (newspaper) 131, 165
Western Australia: Land of Opportunity (film) 129
Western Mail (newspaper) 66
Westralian Worker (newspaper) 185, 186
Wetterliebenschaff, Fritz (fictional character) 231–2
White Butterfly, and Other Fairy Tales, The (book) 102, 114
White, Alan 226–7
White, Bill 134, 177

White, Ernie 226–7
White, Frank 225–8
White, Frank Jr. 226–7
Whitlam, Fred 27
Whittlesea, Vic 189
Whyte, W. Farmer 116
Wice currency 268
Wicklow estate 133
Wightwick, Rev. Humphrey 134
Wildflowers of Western Australia (book) 102, 118, 119
Wilkinson, Rick 171
Williams, Colonel 88
Williamson, J. C. 48
Williamstown, Vic 248
Wimmera 67
Windulva (home) 58, 211–12
Windulva Estate 211–13, 215, 272
Wister, Peter (fictional character) 108
Wittmann, George 47
Wolla Miranda' (Gertrude Poyitt) 107
Wonderland cinema, Mildura 44, 49
Wonga Park, Vic 272
Woodard, Stanley P. 162–163, 165, 169, 254
Woolf, Joseph 7, 214, 221, 238, 240, 243–4, 261, 262
Workman, Charles H. 81

Yallourn, Vic 204
Yanchep, W. A. 274
Yarra (political division) 19
Yarra Street State School 16, 17
You Yangs 250
Young Australia League ('Y. A. L.') 93, 127, 138
Young, O. (fictional character) 225–8, 230–1, 236, 241

Zealandie (ship) 133

The Charles and Joy Staples South West Region Publications Fund was established in 1984 on the basis of a generous donation to The University of Western Australia by Charles and Joy Staples.

The purpose of the Fund is to highlight all aspects of the South West region of Western Australia, a geographical area much loved by Charles and Joy Staples, so as to assist the people of the South West region and those in government and private organisations concerned with South West projects to appreciate the needs and possibilities of the region in the widest possible historical perspective. The fund is administered by a committee whose aims are to make possible the publication by UWA Publishing of research and writing in any discipline relevant to the South West region.

Charles and Joy Staples South West Region Publications Fund titles

1987
A Tribute to the Group Settlers
Philip E. M. Blond

1992
For Their Own Good: Aborigines and Government in the Southwest of Western Australia, 1900–1940
Anna Haebich

1993
Portraits of the South West
B. K. de Garis

A Guide to Sources for the History of South Western Australia
Compiled by Ronald Richards

1994
Jardee: The Mill That Cheated Time
Doreen Owens

1995
Dearest Isabella: Life and Letters of Isabella Ferguson, 1819–1910
Prue Joske

Blacklegs: The Scottish Colliery Strike of 1911 Bill Latter

1997
Barefoot in the Creek: A Group Settlement Childhood in Margaret River L. C. Burton

Ritualist on a Tricycle: Frederick Goldsmith, Church, Nationalism and Society in Western Australia
Colin Holden

Western Australia as it is Today, 1906 Leopoldo Zunini, Royal Consul of Italy, edited and translated by Richard Bosworth and Margot Melia

2002
The South West from Dawn till Dusk Rob Olver

2003
Contested Country: A History of the Northcliffe Area, Western Australia
Patricia Crawford and Ian Crawford

2004
Orchard and Mill: The Story of Bill Lee, South-West Pioneer
Lyn Adams

2005
Richard Spencer: Napoleonic War Naval Hero and Australian Pioneer
Gwen Chessell

2006
A Story to Tell (reprinted 2012)
Laurel Nannup

2008
Alexander Collie: Colonial Surgeon, Naturalist and Explorer
Gwen Chessell

The Zealous Conservator: A Life of Charles Lane Poole
John Dargavel

2009
"It's Still in My Heart, This is My Country": The Single Noongar Claim History South West Aboriginal Land and Sea Council, John Host with Chris Owen

Shaking Hands on the Fringe: Negotiating the Aboriginal World at King George's Sound
Tiffany Shellam

2011
Noongar Mambara Bakitj and *Mamang*
Kim Scott and Wirlomin Noongar Language and Stories Project

Guy Grey-Smith: Life Force
Andrew Gaynor

2013
Dwoort Baal Kaat and *Yira Boornak Nyininy*
Kim Scott and Wirlomin Noongar Language and Stories Project

2014
A Boy's Short Life: The Story of Warren Braedon/Louis Johnson
Anna Haebich and Steve Mickler

Plant Life on the Sandplains: A Global Biodiversity Hotspot
Hans Lambers

Fire and Hearth (revised facsimile edition) Sylvia Hallam

2015
Running Out? Water in Western Australia Ruth Morgan

A Journey Travelled: Aboriginal–European Relations at Albany and Surrounding Regions from First Colonial Contact to 1926
Murray Arnold

The Southwest: Australia's Biodiversity Hotspot
Victoria Laurie

Invisible Country: South-West Australia: Understanding a Landscape Bill Bunbury

2016
Noongar Bush Medicine: Medicinal Plants of the South-West of Western Australia
Vivienne Hansen and John Horsfall

2017
Never Again: Reflections on Environmental Responsibility After Roe 8
Edited by Andrea Gaynor, Peter Newman and Philip Jennings

Ngaawily Nop and *Noorn*
Kim Scott and Wirlomin Noongar Language and Stories Project

2018
Dancing in Shadows: Histories of Nyungar Performance
Anna Haebich

2019
Refuge Richard Rossiter

That Was My Home: Voices from the Noongar Camps in Fremantle and the Western Suburbs
Denise Cook

www.ingramcontent.com/pod-product-compliance
Lightning Source LLC
Chambersburg PA
CBHW031325230426
43670CB00006B/240